NORMAN
COUSINS

Johns Hopkins Nuclear History and Contemporary Affairs

Martin Sherwin, Series Editor

NORMAN COUSINS

Peacemaker in the Atomic Age

Allen Pietrobon

Johns Hopkins University Press
Baltimore

Published 2022
Printed in the United States of America on acid-free paper
9 8 7 6 5 4 3 2 1

Johns Hopkins University Press
2715 North Charles Street
Baltimore, Maryland 21218-4363
www.press.jhu.edu

Library of Congress Cataloging-in-Publication Data

Names: Pietrobon, Allen, 1984– author.
Title: Norman Cousins : peacemaker in the atomic age / Allen Pietrobon.
Description: Baltimore : Johns Hopkins University Press, 2022. | Series: Johns Hopkins nuclear history and contemporary affairs | Includes bibliographical references and index.
Identifiers: LCCN 2021029203 | ISBN 9781421443706 (hardcover) | ISBN 9781421443713 (ebook)
Subjects: LCSH: Cousins, Norman. | Saturday review of literature. | Saturday review (New York, N.Y. : 1952) | Periodical editors—United States—Biography. | Pacifists—United States—Biography. | Press and politics—United States. | Antinuclear movement—United States—History. | Nuclear weapons—Government policy—United States. | United States—Foreign relations—Soviet Union. | Soviet Union—Foreign relations—United States.
Classification: LCC PN4874.C745 P54 2022 | DDC 818/.5409—dc23/eng/20211027
LC record available at https://lccn.loc.gov/2021029203

A catalog record for this book is available from the British Library.

Special discounts are available for bulk purchases of this book. For more information, please contact Special Sales at specialsales@jh.edu.

CONTENTS

NORMAN COUSINS

PROLOGUE

Tail gunner Bob Caron had been counting . . . Seven, eight, nine . . . Soaring 26,000 feet above Japan, Caron was crammed into his shoulder-wide compartment, operating a .50 caliber machine gun perched at the rear of the B-29 Superfortress bomber. The twenty-six-year-old was solely responsible for defending the aircraft from enemy fighters aiming to knock them out of the sky.

On any other mission Caron would have had some help. Usually the B-29 was equipped with ten heavy machine guns piercing the fuselage at strategic points to give nearly 360 degrees of defensive coverage against airborne attackers. But on that morning, eight of the ten guns had been stripped off the plane to save weight in order to accommodate the enormous bomb they were carrying . . . Twenty-one, twenty-two, twenty-three . . .

The B-29 was well suited to this particular mission. In 1945 it was on the cutting edge of military technology, a marvel of aeronautical engineering. Equipped with the latest technologies, at its full defensive complement five General Electric analog computers onboard the aircraft helped to aim the machine guns remotely. As *Popular Mechanics* magazine reported at the time, it was because of these "electronic brains" that a lone B-29 had recently been able to win a four-hour battle with seventy-nine Japanese fighter planes.[1]

None of that was any comfort to Caron, however, because he was manning the only remaining machine gun, located at the rear of the aircraft. If they *did* encounter Japanese defenders on this mission, they would have little chance of survival . . . Twenty-seven, twenty-eight, twenty-nine . . .

The B-29 bomber's engines roared, and vibrations pulsed through the aircraft's polished aluminum body. Upon reaching their target, Caron had started his count the moment the bomb left the plane. Despite being confined to his claustrophobic gunner's compartment, he knew precisely when this happened because freed of its 9,700-pound bomb, the B-29 shot upward in the sky like a rodeo bull trying to buck its rider . . . Thirty-six, thirty-seven, thirty-eight . . .

First officer Colonel Paul Tibbets kept a tight grip on the controls and executed the evasive maneuver that was designed to get them as far away from the shock wave the blast would produce as quickly as possible. No one, not even the physicists responsible for creating the world's first atomic weapon, could be entirely sure how big the blast would be nor what its forces might do to the specially modified plane . . . Forty, forty-one, forty-two . . .

Suddenly, a brilliant white light filled the sky. When the eye-stabbing flash seared through the dark goggles intended to shield him, Caron thought he had been blinded. But when the brightness slowly receded, he witnessed what they had just done. In a split second the city of Hiroshima had been decimated. Copilot Robert Lewis, after watching an entire city disappear in an instant, is reported to have said, "My god, what have we done?" The twelve crew members aboard the *Enola Gay*—named after the pilot's mother—were the first people in the world to witness a city destroyed by an atomic bomb. They were there at the inception of the "atomic age."[2]

Back on the East Coast of the United States, on August 7, 1945, it was around 7:30 a.m. when Norman Cousins, the thirty-year-old editor of the *Saturday Review of Literature,* came down for breakfast in his home in Connecticut. He picked up that day's issue of the *New York Times.*[3] His attention was drawn to the bold streamer headline, three lines deep, announcing, "FIRST ATOMIC BOMB DROPPED ON JAPAN;

MISSILE IS EQUAL TO 20,000 TONS OF TNT; TRUMAN WARNS FOE OF A 'RAIN OF RUIN.'"[4]

The profound effect the events of that August morning had on him would guide his actions for the rest of his life. With the atomic bombing, the purpose of Cousins's life became brilliantly clear to him.

The atomic bomb would consume his thoughts, dominate his writing, and have an immeasurable impact on his family. The dark shadow the bomb cast would follow him until the day he died nearly five decades later. After his passing, his youngest daughter, Sarah, wrote in the *San Francisco Chronicle*, "My father, Norman Cousins, died in 1990. But he was taken away long before that, by the atomic bomb."[5] Neither the world nor Cousins would ever be the same after that August morning.

INTRODUCTION

Norman Cousins (1915–1990) is probably best known today as the longtime editor of the influential American weekly magazine the *Saturday Review*.[1] For a time in the 1960s, the *Saturday Review* was the third most popular news magazine in the country. Cousins was also a leading humanitarian, peacemaker, and anti-nuclear activist who contributed to a wide array of anti-war causes and diplomatic efforts. He stood out among activists during the Cold War because he had a captive audience for his ideas through the *Saturday Review*. The vast network of far-reaching, high-level personal and political connections he built up over the years allowed him to exert influence in the halls of power across the globe despite being a political "outsider."

He never held elected or appointed office (although he was offered a job in the Kennedy White House), but many at the time thought that Cousins's intellect, charm, and growing prominence would one day carry him to the White House as president. Exploratory committees attempted to draft him for presidential campaigns in the 1960s and 1970s. Even though he never became the leader of the free world, his lifelong activities did have an enormous impact on domestic politics and international relations. His contributions to American life and public debate were entered into the *Congressional Record*.[2] He received kudos from numerous world leaders. Even years after Cousins's death, Carter Wilkie, a speechwriter for president Bill Clinton, while drafting a speech to note the anniversary of John F. Kennedy's death, would write, "I took direction from Norman Cousins."[3]

Because of his prominence in the anti-nuclear and peace movements, Cousins has been mentioned in major academic studies by the historians Lawrence Wittner and Milton Katz, but he has mostly been overlooked by scholars, rarely garnering more than a handful of pages in any academic study. In Japan, the memory of him is more poignant. His anti-nuclear activism and success in securing medical treatment for the victims of the atomic bombings is recorded in stone, with a memorial honoring him in Hiroshima's Peace Park.

Cousins himself published a number of books, including two memoirs, one outlining his activities as an emissary for the Kennedy administration (*The Improbable Triumvirate*, 1972), the second reflecting on his many years as editor of the *Saturday Review* (*Present Tense: An American Editor's Odyssey*, 1967). But even his own memoirs are but a narrow spotlight trained on only two episodes in a life full of quiet achievements. This biography, therefore, serves as the first scholarly study of the political life of Norman Cousins and the major impact he had on American anti-nuclear thought, humanitarianism, and international diplomacy during the Cold War.

Cousins's anti-nuclear and humanitarian activism received some public recognition during his life, but behind the scenes he also had a major influence on US foreign policy. He launched successful humanitarian aid programs for the victims of war and took steps to push the United States away from a reliance on nuclear weapons and toward better relations with the Soviet Union. Thus, describing Cousins as simply a peace activist or magazine editor—as previous studies have done—does not even begin to capture the nature of his activities and the scope of his impact. He pursued the more direct and persuasive lobbying effort of someone outside policymaking who managed to wield extraordinary influence. He was a journalist who not only helped to report on but also directly influenced the contours of the Cold War. His magazine played a major role in shaping the American public debate, especially on anti-nuclear issues.

The narrative arc of Norman Cousins's life is sprawling and complex. Cousins was editor of the *Saturday Review* for more than thirty-five years. From the time he joined the magazine in 1940 to 1964 Cousins published just under six hundred editorials—some twenty-five per year on average.[4] In that same time period he wrote or edited ten books. From 1948 to 1964, his archivist later estimated, he delivered at least six college commencement speeches per year and traveled worldwide giving an estimated twenty-one hundred speeches for peace.[5] Transcripts of Cousins's many speeches and radio addresses throughout his lifetime fill more than eighty-one audio reels and 123 videotapes. Cousins himself maintained a voluminous correspondence, which now fills some of the 1,816 boxes that make up his personal papers housed at the Charles E. Young Research Library at the University of California, Los Angeles. (By comparison, the archival collection for Robert F. Kennedy contains just over 2,300 boxes.)[6] Cousins's correspondence is so extensive that his archivist once complained, "He has kept more than any two-term president—because most VIP's [*sic*] throw away routine correspondence before donating their files."[7] Cousin's own ruminations about his public life are captured in hundreds of pages of transcript from his oral history, recorded in 1987–88. In his oral history, though, as in his public life, he was notably mute about his own family. Following his lead, I have chosen to weave in only a small amount of information on Cousins's family and home life, mostly in instances where exploring his personal life adds context to his political activities.

Cousins was deeply immersed in the political affairs and leading intellectual currents of his day. Over the years, he kept in touch with some of the world's greatest thinkers and political leaders, including Albert Einstein, Adlai Stevenson, Nikita Khrushchev, Pope John XXIII, Jawaharlal Nehru, Reinhold Niebuhr, Leo Cherne, John Steinbeck, Martin Luther King, Henry Wallace, Benjamin Spock, Norman Thomas,

Albert Schweitzer, and Leo Szilard. He corresponded with (and frequently provided advice to and wrote speeches for) every American president from Harry S. Truman to George H. W. Bush; he even counted some among his friends. John F. Kennedy's national security advisor, McGeorge Bundy, would later reveal that Kennedy had been deeply pleased by his friendship with Cousins, noting that "their relationship was unusually direct and personal for a notable editor and a modern President." According to Bundy, "Whenever the President did not know Norman's current view of pressing questions . . . he would want to know it."[8]

The life and achievements of Norman Cousins have been previously unexplored largely because his position between diplomacy and activism has kept him from being easily categorized. Mostly, though, he is largely overlooked today because he was engaged in so many diverse causes—abruptly changing direction over the years—that his activities defy traditional scholarly definitions by not fitting neatly into the existing paradigm of either international relations or peace activism.

Because scholars who have previously written about Cousins in the context of peace activism highlight only a very narrow aspect of his life, the snapshot they provide pigeonholes him as being one among many "peace activists" during the Cold War era. Although Cousins *was* working for peace, he never would have called himself an "activist," nor was he one in the traditional sense. In his own words, Cousins considered himself more of a "switchboard operator, keeping lines of communication open." He positioned himself as a "peacemaker in the peace movement."[9] His eldest daughter, Andrea, reflecting on her father's activities in the 1960s, cannot imagine him in a street protest or joining in some chant. "He was in some ways a lone wolf," she said. His approach "was about reasoning with people and talking and convincing them about the rightness of his thinking."[10]

Two of the men he convinced were Soviet premier Nikita Khrushchev and President John F. Kennedy, with whom Cousins worked closely on the 1963 Partial Nuclear Test Ban Treaty. In fact, Cousins played a crucial role, without which, I argue, the treaty might have collapsed. It was Cousins who suggested the idea for Kennedy's now famous American University commencement address of June 1963 and wrote the first draft.

When examining the activities of a man whose life spanned seventy-five robust years, the historian is confronted with the necessity to select and compress a great deal in order to tell that story. I have attempted to bring the story of Norman Cousins to light by focusing on his political life and the impact his work had on both the United States and the international community during the Cold War. As will become clear, Cousins directed most of his attention and efforts toward the international arena, specifically nuclear weapons issues and concerns about war and peace. He worked hard to foster a better relationship with the Soviet Union and the world. Thus, this book will mostly follow Cousins's interest in those fields, mentioning his thoughts on domestic issues and the inner workings of the *Saturday Review* as a company only in passing in order to concentrate on his most impactful international humanitarian, anti-nuclear, and diplomatic activities during the Cold War.

In fact, Cousins's public career tracks the rise and fall of the Cold War itself. The historian Jeff Kingston argues that American use of the atomic bomb in Japan marked the "opening salvo of the Cold War."[11] Thirteen days after the first use of the atomic bomb, Cousins first received wide public attention for his groundbreaking editorial "Modern Man Is Obsolete." He would pass away in November 1990, just a year after the Berlin Wall fell and thirteen months before the Soviet Union collapsed. This book highlights the outsized impact that one individual had on the course of American public debate, international humanitarianism, and citizen diplomacy during the Cold War.

CHAPTER 1

EDUCATOR *for an* ATOMIC AGE

Few Americans were aware that at about the time when many on the East Coast of the United States were sitting down to dinner on August 5, 1945 (or 8:15 a.m., August 6, Hiroshima time), a single plane had dropped the first atomic bomb on the city of Hiroshima, changing the world forever. When President Harry S. Truman first announced the use of the bomb, sixteen hours later, his description of it as "a harnessing of the basic power of the universe"[1] did not make its true nature clear to the average American. Few Americans even knew what an atomic bomb was.

When Norman Cousins first learned of the dropping of the bomb from a headline in the *New York Times* on August 7, he later recalled, he felt "no elation with that headline."[2] That evening he felt compelled to draft an editorial articulating the sense of dread he felt about this powerful new weapon. He would later write that "when on that day a parachute containing a small object floated to earth over Japan, it marked the violent death of one stage in man's history and the beginning of another."[3] The result of his belief that the atomic bomb marked the start of a new "atomic age" in human history was a profound editorial titled "Modern Man Is Obsolete," published in the small cultural weekly the *Saturday Review*. The issue first hit the newsstands on August 18, 1945, just twelve days after the United States bombed Hiroshima and nine days after it bombed Nagasaki. He began his editorial by stating his belief that "whatever elation there is in the world today because of final victory in the war is severely tempered by fear. It is a primitive fear, the fear of the unknown, the fear of forces man can neither channel nor comprehend." He then posited that August 6 had birthed the atomic age, because "the science of warfare has reached the point where it threatens the planet itself." He recognized that while America had been first to win the atomic race, the secret of building atomic weapons would not remain a secret for long, as other nations would race to develop the weapon for themselves. His biggest fear, however, had to do with the already present and growing belief that the atomic bomb was so dangerous, and the terror of retaliation so great, that "we may have seen the last of war." Cousins called this notion "quasi-logical." "Far from banishing war," he wrote, "the atomic bomb will in itself constitute a cause of war. . . . It will create universal fear and suspicion."[4]

Cousins predicted what would later become the tenets of mutually assured destruction and the notion of a first strike: "Each nation will live nervously from one moment to the next, not knowing whether the designs or ambitions of other nations might prompt them to attempt a lightning blow of obliteration." Essentially describing intercontinental ballistic missiles standing on hair-trigger alert more than a decade before they came to fruition, he wrote that nations would "no longer be dependent upon armies but [war] will be waged by push-buttons, releasing radio-controlled rocket planes carrying cargoes of atomic explosives" and that "the slightest suspicion may start all the push-buttons going."[5] Cousins's editorial clearly helped to illustrate to the American public the dangers of atomic weapons and began to shape their thinking about the promise and perils of this new atomic age into which they had just been thrust. His despair may also have been fueled by the fact that his third child was about to be born into this new atomic world—his wife was eight months pregnant at the time.

Praise for "Modern Man Is Obsolete" rapidly flooded into Cousins's New York City office. In less than ten days' time his desk overflowed with more than 150 letters from across the country.[6] A letter writer from San Francisco proclaimed, "You have written a sparkling message which I hope starts a conflagration of constructive thinking and conduct among the peoples everywhere."[7] Even the resident commissioner of the Philippines to the United States, Carlos Romulo, wrote Cousins to tell him that he thought the editorial was "so illuminating that I do not believe there can be people so blind that they cannot see the logic of its conclusions and its unerring prophecy."[8] Many more people wrote to Cousins begging for reprints to send to their friends, relatives, or elected officials. Less than a month after the article appeared in a magazine that had only twenty-two thousand subscribers (and was losing vast sums of money), Cousins apologized to his readers, saying that he had already received thirty-five thousand requests for reprints and the printers were rushing to keep up.[9]

Engaging in some self-promotion, Cousins also sent copies of "Modern Man Is Obsolete" to top US government officials. Secretary of the Interior Harold Ickes responded, "It made a deep impression on me. . . . I wish that every intelligent citizen could read it."[10] A copy of the article even found its way onto a US Navy destroyer returning from the Pacific War, where it was read by a young sailor named Sanford Gottlieb. The article, Gottlieb remembers, so changed his life that he embarked upon a path of lifelong anti-nuclear activism. Years later he would become the executive director of the National Committee for a Sane Nuclear Policy (SANE), an organization that Cousins himself cofounded, which quickly became the nation's top anti-nuclear lobby.[11] Even forty years later, in 1985, when Cousins received a nomination for the Nobel Peace Prize (a prize for which he had received at least twelve nominations, beginning in 1958), "Modern Man Is Obsolete" was still being cited as "a prophetic editorial," one that was just the first installment in his lifelong plea for peace through disarmament and world law.[12]

Cousins's five-page editorial was quickly translated into seven languages and reprinted in international newspapers. Its impact was so great that Viking Press soon approached Cousins and asked him to expand its message in the form of a book. *Modern Man Is Obsolete* went on to sell several million copies in fourteen editions. An estimated 40 million people worldwide read the book.[13] The editorial established Norman Cousins as a leader in anti-nuclear thought. In hindsight, it is also apparent that Cousins presciently defined the basic challenges that would emerge from the nuclear age. His editorial foresaw the tensions that would erupt between the great powers, cautioned against the dangers of placing too much trust in nuclear deterrence, and warned that any future war that involved atomic weapons would certainly mean the end of the human race. The editorial was, as the peace activist and Vatican adviser Father Felix Morlion stated, the "first hit" of the modern peace movement, one that was not easily forgotten.[14]

To Cousins, the atomic bombing of Japan was not just another tragedy in a brutal war. The fires unleashed by the bomb sparked something visceral, something he was completely unable to ignore, something that would spur him to travel the globe in search of solutions. His reaction to it would make him a near household name by the 1960s. The atomic bomb consumed his thoughts and dominated his writing. Cousins claimed that 95 percent of his position on the bomb had emerged the moment he read that *New York Times* headline announcing the atomic bomb's use. Everything after that had simply corroborated it.[15] But it would be misleading to claim that this sudden epiphany about the bomb came to him all at once and in isolation.

In order to understand both Norman Cousins's thinking and how he managed to have such a lasting impact on American culture, foreign policy, and anti-nuclear thought, we must first examine how a promising thirty-year-old magazine editor came to write an editorial like "Modern Man Is Obsolete." This will provide some broader context for the American public's receptiveness to Cousins's ideas. Although he claimed that 95 percent of his position on the bomb emerged on that fateful morning, in reality the basis of his position had begun to form nearly a decade earlier.

CHAPTER 2

THE FORMATION *of a* VISION

Born fifteen miles outside Manhattan, in Union Hill, New Jersey, on June 24, 1915, to the Russian-born Samuel and Sarah Cousins, Norman was raised in an industrious household. His Jewish immigrant parents seized every opportunity that their adopted country afforded them. Samuel, a carpenter of modest means, became a shopkeeper. With the help of his wife, Cousins later recalled, his father "progressed upwards in business until [they] had acquired a department store of fairly substantial proportions," which allowed them to have "the comforts and advantages of an average American middle-class family." Norman later wrote of his mother as being a "remarkable woman" of compassion and integrity whom everyone trusted and respected.[1]

Theirs was a fraught marriage. Norman's daughter Candis describes it as more an arranged marriage than a marriage of love—a commonplace practice in that era and culture. According to Norman, his parents fought frequently and would fall into periods of not speaking. Norman, as a young boy, would carry messages back and forth between them. His eldest daughter, Andrea, thought her father's concern for peace might have had roots in his parents' quarreling.[2] He told Candis a few years before he died that he still felt responsible for their separation. He thought that perhaps he could have done more. "My father's sense of responsibility for peace between warring parties was profound," Candis said.[3]

Cousins (*on chair*) with his parents, Samuel and Sarah, and his sister Sophie, ca. 1917.

(PHOTO COURTESY OF CANDIS COUSINS KERNS)

At the age of ten, Cousins, who had always been a rather frail child, was misdiagnosed with tuberculosis and sent to a sanatorium to recover. He would later recall "the exposure to that particular experience where you had to think about life in a rather basic way—not all the kids who were there survived the experience or survived their TB." That experience taught him that life was precious but also fragile.[4]

By the time Norman reached high school, his father's business had become a casualty of the Great Depression. The family lost all but a few meager investments and struggled to get by, maintaining ownership of just a garage and a gas station. "Like most other American families," Cousins observed, "ours suffered severely from the Depression." When he wasn't in school, he worked at his father's gas station. As a youngster Norman had been seen as a precocious child, earning him the nickname "The Professor." His mother thought he was destined for higher education. Despite his intelligence, though, Cousins was not a strong student. Later in life he told Candis that he thought he might have had dyslexia. He also suffered from a fairly severe stutter.[5]

Upon completing high school in the spring of 1933, Norman applied (twice) to the City College of New York, but he was rejected both times on account of his poor grades. Therefore, to contribute to the family income however modestly, he took a part-time job as an editor for the trade publication *Master Plumber*.[6] It was a natural progression from the writing he had done for his high school newspaper. With his budding career in the publishing world established, in the spring of 1934 he accepted a position as the education editor for the *New York Post*.[7] Still, he longed to go to college.

In 1935, Norman filled out an application for Columbia University's Teachers College. It is unclear whether he applied and was rejected or never submitted the application in the first place, but he did not "officially" enroll at Columbia.[8] Instead, he got his college education in bits and pieces. In September 1935 he left the *New York Post* and started auditing classes at Teachers College. Cousins would later explain that while he thought he might like to be a teacher, that was not what drew him to the field. He started sitting in on classes because at the time Teachers College was, he thought, intellectually the most exciting place in the country to get an education.[9] One of the classes he took was taught by John Dewey, a philosopher, psychologist, and reformer and one of the most prominent American scholars in the early twentieth century.[10] Cousins later described the faculty as thinking hard about life at a time when everything nailed down was coming loose, philosophically, politically, and intellectually.[11] His professors were concerned about more than just the field of education, exploring the world of ideas in a troubling time.[12]

Dark political clouds gathered worldwide throughout the 1930s, and nations confronted not only economic depression but the emergence of totalitarian regimes. Cousins described it as a "terrifying time" when "people were living near the edge" but also a "vastly exciting experience."[13] Being immersed in the intellectual milieu of Teachers College provided Cousins with a fertile atmosphere in which to indulge his fascination with the history of political ideas. Although he was only auditing classes, Cousins's sophisticated intellect attracted the notice of a faculty member who saw him as an individual of unusual promise. The prominent professor William Kilpatrick became Cousins's champion, approaching the administration and negotiating an arrangement that allowed Cousins to continue to attend classes without paying, albeit without earning academic credit.[14]

Cousins was attending college in New York City during a veritable golden age of intellectual thought. New York's Greenwich Village had been a hotbed of intellectual and cultural experimentation for decades. Freethinkers from all over the country were attracted by its cheap rents and plethora of like-minded people at a time when New York City formed the center of public intellectual culture in the United States. The Depression years provided endless fodder—rapid industrialization, urbanization, economic depression, war, the rise of Fascism, and the threat or promise of Communism—for thriving debates about alternative ways of life.[15] Later, in a 1949 editorial, Cousins reflected on the trials of his generation:

> From the moment we were born, history laid siege to our times and our affairs. Our earliest memories were of World War I, of brothers and sisters or uncles who said goodbye and who never came back. . . . When we were old enough to think creatively about politics and philosophy, the Depression laid strong hands on our ideas, and the old and accepted systems of thought and

politics seemed feeble and irrelevant, fit for museums or testbooks [*sic*] but not for the throbbing issues of the day. We groped for economic footing and for intellectual change.[16]

Many of these leading thinkers pushing for change were members of a distinct group of Jewish intellectuals who would rise to prominence in the postwar period. They included Lionel Trilling, Whittaker Chambers, Alfred Kazin, Paul Goodman, Harold Rosenberg, Norman Podhoretz, Sidney Hook, Daniel Bell, Richard Hofstadter, and Irving Howe. Many of these Jewish intellectuals embraced political radicalism during the 1930s.[17] Cousins was Jewish by birth but had been raised in a non-practicing secular family. While he claimed that he valued his religious heritage, he never publicly self-identified as Jewish. From a young age he was implored by his mother not to present himself in public as Jewish. His parents had suffered from the rampant anti-Semitism of prewar Europe before emigrating, and they had experienced traces of the same in New York City. To protect her son, she instructed him to hide his Jewish identity and instead celebrate Christmas.[18]

When it came to religion, Cousins sought an inclusive spirituality. Writing to a reader, he explained, "To the extent that I can define a religious purpose for myself I would say that it is to find a way to lower and erase the barriers that tend to separate men."[19] Whenever he was directly asked to specify what religion he identified with, as he was once by a *Saturday Review* reader, he answered, "Universalism with a lower case 'u,' meaning that I felt I could not bind myself to any single religion since I was aware of the many things they all had in common. Besides, I had the feeling that I had to find a Church which would welcome *any* man."[20] That being said, once he had children of his own, he would go out of his way to help them explore their faith. Andrea recalls her father taking them to the Unitarian Church as well as to a Quaker meeting. "His idea for all of us was that we should visit different places of worship and decide for ourselves," she explained.[21]

Politically, Cousins also steered well clear of any affiliation with the Communist Party during this time. The FBI conducted multiple investigations of him later in his life but found no evidence of any Communist connections save for a distant sister-in-law.[22] Regarding Communism, Cousins would later write, "The idea that you judge a man by what he does, not by what he is supposed to believe, is sound. But a man who is a Communist has done certain things. Being part of the Communist Party is doing something." Defining himself only as "liberal," Cousins made clear that being a liberal did not equate to being a Communist. In fact, they could work at odds. "I believe it is possible to oppose Communism and still be a liberal," he wrote. "Indeed, I would say, perhaps pompously, that I could not take a liberal position without opposing Communism."[23] This position likely stemmed from the fact that Cousins fully supported the New Deal and credited Roosevelt's social and political reforms with saving the United States from a potential Communist victory. Cousins explained, "I think it is quite possible that Roosevelt saved this country from a revolution by proving that a democratic nation such as this was able to meet its problems."[24]

Although he never received a degree, Cousins left Columbia fundamentally changed by the experience. By his early twenties, his personal charm, drive, and intellectual curiosity were sufficiently developed to enable him, with only a high school degree, to secure a job as a book reviewer at the magazine *Current History* in 1937. Having been exposed to debates about the very nature and meaning of democracy in an era when the world seemed to be pulling apart at the seams in the lead-up to World War II, Cousins could see growing evidence all around him that forced him to reevaluate his own beliefs. His new job allowed him the opportunity to self-educate through the extensive reading he was required to do as a book critic. It was in 1937, Cousins writes, that the sense of disillusionment that marred many of his contemporaries finally cleared for him. He dove into studying Eastern philosophy, where he encountered the Indian poet Rabindranath Tagore's philosophy of universalism and the belief that man can overcome the dangers of nationalism. Tagore recognized that nations could only find salvation by coming together in common cause.[25] Cousins was also taken with the writings of the American revolutionary Thomas Paine, who showed him that there need be no conflict between allegiance to one's country and allegiance to mankind.[26] Finally, Cousins found inspiration in the works of poet Ralph Waldo Emerson, who, he explained, "drove the final nail into the coffin for my disillusion; he defined both the power and responsibility of the individual in a complex society."[27]

Cousins felt in Emerson "a sense of purpose and usefulness to my fast developing interest in and concern with the philosophy of universalism, for it added political form to ideological substance and served to translate important aspects of universalism into their direct political expression."[28] He wrote to a reader that he had "been attempting to wrestle with some basic philosophical and religious questions, and I find myself veering off from many of my beliefs of long standing."[29] In his ongoing attempt to understand and define his own worldview, Cousins took to heart the ideals that would come to form the basis of Western humanitarianism after the war. He believed that the individual held both the power and the moral responsibility to act in service of the general welfare.

Despite the doldrums of the Great Depression still present around him and the increasingly troubling situation in Europe in the late 1930s, his personal life was about to be greatly enriched. It was Memorial Day weekend, 1938, when Cousins went up to the Catskills for a weekend social.[30] One evening Cousins ended up dancing with a young woman named Pearl, who in turn introduced him to her older sister Eleanor. The rest of the evening, Norman and Eleanor danced only with each other. The next day, finding themselves in the pool together, they jumped up in the same moment onto an inflatable raft. The raft capsized, and when Norman and Ellen came up on opposite sides of the raft and made eye contact, Eleanor knew, she said, that Norman was the one and only one for her. She told him soon after they met that she was going to marry him in two years.[31] It turned out to be a lot sooner.

Ellen and Norman on their wedding day.
(PHOTO COURTESY OF CANDIS COUSINS KERNS)

Ellen—who, like Norman, was the child of Jewish immigrants—had grown up in Utah and was now living with her sister in New York, working for the Newspaper Guild. She was later described by a *Saturday Review* employee as "unaffected, natural, and genuine." Ellen and Norman were married on June 23, 1939, the day before Norman's twenty-fourth birthday, in a "simple and moving" ceremony in the rabbi's study at the Temple Emanu-El in New York City, followed by a small reception in their apartment.

Both Ellen and Norman were hardy types who loved being outdoors. After their marriage, they decided to move from New York City to somewhere closer to nature. They settled in Norwalk, Connecticut, a small industrial town on the shore of the Long Island Sound, about forty miles from Manhattan.[32] Their new home was in just the kind of greenspace they were looking for. Cousins enjoyed going for walks in the woods, but from Norwalk he was still able to commute in to the city by train each day.

Three months after their wedding, on September 1, 1939, Hitler's Germany invaded Poland, sparking World War II. Despite this looming catastrophe, Cousins's personal fortunes continued to improve. Newly married, he was considering a new job prospect. The offices of Cousins's employer, *Current History*, happened to be in the same building as the *Saturday Review*, which advertised an open position for executive editor. One would be reasonable in thinking that a twenty-five-year-old stuttering Jewish kid without a college degree would probably not be anyone's first pick for an executive editor's job. But Amy Loveman, one of the founding editors of the *Saturday Review of Literature*, saw something in Cousins and took him under her wing. It likely helped that Norman was, according to Candis, enormously charming and had a way of winning people over.[33] With the March 9, 1940, issue Cousins joined the masthead.[34]

Candis Cousins recollects that her father's true education really came in those early years at the magazine. Loveman, Jewish herself, helped Cousins become who he wanted to be, sheltering him from the anti-Semitism still prevalent in New York at that time and teaching him how to write and edit. Says Candis, "I don't think he would have had the kind of career that he had [if not for Loveman]. She protected my father. He was a diamond in the rough."[35]

Within two years that diamond was shining, and Cousins was promoted to the editorial helm in 1942. When he was first offered the promotion, Cousins—just twenty-seven and carrying no weight in the New York literary world—considered himself unqualified for the job. He agreed to take the position as an interim placeholder, only until someone more qualified could be found. The search for a new editor ultimately proved futile. No one of any literary or intellectual stature wanted to join the small, financially struggling magazine. Cousins would say that he ended up keeping the position because no one else wanted it.[36] It proved to be a perfect match.

CHAPTER 3

WORLD WAR II

Cousins's new position editing a national, albeit small magazine gave him a public platform from which to put his newly solidified worldview into practice. The editorial pages of the *Saturday Review* would quickly come to reflect Cousins's belief that with the world at war, it was no longer enough for American intellectuals and writers to remain detached and aloof; they had to become involved in supporting the war effort.[1] But the outbreak of war also challenged one of Cousins's core principles, pacifism; and his struggle to reconcile his pacifism with his belief that the Nazis needed to be stopped played out in the pages of the *Saturday Review* in some of his earliest editorials. "There is no paradox, no contradiction, no inconsistency," Cousins wrote in June 1940. "In the [first] World War liberals led the interventionist movement; in the years that followed they led the anti-war movement; today the trend seems to be returning to intervention again. Have the liberals changed sides? No; only targets."[2]

Cousins claimed that his core pacifism had not changed, only its form: he had been against war before, but now he was against the barbarism he saw in Nazi actions. In August 1940, Cousins turned his opprobrium on those who claimed the United States needed to remain neutral in this conflict. Writing that the isolationist stance was a "deadweight idea," he explained that "our favorite dogmas or ideas of only a few years back have been obscured or obliterated under the pressure of changing events" and that isolationists needed to reevaluate their position.[3] The very reevaluation Cousins called for would be foisted upon isolationists when Pearl Harbor was attacked the following December, largely obliterating support for the isolationist position.

In his first article following the attack, with the full benefit of hindsight, Cousins took to the editorial page to eviscerate the United States' isolationist policies. "This isolation would have been wonderful, except that we were the only ones who believed it," he wrote in January 1942. "It played a large part in not only making a new and greater war possible . . . it became, in large part, a substitute for intelligent action."[4] But Cousins recognized that he shared some of the blame. He would later confess to a sense of personal guilt for what happened in Germany, writing, "Before the war I had been doing a lot of fancy talking and writing against Nazism, but that was easy enough to do from the safety of America. . . . If my convictions were worth anything, I should have been in Germany, taking my chances with the others on the firing line against Nazism. . . . I felt guilty because so much of my anti-Nazism had been just talk."[5] Ultimately, though, he would have to continue to "just talk." He was classified by the Selective Service Board as being fit for only "limited military service" due to concerns about his health. After his misdiagnosis of tuberculosis as a child, when he was sent to a sanatorium he actually *contracted* TB there as a result of being in close proximity to other infected children. He recovered, but the illness left calcification in his lungs, so that intense military service was impossible.[6]

He may have breathed a sigh of relief that he would not be heading to the front lines alongside so many other young men. On July 25, 1941, five months before Pearl Harbor, he and Ellen had their first child, a girl they named Andrea. Although he could not serve in combat, he took action to devote his talents to the war effort. Cousins wrote to his local Selective Service Board explaining that the service he was able to provide as a civilian might be of greater use than the limited service he could provide as a soldier.[7]

In June 1943 Cousins was asked by the Office of War Information (OWI) to become the chief publication editor for the prodemocracy circular *U.S.A.*, a pocket-sized propaganda pamphlet that was dropped by US airmen over territory occupied by the Nazis.[8] It typically included classic American literature and articles about democracy to educate foreign citizens about American culture and democratic values. Under a special arrangement, he was able to continue his job at the *Saturday Review*, where, as a point of personal honor, he reduced his salary sufficiently that he would not end up profiting from his wartime service.[9]

In January 1944 the Cousinses welcomed a second daughter, Amy, named after Norman's mentor Amy Loveman. By then Cousins had added his voice to a fierce debate that was raging in both British and American society over the morality of bombing civilian populations rather than just military installations. After German planes lost their way and accidentally bombed London in August 1940, the British were the first to launch large-scale bombings of German cities. According to historian Michael Bess, when the Americans entered the war, some officers believed that area bombardment of cities (as opposed to precision bombing of military targets) would never be acceptable to the American public.[10] Arthur Harris, head of the British Bomber Command, argued that as cruel as it might be, the bombing of enemy cities was proving to be highly effective in degrading the enemy's military capabilities and offered the best chance of winning the war as quickly as possible. The American command quickly adopted Harris's view, stating that bombarding civilian homes, even if it meant killing of noncombatants, would further the goal of concluding the war swiftly and thereby saving lives.[11]

Prominent writers and clergymen, however, joined prominent British writer Vera Brittain in a growing movement that called this policy the "obliteration bombings." In the United States the Fellowship of Reconciliation published similar critiques under the title "Massacre by Bombing." They argued that there was no moral justification for the bombings; that they only further engendered hate and a desire for revenge on the part of the German people; they increased the German will to resist. Cousins waded directly into the argument, writing that he "disagreed violently" with this position.[12] In an editorial attacking Brittain's position, he argued that the Germans had brought this upon themselves: "The bombing of [German cities] was not ordered by the American people or the British people or our military leaders. It was ordered by the Nazis themselves. . . . If Germany dislikes these bombings, if she would prefer that we cease and desist, she has only to tell us that she has had enough."[13]

Although Cousins was supportive of mass aerial bombing, he was especially concerned about the advanced new weaponry both sides were deploying. Given his position in the Overseas Department of the OWI, Cousins was well aware of the overwhelming destruction in Europe. His work afforded him the opportunity to speak with many people about the long-term implications of the role science played in destructive warfare, which left a powerful impression on him. Cousins believed this experience was an important part of his personal growth, because his bird's-eye view of the war sparked a passionate connection to the larger issues.[14] On March 3, 1945, he decided to air his concerns in an editorial addressing his assessment that the postwar peace was not a foregone conclusion and that given the advancements of science, should another war break out, it would likely be the world's final war. Presciently envisioning what would soon come to pass in the atomic age, he wrote,

> It will be a war operated by means of push-buttons and levers, releasing and directing armadas of high detonation through the sky. It will be a canopy of death making the present V1 and V2 robombs and rocketbombs seem like flimsy kites alongside the B29 Superfortresses. There will be switchboards of annihilation, with one button for a large city such as Detroit, and another for New York. . . . The moment [the next war] starts each nation

> will run to its own switchboard—that will be the end of everything, literally, figuratively, definitively.[15]

Of course, despite nations' possessing nuclear weapons after 1945, countless subsequent wars have not (yet) led to global destruction, but what Cousins correctly anticipated was the terrifying power of modern weaponry. Cousins's vision of the future would ultimately become a reality just months later, unleashed by the dropping of the first atomic bomb on Hiroshima on August 6, 1945.

The day that Cousins learned of the atomic bombing, he was scheduled to speak before a business group at the Waldorf Astoria Hotel in New York City. Throughout the war Cousins had devoted a lot of time to giving lectures both to public audiences and to soldiers at army camps.[16] Despite the stutter that had plagued his youth, Cousins had become a gifted and engaging speaker, drawing increasingly large audiences.[17] In his wartime speeches he typically extolled the virtuousness of the American war effort and implored citizens and soldiers alike not to become defeatist. If the businessmen gathered at the Waldorf that afternoon expected more of the same from Cousins, they were in for a surprise. Still stunned by the news of the bomb, Cousins scrapped his original speech and instead talked about the world-altering events of the previous evening. Cousins told the group that he had never known such sadness as he felt about the decision to use such a terrible weapon on human beings. He believed that "the decision to use the atomic bomb was perhaps the greatest single mistake in American history."[18]

Although there is no record of how the crowd reacted to this bold statement, by Cousins's own admission it was an unpopular position to take on that day. Not just bold but hypocritical, some might say. How could a man who fervently supported the firebombing of German cities suddenly be against the bombing of Hiroshima? Cousins would later explain,

> One of the dangers and perhaps flaws in my position about the mass bombing of Germany was that having started down that road we could justify almost anything that we did. . . . But the situation in Hiroshima was, it seems to me, basically different. We didn't have to do it. Would it really . . . bring us closer to victory? Or is it random and extraneous destruction, where the loss of lives becomes more than a wartime fact, but something that is the result of a political—rather than military—decision?[19]

Cousins would counter that he had supported the bombing of German cities because he saw it as the quickest way to bring an end to Nazi barbarism. But in this case it was the United States that had perpetrated the barbarism. Even though the end result of the destruction might look similar, the atomic bomb, he argued, was a fundamentally different weapon than conventional bombs. The advent of atomic weapons marked the end of one period in the history of man and the beginning of a new, unknown, much more dangerous era.[20] The dropping of the atomic bomb on Japan was entirely different from the bombing of Germany because it signaled a paradigm shift. Cousins later stated that the astonishing power of the atomic bomb had been such that "history had come around to the point where it was no longer possible to use force as a way of protecting yourself against force."[21]

In the aftermath of the bombing, Cousins wrote that he felt that humanity had "fixed a sword with the point over his heart, and he was stumbling around in a darkened arena full of pits, holes, and knee-high obstacles."[22] His means of sorting out these thoughts was to write "Modern Man Is Obsolete." Cousins, though, recognized the contradiction he faced in publishing that editorial. Cousins would later admit that to that point in his life he had been a gradualist, but with Hiroshima it had become clear to him that a long-range ideal had become an immediate necessity.[23] "Modern Man Is Obsolete" was a call to action, imploring people around the world to finally embrace a true world government that could control atomic energy and prevent future wars. Cousins's was among a growing cacophony of voices that, post-Hiroshima, believed that the bomb had rendered current political and economic nationalism meaningless and called for a new international order.[24]

Because of this new reality, Cousins would make sure that his newfound anti-nuclear work was not "just talk," as it had been before the war. This time Cousins was determined to use his talk to spur action. On that August morning, he resolved to dedicate the rest of his life to the anti-nuclear cause.

CHAPTER 4

AN ANTI-NUCLEAR CRUSADE

Norman Cousins truly believed that with inspired leadership the dawn of this new atomic era could be the moment when humanity broke through to a new awareness and, in doing so, entered what could easily be a golden age of peace. This world, however, would have to be consciously built.[1] In order to achieve this rather idealist and lofty goal, his first order of business was to make the *Saturday Review* a weekly mouthpiece of atomic-age awareness by changing its editorial approach to highlight the cause of peace. "I feel very deeply," Cousins explained to a reader, "the responsibility of an editor to carry the message of peace to his readers."[2] He also believed that peace could only be lasting if there was some mechanism of world law through which to enforce it. Explaining his position, Cousins wrote, "I believe deeply that the basic and urgent need of our time is for world law in time to stop world war. I believe everything else is secondary until this one basic problem is solved."[3]

Much as he had in previous years, Cousins dove into educating himself about the challenges and possibilities of the atomic age. His office filing cabinets soon filled with the latest pamphlets, reports, books, and statements regarding atomic energy. Interestingly, though, despite being the editor of a literary magazine and a former book reviewer, Cousins was not a voracious reader. Later in life when his daughter Candis asked him about reading, he responded, "No, I don't *read* books, I *use* books." At the magazine, Cousins had his staff do much of the reading for him.[4] Even the president of the *Saturday Review*, Hal Smith, once wrote that reading and reviewing books "was never Norman's real function because however much he knew of the scientists, historians, and statesmen with whom he has been most concerned," he did not have time to know the world of books.[5]

Week after week in the *Saturday Review*, one can see Cousins's sense of increasing urgency that with peace would come apathy among the American people. Even before the use of the bomb, drawing from historical lessons (which he often did to reinforce his arguments), Cousins reminded his readers that although Thomas Paine had rejoiced at the 1783 Treaty of Paris, which ended the American Revolution, later he had realized that the most important period actually had been after the peace, from 1783 to 1787, when vast political change was necessary.[6] Cousins saw Paine's sentiment reflected in the post-1945 era. Given the existence of the atomic bomb, the need for change was especially urgent in the United States, which would have to quickly embrace new thinking and new laws in order to safely control this ghastly superweapon.

In the fall of 1945, as "Modern Man Is Obsolete" was read worldwide and received rave reviews, Cousins's worst nightmare seemed to be coming true. Two months after the war ended, Cousins wrote of the "shocking failure thus far to accept the responsibility for moral leadership that was laid at our door at the end of the war. . . . The world is slipping, too, back into old systems of isolation and power politics and spheres of influence."[7] Cousins was especially exasperated following the war because, as he wrote, "I still can't understand, even now, how it is that the American people were not sickened by the action of their leaders in authorizing the dropping of the bomb."[8] He argued both in private and in public that "we came out of the war thinking that peace falls like fruit, over-ripe fruit, from trees. . . . We came out of the war with an anesthesia of conscience, a paralysis of responsibility. We came out of the war with bankrupt leadership."[9]

This was a rather harsh indictment of a country that in fact *was* attempting in many ways to exercise moral leadership through initiatives such as the denazification process; seeking justice for war crimes through the Nuremburg Trials; flooding Europe with material and monetary aid; and attempting to establish an occupation zone that fostered greater freedom and civic representation, especially in contrast to what the Soviets were offering.

Cousins was not so much criticizing American actions as he was condemning the limited application of American power. He believed that the United States should use its position of postwar superiority to engage even more heavily in world affairs. In reality, the United States *was* doing what Cousins wanted. The nation rapidly shook off its previous isolationism and took on the task of creating the world anew. In fact, as historian Geir Lundestad argues, America's expanded role after the war was "striking" and "could be felt strongly in most corners of the world."[10] Cousins seemed to want even more. In addition to calling for American moral leadership in controlling atomic weapons, Cousins also proposed that the United States should essentially continue its total war footing. Cousins wanted the country to devote as much of its resources toward peace and humanitarian aid as it had toward fighting the war, going far beyond its current efforts to secure peace and democracy for all. He called for "an immediate and complete mobilization of America's industrial and agricultural resources, a mobilization for mercy."[11]

Cousins was not alone in these calls for American global leadership at the time. As historian Stephen Wertheim writes in *Tomorrow, the World*, a small group of prominent Ivy League intellectuals and scholars were advocating for the same thing.[12] Scholars like James Shotwell, Yale professor Nicholas Spykman, and economist (and author of the UN charter) Leo Pasvolsky may have differed over the details, but they all agreed that global leadership was an American birthright.[13] But while Cousins's larger "mobilization for mercy" overlooked the public's war-weariness and its desire to put hardship behind it and return to normalcy, he was not the only one who recognized the lack of awareness of the atomic threat. His increasingly forceful editorials were about to gain him some notice in high places.

Even though he had no scientific training, Cousins's understanding of the dangers that atomic weapons posed and his espousal of what should be done to head off catastrophe caught the attention of the preeminent physicist Albert Einstein. Einstein had lent his intellectual stature to the effort to persuade President Roosevelt to launch the Manhattan Project in the first place, but he had regrets after seeing the results of the bomb. Einstein read "Modern Man Is Obsolete," which resonated with him deeply enough that the famous physicist wrote Cousins asking to meet so that they could consider what ought to be done in the future.[14] Cousins arranged to meet with Einstein, and during their two-hour parlay Einstein attempted to draw Cousins out and encourage him to be even bolder with his editorials.[15]

Cousins was a champion of the United World Federalists, an organization created in 1947 that advocated for a strong, enforceable world law that could resolve national disputes and prevent wars. It fit with Cousins's belief that the atomic bomb made national sovereignty obsolete. Einstein too was an advocate for world government. Einstein outlined his concern that one of America's vulnerabilities was the belief that the country was powerful (and thus invincible). For this reason, he believed there was an urgent need to persuade people of the danger posed by atomic weapons, which, despite a nation's conventional military power, were nearly impossible to defend against. Einstein told Cousins that he would like to do what he could to help and specifically offered to meet with influential people who needed to be convinced.[16]

Einstein would be just the first of many atomic scientists who would soon gravitate toward Cousins. Cousins's public statement of his frustration that America was failing to demonstrate moral leadership equal to the atomic threat drew to him equally frustrated scientists who shared this sentiment. The Association of Los Alamos Scientists, which took keen interest in Cousins's editorials, wrote to him expressing their eagerness "that there should be the closest of cooperation between us." They offered their scientific expertise to "arrange for the maximum assistance which we can give you."[17]

From the day "Modern Man Is Obsolete" was published, the *Saturday Review* was the nation's only periodical to continuously champion the cause of international law and atomic control, which turned the magazine into a sort of clearinghouse for the atomic scientists. Following Hiroshima, many scientists realized that it was not enough to simply "stick to the science," especially if modern science could create something as horrific as an atomic bomb. Many scientists recognized that there needed to be a public reckoning in the aftermath of the bombings and that scientists' opinions should help to inform the public and serve to influence policy. According to Cousins, "The first of them to approach us was Harrison [S.] Brown, and he brought in [Leo] Szilard. That was the beginning of a fairly intensive association and certainly a warm friendship."[18] Eventually joining the ranks was a veritable who's who of the Manhattan Project: Alexander Sachs, Eugene Wigner, Lee A. DuBridge, Arthur Compton, and the "father" of the Manhattan Project himself, J. Robert Oppenheimer.

At the request of atomic scientist Leo Szilard, Cousins actively helped to raise funds to launch the *Bulletin of the Atomic Scientists*, a dedicated publication through which scientists could compound their voices.[19] Cousins also supported the creation of the Federation of Atomic Scientists, an organization devoted to the belief that scientists have an ethical obligation to ensure that the technological fruits of their intellect and labor are applied to the benefit of humankind.[20] Cousins personally donated five thousand dollars to the federation, a substantial amount at the time (nearly $73,000 in 2020 dollars), large enough to draw the attention of the FBI, which noted it in a report.[21] Cousins, however, was quite financially secure. His 1943 tax return shows that in that year he had earned $6,423.53 (nearly $94,000 in 2020 dollars).[22] This was more than double the approximately $3,000 average income for non-farm families around that same time.[23]

In addition, Cousins took the lead in organizing a major fundraiser, the Atomic Age Dinner at the Waldorf Astoria Hotel. The purpose of the dinner was, as organizer Ulric Bell explained, to "draw attention to the impact of atomic energy upon our thinking."[24] Seventeen hundred people showed up on the night of November 28, 1945, to hear the guest of honor, the director of the Los Alamos National Laboratory, J. Robert Oppenheimer. Also on the speaking docket were Leo Szilard and Colonel Paul Tibbets, the pilot of the plane that dropped the first atomic bomb.[25] Tibbets concluded his speech by explaining that he had since been on the ground in Hiroshima and wanted to make clear that the aerial photographs did not show the vast extent of the damage done to the city.[26] Hosted by the prominent radio personality Raymond Swing, the dinner succeeded in raising thirty-seven thousand dollars to help finance the activities of the Federation of Atomic Scientists.[27] Following the dinner, the founder of the Simon & Schuster publishing house, Lincoln Schuster, would write that "Norman has become the editorial nerve center for a whole group of scientists that developed the atomic bomb—from Urey to Oppenheimer and Smythe right down the line."[28]

Spurred on by his professional connections and budding friendships with these prominent atomic scientists, and recognizing that the world desperately needed to understand the dangers of atomic weapons, Cousins decided to dedicate an entirely new feature in the magazine to the cause. On November 17, 1945, the *Saturday Review* launched a new section called "The Atomic Age," recruiting nuclear physicist Eugene Wigner to pen the first article.[29] Oppenheimer followed up with an article in the next issue. Cousins's hope was not only to have atomic experts explain to the layman the science behind the atomic bomb but to address the myriad problems the nation was forced to consider because of the existence of such a weapon, as Oppenheimer explained in his article, "Atomic Weapons and the Crisis in Science."[30]

Cousins's credentials as an anti-atomic campaigner grew exponentially as the *Saturday Review* tirelessly addressed these issues in a way that no other mass-consumption periodical did at the time. Because of his campaigning and his expanding professional connections in the scientific world, in October 1945 Cousins received an invitation to attend and participate in the Dublin Conference in New Hampshire. The conference was arranged as an unofficial meeting to gather top experts to consider how best to remedy the perceived weakness of the United Nations Organization to maintain international peace in the face of the new challenges atomic weapons presented.[31]

As Cousins explained in an editorial, the conference was necessary because "the world which the San Francisco Conference met to consider [before the atomic bombings] no longer exists, even though the same nations and same people represented at the Conference belong to both the old and new worlds."[32] The organizers of the Dublin Conference recognized that time was a luxury the world could little afford in the face of the atomic threat. Even an article that made the front page of the *New York Times* declared that "it was obvious that the atomic bomb . . . had tragically revealed the inadequacy of the United Nations Organization to maintain international peace."[33]

After five days of private debate, the majority of the Dublin Conference delegates signed a declaration outlining their conclusion that the only effective means to prevent a future war was through the international control of atomic weapons.[34] The only way to truly achieve a lasting peace, the declaration outlined, was to create "a world federal government . . . with closely defined and limited power adequate to prevent war and designed to restore and strengthen the freedoms that are the inalienable rights of man."[35] Norman Cousins, whose signature can be found among those endorsing the declaration, was later put in charge of the committee tasked with drafting the amendment to strengthen the UN Charter.

The Dublin Conference actually accomplished little toward reforming the United Nations. In terms of Cousins's atomic education, however, it proved to be an immensely fruitful five days. He met a number of men there who would soon become prominent; he would remain in touch with them, and they would greatly expand the profile of his anti-nuclear work going forward. Grenville Clark would go on to become a prominent organizer for peace and world government; Alan Cranston would have a long career in the US Senate and would be particularly supportive of Cousins in the years to come; and Thomas K. Finletter, who was to become Truman's secretary of the Air Force and later Kennedy's ambassador to NATO, would prove especially important to Cousins. Cousins's friendship with Cranston and Finletter would soon result in Cousins joining a meeting with President Harry Truman to help lobby for the international control of nuclear weapons. Cousins had come a long way, from being an unknown junior reporter standing at the back of the room during a White House press conference with Franklin Roosevelt in 1938 to sitting at the table with President Truman in 1945.

Cousins first met with Truman at 12:30 p.m. on December 21, 1945, when Cranston, Finletter, Cousins, and a few other participants sat down with the president to, as Cousins recalled, "assure him of public support for a position on world organization he might take far in advance of any position he has taken previously," as well as to discuss how to implement enforceable atomic safeguards. As spokesman for the group, Finletter outlined for the president the current weakness of the United Nations and spoke of ways to develop "enforceable safeguards" applicable to atomic energy. According to notes Cousins took, Truman listened intently before responding, "I am not wringing my hands about this thing. I think we are going to be able to work it out alright. . . . We are working on a step by step plan to achieve the necessary international controls." The president concluded that he was "pretty confident that we will be able to control this thing."[36] "This thing" was the atomic bomb.

Cousins interjected at that point, pressing the argument that it was the time to anticipate the long-term problems that the atomic bomb presented for peace. The United Nations as then constituted was incapable of doing the job. International control required the power of enforceable world law, a point that the president readily agreed with before he stated that he was unwilling to go on the record in support of world law out of fear of being labeled a Communist.[37]

Cousins admitted to spending much of the meeting trying to get a "personality impression" of the president. He wrote that he had come away with a much more favorable impression than he expected. At the same time, however, Cousins noted, "I don't think he saw atomic energy as the beginning of a new age in human history. . . . or the fact that we were dealing with absolute power and what the implications of absolute power meant."[38] This did not sit well with Cousins, who believed that the existence of atomic weapons was indeed a crisis that the American leadership and the American public in general were not taking seriously enough—a charge he would level regularly in his editorials.

Cousins's impression of the president declined further when, despite Truman's assurances that he agreed with the Dublin Committee's goals and would work toward controls on atomic weapons, the months dragged on and the president failed to take any further steps toward increasing the strength of the United Nations. In 1948, Cousins and a number of his associates, backed by Senator Brien McMahon (D-CT), decided to take another shot at persuading Truman. They met with him on January 20, 1948, to present to him the Norwalk Petition, which called for strengthening the United Nations into an organization that could enforce world law.[39]

The United Nations was created partly as an avenue for nations to work together to prevent conflicts from becoming full-scale wars—an imperative that the existence of atomic weapons had made even more important. The United Nations, however, was falling short. Cousins and others had hoped to encourage Truman to strengthen the organization, but the editor of the *New Yorker*, E. B. White, for one, reflected a widespread feeling that nation-states were incapable of "applying law and justice to each other. . . . Under all is the steady throbbing of the engines: sovereignty, sovereignty, sovereignty."[40] Cousins attempted to apply further pressure through public opinion. On March 27, 1948, he published in the *Saturday Review* an eight-point open letter to the president explaining why a weak United Nations would not be able to keep the peace.[41]

While Cousins's initial impression of Truman was favorable, it seems to have quickly worn off. He would later write in a letter that he thought Truman was a void when it came to generating grand inspiring ideas and that his sense of goodwill was "insular and independent of any central purpose or mission."[42]

CHAPTER 5

1946: A NEW YEAR *in the* ATOMIC AGE

As the winter of 1945/46 descended, a ruined Europe was witness to millions standing in line to receive meager rations with which to fend off the cold, starvation, and disease that followed the end of the war. Cousins bitterly noted in the *Saturday Review* that at the same time millions of Americans also stood in line, but to purchase expensive luxury goods. America's throbbing prosperity juxtaposed to Europe's and Asia's impoverishment and despair was, Cousins charged, "as tragic as it is grotesque."[1] That this disparity was allowed to exist Cousins largely blamed on the American people, who, comfortable in their own material excess, had not demanded that their leaders do more.[2] Secretary of State George C. Marshall would use much the same language when he announced the Marshall Plan the following year: "The people of this country are distant from the troubled areas of the earth and it is hard for them to comprehend the plight and consequent reactions of the long-suffering peoples."[3]

With two editorials in early 1946, "Reading Between the Lines" and "For Murderers Only," Cousins delivered one of the earliest articulations of what would become one of his oft-stated positions: that the US government was not doing enough to help alleviate humanitarian crises around the world. Since the United States had the resources and the financial ability to help, neglecting to do so amounted to a shirking

Cousins in 1946.

(PHOTO BY FRED STEIN / ALAMY STOCK PHOTO)

of its moral responsibility to humanity. In Cousins's view, any able individual or entity, especially the US government, had the moral obligation to help in the face of injustice. He harbored a great fear that if America shirked this responsibility, the rest of the world would come to resent it for its selfish apathy in the face of global deprivation. He believed this would be especially true in the case of Japan. In Cousins's estimation the United States, having set the precedent of destroying human life with atomic weapons, was obliged to demonstrate moral leadership by making amends.[4]

Although the United States had not set the precedent of aerial bombardment of cities, as Cousins's many wartime editorials pointed out, he supported the tactic when used against Germany. It is clear that Cousins was anti-Nazi from early on, and his focus on Europe while working for the OWI seems to have nurtured a special hatred toward

Nazi Germany. He had already argued essentially that *they* had started it and therefore deserved what they got in terms of Allied bombing during the war. But Cousins's tone toward Japan suffered from a bit of cognizant disconnect. He ignored the violent imperialist expansion Japan had been involved in throughout the 1930s, not to mention the Japanese surprise attack on Pearl Harbor. He argued that the United States needed to atone for its atomic bombing of Japan because it was a wrong that *we* had done to *them*.[5] Cousins's editorials painted the picture that the US use of the bomb had been so horrific as to negate anything the Japanese had done during the war to that point. His was a minority view: in August 1945 a Gallup poll reported that 85 percent of the American public approved of the dropping of the atomic bombs on Japan.[6]

In addition to his writing, Cousins maintained a robust public-speaking schedule. He typically spoke to audiences about new books and emerging literary trends, with brief forays into discussions of world affairs.[7] The many hours of Cousins's speeches from the 1940s and 1950s that the UCLA archivists have preserved on the original reel-to-reel tapes offer an education in excellent oratory. He skillfully translated his editorial vision into speeches that commanded an audience. On the tapes one can sense the audience's rapt attention. He knew how to be self-deprecating and how to entertain with humor and anecdote. His deep, warm, resonant voice had the rhythm and music of poetry. He spoke truth as he saw it, with a sincerity that was audible and to my mind beyond question. On any podium, he shared what he regarded as crucial for those listening to hear and understand, for their own good and for the good of the planet. His daughter Sarah remembers "sitting in an audience somewhere and feeling proud, as his voice rose to a crescendo, that his impact as a public speaker lay, above all, in the force of his conviction, the power of his belief."[8]

Despite the great skill her father developed in public speaking over the years, Sarah recalls her mother telling her that he initially took up lecturing to pay back their friends Henry and Bertie Myers, of Norwalk,

Connecticut, who had lent him the money for the home they purchased.[9] Public speaking was more lucrative than writing for the financially struggling *Saturday Review.*

While he maintained a busy work schedule and was away for many extended periods, Cousins's wife, Ellen, proved to be his champion and strongest supporter. His daughter Sarah says that her mother supported her father's projects "unhesitatingly, uncomplainingly." Candis recalls that Ellen "was the Hercules of the family. She held everything up."[10] Ellen did not work outside the home, but Sarah says that their mother was anything but a conventional American housewife—with the fifty chickens that she raised in order to serve her family organic eggs and the large organic garden that she cultivated by herself. "I do remember," Sarah recalled, "my mother telling me that she had wanted to have a cow [at the home to provide fresh milk] and to this, my father had said no. If I recall the story correctly, he said he could just imagine calling her to come into the city to attend this or that event, and she would say, 'Norman, I can't. I have to milk the cow.'"[11] The Cousins house was open to one and all. Both Ellen and Norman seemed to regard all of humanity as their responsibility. "I love that about them. I think that was their primary value in life: their sense of personal responsibility for just about anyone whose path crossed theirs," Sarah recalls.[12]

In 1946, with Cousins's intense focus on spreading awareness of the danger to humanity posed by atomic weapons, he undertook an entirely new, intensive lecture tour titled "Living in an Atomic Age." In response to a request from a bookstore owner who wanted him to lecture on current books, Cousins politely declined, explaining, "When I talk these days, it is strictly in an attempt to plant dynamite under the seats of people who think that the peace represents less of a challenge than did the war."[13] For the next four months Cousins immersed himself in his lecture tour. He also continued to deepen his connections with the atomic scientists in order to further the magazine's Atomic Age feature. Atomic scientists like Leo Szilard and Harrison

Brown were known to join Cousins at his home in Connecticut for discussions.[14]

In March 1946, Cousins was compelled to return to his desk to pen an editorial responding to an important development in international affairs. Typically, though, writing from a desk was not Cousins's style. With a seemingly incredible ability to multitask, he would most often sit in a recliner in front of the television and write his editorials on a steno pad while watching baseball.[15] A secretary at the *Saturday Review* would later type them, since Cousins, for his entire life, used the hunt-and-peck (two-fingered) method of typing. From time to time while at home Cousins would tell his wife that he needed a quiet place away from the children to write. She would oblige and create places in the house, decorating them expertly and transforming them into cozy offices. Cousins rarely used them. Invariably he would end up back in front of the baseball game. Sarah remembers fondly the sound of her father's exultant cheers of victory and pained cries of "Oh no!" in response to the games.[16]

On March 30, 1946, Cousins decided to take on former British Prime Minister Winston Churchill. On March 5, in Fulton, Missouri, Churchill had delivered his now-famous "Sinews of Peace" speech, in which he claimed that an "Iron Curtain" had descended across Europe and called for a tougher stance against the Soviet Union. Cousins, concerned that Churchill's aggression might put further stress on the already shaky and quickly crumbling foundations of postwar US-Soviet relations, blasted the former prime minister in the *Saturday Review*.

Cousins lamented that Churchill's speech encouraged the war hawks to provoke a showdown with Soviet Russia. Cousins stated that he had considered Mr. Churchill's points and sharply disagreed with most of them. He suggested that Churchill was confusing strength with hostility and equating firmness with bellicosity.[17] "Can there be any doubt," Cousins asked, "that what is needed today is not hot needles but cold compressors? Not side-choosing but genuine statesmanship? . . . not drifting but leadership and initiative?" Cousins argued that Russia was not the problem but only a symptom of the larger issue. That issue was the lack of any higher authority to ensure global security. The disease was each nation deciding for itself what was necessary for its own security, leading to universal fear and suspicion, as he articulated in "Modern Man Is Obsolete." The blame for the quickly deteriorating international situation, Cousins argued, fell largely on the United States for clinging to its atomic superiority, thus fueling Soviet suspicions. If peace was to be ensured, this cycle had to be broken, and in Cousins's estimation it could only be broken by means of an enforceable world law.[18]

Cousins had discussed these very problems with President Truman just months before, and now Truman, who sat to Churchill's right during the entire address, seemed to be adding an air of official legitimacy to a much more aggressive stance toward the Soviet Union. The Churchill speech, which led Cousins to publicly challenge Churchill on US-Soviet relations, was just a temporary diversion from Cousins's focus on the atomic issue, about which he would soon publish another article, one that sparked even greater controversy.

In January 1946, Secretary of State James Byrnes created a special committee under the direction of Under Secretary of State Dean Acheson and chairman of the Tennessee Valley Authority David Lilienthal, with J. Robert Oppenheimer as their chief scientific consultant.[19] Established on January 24, this committee was tasked with composing a report that would propose possible methods for the international control of atomic weapons. That report, which would become known as the Acheson-Lilienthal Report, was presented to the State Department on March 16. Kept in the loop through his contacts with Szilard, Einstein, and Oppenheimer, Cousins managed to arrange a telephone interview with David Lilienthal on March 15, the day before the report was sent to State. Cousins, meanwhile, was gathering as much background on the Acheson-Lilienthal Report as he could for an important article he and Thomas Finletter were collaborating on.

Timed to coincide with the first meeting of the United Nations Atomic Energy Commission on June 15 and disguised ostensibly as a review of the Acheson-Lilienthal Report, Cousins's article, "A Beginning for Sanity," coauthored by Thomas K. Finletter, began by expressing the authors' irritation that since the war's end, "instead of a bold, affirmative program whose dimensions bore some relationship to the size of the problem, America has exhibited a policy of drift, default, and delay."[20] Mincing no words, Cousins and Finletter then definitively stated their belief that the Truman administration's decision to drop the atomic bomb had been a "mountainous blunder." Importantly, though, they also excused Roosevelt's decision to fund the Manhattan Project in the first place and absolved the atomic scientists working for it of moral responsibility by claiming that they had not known what they "were forced to do out of sheer national preservation, for the enemy was working on atomic weapons as well."[21] This assumption by Cousins, however, was wrong. Although it was accepted reasoning at the time, we now know that Japan's nuclear program was nonexistent, and Germany's had been greatly diminished by mid-1942 and mostly scuttled that fall.[22]

This statement absolving the scientists presents an intriguing dichotomy since a common theme in Cousins's writing is that citizens cannot expect to escape blame if they fail to exercise their own individual moral responsibility. Given this fact, one wonders whether he tempered his criticism of the scientists working on the project because of his close friendship with many of them. When later pressed on the issue of the moral responsibilities of the atomic scientists, Cousins responded, "I don't know what more they could have done. Should they have immolated themselves?" Asked whether they could have withheld their labor, he answered, "I don't think they would have gained any credibility by such dramatic tactics."[23]

Recognizing the highly volatile nature of the assertion that using the bomb had been a "mountainous blunder," Cousins and Finletter went on to support their contention with evidence they had gathered over the past year. The source for their conclusion was the Franck Report.[24] Virtually unknown to the public at the time, the report revealed that a number of top atomic scientists had urged Truman to conduct a public demonstration of the bomb rather than using it against a city. Failing to do so would jeopardize the United States' standing and degrade trust, especially in regard to Russia, according to the scientists. "The military advantages . . . may be outweighed by the ensuing loss of confidence and by a wave of horror and repulsion sweeping over the rest of the world," the report argued.[25] If this was the case, Cousins and Finletter asked, why then drop the bomb?

Decades before it would become a hotly contested argument in academic circles and nineteen years before historian Gar Alperovitz would posit the same argument in his 1965 book *Atomic Diplomacy*, Cousins and Finletter made the controversial claim that the bomb had been used because the United States was, they claimed, "more anxious to prevent Russia from establishing a claim for full participation in the occupation against Japan than we were to think through the implications of unleashing atomic warfare." They argued that the Franck Report and its call for an atomic demonstration had been ignored because "any test would have been impossible if the purpose was to knock Japan out before Russia came in."[26] Historian Barton Bernstein points out that this idea that the bombs were dropped to forestall Russia, the so-called atomic diplomacy argument, was "first suggested by Norman Cousins."[27]

What Cousins and Finletter willfully ignore in "A Beginning for Sanity," however, is the question of an invasion of Japan as an alternative to dropping the bombs. As historian Richard Frank points out, any American citizen who read the newspaper could have easily concluded based on publicly available information that an invasion of the Japanese home islands would have resulted in potentially staggering American losses.[28] Historian Michael Bess writes that throughout the war the Japanese endured a fatality rate rarely seen in the history of warfare. Japanese soldiers fought to the bitter end and preferred death or suicide over capture or surrender.[29] Newspapers of the day dwelt on the immense cost in lives—anywhere from five hundred thousand to a million casualties, one correspondent supposed—that an invasion might result in.[30] Today, however, these numbers do not stand up. Samuel Walker, a former historian of the US Nuclear Regulatory Commission, acknowledges that the idea that an invasion would bring hundreds of thousands of casualties was a rationalization after the fact to justify a terrible act; the estimates made at the time were much lower.[31]

Cousins never joined the debate over an invasion of Japan in any of his 1944 or 1945 articles. This is somewhat unsurprising, though, as both his editorials and his work with the OWI kept him quite focused on the war in Europe. His attention turned to Japan only after the bombing. Years later Cousins would claim that before he read the Franck Report, "the argument that [the atomic bomb] was dropped to spare the casualties of an invasion was even more ludicrous to me."[32] Although Truman stood by his claim that the use of the bomb saved from half a million to a million lives, most scholars now agree that after six decades of accruing evidence, this estimate of half a million casualties has been completely discredited.[33]

At the time of its publication, "A Beginning for Sanity" was one of the most poignant and hard-hitting critiques yet to be published about the decision to use the atomic bomb. It would be the first of an increasing number of articles that directly confronted the Truman administration's stated reasons for using the bomb. In 1948, the British physicist P. M. S. Blackett published his thesis that the bomb had been dropped to impress the Soviets, as the first salvo of the Cold War. The prominent American writer and intellectual Lewis Mumford claimed that the bomb was nothing more than genocide wrapped up in a neater and cheaper package. In 1947, labor activist and pacifist A. J. Muste labeled the bomb a "sin of the most hideous kind.[34] But it was journalist John Hersey who, in the summer of 1946, would provide Americans with a stunning picture of the effects of the atomic bombs.

On August 31, 1946, the *New Yorker* published Hersey's "Hiroshima," in which he put a human face on the devastating effects of the bomb by telling the gripping stories of six survivors.[35] Although the media coverage of the bombing had initially been heavy, the details of the aftermath were hard to come by. Immediately after the bombing, the newly arrived American occupation forces embarked on a concerted (and mostly successful) effort to contain the story of the aftermath of the bombing.[36] Hersey's "Hiroshima" gave Americans their first exposure to the bombings in human terms. In 1999, New York University's journalism school voted John Hersey's "Hiroshima" the twentieth century's most important work of journalism.[37] According to journalist Lesley Blume, Hersey alerted Americans to the fact that they were facing a full-blown crisis and that everyone in the country needed to acknowledge the Pandora's box the United States had opened.[38] Cousins would praise Hersey's article in a 1946 editorial of his own, while also writing again about the "crime" of Hiroshima.[39]

It was this increasing level of public criticism and questioning of the use of the atomic bomb in late 1946 that finally forced a public defense of the Truman administration's decision to use the bomb. Bart Bernstein contends that it was Cousins's September editorial that especially alarmed atomic policymaker James B. Conant.[40] He wrote to Harvey H. Bundy, formerly a special assistant to the secretary of war, to complain that there had been a lot of dangerous "Monday morning quarterbacking" about the Japan bombings. Clipped to his letter was a copy of Cousins's editorial.[41]

Wanting to shape popular opinion and eradicate this "wrong kind of thinking" by this "group of so-called intellectuals"—writers like Hersey and Cousins—who might negatively influence opinions about the bombings, Conant persuaded former secretary of war Henry Stimson to pen an article setting the record straight (from their perspective at least). William Burr, senior analyst at the National Security Archive, agrees that it was primarily Norman Cousins's explicit and continued criticism of the decision that prompted Stimson to respond with an article of his own.[42] Bernstein's research reveals that Stimson's article, "The Decision to Use the Atomic Bomb," was largely ghostwritten by twenty-seven-year-old McGeorge Bundy (Harvey H. Bundy's son), who decades later would become President Kennedy's national security advisor.[43] Interestingly, Cousins had actually been advised earlier in 1946 by one of his *Saturday Review* colleagues, John Mason Brown, to hire the "brilliant young man" (Bundy) to write for the *Saturday Review*.[44]

In February 1947, *Harper's Magazine* published Stimson's article, in which he outlined the reasons why the United States had been justified in dropping the bomb on Japan.[45] Stimson's attempt to counter the growing accusations of atomic critics like Cousins cemented the ideological divide and established the parameters of the debate over the atomic bomb that would rage for the next sixty years. But before Stimson's article came out in 1947, months after "A Beginning for Sanity" was published, Cousins had already embarked on yet another atomic experience. He was not at his New York City office to gauge the reaction to his charges against the Truman administration's reasons for using the bomb, for he was already on his way to the South Pacific, where he would witness an atomic explosion firsthand.

CHAPTER 6

WITNESS *to a* CATASTROPHE

Earlier in 1946 Cousins had applied for press credentials in order to be an observer at Project Crossroads. It would be the first postwar test of an atomic bomb, scheduled to take place that July in the Bikini Atoll chain of islands in the South Pacific. Aboard the USS *Appalachian* steaming toward the islands, Cousins explained his feelings about what he would soon witness as a response to a "primitive overwhelming lure of the spectacle," a "morbid curiosity," a "perverse fascination."[1] But weighing on his mind even more heavily was the fact that while he was en route to the spectacle of a live nuclear test that he called a grotesque, authorized insanity, he recognized that this "deliberate catastrophe" helped to dramatize the real issue that was being discussed at that very moment at the United Nations. He saw the irony in the fact that these two acts in the global atomic drama were playing simultaneously. One act took place in New York, where Bernard Baruch was presenting a modified version of the Acheson-Lilienthal Plan (a push to establish an international body to oversee the use of atomic energy), while the concurrent act was to be a US expression of atomic might. To Cousins these two acts symbolized both the problem and the choice: the world was racing to control atomic weapons, while he was steaming toward a man-made atomic catastrophe. The US government had already decided which act to attend, having signaled its chilling intention by proceeding with the test.[2]

There was one positive side to this test, Cousins realized. Although less than a year had passed, he thought that the world had already forgotten too much about Hiroshima. En route to Bikini, Cousins wrote to David Lilienthal that he saw a perceptible improvement in the global opinion regarding atomic control and was hopeful that things would "break the right way."[3] At the very least this test would be a reminder, however costly, of what the world faced.[4]

The Bikini test marked the fourth atomic bomb to be exploded in the world in less than a year, but this one was different from the previous three, shrouded in their wartime secrecy. This time the eyes of the world were watching through surrogates like Cousins, who took his position on the third deck of the USS *Appalachian* at 7:30 a.m. on July 1, 1946. The bomb was detonated, and Cousins ripped off the goggles that protected his eyes from the blinding flash to see the rising mushroom cloud. He reacted with a shudder at the thought that this was now a familiar symbol. One of his fellow correspondents, unimpressed by the explosion, turned to him and said, "I was just thinking that the next war's not going to be so bad after all."[5]

Racing to meet a deadline, Cousins and his fellow reporters would have just ten minutes from the moment of the explosion to file their stories—before the mushroom cloud even reached its ceiling (which happened fifty-seven minutes after the detonation). For that reason, the initial reports Americans would receive were mostly prewritten. The reports were eyewitness accounts only in the most cursory sense. The prominent *New York Times* journalist William Laurence, who had already witnessed the Trinity test in New Mexico, as well as the Nagasaki bomb, wired back to the *Times* that what he saw was an "awesome, spine-chilling spectacle," but that day's headline also reported that it was "less than expected."[6]

Cousins later revealed his concern that "we—those of us at Bikini—did a bad job of reporting" because it was not until two days later that they were allowed to enter the lagoon and inspect firsthand the vast extent of the damage, which had not been immediately visible from the ship, anchored miles away.[7] By the time the reporters were able to file more thorough, evidence-based articles, Cousins lamented, it was already too late to change the public's perception that atomic bombs were merely another combat weapon. A more powerful one, sure, but nothing to be shocked by. Unimpressed, the public moved on to other stories, and the follow-up reports outlining the true extent of the bomb's damage had already missed the news cycle.[8]

Even after the long sail back to the United States, Cousins still believed that the public deserved to know what had truly transpired at Bikini. In an editorial on August 17, 1946, Cousins called upon the US government to "perform a valuable public service" by letting "the *Independence* [a target ship heavily damaged during the test] be towed back to the United States. Let it be anchored off each of the coastal cities, East and West both. Let its meaning soak in as only seeing it at first hand can do."[9] Instead, the US government would later sink all thirty or so target ships that remained afloat after the test. Eighteen had already succumbed to the blast damage and sunk.

Returning to New York City after his trip to the South Pacific and staying closer to home throughout 1947, Cousins maintained a rigorous schedule of publishing that engaged with the key issues of the day. After the flurry of articles surrounding the Bikini test, the *Saturday Review*'s editorial pages moved away from atomic issues while still encouraging peace through world law. Letting his Atomic Age feature speak for itself, Cousins noted that he was increasingly "impressed with the emergence of many of the leading scientists of this country as public citizens."[10] He also wrote in an editorial early that year that he was "afraid that the public climate in America is rapidly working itself around to the point where it will be impossible to enlist reason and intelligence in dealing with Russia."[11]

The deepening divisions between the United States and Russia especially in regard to Berlin were most concerning to Cousins. The United States' growing aggression in dealing with the Soviet Union prompted Cousins to write that he did not see "how it was possible for

Americans . . . to achieve security by developing security zones in the traditional manner of diplomacy and militarism."[12] And yet, security zones were what the United States was rapidly moving toward. In July 1947, the sensational "X article" was published in *Foreign Affairs.* In "The Sources of Soviet Conduct," State Department official George Kennan, writing under the pseudonym "X," called upon the United States to forcefully resist Russian expansion. "In the face of superior force," Kennan wrote, the Russians would retreat.[13] Kennan's earlier "long telegram" sent to the State Department was interpreted by the Truman administration as a call for a more aggressive policy against the Soviet Union.

Cousins revealed in a 1951 private letter to one *Saturday Review* benefactor that he essentially agreed with the prevailing American thinking at the time. He wrote that Americans must recognize "the Soviet's objectives, which at its minimum is to control the balance of power in the world, and at its maximum is to impose a single totalitarian system and ideology on all peoples."[14] Cousins had clearly fallen into the same trap as many American (and other Western countries') policymakers who, according to historian Marc Selverstone, had come to believe that international communism was monolithic, expansionary, and directed by Moscow toward a clear goal of world domination.[15]

Cousins in fact believed that the United States needed to go *further* in its containment policy, to be more proactive. "The problem with the containment policy," he wrote, "is that it has put us in the position of chasing after the Soviet after the damage has been done. . . . [We need to] start thinking in terms of seizing the initiative."[16] This myopic thinking—from a man who believed in the pursuit of peace and better relations between nations—was precisely the type of thinking that accelerated Cold War tensions. Cousins was reacting to growing tensions over the past few years. In the spring of 1947 a financially strapped Britain had announced that it could no longer afford to support Greece and Turkey and asked the United States to step in. Truman had responded by going before Congress and requesting $400 million, arguing that it was the duty of the United States to protect free peoples everywhere from aggression or subjugation from outside powers.[17]

This new Truman Doctrine vastly expanded the scope of US political and military involvement on a global scale. Despite privately supporting "seizing the initiative" against the Soviets, Cousins blasted Truman and his new doctrine. "The President of the United States," he wrote, "openly and directly violated the letter and spirit of the United Nations Charter by calling for American intervention in Greece and Turkey." He explained that Truman "did the American people and the cause of world security grievous damage in using a unilateral approach."[18] Clearly, Cousins was not against aggressively confronting the Soviets; he just wanted it done through the United Nations. Cousins did not say how an attempt at that might have played out given the Soviet veto in the UN Security Council.

Also left unsaid was how he reconciled his private assertion that the Soviet objective was "to impose a single totalitarian system and ideology on all peoples" with his public position that the US attempts to staunch any domestic communist subversion were overblown. In 1947, concerned about Soviet infiltration of the US government, President Truman signed an executive order requiring background investigations of people suspected of communist leanings. Disgusted by this development, Cousins wrote, "It will hardly advance the security of this country . . . by having the country overrun by over-zealous loyalty bulldogs competing with each other for victims."[19] The increasingly virulent anti-Communist sentiment that seemed to be sweeping the nation led the US Congress to ramp up the House Un-American Activities Committee (HUAC) investigations, which sought to root out Communist threats. At times HUAC called in academics who had simply criticized US foreign policies.

Cousins especially took issue with these HUAC attacks on academic freedom. Believing that educators had a legal, moral, and political responsibility to resist HUAC's witch hunts, in 1949 he took a bold stand against the US government. Cousins put out the notice that "so strongly do we feel that we are prepared to furnish legal counsel at our own expense to any school superintendent or college or university president who decides to stand his ground."[20] Cousins's stand against HUAC demonstrated his engagement with domestic issues, but more important was an August 2, 1947, editorial in which Cousins addressed an international issue, which would gain him recognition in important circles. Drawing from his experience on the New England Education Commission, Cousins wrote about the German school system and the issue of eliminating the lingering remnants of Nazi habits of thinking and teaching.[21]

Following up a month later, Cousins pressed his belief that "only education can promote the understanding among peoples that can break the long habits of war, or make better human beings."[22] Cousins's focus on education may have been driven by the fact that as an adult he had come to see himself as having been "miseducated." He would later say that he had been educated in a milieu that "fostered disillusion and cynicism," one that taught him to see historical events as inevitable and deterministic. Therefore, he had "re-educated" himself to see that humans could change the course of history.[23]

The essential role that education played in helping to build democracy and a lasting peace was not a new subject for Cousins. During the war he had been a sponsor of the Council for a Democratic Germany.[24] He also lectured on public education's effect on fostering democracy, explaining his belief that World War II had emerged partly because after World War I many European nations—France and Germany especially—had lacked a coordinated educational policy. The result, as Cousins wrote, had been that "history's lessons [were] mistaught, misunderstood, or ignored." Cousins asked if there was any doubt "that the educational vacuum existing in Germany after the last war was an open invitation to Adolf Hitler?"[25] Cousins's thoughts and arguments about education's vital role in fostering (or undermining) democracies garnered him some attention in high places and contributed to what would be Cousins's first official mission on behalf of the US government.

CHAPTER 7

AN EDUCATIONAL FIELD TRIP *to* GERMANY

By the summer of 1948, with Marshall Plan aid just beginning to pour into Europe, the United States' highest priority in Europe was democratizing Germany. General Lucius D. Clay, the commanding general of the Office of Military Government for Germany, was concerned with the human rights obligations of the occupation. Thus, he requested that the American Civil Liberties Union (ACLU) send a committee to Germany to investigate the situation and make recommendations.[1]

Cousins had been asked to join the national board of directors of the ACLU in 1944. He cut his teeth on German issues by debating legal cases involving the free-speech protections of Nazis and right-wing totalitarians. Some lawyers at the ACLU believed that they had the obligation to protect the free-speech rights of Nazi sympathizers who denounced the United States. Cousins, however, believed that "to protect the legal and human rights of those who would destroy the legal and human rights of others was stretching it a bit." It led, in his words, to "some interesting debates."[2]

Because of Cousins's experience with the ACLU, the fact that his 1942 book *The Good Inheritance, The Democratic Chance* sought to combat authoritarianism by extolling the virtues of democracy, and his most recent editorial musings about fostering education in Germany, General Clay requested that he be part of the committee that was being sent to Germany.[3] Cousins, along with Roger Baldwin and Arthur Hays, respectively the director and general counsel of the ACLU, departed in August 1948 for a seven-week tour of Germany.

While in Germany, Cousins had an opportunity to witness the emerging Cold War tension firsthand. The Berlin Blockade, the first international crisis of the Cold War, had erupted just weeks before his arrival. The Soviet Union, in an attempt to force concessions from the Allies, cut off access to the city via their land corridors. In response, the Allies began to airlift supplies into the city. Cousins had the opportunity to hitch a ride on the airlift, making several round-trips aboard a coal transport aircraft in the air corridor between Frankfurt and Berlin.

After later visiting East Berlin, Cousins became concerned about those who said that the greatest argument being provided for a free society was being supplied by the Russians in East Berlin. He felt that it was foolish to expect people to learn about the virtues of democracy simply by comparing it with Soviet rule.[4] Cousins noted that the airlift was doing more than anything else to make a positive impression on the Germans.[5] The vast American-led humanitarian effort of the Berlin Airlift was far more effective than any show of military force, which some supported. The airlift represented the exact type of moral leadership role that Cousins had been imploring the United States to take in its approach to the world. It also proved that the United States could use its financial resources and military force as instruments for good.

Reporting about his experiences in Germany in a series of four John Hersey–style articles upon his return, Cousins stayed well clear of policy and portrayed a very human story that centered on many of the people he had interviewed while in Europe. He wrote of a young girl he had met in one of the many displaced persons camps he toured;[6] an interview with the German industrialist and former Hitler supporter Fritz Thyssen, who was then on trial at Nuremberg;[7] and a conversation with a French child to whom he had struggled to explain why

Americans had so much, while Europeans had so little.[8] The articles culminated with "Dinner for 26 in Berlin," an account of the difficulties he encountered in trying to secure enough food to host a large dinner for German university students.[9]

But even after Cousins returned home, an experience he had had during a tour of the displaced persons camp in Bad Nauheim stayed with him. There he had met a seven-year-old orphaned girl named Brisca, whose parents had been murdered at the Majdanek concentration camp. After spending the day with young Brisca, Cousins was troubled when she asked him to take her out of this camp and back to America with him. Cousins had long argued that America, the land of comfort and plenty, should be doing more to help alleviate this humanitarian crisis in Europe. He was personally dismayed at his inability to help young Brisca or the millions of others in her situation. "On the way back to Frankfurt that afternoon," he would write, "I knew a sadness heavier than I had felt for many years."[10]

Cousins's seven weeks in Germany proved to be a success. The ACLU's report to General Clay was well received.[11] According to Cousins, General Clay was "very appreciative of that visit. . . . They did accept some of our key recommendations."[12] On a personal level, what Cousins saw proved to him the positive effect of moral leadership. He witnessed how the Berlin Airlift concurrently served a humanitarian prerogative and improved German citizens' opinion of the United States. At the same time, he was also struck by the harm that misguided government policies inflicted on individuals like Brisca, who needed help the most. It made clear to him the human impact of government policies. These experiences may have inspired him to take more public action to promote peace.

In January 1949, Cousins received an invitation from Dr. Harlow Shapley, head of the Harvard Observatory, inviting him to speak at the upcoming Cultural and Scientific Conference for World Peace. The conference would see eight hundred prominent literary figures descend on New York's Waldorf Astoria Hotel to call for peace with the

Soviet Union. The problem, as Cousins (and countless others, including the State Department and the CIA) saw it, was that the conference was dominated by Communists. *Newsweek* argued that the conference was nothing more than a Soviet attempt to win the minds of the world's intellectuals.[13] *Life* claimed that any American who chose to participate would be a "superdupe."[14] Not wanting to be labeled such himself, Cousins wrote that he declined his invitation based on evidence that the conference would be "used as a sounding board for blasting American policy and for vindicating Soviet policy."[15]

However, as the date drew nearer and Cousins saw the advance list of participants, he reconsidered, explaining to his readers that he believed that if only the Communist side was represented, it "would actually retard the chances for peace by intensifying the [negative] feeling between the two countries."[16] Other American intellectuals felt the same way. Biophysicist Eugene Rabinowitch would write in the *Bulletin of Atomic Scientists* that he and others had had no illusions about the political bias of the conference but had attended anyway because they believed atomic weapons should be abolished.[17]

On the fence about what to do, Cousins contacted the State Department for advice. George V. Allen, assistant secretary of state for public affairs, replied explaining the government's position to Cousins: "While the department has no illusions concerning the manner in which communists will attempt to use the conference for their own ends, the department is hopeful that an adequate and vigorous presentation of the democratic and anti-totalitarian point of view will be made."[18] Cousins, never one to shy away from defending democratic ideals, responded to Allen that he had been "undecided until the last minute about going ahead, but your encouragement swung the balance."[19]

Cousins's determination to take a strong stand at the conference cloaked his considerable anxiety when the date finally came. On the morning of his speech, Cousins telephoned the New York office of the FBI and reported that he was going to "blow the lid off the conference" in such a manner that he thought it prudent to have FBI protection at the event. Despite being informed that the FBI could offer him no such advice or protection, Cousins went ahead with his speech.[20] Speaking before the gathered delegates, Cousins proceeded to give a thorough defense of American democracy and spoke of the Communist Party of the United States (CPUSA) as a group "without standing and without honor."[21] Clearly unpopular with this audience, his speech was interrupted at least a dozen times with what the FBI, which did after all place informants in the crowd, reported back to Washington was "considerable booing and hissing."[22]

In the aftermath of the Waldorf Astoria speech debacle, the Soviet newspaper *Novy Mir* published an article charging Cousins with "attempting to whitewash the United States and to distract the American people away from their misery by calling attention to all the good things that are happening in this country."[23] By contrast, *Life* described Cousins as an "absolute ringer," saying that he had made a "ringingly pro-American speech."[24] Letters of praise for Cousins's "brave" stand poured in from the public and the government alike. The chief of the Army Security Agency wrote, "Permit me to congratulate you on your personal courage and your forthright Americanism in standing up for those ideals."[25]

While Cousins's Waldorf Astoria speech was likely one of the least well received of his career, it would prove to be an important moment in firmly establishing his anti-Communist credentials. Putting himself in the undesirable position of defending the United States and attacking the CPUSA at an event full of Communist sympathizers served to increase his stature within government circles and especially helped to insulate him against later charges that he was too supportive of the Soviet Union. For the next four decades, whenever Norman Cousins aroused the attention of the FBI either because of a citizen's "tip" that his ideas were subversive or because of background checks owing to his proximity to presidents and world leaders, his FBI investigators would reference his speech as "proof" that he was indeed an anti-

Communist, patriotic American who supported the values of the United States.[26]

In his search for a way to promote world peace in the atomic age, Cousins's steadfast belief in the ideals of democracy, peace, freedom, and improved international relations would inform him when he faced these issues head-on in Japan the following year.

CHAPTER 8

FROM EDITOR'S DESK *to* WORLD STAGE

Norman Cousins returned from his government mission to Germany in late 1948 bolstered by the knowledge that the report he had helped draft had been well received by General Clay and the US occupation administration. Soon an opportunity would present itself that would change the course of his life.

In early 1949, one of the survivors profiled in John Hersey's *Hiroshima* reached out to Cousins. Reverend Kyoshi Tanimoto, a Methodist minister in Hiroshima who was an outspoken activist for the postwar reconstruction of the city, was working hard to establish Hiroshima as an international city for peace. Because of his church affiliation, Tanimoto was invited by the Overseas Methodist Mission Board to make a speaking tour of the United States, where he hoped to raise money to help rebuild his bomb-damaged church in Hiroshima.[1] Tanimoto's more ambitious goal, as he later told *Saturday Review* readers, was to establish an "international and non-sectarian [peace center] which will serve as a laboratory of research and planning for peace education throughout the world."[2]

Tanimoto hoped to find a US partner who could help publicize his efforts and raise funds for this international peace center. Already acquainted with the American writer and humanitarian Pearl S. Buck (because of her own humanitarian work in Japan), Tanimoto asked her if she could gather a group of Americans to help support his efforts. Buck, though only fifty-seven, considered herself too old to be of much help; she instead recommended Norman Cousins as someone who might be of assistance.[3] Publishing Tanimoto's proposal for the establishment of a world peace center on March 12, 1949, Cousins informed his readers that the *Saturday Review* enthusiastically supported the initiative.[4]

Tanimoto's goal resonated with Cousins's longstanding concern that millions of dollars were being spent on research for war, with relatively little allocated to research for peace. The peace center's first focus, however, would be on meeting more immediate needs by establishing a health center and an orphanage in Hiroshima. Within six months of the publication of Tanimoto's article "Hiroshima's Idea," through the *Saturday Review* appeal and Tanimoto's US lectures he managed to raise ten thousand dollars. With these funds the Hiroshima Peace Center Associates was established, with Norman Cousins named chair of its board of directors.[5] According to Japanese historian Naoko Shibusawa, this first contact with Tanimoto marked an early episode of stateside American humanitarian aid to the victims of the atomic bomb.[6] Cousins was invited to attend the groundbreaking ceremony for the Peace Center, which took him for the first time to the city that had loomed so large in his mind since 1945.

Eager to report on the fourth anniversary of the bombing, Cousins made arrangements to visit Japan in August 1949. That he was able to travel so readily and for such long stretches despite running a magazine was partly owing to the formidable team at the *Saturday Review.* Shortly after he took the reins, he used his many connections and his persuasive power to recruit some top-tier people despite the fact that he couldn't offer them substantial compensation. He persuaded the hard-driving Jack R. Cominsky to leave an advertising position with the *New York Times* in order to become vice president and publisher of the *Saturday Review.* Cominsky had the business acumen that Norman (admittedly) lacked, and the two men quickly developed a close chemistry.[7] Cominsky brought aboard Hal Smith, who is credited with discovering William Faulkner and helping develop the literary talents of

Sinclair Lewis. The respected literary critic Henry Seidel Canby served as chairman. Pulitzer Prize–winning poet William Rose Benet and American Theater Hall of Fame inductee John Mason Brown rounded out the associate editor positions.[8] Cousins's champion, Amy Loveman, was in her twenty-fifth year at the magazine. The team kept the magazine functioning while Cousins headed to Japan.

Cousins arrived in Japan in 1949 already believing that the US government needed to atone for the unnecessary atomic bombings, but what he learned while there on his first trip catalyzed his moral indignation. The destruction and hardship he witnessed in Hiroshima even four years after the bomb would arouse in him a strong sense of connection to the city. Cousins's reaction to the troubling and inspiring encounters he experienced in Japan and the humanitarian programs he launched in response thrust him onto the global stage as a man who had the conviction to act on the beliefs he publicly espoused.

One of Cousins's primary editorial themes was that the United States needed to do more to help the disadvantaged people of the world, but it was in Japan that he would turn his words into actions. Upon arriving in Hiroshima, Cousins was met by Mayor Shinzo Hamai, who served as his personal tour guide. Hamai had taken over as mayor of the rubble-strewn city two years earlier and was one of the driving forces in the rebuilding of Hiroshima as an international city for peace at a time when the city's continued existence was in question.[9] Cousins was inspired by the new city he saw rapidly rising from the atomic ashes and dedicating its entire existence to promoting peace, under the direction of the indefatigable mayor. Cousins later wrote that he had come to Hiroshima expecting to see the end of the world. Instead, what he saw was the beginning of a new world.[10] Despite the disconnect between what he expected and what he saw, daily life in the city was still a harsh reality.

Hamai first took Cousins on a tour of some of the area hospitals. Cousins later wrote that "it was an experience difficult to put out of your mind, and you tried hard to put it out of your mind because you saw things that whatever sanity you may have had cried out against." One of the operating rooms, he wrote, looked "little better than a crude abattoir."[11] Hamai took Cousins to the hospitals in order to poignantly illustrate Japan's desperate need for America's help in taking care of Hiroshima's sick and wounded. Horrified by what he witnessed in this crude hospital struggling and failing to adequately treat patients, Cousins would later write a personal check for $1,565 (more than $17,000 in 2020 dollars) to help fund medical treatments.[12]

During his tour of the city Cousins noticed the large number of children roaming the streets of Hiroshima. Thousands of young children had been orphaned as a result of the atomic bombing, and caring for them was difficult in a city of limited resources already being stretched to the limit. The next stop on the tour was an orphanage that was home to some one hundred children who had lost their parents to the atomic bomb. That the atomic bomb had made orphans of so many children was especially troubling to Cousins, but what he saw also pressed him into action. After the shock he felt at the hospital conditions, Cousins wrote, "The Yamashita Orphanage was, I think, the high spot of my visit to Hiroshima. . . . There was only one thing wrong with the Yamashita Orphanage. There was not enough of it. It ought to be five times as large, and it would be, if outside help were forthcoming."[13] Encountering these orphans clearly had a lasting impact on Cousins. His daughter Andrea remembers her father telling her when she was young that he wanted to "go around the world and gather up all these children who needed homes." He talked to her about great people in the past who, like Gandhi, had taken vows of poverty. He was very concerned, Andrea recalls, with conveying these humanitarian ideas to her.[14]

Cousins's first tour through Hiroshima exposed the horrors of daily subsistence and suggested what could be done if the city received just a little more outside help. The United States was already making progress toward reforming Japan politically, but it was not doing enough, in Cousins's estimation, to alleviate the daily suffering of the Japanese people, in particular victims of the atomic bomb, to whom Cousins believed the United States owed a special debt. Addressing the larger problem faced by local authorities was beyond Hiroshima's own capabilities. It was a grave problem that Cousins swore to remedy when he returned to the United States.

With transpacific passenger air travel still in a fledgling state in 1949, it took Cousins nearly three days and multiple plane trips to get back to New York, affording him plenty of time to think about what he had witnessed in Hiroshima. Cousins relished the long flights. To him, flying was a "dining room for the imagination," provided the ideal conditions for sustained thinking. "You get a sense of stretch up here," wrote Cousins, "you have the feeling that this is the natural habitat for men who think they'd like to work together."[15] Mostly he loved flying because there were no interruptions and no one could bother him.[16]

It was while airborne that Cousins hatched a plan to provide some of the outside help that Hiroshima desperately needed. During his visit to the Yamashita Orphanage he had suggested to its director that Americans should be invited to contribute to the support of the orphans.[17] While flying home, Cousins worked out the details. He would launch a "Moral Adoptions" program through which American citizens could donate $2.25 a month (about $25 in 2020) to help pay for the education and care of Hiroshima's orphans. A "moral" adoption was necessary in 1949 because the Immigration Act of 1924, which prevented immigration from Asia, still the law of the land, made it extremely difficult to legally adopt a Japanese child and bring him or her to the United States. During the occupation, it was even a challenge for Japanese citizens to visit the United States for a short time. Cousins's intention was for Americans to "morally" adopt these children, providing money for their care until they were of age. Cousins did not pioneer this idea. The Christian Children's Fund had launched such a fundraising program in 1938 to help Chinese orphans during the Sino-Japanese War.[18]

Acting as the middleman in soliciting funds, on September 17, 1949, Cousins appealed to his *Saturday Review* readers to donate what they could, hoping for a modest response at best.[19] The response was more than modest, but it caught Cousins off guard because his plea was also met with outrage. Many Americans still bristled with wartime hatred toward the Japanese people, and some of Cousins's own readers expressed their indignation toward an initiative that would help the very people who had been their sworn enemy just four years earlier. One reader from New York wrote that before she got worked up about the orphans of Hiroshima, she would "like to know what happened to those [orphans] made by the attack on Pearl Harbor?"[20] Another incredulously asked whether it could "be possible that all your readers have forgotten so soon how the little men of Japan treated those whom they conquered?"[21] Cousins was even derogatorily labeled a "softie" by one of his own friends.[22]

But instead of backing down, Cousins directly confronted these critiques in an editorial the following week titled "On Being a Softie," in which he maintained his convictions, standing by his belief that Americans had a special responsibility to the Japanese people in general and especially to those blameless children orphaned by the atomic explosions. While many Americans still harbored resentment toward the Japanese, others were deeply moved by Cousins's reporting on Japan and his call for help on behalf of Japan's atomic orphans.

In short order donations and letters began pouring into the *Saturday Review* offices from readers who shared Cousins's sentiments about America's need to atone for the bomb. One reader wrote that he was making a donation as "partial recompense for the immoral act of dropping the atom bomb."[23] Another said that she wished to make "this small atonement toward a monstrous military 'expedient' for which we, as a nation, are guilty."[24] A reader from New York wished to reconcile the fact that her country had "[cast] aside all decent scruples and committ[ed] mass murder in the name of military necessity."[25] The most potent letter of all came from a former B-29 pilot, Lawrence Malis, of Philadelphia, who wrote, "Having flown twenty-six B-29 missions over Japan, I have carried a guilty conscience for several years. First, because of the indiscriminate fashion with which we used to burn out the slum areas with firebombs; second, because of the atom bomb itself, and what I feel was its unwarranted and needless use."[26] The voices of the early naysayers were quickly supplanted by letters like Malis's, and the Moral Adoptions program proved to be a resounding success. Within two months Cousins was able to write to Mayor Hamai that all seventy-six children at the Yamashita Orphanage had been "adopted."[27] But Cousins was just getting started.

With this outpouring from donors, Cousins was able to quickly expand the Moral Adoption support to provide funding for eighty-six more children in four other Hiroshima orphanages.[28] Even the famous American author and political activist Helen Keller sent twenty-five dollars to support the program, writing that she wanted to help repay a debt that "remains immeasurable."[29] At one point the number of Americans wanting to participate exceeded the number of children ready for adoption.[30] Cousins later recalled, "Few things in my life have touched me more deeply than the response of Americans to the moral adoptions proposal."[31]

Cousins's program had a widespread positive ripple effect as news of it reached far beyond the *Saturday Review* readership. Raymond Ciacio, of the Cooperative for Assistance and Relief Everywhere (CARE). wrote to Cousins that his organization had seen a surge in donations as a result of the growing awareness of the Japanese atomic bomb orphans.[32] Since to this point US policy had forbidden official American aid to the victims of the atomic bombs, Cousins's program—the most notable and successful American-led charitable initiative launched in Japan during the period—was the first to generate this outpouring of public support.[33]

Hoping to further capitalize on the unexpected success of the Moral Adoptions program, the Hiroshima Peace Center Associates funded a trip for Tanimoto to return to the United States in September 1950 for a six-month lecture and fundraising tour.[34] A unique and surreal moment on his tour came when Reverend Tanimoto stood in the US Senate and led the chamber in prayer as the guest chaplain on February 5, 1951. Tanimoto's prayer so inspired Virginia senator Willis Robertson (D-VA) that the distinguished war veteran rose after the prayer was concluded and stated, for the record, "We tried to kill him, but he has come here today and prayed for us. . . . The atomic bomb did not kill him. It did not break his will."[35] Clearly, Senator Robertson was not the only American on whom Tanimoto's story had a deep effect. Tanimoto's fundraising tour was quite the financial success: he returned to Japan at the end of his stay having raised $4,390.43, more than enough to finish rebuilding his bomb-damaged church.[36]

As successful as the Moral Adoptions program was proving to be, Cousins considered it only the first phase of what he hoped would become a much larger program. Cousins's aim was for these "moral" adoptions to become real adoptions, with the orphans being brought to the United States to live with the families who sponsored them. With the US occupation of Japan ending in 1952, the same year that Congress ended the Asian immigration exclusion and thus Japanese citizens could immigrate to the United States, Cousins wrote that he felt "some obligation to begin the next phase of the moral adoptions program."[37] Determined to lead by example, Cousins explored the possibility of adopting a Japanese child himself and bringing the child to America. Choosing from a number of candidates the orphanages provided him with, Cousins selected a seventeen-year-old gifted pianist named Teruaki Shimaguchi, whom Cousins believed would greatly benefit from conservatory training in the United States. Unfortunately for Teruaki, Cousins had become something of a celebrity in Japan, and word quickly leaked out that *the* Norman Cousins was going to adopt a Japanese boy. The spotlight on Teruaki became overwhelming. He refused any further assistance from Cousins, writing that the attention and the expectations being placed on him were overwhelming.[38]

In pushing the Moral Adoptions scheme Cousins seemed to overlook the turmoil it might bring to his own family. He wrote to William Maloney, the medical director of the Atomic Bomb Casualty Commission (ABCC), that he had "no uneasiness about any sense of displacement our own girls might have as a result of a senior [Japanese] child being brought into the family."[39] While the plans for Teruaki ultimately did not work out, in 1955 Cousins would adopt Shigeko Sasamori, a Japanese woman who had been disfigured and scarred in the atomic bomb, who would live with the Cousins family while continuing her studies in the United States. His daughter Sarah says that she did indeed come to love Shigeko as a sister, though she would later write, "I felt there was nothing I could do, no suffering I could ever hope to come up with there in slick, comfortable New Canaan, that could ever make me as worthy of my parents' attention as were my Japanese counterparts."[40]

In most years, Cousins was away from home for months traveling. Ellen sometimes traveled with him. Sarah writes that "it felt as if the whole house had been unplugged from its power source each time my parents went away on one of those trips."[41] Candis remembers that even when her father was home from his travels or from work he used the time to unwind. "When he was at home he'd usually be playing chess or playing golf or playing tennis. So there really wasn't an opportunity to talk to him that much." Candis envied her friends for their fathers, who "were home much more. It just seemed amazing to me that they had fathers like that."[42] "The last time I saw my father, during one of his visits to us in Jerusalem," says Sarah, "he spoke of his 'saturating remorse,' for not having given up everything—all his writing and lecturing around the globe—to spend more time with the family. It pained me to hear this. I wanted him to know what a wonderful father he was, and the ideals he and my mother gave over became my own north star." "My father wanted us to know about the world. . . . It was an intellectually vibrant home," says Sarah. "I experienced my parents as role models of hospitality, kindness, and generosity. My father personified the dignity of the spoken word. Gossip and frivolous putdown would not find in him a listening ear."[43]

Cousins does seem to fit the traditional notion of the 1950s "man of the house." He was extremely focused on world affairs, leaving the primary job of caring for the family to his wife. Her mother, Sarah remembers, was "a giver beyond normal limits. Virtually anyone who walked through their door became a relative for whom she felt responsible. She wanted her husband to accomplish what he wanted to accomplish, and protected his freedom to work and to play."[44] "He was doing whatever he wanted to do because my mother made it possible," Candis remembers. "It was she who was backstage." In fact, Candis remembers her father once saying, "If it weren't for Ellen there would be no Norman Cousins." Candis remembers the family sitting down to a Sunday meal when all of a sudden her father said, "Ellen! I think I'm supposed to be giving the commencement speech at such-and-such a college!," to which Ellen responded, "Don't worry, Norman. Go upstairs, get dressed, and I'll get the car! We can do it!" This type of scene played out on many occasions.[45]

Cousins himself would tell his archivist in the early 1980s, "Everything I know I've learned from Ellen. . . . She's a remarkable woman who has the gift of cheerfulness." He said that he had been lucky to live with someone who was "solution minded and willing to tackle the tough problems in life."[46] There would be times, Candis remembers, when her father would call and say he couldn't come home from the city that night. Ellen would make dinner, drive the nearly fifty miles into Norman's New York City office, set the dinner down in front of him, give him a kiss, and then drive back home to take care of the children.

CHAPTER 9

IN SEARCH *of* PEACE, COUSINS RALLIES *for* WAR

The outpouring of praise Cousins received for the Moral Adoptions program may have provided him with a morale boost, but Cousins found himself increasingly burnt out and distressed at the state of the world as 1950 approached. These feelings had been building slowly over the previous three years. In 1947, writing to Lewis Mumford, Cousins lamented that "any appearance of fatigue is no coincidence. For about six months now my psyche has been trying to generate a second wind—trying to tell itself that hope has real dimensions . . . but the grotesque senselessness within which life must be lived these days makes one, at times at least, somewhat tired if not hopeless."[1] Mumford wrote back to tell Cousins that he was not the only one who felt disillusioned. "We're all in the same boat," Mumford wrote. "I don't know anyone worth his salt who hasn't been going through the same experience that you've been going through: not to have been touched by the catastrophes behind us, the villainies around us, and the more awful events that may lie ahead."[2]

Even as the outpouring of support for the Moral Adoptions program helped enliven him, Cousins still felt drained physically, intellectually, and emotionally. After spending the past ten years at the helm of the *Saturday Review*, he felt as if he had run out of ideas and energy.[3] Overwhelmed and exhausted, Cousins decided he should have a fresh start to the decade of the 1950s. He tendered his resignation as editor of the *Saturday Review* in January 1950. Cousins wrote that "the editor's chair (and hence editorial page) ought to be occupied by someone with a new ten-year supply of adrenalin for his own causes and ideas."[4] The magazine, however, was in such a precarious financial position that the staff persuaded Cousins to stay on as editor at least until things were more stable. Two years earlier, in 1948, the magazine had still been operating at a loss despite its seventy-one thousand subscribers, up from fifty thousand in 1945.[5] The *Saturday Review*'s financial insecurity ended up being its (and his) saving grace. Within months of his decision to stay with the magazine the outbreak of the Korean War would reinvigorate Cousins and give him something new to campaign for.

On June 25, 1950, seven divisions of elite North Korean troops streamed across the 38th parallel into South Korea, clashing with South Korean troops and a tiny contingent of US military advisors, who were completely overwhelmed by the attack. It was a Saturday night in Washington when news of the attack reached the capital.[6] Monday's edition of the *New York Times* reported that the president had met with his top advisors over dinner the previous evening but had issued no statement except that they would "continue conferring."[7] Truman, an anti-Communist hardliner, had already made up his mind. "There's no telling what they'll do if we don't put up a fight now," he argued.[8] Within a week, Truman would announce the deployment of American ground troops to Korea in what he declared was a "police action." The American troops would in time be joined by UN forces to draw a line against Communist aggression in Korea.[9]

The North Korean troops had extensive battle experience, many having recently returned from the Chinese civil war, and they enjoyed stunning success in the early weeks of the war. The US war planners had grossly underestimated their strength and abilities.[10] The chairman of the Joint Chiefs, Omar Bradley, would later testify that "no one believed that the North Koreans were as strong as they turned out to be."[11] The Joint Chiefs thought the invasion could be quickly turned back by American air and naval power. Instead, the combat would drag on for more than three years.

Paradoxically, although he claimed that his driving goal in life was to pursue a sustainable global peace, for the second time Cousins threw his support behind a war. The war provided the opportunity to further the cause of peace, albeit in a somewhat convoluted way. Victory in Korea, Cousins argued, would be a victory against war itself. Four weeks after the outbreak of hostilities, Cousins penned an editorial expressing his fear that this war might be the "sputtering fuse that may crack open the brittle flooring of the twentieth century." But immediately after that brief caveat he took the position that the war was actually a grand opportunity. "Victory in Korea for the UN forces," Cousins wrote, "can be a sturdy platform on which something more than a tentative peace may be built."[12] Cousins had spent the previous five years tirelessly arguing that the United States (and the world) had missed a historic opportunity by not giving the United Nations the type of enforcement powers that would allow it to field a supranational military force capable of preventing exactly the sort of aggression that happened in Korea. Now, with troops from many countries all fighting together in Korea under the UN flag, Cousins argued that a victory in Korea could be a victory against war itself. A future historian might point out, Cousins hoped, that the Korean War was the moment when the United Nations was truly born because it forced Americans to face up to the fact that the United Nations needed to be given effective peace enforcement powers.[13] He believed that if the United Nations had commanded troops of its own, the aggression in Korea would not have occurred.

Although he believed in the ultimate goal of peace, Cousins was not sympathetic to the pacifist position. He provided a clear definition of his reasoning in April 1948, when the famed pacifist A. J. Muste wrote Cousins to ask him where he stood on the question of pacifism and

Gandhian principles of nonviolence.[14] Cousins responded: "I do not believe in violence. But I believe that violence is not met effectively through non-violence. I believe that what is necessary is the creation of workable law on a world level and that every effort ought to be turned towards that end. . . . World law may at least give us the chance to work towards the ultimate objective—peace with justice."[15]

Cousins's position on peace can best be described along the lines of the more traditional notion of "peace through strength." According to Cousins, the United Nations was ineffective because it was toothless, and it was precisely that toothlessness that the Soviet ally North Korea exploited when it started the war.[16] In a radio broadcast, Cousins proclaimed that "the fundamental danger of the U.N. as presently constituted is not only that it is too weak to cope with an actual crisis but that this very weakness tends to create crises."[17] On this point Cousins was off in his assessment. The North Korean decision to attack had little to do with its perception of the United Nations.

Cousins also thought that the Soviet Union was the nefarious provocateur behind North Korea's aggression. He wrote in a private letter that he believed that the Soviets had directed the war in order to draw in the United States so they could "sit back and see American blood drained off in an interminable military operation. . . . Thus in Korea the Soviet created a dilemma for us in which our choice was between something incredibly costly and something disastrous."[18]

Cousins was not entirely off base. Historian Bruce Cummings writes regarding the Soviet decision to abstain from the UN vote for war that Stalin "may have hoped to facilitate the entry of U.S. forces. . . . Thus to waste blood and treasure." But he might also have hoped "that American dominance of the UN would destroy the perceived universality of the international body."[19]

On the flip side, the United States' own value-laden public pronouncements often hid deeper (and more sinister) geopolitical strategizing. According to Cummings, the US decision to intervene "had little to do with Korea's strategic value, and everything to do with

American prestige and political economy."[20] Cousins harbored similar thoughts. In March 1951, he wrote in a private letter to a friend that "if we failed to act decisively in meeting the threat of Communist aggression in Korea, then the vast area of Southeast Asia would have become unhinged, and America would have been effectively cut off from areas vital to the security of the free world."[21]

Cousins's statement is eerily similar to one that President Eisenhower would make two years later at the Governors' Conference in August 1953. "Now let us assume that we lose Indochina.... The Malayan peninsula, the last little bit of the end hanging on down there, would be scarcely defensible. All of that weakening position around there is very ominous for the United States, because finally if we lost all that, how would the free world hold the rich empire of Indonesia?"[22]

For all of Cousins's praise of Eastern philosophy, his writings about how Americans should learn about, respect, and celebrate other cultures, and his calls to be understanding of other people's opinions, he never fully acknowledged that his vision for the world was, naturally, an *American* view of humanity. An American view of "the good." An American view of how societies and governments should be run and what they should value. Aside from espousing the view that the United States and the Soviet Union need not be in a cold war, he did not address how the East-West ideological conflict should be overcome, aside from other countries becoming more like the United States. Cousins subscribed to the American mind-set of the era that painted the Soviets as dangerous actors in the world, striving for domination and willing to achieve it through violence. That the United States was the "good" nation and a necessary bulwark against Communist tyranny.

Cousins wrote to a friend that "we have a great deal to offer to the world in terms of technological know-how, industrial organization, distribution and development of resources and raw materials.... The United States is in a powerful position to exert pressure." Of course, the Soviets had long argued that the American vision for the world was nothing more than capitalist imperialism. And yet, in that same letter,

Cousins criticized the Soviets for doing effectively the same thing he wanted the United States to do: "Russia comes along in the role of champion and uses propaganda to convince them that Communism can give them food, land and jobs," he complained.[23] He evidently gave little thought to whether the people in those countries he sought to "exert pressure" on even *wanted* American help (or Russian help, as it were). Cousins, although to a lesser degree than some, clearly shared the "liberal cold warrior" worldview of those who supported democracy, international engagement, and equality, while vehemently opposing the Soviet Union and Communism in general.

When it came to the Korean War, Cousins saw a large and powerful standing army under the UN banner as the supranational force that could ensure peace by serving as an effective deterrent against any military aggression launched at the national or international level. This was not just Cousins's public platform; he expressed it privately as well. Responding to a US serviceman's letter, he explained, "The military *does* serve a critically important purpose. While it cannot in itself create peace, it can at least help to create the conditions under which it may never be used."[24] In effect, Cousins was in favor of the creation of a large international conventional military force under the auspices of the United Nations to serve as a deterrent to aggression in much the same way that the United States would later come to rely heavily on nuclear weapons for that same purpose. Cousins also left out of his grand idea any mention of where Soviet or Chinese troops would fit into these UN forces. They, too, were Security Council members, after all.

Cousins would later liken the world without a strong United Nations capable of enforcing the peace to the American Wild West. "Here in the American West," he wrote, "we knew the insecurity that once came from lawlessness, and we kept close our six-shooters because this was the only security we had. But we gave up those six-shooters when law and the machinery of law were instituted. The same holds true for the world today. Instead of six-shooters, we now have guns with nuclear bullets."[25] Cousins saw a UN force existing to defend the machinery of a world law, which would increase global security because no nation would need its "six-shooters" anymore. While this fitting anecdote was Cousins's own, the larger idea behind world government was not his alone.

In February 1947, delegates from the six major world government groups agreed to merge into one organization to be known as the United World Federalists (UWF). The organization advocated for the establishment of a global democratic government as a step toward preventing wars. Cousins believed world federalism was "central to the welfare of the American people."[26] Cousins, a central member of the new organization and its chief spokesman, would go on to become the UWF president in 1952. According to historian Lawrence Wittner, Cousins became "perhaps the most effective of the new advocates for world government."[27] The UWF enjoyed surprisingly rapid success. By 1949 its membership had swelled to nearly fifty thousand in some 720 chapters nationwide.[28]

The UWF scored some major early wins. In June 1949, ninety-one members of the US House of Representatives tendered a resolution supporting world federation as a "fundamental objective" of US foreign policy.[29] In the two states (Massachusetts and Connecticut) where the proposal to turn the United Nations into a world government appeared on the ballot, it was overwhelmingly approved by voters. This early momentum, however, would dissipate rapidly, and Cousins would ultimately fall on the wrong side of public opinion. Almost immediately after its peak in 1949, membership in the UWF fell off rapidly, partly as a casualty of the Korean War.

Even with Cousins's tireless urging that the Korean War represented a golden opportunity for world government, the war caused many to rally around the flag rather than a hypothetical world organization. The anti-Communist crusade launched by Senator Joseph McCarthy (R-WI) in February 1950, preceding the war by five months, would provide another nail in the coffin. International organizations such as the UWF were perceived to be rife with Communist sympathizers, further scaring away members who did not want their name attached to anything the FBI and the House Un-American Activities Committee were actively investigating. By June 1951 membership had plummeted by more than half, to around twenty-two thousand.[30]

That same month, under intense pressure from "patriotic" groups, all but eight of the twenty-two states that had passed resolutions supporting world government decided to rescind them.[31] In this moment Cousins failed to recognize (or simply chose to ignore) the changing public mood that saw world government as a quickly fading dream. Having lost half its membership in less than two years, the UWF found itself in dire financial straits and on the verge of collapse in 1952. Cousins took over the presidency from Alan Cranston, who had held the position since 1949. Even if Cousins did recognize that public support for the idea had waned, he was so unwilling to see the movement fail that he made a substantial personal donation of fifty thousand dollars ($546,000 in 2020 dollars) to keep the organization afloat.[32] This was in addition to the more than three thousand dollars ($33,000 in 2020 dollars) he had already given over the previous two years.[33] It was a good thing that he had J. R. Cominsky looking after the business side of the *Saturday Review*, because in his personal life Cousins would fund many successful initiatives, certainly, but he also quixotically poured substantial sums of money into initiatives that quickly fizzled. Journalist Arthur Herzog once claimed that "in giving to peace, at one time [Cousins] almost destroyed himself financially."[34] It is little wonder that around this time collection letters from creditors arrived in his mailbox frequently, and Cousins had to write to businesses apologizing for late payments or for payments he had to temporarily withhold because of his low account balance.

Sarah remembers her parents' relationship with money as never being about the acquisition of money itself; rather, they only thought about the good one could do with it. Candis says that her father "had the mind of a visionary. He would have an idea and with very little support he would stand on nothing but a vision, then create the evidence around that vision. That's what made him so special."[35] A visionary he certainly was, especially in later decades, but it seems that in these early years he was still finding his footing, and many of his visions did not pan out. A close associate of Cousins's later mused that he was loath to close off options. At times this led to consequences that were "sometimes disastrous in terms of money and the aftermath of the troubles that result."[36]

Regarding her father's use of money, Candis recalls that "without a doubt, my parents were enlightened in their approach to money. Their life was consistent with their belief that money should be used to relieve suffering, to promote authentic intellectual development and creativity, and to do nothing less than save the world from nuclear destruction. How they made these sort of financial choices while raising their children in progressive schools, living in a large house surrounded by acres of Connecticut forest with organic gardens, chickens and horses, and ongoing adventure and travel I will never know."[37] It was probably made easier by the fact that by 1961 Cousins's *Saturday Review* salary would balloon to $36,875 (equivalent to $324,000 in 2020). His perks also included his travel expenses, a personal vehicle that the magazine paid for, and a generous expense account.[38]

For the next nine years Cousins would sink enormous personal and financial sums into the promotion of the UWF agenda. His archivist would later write that he did it because he found in the group a commonality of spirit and dedication to the movement that matched his own.[39] But even Cousins's confidence, faith, and tireless dedication could not sustain the movement. In 1961, Cousins sadly admitted that he could not see the development of a world government in the foreseeable future.[40] Although blinded to the reality of the national mood by his enthusiasm for world government, Cousins soon did recognize that using the Korean War as a platform to strengthen the United Nations might be more difficult than he had initially expected. Few people in the United States seemed to be paying much attention to the war. Picking up emerging threads of what historian Clay Blair would later name the "Forgotten War," Cousins wrote that with regard to Korea, "there is a strange sense of detachment and compartmentalization. . . . [The war is] largely unrelated to the life of a people enjoying the greatest prosperity in human history."[41]

Cousins's insight was on the mark. An August 1950 Gallup poll confirmed that only 6.5 percent of respondents listed the Korean War as the most important issue facing the country.[42] Even after Chinese Communist troops launched a massive counterattack in November 1950, driving the Allied forces back and putting an end to any thoughts of a quick or conclusive US victory, 54 percent of respondents agreed with the statement that the Korean War was "an utterly useless war."[43] But Cousins did not believe that the war was useless—it was the great battle for the future of the United Nations—and he was not about to let it fade from the minds of Americans. In order to bring the war to life for his readers, in January 1951 he set off across the Pacific to report directly from the battlefields in Korea.

Cousins filed his first report from Korea in February 1951. Following the model of his visit to Berlin, he toured the country, combat zones and rear areas alike, while reporting on the human tragedy that he encountered. From Taegu, South Korea, he wrote about the humanitarian crisis caused by hundreds of thousands of refugees streaming south. The throngs of those fleeing the fighting were so thick that military vehicles carrying supplies north became moored in the mass of humanity clogging the narrow roads.[44] His firsthand introduction to combat quickly sapped the prowar enthusiasm apparent in his earlier articles and exposed him to the perilous situation the UN forces were in. He admitted feeling that "we are facing great odds and we may not be able to hold on."[45]

On his return trip from Korea Cousins chose to stop over in Calcutta to give a few lectures, see some old friends, and expand his network there. He relished having dinner at the home of the American consul in Bombay, at which, he reported, "there was a fairly impressive assortment of big wigs."[46] While in India he picked up a case of amoebic dysentery, which put him out of commission for about three weeks and threw him far behind in his writing schedule. He wrote to a friend that "I could not sit at the typewriter long enough to type my own name." On the bright side, he noted, "it is a sure fire way of cutting off surplus poundages. I sheared off 17 lbs in three weeks and about 300 sittings."[47]

Cousins's trip overseas overlapped with his wife's birthday, a fact not lost on him. As her gift he sent her a plane ticket to meet him in Paris. He had booked a few days in the city to catch his breath after his exhausting journey. It was Ellen's first trip to Europe. While they toured the sights Cousins noted that he was "getting the biggest kick in my life seeing [Paris] through her eyes."[48] When the couple traveled together, they always had a great deal of fun. They were extremely adventurous, Candis recalls. They rarely planned; they would just pick up a map and go somewhere.[49] But as the Cousins's explored Paris, the Korean War dragged on.

With US casualties mounting, General Douglas MacArthur grew increasingly unhappy with the progress of the war and began issuing statements from his command in Tokyo criticizing the administration's war policies as well as pushing for an all-out war with China.[50] With advance knowledge that Truman would soon make a major speech suggesting that both sides head to the negotiating table, MacArthur sabotaged the president by preemptively issuing his own ultimatum to China.[51] Truman, finally fed up with his top general's rogue statements, chose to fire him. A national furor erupted when the White House announced on April 11, 1951, that MacArthur would be relieved of his command.

Cousins responded to the dismissal of MacArthur by writing, "The seriousness and scope of the issues involved are as great as any foreign policy question in our history."[52] *Time* magazine entered the fray and eviscerated Truman by describing him as a "professional little man."[53] The *Chicago Tribune* called MacArthur's dismissal "vindictive" and charged Truman with being "unfit, morally and mentally, for his high office."[54] Other papers sided with the administration. The *New York Herald-Tribune* wrote that MacArthur had "virtually forced his own removal," and characterized Truman's announcement as "one of those strokes of boldness and decision."[55] Cousins too weighed in. He deftly summarized the national mood before paying ringing tribute to MacArthur's war record. But ultimately he said that "the President took the only course open to him in relieving General MacArthur of his command." He criticized MacArthur for breaking the chain of command and pursuing his own view on how the war should be fought, while also pointing out that "the Government's own position is too indecisive and sketchy to offer reasonable hope that stalemates can lead to settlement."[56]

On April 19 MacArthur, having just returned from Japan, addressed a joint session of Congress. In his thirty-seven-minute speech he complained that he had "constantly called for new political decisions essential to a solution."[57] There could be no substitute for victory in Korea, MacArthur concluded, no matter the cost. Cousins agreed. Mirroring MacArthur's aggressive stance, he opined that the United States (and the United Nations) needed to meet the threat adequately and decisively. If that meant a "force of two million men or five million men or twenty million men, then that is what it means."[58] Here was Norman Cousins, a man for whom peace was paramount, calling for a military force of 20 million men. This was not his finest moment.

It was clear to Cousins that bold new leadership was necessary. A new policy for the war as well as new leadership for the country at large. While the war would remain a quagmire until an armistice was signed in July 1953, Cousins took an active role in developing the potential new national leader he sought.

CHAPTER 10

CANDIDATE *of the* INTELLECTUALS

Adlai Stevenson, 1952

Embattled over the firing of MacArthur, weighed down by the quagmire in Korea, and under fire for being unable to deal effectively with Congress, President Truman quietly decided that he would not seek reelection in 1952. Impressed by Illinois governor Adlai E. Stevenson, Truman approached him in March about considering a run for president.[1] Stevenson, however, made no commitments even after secretly meeting with Truman twice on this issue. Stevenson preferred to remain governor of Illinois for another term, setting his sights on a presidential bid in 1956 instead.[2] Although he remained coy in public about the possibility, privately he was seriously considering it. Ultimately he decided to throw his hat into the ring and won the Democratic nomination.

Stevenson hastily assembled a campaign team of relative newcomers to politics, hoping to avoid the Washington establishment and build his own team from scratch. The majority of those he recruited came from the liberal intellectual and academic world. David Bell, Arthur Schlesinger, John Kenneth Galbraith, and Bernard DeVoto all joined Stevenson's team.[3] Major names in the New York publishing world soon joined the cause as well. Bennett Cerf, of Random House, agreed to hastily publish a biography of Stevenson—famed novelist John Steinbeck wrote the introduction. Poet Archibald MacLeish helped organize volunteers, as did journalist John Hersey. *Atlantic Monthly* editor Robert Manning pitched in as well.[4] Stevenson biographer Porter McKeever describes the team as being made up mostly of "bright young professionals getting their first taste of politics."[5]

A bright young professional in the New York intellectual and publishing world in his own right, Norman Cousins was not part of the group of initial recruits brought in that summer. In the last week of August 1952, however, Stevenson personally called upon him to come to Illinois to help.[6] The impetus for this could have been an editorial Cousins published earlier that month titled "Speech for a Presidential Candidate," in which he argued, "The real issues of this campaign, it seems to me, are far broader and potentially far more inspiring than the usual issues over which we argue so mightily in a Presidential year. The real issues center around the meaning of America in the present human crisis. They concern our ability to understand what moral leadership and moral responsibility mean."[7] Cousins's editorial appealed to Stevenson's desire to "talk sense to the American people" and run a campaign that tackled big ideas, but he was struggling to define what these big ideas and campaign issues might be.[8] Stevenson called in Cousins to elaborate on some of the ideas he raised in the article that could form the basis for a foreign policy platform.[9]

Cousins's participation in Stevenson's election campaign provides a unique window into what the ideal American leader might look like in his eyes, as well as his prescriptions for how US foreign policy should be conducted. Stevenson's appeal to the mind offered Cousins his first real chance to take his editorial prescriptions and thrust them onto the national stage, putting his own ideas at the forefront of public debate as they were broadcast nationally through the megaphone of Stevenson's campaigning.

Cousins explained to Stevenson that in 1952 Americans suffered from a profound sense of national frustration. They were restless because of conscious and subconscious fears resulting from a foreign policy that "has averted what could have been disaster, but it has yet to come up with something so positive and so striking that people can have a sense of direction and a sense of destiny. They are waiting for big ideas. . . . They know the big dollars and the big bombs aren't enough."[10] Cousins made the same point in his editorial "Speech for a Presidential Candidate," arguing that his generation was "a generation looking for spiritual and intellectual anchorage at a time of uncertainty and upheaval." Cousins saw in Stevenson the "intellectual anchorage" he sought, and he implored the governor not to let his staff "talk you into abandoning your soul-searching in public in favor of an 'I've-got-all-the-answers-and-the-other-fellow-hasn't' type of campaign." Reflecting upon the country's rapidly expanding role in the world, Cousins pointed out that the biggest challenge Stevenson would face as president "has to do with the meaning of America in the world today."[11]

Cousins's prescriptions for American foreign policy expose his own long-standing personal beliefs. He implored Stevenson to consider that "on the operational level of our foreign policy it is not merely idealistic but mandatory to earn and maintain the good will and support of the preponderance of the world's people. . . . [America] justifies its good fortune only as it speaks for the cause of man."[12] Despite Cousins's rather lofty ideals, Stevenson was thoroughly impressed, writing Cousins to tell him that "your material is by far the best that I receive."[13] This was not a mere platitude from Stevenson. Their extensive correspondence reveals that Stevenson felt a particular appreciation for Cousins's talents and ideas.

Not all of Cousins's advice was sound, however. One of the recommendations he made was that Stevenson need not apologize for his intelligence. Cousins believed that "the hackneyed political fear of a literate and articulate candidate is feeble stuff and badly dated." While he cautioned Stevenson not to brandish his mastery of facts like a club, he called his clear intelligence a "fresh note."[14] Unfortunately, Stevenson's intelligence was the very club with which his opposition hit him. Newspaper columnist Stewart Alsop coined the word *egghead* as a term of derision to describe Stevenson, and the insult stuck.[15]

Regardless of any minor missteps, Stevenson still thought Cousins's ideas had merit. After reading Cousins's "six-senses" policy memo, Stevenson paid him three hundred dollars for his services and asked him to become much more involved in the campaign. (Cousins donated his payment back to the campaign.) Cousins embraced the assignment with gusto. He immediately reached out to his contacts in the publishing world and solicited a large donation on Stevenson's behalf from Harold Guinzburg, president of Viking Press. Cousins wrote policy speeches on youth and education.[16]

As the campaign entered its final month, Stevenson turned to Cousins for advice more frequently, recognizing that because of Cousins's exhaustive national lecture circuit he could serve as a good judge of the public mood. Cousins noted as much when he reported back directly to Stevenson at the Governor's Mansion that everywhere he went in the country he saw that people wanted change. Independent voters especially were siding with Stevenson because he represented the qualities of "a largeness of spirit, affirmativeness, and a sense of values that places national unity above personal advantage." Stevenson's best hope for election, in Cousins's estimation, was to persuade more of those independents to vote for him.[17] But both Cousins and Stevenson seemed not to recognize the self-reinforcing bias in Cousins's measure of the national mood. His lecture appearances through 1952 took him mainly to colleges, major urban areas, peace rallies, UN and UWF functions, and literary circles, all demographic groups that tended to be in Stevenson's camp anyway.

Although Cousins refrained from telling Stevenson this, he wrote to his friend the former governor of Connecticut (and Stevenson supporter) Chester Bowles that "[in] travelling around the country, especially in the Midwest, I find an astonishing amount of support for Eisenhower among the very working and white collar people that Roosevelt used to count on for a large part of his voting strength." Still, said Cousins, "I'm [not] discouraged; it's just that I myself have seen very little of the evidence which causes some of our friends to predict an

Eisenhower rout."[18] Cousins was most certainly wrong on this point. Eisenhower would ultimately win the election with 442 Electoral College votes to Stevenson's 89 and nearly 7 million more in the popular vote.

Throughout the election season Cousins kept his involvement with the Stevenson campaign a secret. In two separate letters he later explained that he was always very careful not to criticize the people in government he had to work with and thus his work required that he navigate largely in nonpolitical waters. Although he (privately) identified as a Democrat, he took pains not to make his political allegiances publicly known.[19]

Eisenhower carried all but nine states, sweeping the Republican Party back into office after twenty years on the sidelines.[20] The election results were so overwhelmingly clear that just after midnight Stevenson conceded to Eisenhower in a short but eloquent speech. The *New York Times* reported two days after the election that Stevenson's loss was largely the political fallout from the Korean War but also a consequence of voters' resentments after twenty years of Democratic rule.[21]

Far from devastating Stevenson, the presidential campaign only whetted his political ambitions. He was already looking ahead to 1956. Immediately after the election, Stevenson sent Cousins a letter soliciting his advice as to what he should do next. Cousins advised Stevenson to stay in the public spotlight through the lecture circuit as well as TV and radio spots. Within weeks of the election Stevenson resumed his position on the speaker's dais, even delivering the prestigious Godkin Lectures at Harvard University.[22] He also accepted a lucrative proposal from *Look* magazine to embark on a world tour and submit eight 3,000-word articles about the countries he visited. The assignment allowed him to get away from the political scene and avoid the partisan squabbles among Democrats back home.[23]

Cousins, inspired by the political world he found himself immersed in during the campaign, decided to reformat the *Saturday Review*, shortening its name from *The Saturday Review of Literature* to simply *Saturday Review* to note its move away from being a literature review and reflect its new focus on politics and international affairs. It would seem that the presidential campaign had completely erased Cousins's 1950 apathy-driven attempt to leave the magazine. He was now fully committed to making the *Saturday Review* a fixture of national importance.

CHAPTER 11

FROM ADVOCATE *to* DIPLOMAT

On January 20, 1953, Dwight D. Eisenhower placed his right hand on the Bible his parents had presented to him upon his graduation from West Point in 1915 and took the presidential oath of office.[1] As historian Benjamin Greene points out, embedded in his twenty-one-minute inaugural address was an insightful passage that demonstrated his concerns about the atomic age: "Science seems ready to confer upon us, as its final gift, the power to erase human life from this planet."[2] But the growing fear of nuclear weapons erasing human life did not stop Eisenhower from greatly increasing the US reliance on those weapons as a means of defense throughout his two terms in office.

The early 1950s saw a major shift in Cousins's worldview that marked the beginning of his evolution from an advocate for international control of atomic weapons and an increased focus on humanitarianism worldwide into someone who directly challenged US government policy. Working on Adlai Stevenson's presidential campaign in 1952 helped Cousins sharpen his ideas about America's role in the world, but it also reinforced his belief in the strength and importance of individual action. Rhetorical persuasion through his *Saturday Review* editorials was a great way to hone his ideas, but words alone were not enough to drive the kind of change Cousins desired. He began to move from being a magazine editor who sponsored a charitable humanitarian aid mission to a private diplomat who directly challenged US policies instead of just editorializing about them. Cousins's actions overall in the 1950s put him at odds with the Eisenhower administration and carried geopolitical implications.

Through his work in Japan, Cousins had learned that as a matter of policy the government was not providing medical treatment to those who suffered from the effects of the atomic bombings. In fact, archival evidence shows that the State Department was actively seeking to prevent the treatment of Japanese atomic bomb victims in hopes of maintaining access to them as research subjects. Thus, in an attempt to shame the US government into changing its (nonexistent) treatment policy, Cousins would launch the Hiroshima Maidens project in 1955. It was an initiative that brought twenty-five women from Hiroshima who suffered from lingering atomic bomb wounds to the United States for advanced medical treatment. The US government responded to his involvement in the Hiroshima Maidens project by labeling him a "potential troublemaker," and the issues raised by the project proved so troublesome to US political goals that the State Department pursued a (failed) last-minute attempt to cancel the program.[3] Attempts to influence sensitive international relations came to be an increasingly important part of Cousins's activities going forward.

There have, of course, been private, citizen, and other "unofficial" diplomats as long as there have been communities interacting with one another across some form of recognized (or unrecognized) border. By the twentieth century, the state had come to dominate all things diplomatic, but private actors still made up, as British diplomat J. D. Gregory put it, the "harlequinade" of confusing and diverse private actors who could still have an impact on diplomacy.[4] However, it was during the second half of the twentieth century, when matters of war and peace took on apocalyptic dimensions (and the cost and difficulty of international travel improved), that citizen diplomacy gained more purchase.[5] American diplomat Joseph Montville describes President Eisenhower as "the father of Track-II [citizen] diplomacy."[6] It was Norman Cousins who made that moniker possible. While he was by no means the *only* citizen diplomat during the Cold War, he would become recognized as one of the first of the atomic age.

Even after Adlai Stevenson's 1952 election loss, Cousins did not abandon his campaign of imploring American politicians to embrace a platform of moral leadership and speak not just for Americans but for all humanity. Clearly, he had been deeply pondering and honing his position during the campaign, and in the same month that Eisenhower took his oath of office Cousins greatly expanded his audience by publishing a new book, *Who Speaks for Man?*, in January 1953.

The first half of the book is a partly autobiographical exploration of world culture and events based on Cousins's many international experiences since 1945. The second half of the book outlines his idealistic worldview. The notion of national sovereignty in the atomic age, Cousins argued, was a myth. Under modern conditions not only was the nation-state's ability to protect its people thoroughly compromised but the aggressor nation now made our decisions for us, he claimed. Witness Pearl Harbor, Korea, the US armament program, and the tax policy required to pay for it all.[7] When individual nations and often individual leaders possessed the awesome power to expunge life from earth at the push of a button, humanity had no spokesperson, no collective voice, no effective representative of its most vital interests, he argued.

Within months of its publication, *Who Speaks for Man?* received widespread critical acclaim. A national board of twenty-nine literary critics chose it from a list of 115 books as its most recommended work of nonfiction for 1953.[8] Even the famed astrophysicist Carl Sagan, whom the *Atlantic* called "one of the greatest minds of all time," listed *Who Speaks for Man?* as one of his top ten literary influences in 1954.[9] While Cousins's book was making waves nationally and getting Americans to ponder the pathways to a more peaceful world, the Soviet leader Joseph Stalin's sudden death on March 5, 1953, caused Eisenhower to ponder the same thing.

Stalin's death provided an unprecedented opportunity for his successors to move away from his confrontational ideology and reliance on the theory of inevitable conflict.[10] It also presented a potential opening that Eisenhower, just over a month into his tenure, could use to reduce global tensions and warm the frosty relationship with the Soviet Union. When Eisenhower learned the previous morning that Stalin had suffered a stroke and was likely dying (or perhaps already dead), he was shocked to learn that neither the State Department nor the Defense Department had any contingency plans. He worked with his staff for two hours to draft a statement neither praising nor vilifying Stalin (nor even mentioning him by name) but expressing the sympathy of the American people. It was designed to appear to extend an overture for peace without explicitly doing so.[11]

In the turmoil following Stalin's death, two men, Deputy Prime Minister and Head of State Security Lavrentiy Beria and Second Secretary of the Communist Party Georgy Malenkov, stepped into the fray and immediately moved to switch Soviet foreign policy to a less dangerous track, even announcing at Stalin's funeral that they would pursue a new "peace initiative."[12] Following up on this notion, on March 15 Malenkov took Washington by surprise when he announced to the Supreme Soviet that "there is no dispute or unresolved question that cannot be settled peacefully by mutual agreement of the interested countries. This applies to our relations with all states, including the United States of America."[13]

Eisenhower, not about to let this golden opportunity slip by, indicated to his staff that he was tired of the indictments of the Soviet Union. He wanted to do something to improve the chances for peace. "The past speaks for itself," he claimed. "I am interested in the future. Both their government and ours now have new men in them. The slate is clean. Now let us begin talking to each other."[14] After a long silence, Eisenhower chose his very first formal address to the American people as the occasion for this opening to the Soviets.

At a luncheon of the American Society of Newspaper Editors, Eisenhower explained that he wanted to speak about the issue of peace. Without it the United States would be subjected to "a life of perpetual fear and tension; a burden of arms draining the wealth and the labor of all peoples; a wasting of strength that defies the American system or the Soviet system or any system to achieve true abundance and happiness for the peoples of this earth." Eisenhower went on to propose placing atomic weapons under international control and greatly reducing the arms race by limiting the size of military forces and restricting weapons production. He characterized excessive military spending as a wholesale theft from the American people, indicating that this money could better be spent on schools and hospitals. He concluded that if this could be done, humanity might find before them "a golden age of freedom and peace."[15]

The speech was a triumph. The *New York Times* called it "magnificent and deeply moving." The *New York Post*, a staunchly Democratic newspaper, praised the Republican president, writing that the speech was "America's voice at its best."[16] Cousins must have been elated when he read the speech; it was exactly what he had been advocating for. In an editorial three weeks later he referred to "President Eisenhower's historic statement on peace" and said that it "reflected moral imagination and an inspiring awareness of the need for the United States to talk about the conditions of peace on a somewhat higher level than the mathematical equations of military force."[17]

Cousins may also have been heartened by Eisenhower's pre-presidential public stance on nuclear weapons. After the war, he had gone on record to oppose the atomic bombing of Japan on both military and moral grounds. In 1947 he had told an audience, "I decry loose and sometimes gloating talk about the degree of security implicit in a weapon that might destroy millions overnight."[18] Eisenhower apparently maintained this unease even in 1956 when he wrote Cousins on the eleventh anniversary of the bombing of Hiroshima to tell him that he was still deeply disturbed about what nuclear weapons meant for civilization. "[I was troubled] when I learned that the first atomic bomb had been successfully tested in 1945 and that the United States planned to use it against a Japanese city. Never has the matter ceased troubling me."[19] Yet, his actions as president did not reflect his words when it came to nuclear weapons.

CHAPTER 12

EISENHOWER'S NEW LOOK

Although President Eisenhower spoke in his April 16 speech of greatly reducing the arms race by restricting the production of atomic weapons, in October 1953 he approved a policy that would see America's defense stance redeveloped around nuclear weapons.[1] Eisenhower came to think that the rapid technological leaps in nuclear weapons design in the postwar period, as well as their proliferation, had effectively rendered conventional armies obsolete. Eisenhower recognized that the United States would never be able to cost-effectively match the size and power of the Red Army. Thus, nuclear weapons were vital to offset superior Communist manpower.[2]

The administration argued that this was a defense posture that could be sustained over the long run without bankrupting the country. Most alarmingly, this "New Look" defense policy stated that "in the event of hostilities, the United States will consider nuclear weapons to be as available for use as other munitions."[3] This was a fundamental departure not only from previous US policy, according to which nuclear weapons would be used only in the most dire of circumstances. Eisenhower's New Look sought to make nuclear weapons more usable, with the president stating that in his mind there was no distinction between conventional and nuclear weapons.[4] The United States' European allies were spooked by Eisenhower's cavalier attitude toward using nuclear bombs, and they pressured him to slow down the arms race.[5] Unfortunately, the New Look's increased reliance on nuclear weapons instead inaugurated a greatly increased nuclear arms race between the United States and the Soviet Union.

The race had already entered a new stage before Eisenhower became president. The United States had started down its own path to developing a hydrogen bomb in 1952, after a contentious debate during the Truman administration. If successful, an H-bomb would be many orders of magnitude more powerful than the existing atomic bombs. Recognizing the increased public alarm fostered by the New Look, Eisenhower announced the Atoms for Peace program at the United Nations on December 8, 1953. This was a program that attempted to put a smiley face on the atom and sought to find a way to spread the benefits of peaceful atomic power at home and abroad.[6] The speech, broadcast worldwide on the Voice of America, received enthusiastic responses from nearly every capital except Moscow, which viewed it with suspicion. Domestically the speech garnered much praise among citizens and politicians alike.[7] Cousins, however, thought otherwise.

Launching a series of articles, Cousins blasted Atoms for Peace and the development of the H-bomb with equal force. Claiming that the United States had entered a "period of total danger," he made clear that despite what the politicians might say, the country had no adequate defense against a hydrogen or an atomic bomb attack. Cousins argued that the New Look meant that the nation's defense was now largely limited to the striking power of massive nuclear retaliation. This was a special kind of madness given that the bulk of the US population and industry were concentrated in a few key cities (in contrast to the Soviet Union's more widely distributed population and industrial base). Therefore, Cousins argued, "the United States carries a higher war hazard than any major nation in the world."[8] The New Look, he claimed, actually made the country *more* vulnerable to attack, not less.

But there was more to the problem than just a war hazard. Cousins's article came on the heels of the disastrous Bravo nuclear test. On March 1, 1954, the first US test of a high-yield hydrogen bomb, conducted in the Marshall Islands, exposed a number of US soldiers stationed nearby, hundreds of Marshall Islanders, and, infamously, the crew of a Japanese fishing boat named *Daigo Fukuryu Maru* (Lucky Dragon Five) to radiation. Although the boat was safely outside the restricted zone, twenty-three Japanese fishermen were exposed to high levels of radiation, and one received a fatal dose.[9]

To this point there had been a public debate over the level of danger from radioactive fallout. The Bravo test made clear to the world that through radiation exposure nuclear weapons could be unintentionally deadly even to those at a "safe" distance. To Cousins, this was evidence enough that "no Government can any longer say that radioactivity in another war can be controlled or that the human genes can somehow be shielded from the mangling effects. . . . The Government cannot provide such reassurance because there is no reassurance to be had."[10] Honing in on this idea of radiation affecting not just those directly exposed but all future generations of humanity through the genetic damage it also causes, Cousins's November 27, 1954, editorial put forward the treatise that would soon come to define and direct the next phase of his anti-nuclear career:

> The rights of the state are many. They include the right to sacrifice human life or to take human life in the defense of the nation. But there is nothing in the political rights of the state or its rulers that includes the right to strike at the nature of man or to disfigure the face of man or to toy with the vital balances that make life possible. For if the state has political rights then man has natural rights. These natural rights are above the rights of the state and beyond the reach and the authority of the state. The good society exists to serve and protect these rights. Man has a right to keep himself from being cheapened, debased, or deformed. He has a right to creative growth. He has a right to individual sanctity and sovereignty. He has a right to make his life purposeful. If these natural rights should die, though human flesh in some form re-

> main, then the survivors will not be the lucky ones. To dismiss all this by referring solely to the threat of Communist Russia is to dramatize folly.[11]

Cousins's November 1954 editorial marked a major turning point in his nuclear thinking. He evolved from a nuclear control advocate into an anti-nuclear activist and in doing so also helped to bring the perils of nuclear radiation to the forefront of the public consciousness. Cousins's contention about the existence of radiation meant that decisions about nuclear weapons were no longer solely a national political issue; they were a moral and ethical issue of international scope. Cousins's message was also reaching a much larger audience. The *Saturday Review* had around 20,000 subscribers when Cousins arrived in 1940. By 1956 it had 190,000.[12] These discussions about the dangers of nuclear war and radiation exposure even impacted Cousins's family. His daughters recall the atomic bomb casting a long shadow over their lives in the 1950s and 1960s. Sarah says that when she was a child, the fear of the atomic bomb was her central preoccupation. Andrea too, recalls the pall cast by the bomb. It was a frequent dinner-table topic.

With a growing family, Ellen and Norman had started looking for a larger home in late 1953, and in 1954 the family moved to a new home in the neighboring city of New Canaan, Connecticut. They had come across a stately old house with more than forty acres of wild woodland and grassy fields and fallen in love with it. The property came with an old barn, an overgrown riding ring (the two older girls would soon get horses of their own to care for), a pasture, and woods. They very soon built a tennis court, which was "very important for my parents," according to Candis. "They were tennis aficionados."[13] "I think that my father had faith in the beauty and truth of nature," Sarah said, "and that by putting us in this beautiful wild spot of trees and fields and grass and open sky, his children would be alright. It seems to me that my parents thought that if they provided us with this oasis of nature, we [girls] would find our own way in life our own truth . . . that the natural world can lead a person to truth."[14]

Moving from the more working-class Norwalk to the upper-middle-class New Canaan did mean a cultural change for the family. Sarah recalls being the only Jewish child in her class. "In those years so soon after the Holocaust, what it meant to be a Jew was an inwardly overwhelming—though never articulated—question, under the surface of our childhood."[15] Andrea remembers that when she was in elementary school before they moved, she was in the Norwalk public school system for a time before her parents enrolled all the daughters in the New Canaan Country Day School, which was of higher quality than the local public schools After the move to New Canaan, Norman, being at the time on the New England Education Commission, took the girls out of the Country School and returned them to the public school system in New Canaan, which was known to have a higher-performing public school system. Andrea recalls that "this was sort of a trauma for me, just terrible! My father didn't understand what it would mean socially to change schools, and he didn't really understand the difference in the two cultures. . . . He just wasn't involved in our social lives at that level."[16]

But even in the bucolic hills of New Canaan, the latest scientific research was making ever clearer, the nuclear bomb threat could still reach them. Previously, it had been easy for many Americans to accept the necessity of increasing the nuclear stockpile in order to keep the country safe. It was understood (mistakenly) that in the event of an attack only those directly in the blast zone would be affected, as would be the case with conventional weapons. The US Atomic Energy Commission (AEC), however, was aware as early as 1950 that radioactive fallout from its nuclear tests presented a serious health risk to those who came in contact with it. The growing awareness of radioactive fallout, coupled with the sharp increase in the number of atmospheric nuclear tests conducted in the United States after 1950 (with the level of atmospheric radiation increasing with each new test), exposed a new threat. The atomic bomb had transformed every citizen into a potential casualty regardless of their proximity to the blast zone.[17] Despite this knowledge, the AEC remained adamantly opposed to any changes to its testing regime. Commissioner Willard Libby callously stated that "people have got to learn to live with the facts of life . . . and part of the facts of life are fallout."[18]

For this reason, beginning in 1951 the Federal Civil Defense Administration (FCDA), the federal agency that coordinated defense preparedness, began a program of saturating the newsstands and airwaves with civil defense planning procedures in order to prepare Americans for these "facts of life" and protect the population from the deadly radiation that would accompany a nuclear attack. In 1952 the FCDA set up a liaison program with national magazines that offered prewritten editorial statements and articles that could be easily published. By 1955 this propaganda effort had achieved so much success that the lines between government-sponsored civil defense stories and the free press became disturbingly blurred. Historian Laura McEnaney contends that press cooperation was so thorough that it was virtually impossible for American citizens to discern the difference between FCDA spin and independent journalism.[19]

Cousins, however, refused to follow the lead of some FCDA mouthpieces, such as *Life* magazine, which would later run an article about bomb shelters proclaiming that "fallout can be fun" and that nuclear war was survivable.[20] This whitewashing of nuclear dangers stemmed from a key tenet of the Atoms for Peace program, which aimed to persuade the American people that there was nothing unique about nuclear weapons: they were simply a normal tool of the defense arsenal. Secretary of State John Foster Dulles specifically called for the program to break down the "false" distinction between conventional and nuclear weapons.[21] To Cousins, the distinction was glaringly clear, and not recognizing it might mean the end of humanity.

Cousins did not allow the *Saturday Review* to participate in the FCDA's program of psychological inoculation against the horrors of atomic warfare. In a February 1955 editorial, he claimed that the civil defense procedures the US government was insisting upon were "as outmoded as a knight's suit-of-armor in front of a howitzer. The raw fact is that our cities are indefensible."[22] He mocked the FCDA's recent announcement that an effective survival measure in event of a nuclear attack was simply to evacuate the major cities. Cousins asked how the million people in Manhattan would scramble across the few bridges connecting the island to the mainland in the short period after they were warned.[23] This completely ineffective panacea being sold to the American people meant that "mass evacuation might well become a term for mass incineration."[24]

In the midst of this roiling controversy over the hydrogen bomb tests, nuclear radiation, and thoughts of mass incineration, Cousins also found time for family fun. Albeit, mixed with work. Andrea remembers that most of their family vacations when she was growing up were connected to her father's work. He would get invited to speak somewhere (like the University of Toronto in July 1954), and he might take the whole family along and make a vacation of it.[25] On this particular summer road trip, just before crossing into Canada they stopped to take in the sights of Niagara Falls. After surveying the scene, young Candis earnestly said, "Daddy, it's wonderful and all that, but just between you and me, don't you think it's a little overrated?"[26] They spent some time in Toronto before taking a leisurely sightseeing drive back through upstate New York, where Cousins was eager to stop at historic Fort Ticonderoga. He had always been fascinated by the philosophy and beliefs of the Founding Fathers, particularly their religious beliefs, which he would discuss in a book about four years later, *In God We Trust: The Religious Beliefs and Ideas of the American Founding Fathers* (1954).

Cousins later wrote to a friend that he took great pleasure in taking his daughters through the same passageways that George Washington and other historic American figures had walked through. After exploring the fort, the family sat down near a big cannon overlooking the valley and Cousins took on the role of the professor, telling his girls the story of the fort up until the time it was taken by the Americans.

Perhaps seeing the world as only a nine-year-old could, Candis chimed in: "Daddy," she asked, "did you say the Americans *took* this fort from the British?" Cousins nodded. "How rude of them," she observed with some indignation. Cousins reflected on his daughter's interjection and how ethics could foul up history, making demons out of heroes.[27]

The family trip was a welcome respite from Cousins's days at the office, which were typically punctuated by constant pressure made worse by endless interruption. His daughter Sarah got a firsthand look at this when, as a college student, she got a job working in the Classified Ads Department of the *Saturday Review.* On weekday mornings she would join her father for breakfast in the city. Sarah would order a cup of coffee, while her father enjoyed two eggs over easy and two slices of whole wheat toast before they caught a cab to the office.

Sarah later wrote that it was a revelation to see how hard he worked to get the magazine out each and every week when all day long people never stopped knocking on his door, "complaining, beseeching, imploring, and demanding."[28] Cousins, too, frequently complained in letters to associates that his phone never stopped ringing and the correspondence just kept piling up. He frequently took letters home to respond to after hours, but the backlog grew there too. His archivist later lamented that Cousins was like a squirrel. In his study at home letters and papers were stuffed everywhere. In one drawer, scattered between shirts she found plane tickets, vouchers, invitations from Khrushchev, his will, and letters from famous people from around the world.[29] Cousins was fond of telling people that his desire for order was exceeded only by his inability to create it.[30]

CHAPTER 13

A NEW PROJECT

The Moral Adoptions program, which had enjoyed such success in 1949, was faltering. It was difficult to keep people interested in the ongoing program, and by 1953 donations had inevitably waned. Reverend Tanimoto, who was aware that there was still much more to be done to help the victims of the atomic bomb, had taken it upon himself to assist a group of atomic bomb victims who suffered a particular hardship.

Soon after the bombing, young women who had been badly burned and scarred by the bomb began to wander into Tanimoto's church, the Nagarehawa United Church of Christ in Hiroshima, seeking refuge because they did not know where else to turn. Their physical deformities meant that they were forced to live as near outcasts. In many cases their families kept them hidden away from public view. Wanting to help, in August 1951 Tanimoto started hosting a support group for these women in the basement of his church. It began as a simple sewing circle where the women could interact with others like themselves, but Tanimoto sought to help them find jobs in order to rebuild their self-confidence after years of living as pariahs.[1] Their sense of alienation from their community caused them to avoid moving about the city during daylight.[2] Tanimoto recognized that if these women were to ever lead normal lives, their physical wounds would have to be treated. These women were different from the multitudes of injured

Japanese victims of war. Because of the unique nature of their injuries, they required advanced and ongoing care.

Tanimoto struggled to find effective medical treatment for the girls, though not for lack of trying. Through hard work and with the sponsorship of Japanese author Shizue Masugi, Tanimoto managed to take many of the girls to Tokyo in June 1952 for plastic surgery to repair the damage to their skin.[3] Unfortunately, plastic surgery was still rather experimental, and given the Japanese doctors' lack of knowledge about treating radiation burns, the results of the surgeries were disappointing. Without the advanced plastic surgery techniques that were only available in the United States, nothing more could be done.[4]

In July 1952, Pearl Buck wrote to Cousins informing him about Tanimoto's hope that perhaps they could find a way to bring some of the girls to the United States for treatment, for he "fears that the surgeons in Japan do not have the best methods."[5] Haunted by the conditions of the hospital he had visited in 1949, Cousins admitted that ever since his first visit he had desired to establish some sort of medical program.[6] But even after Tanimoto's pleas, Cousins showed no personal interest in the plan.[7] He may have been reluctant to add another major commitment to his already overwhelming schedule, but Tanimoto was not to be discouraged.

The official US occupation of Japan having ended the previous year, Cousins returned to Japan in August 1953 as part of a world tour that he undertook for the *Saturday Review*. During a visit to Tanimoto's his newly rebuilt church, Cousins was introduced by Tanimoto to the women he was assisting. Tanimoto told him about the difficulties their injuries caused them and the need to get them the advanced treatment that was unavailable in Japan.[8] Cousins listened intently as they spoke about the articles they had read regarding advances in plastic surgery and their hope for the miracle that might help them return to a more normal life one day.[9]

Cousins with Kyoshi Tanimoto's daughter, Koko.

(PHOTO COURTESY OF KOKO KONDO)

In a 1984 interview, Cousins recalled that he had been "profoundly disturbed, not just by the conditions of the girls but by what the atomic bomb had done." He remembered being speechless and very much moved.[10] Touched by their struggles, he knew firsthand the hospital conditions these women had already endured, and he also knew what would be required to fully heal them. The women's struggles were especially tragic to Cousins since Japan was reportedly already producing some of the world's leading research on treating atomic injuries.

The Atomic Bomb Casualty Commission (ABCC) was established in Hiroshima in 1947 and in Nagasaki in 1948 to investigate the effects of radiation on the atomic bomb victims. Although funded by the United States, the ABCC was intended to be a largely Japanese-run institution. It would also quickly become a lightning rod because its mandate was to simply study the effects of radiation, not to offer treatment. Those who required medical treatment were referred to local Japanese hospitals.[11]

The ABCC kept secret most of its research findings and placed restrictions on the dissemination of any atomic bomb–related information. These restrictions prevented Japanese doctors from accessing the information generated by the ABCC about how to treat atomic victims at the local hospitals they were referred to.[12] Despite frequent Japanese Ministry of Welfare requests that US doctors give advice on treatment, State Department memos confirm that much of the knowledge that Japanese scientists had gathered on nuclear illness and treatments was taken away to the United States during the occupation.[13] When challenged, ABCC director Carl Tessmer explained that the commission's primary purpose was medical investigation, a task that was "so large that our efforts and resources would have to be kept in this one direction." He also turned the argument back on the Japanese, claiming that if the ABCC offered free treatment, it would threaten the livelihoods of physicians in Hiroshima and Nagasaki.[14] Already affected by the American bombs, many survivors believed that they were being victimized a second time, turned into research subjects by American scientists.[15] In a 1949 editorial Cousins addressed this contentious issue of nontreatment. He wrote that it was a "strange spectacle" that an atomic bomb survivor got "thousands of dollars' worth of analysis but not one cent of treatment."[16]

Although there was widespread discontent and suspicion among the survivors being studied at the ABCC, outcry from the general public was limited at first. During the occupation the Japanese press was prohibited from publishing any "destructive" criticism or any news that "might, directly or by inference, disturb the public tranquility."[17] However, with the end of the occupation in 1952 and the lifting of the restrictions on the Japanese press, complaints spread quickly. John Beatty, a philosophy of science scholar, points out that with the end of the occupation-enforced censorship, the ABCC grew increasingly concerned that the Japanese press was spreading the idea that the patients studied at the ABCC were simply "guinea pigs."[18] Cousins believed that the ABCC pursued an important scientific purpose, but he also felt that any doctor who examined a patient had an obligation under the Hippocratic Oath to treat that patient.[19] Cousins had seen firsthand that the local hospitals the ABCC referred patients to had neither the equipment nor the advanced medical knowledge required to treat the bomb victims.

After meeting Tanimoto's charges, Cousins recognized that these victims of the atomic bomb would never receive the help they needed without outside assistance, given the ABCC's de facto policy of nontreatment despite its access to advanced research and medical equipment. Nor would any help be forthcoming from the US government. A condition of the peace treaty signed by Japan in 1951 was that the Japanese government relinquished the right to seek compensation from the Allied powers.[20] In reality, a 1956 report put the cost of initiating a treatment program at approximately thirty thousand dollars a year.[21] Despite this relatively low cost, the State Department maintained that no money could be found for treatment.[22]

If the US government was unwilling to change this reprehensible policy of nontreatment even when the occupation was officially over, Cousins told author Rodney Barker, then his goal was to "shame the bastards [the ABCC]" into behaving more compassionately.[23] He asked Tanimoto if he would welcome efforts to bring the girls to the United States. Tanimoto replied that "this had been his dream from the first moment."[24]

CHAPTER 14

THE HIROSHIMA MAIDENS

Newly inspired by the possibilities of directly treating atomic bomb victims, upon returning to the United States Cousins wasted no time in approaching multiple private organizations and companies seeking sponsorships to launch the Hiroshima Maidens initiative. With the success of the Moral Adoptions program to his credit, Cousins thought he would have no trouble securing corporate sponsorship for the Maidens project. Discouragement came fast and early.

Every organization he approached for funding to bring Japanese women to the United States for medical treatment expressed concern over the possibility of negative publicity or liability and ultimately turned him down. Forced to turn to more personal contacts, Cousins, through his personal physician and longtime friend Bill Hitzig, was eventually able to persuade the board of Mt. Sinai Hospital in New York City to at least provide modest facilities at no cost. Two top plastic surgeons also agreed to donate their time.[1]

Even after medical facilities were secured, the entire project was held up for six months over the prohibitive expense of air transportation for such a large group of people. Cousins first approached Pan American Airlines about donating flights. Its spokesman replied that official airline regulations prevented them from offering free passage regardless of the humanitarian nature of the mission. He appealed to the Civil Aeronautics Board for an exemption from this rule but was denied.[2]

When all else seemed to have failed, Cousins was advised to approach Kiyoshi Togasaki, president of Japan's *Nippon Times.* Togasaki had the bold idea of appealing directly to General John E. Hull (US Army, Far East Command). With the approval of the US Embassy in Tokyo, Togasaki asked whether the US Air Force might be willing to fly the girls. After some deliberation, finally convinced of the humanitarian nature of the project, General Hull agreed to donate a large Air Force plane to fly the girls to the United States.[3]

General Hull's memoir published in 1978 makes clear that he was very concerned about conditions in Japan, and as Far East commander he was personally dedicated to improving US-Japanese relations.[4] Hull's donation of the aircraft not only saved the project from floundering but also meant that the US government was directly involved in supporting Cousins's efforts. This act served to greatly increase the project's profile, giving it the aura of being officially sanctioned. After the Air Force plane was secured, Pan American Airlines reconsidered its initial refusal and agreed to pay $1,275 toward the return flights.[5]

By January 1954, with the project coming slowly together, the Hiroshima Peace Center Association (HPCA) sent its treasurer to inform the State Department of the association's intentions. State Department officials were less than enthusiastic about the prospect of bringing atomic bomb victims to the United States and expressed many concerns. For one, the United States maintained a policy that avoided any gesture that would indicate a sense of guilt or liability for the plight of the atomic bomb victims.[6] Treating victims in the United States might imply that the United States was responsible for them. The State Department expressed much concern over the possibility that the project would generate negative, or worse, Communist propaganda. Officials at State also worried that treating atomic bomb victims in the United States might jeopardize the department's policy of deemphasizing the negative aspects of nuclear weapons.[7]

After a two-hour discussion with the HPCA treasurer, the State Department, although still leery, agreed not to stand in the way on the

The Hiroshima Maidens prepare to travel from New York to California before returning to Japan.

(PHOTO BY JACOB HARRIS / ASSOCIATED PRESS)

condition that Cousins ensured that the Maidens maintained as low a profile as possible in order to avoid any public relations issues. The government's preference was for the girls to come one at a time and not as a group in order to minimize the potential for media exposure.[8] Cousins was informed by the committee members helping to arrange the project that the State Department "strongly urged that we sneak the girls into the country as quietly as possible."[9] Since the Air Force was only providing one flight, it was impossible to bring the girls over one at a time, but Cousins did promise that they would stay out of the spotlight as much as possible. With the State Department placated (for the time being), the Maidens project moved into its final planning stages just as international furor erupted that would suddenly make nuclear issues much more prominent.

The Bravo bomb test took place just three weeks after the State Department meeting. For the third time in a decade, Japanese civilians were exposed to radiation caused by atomic weapons, sparking a firestorm.[10] Interestingly, none of Cousins's *Saturday Review* editorials written at the time mentions the failed Bravo test or the radiation poisoning of the Japanese fishermen. One could speculate that with his Hiroshima Maidens project about to launch, he did not want to draw any negative attention to himself or to anger the State Department after agreeing to keep a low profile.

The *Lucky Dragon* incident completely changed the diplomatic atmosphere. In the days that followed the disastrous test, Japanese doctors accused the United States, and specifically the ABCC, of refusing to provide them with information necessary for treating the *Lucky Dragon* victims and atomic bomb victims in general. The extremely vocal reaction in Japan made it especially imperative that the United States receive no more negative exposure regarding nuclear issues. The US government tried to downplay the incident, with AEC chairman Lewis Strauss going as far as to claim that it was all a Communist plot to discredit the United States.[11]

In April, the Japanese Ministry of Welfare released an open letter stating that it had frequently called on US doctors for advice on treatment but had received no reply.[12] A bitter statement appeared in a Japanese newspaper from a doctor involved with the case. He claimed that US officials refused to provide information because they intended to use the fishermen as "experiment material."[13] In this tense new atmosphere the issue of treating the victims of atomic bombs (or not treating them, as it were) took on new pertinence.

With the Maidens project scheduled to begin in early May 1955, Cousins traveled to Hiroshima with his entourage in late April to help brief and prepare the girls. When information prematurely leaked to the Japanese media about his newest initiative, especially the fact that he was partnering with Reverend Tanimoto, the media descended on them in droves. Naturally, the Japanese were both curious and a little suspicious when they learned of the Maidens project. Cousins characterizes the Japanese media as "constructive and friendly," but they also posed questions that were often "severe."[14] In the post-Bravo atmosphere the Japanese were extremely wary of US attempts at subterfuge. Many wanted to know why Cousins was *really* doing this and who was putting up the money. Some accused the US government of secretly sponsoring and paying for the project as a means of building goodwill to offset the bad impression caused by the ongoing nuclear tests in the Pacific.

Fortunately, Cousins was able to carefully avoid most of the questions and accusations, but he admitted that he struggled to find an adequate answer to the question why they were doing it. Cousins wrote, "As individual citizens we no doubt felt a strong personal responsibility for the first atomic weapon to be used against human beings. . . . The feeling of guilt, while real enough, was not the whole answer. . . . Finally we told the newsmen . . . each of us happened to be in a position where we might be of some help and we were responding the best we could, simply because we wanted to."[15] But Cousins's after-the-fact recollection belies his deeper drive. Although he publicly claimed this was simply a humanitarian aid project taking advantage of American benevolence to aid the victims of war, Cousins had powerful ulterior motives. Although Cousins may not have seen himself (yet) as a private diplomat, both he and Tanimoto agreed that the project might positively influence larger geopolitical issues. For Cousins it was an opportunity to create a powerful symbol of goodwill and show the Japanese people to Americans in a sympathetic light.[16] He was also extremely critical of US policies in Japan, especially the ABCC's nontreatment policy. He was determined to directly challenge the US government by forcing it to take some responsibility for the treatment of the atomic bomb victims, a position he had held since 1945.

While Cousins won over the Japanese press, he did not have the same success with the ABCC. While in Hiroshima he paid a visit to the ABCC, much to the chagrin of its director, Charles Dunham. Dunham complained, "Norman Cousins arrived in town to collect his A-Bomb maidens. . . . [He] seemed to be trying to get as much for nothing as he could. He invited himself and his crowd to dinner the first night he was in town, and proceeded to do it again for breakfast."[17] All this renewed focus and growing media attention was making the State Department increasingly nervous in the wake of the *Lucky Dragon* incident.

The day before the group was scheduled to leave, Ralph Blake, a US Foreign Service officer, sent a cable to the State Department questioning whether the Hiroshima Maidens program was in keeping with "our worldwide efforts to de-emphasize the destructive effects of nuclear weapons."[18] Never enamored with the Maidens project, now with mounting concern in the wake of the *Lucky Dragon* incident the State Department decided to withdraw its approval on the very day the group's plane was set to depart from Japan. A cable was sent from Washington to the Far East Command withdrawing authorization for the flight. The US Air Force plane, already loaded and ready to depart with the group, was idling on the taxiway when the telegram canceling the flight arrived and was rushed outside to General Hull, who was standing on the tarmac to see the plane off. Hull looked at the telegram for a long moment before telling the aide who had handed it to him that he did not have his reading glasses and would have to look at it later. The plane departed as planned.[19]

The whole "glasses trick" was almost certainly a feint, since General Hull clearly was proud of the role he played. The following month, he wrote Cousins a personal letter in which he stated, "This is one of the finest things which has been done, and the future returns from this act of goodwill will pay tremendous dividends, I'm sure, to the United States. I am very happy that I was privileged to assist."[20] Cousins would later state that "it must have been a very difficult decision [for General Hull,] requiring a lot of courage to make. . . . He was wise enough to know that the human principle was more important than political principles."[21]

The flight was long and grueling. The Douglass C-124 model that was ferrying the Maidens to America, although introduced only three years earlier, was aptly nicknamed "Old Shaky." It had a range of just over thirty-five hundred kilometers. The refueling stops necessitated by the flight from Japan of more than ten thousand kilometers meant it would be a three-day journey to the United States. (Still it was an improvement over the fifteen days it typically took an ocean liner to make the same journey in that era.) State Department officials realized that the negative public reaction to forcing the plane to turn around after it had started out would have been too great, so they let it continue.[22] Since they had been unable to stop the program before it literally got off the ground, a flurry of activity ensued about how to handle damage control.

The day after the plane departed, the State Department sent a memo to the American Embassy in Tokyo expressing its concern that the "Hiroshima girls [*sic*] medical treatment in U.S. can generate publicity harmful not only [to] our relations with Japan but particularly our worldwide efforts [to] avoid playing up [the] destructive efforts [of] nuclear weapons."[23] However, the State Department was wrong on this count; the project seemed to be having the opposite effect. On the day the girls departed, a front-page story in the *Japan Times* proclaimed that the Hiroshima Maidens "will also erase some of the wrinkles and scars on the popular attitude of Japan to America. In short, the unprecedented project will undo what the Bikini fallout did to the relations between the two nations."[24]

Two days after their arrival in New York, Tanimoto and two of the Maidens flew out to California to appear on the television show *This Is Your Life*. The episode had been arranged by Cousins as an opportunity to solicit donations to help cover the living expenses of the Maidens while they were in the United States. The surreal episode began with Tanimoto's wife and children appearing in the studio, to his complete surprise as he had left them back in Japan. After the surprise reunion, another shocking twist introduced Captain Robert Lewis, copilot of the *Enola Gay*. Apparently, Cousins himself had persuaded Lewis to appear on the show after Lewis telephoned the *Saturday Review* office and reportedly said, "I just wanted to say how personally grateful I am for this project. . . . I was the captain of the plane that dropped the bomb."[25]

On the air, Lewis described the events of the morning the bomb was dropped and appeared to express remorse for his actions before presenting a fifty-dollar check from him and his fellow crewmember to help the Maidens.[26] Instantly the telephone switchboard at the NBC studio lit up with angry callers. In addition to horrifying the State Department, Lewis's appearance on the show and implied apology outraged veterans. In the end, though, only fourteen critical letters were received, in contrast to more than twenty thousand letters of support. Viewers also donated an astonishing fifty-five thousand dollars to the Maidens project.[27] The *This Is Your Life* episode was a stunning success. It was reported to Cousins that the show's host, Ralph Edwards, had told a colleague that "of all the shows he has ever done he believes this one will have the most far-reaching influence for good."[28] From the perspective of the State Department, however, it was a public relations disaster.

Growing increasingly concerned that the rash of publicity would evolve into open criticism of America's nuclear policies, the State Department requested a meeting with Cousins. Knowing that he was a leading critic of US nuclear policies, officials sought assurance that he would not attempt to use the Maidens for his own political objectives. Cousins met with Walter Robertson, assistant secretary of state for the Far East, on June 2, 1955. Robertson stated that while the United States endeavored to help the "victims of misfortune" (State Department employees had been instructed in an internal memo not to refer to the woman as victims of the nuclear bomb), Cousins was to keep "the Hiroshima girls from stirring up propaganda against nuclear weapons."[29] Cousins would later recount that during the meeting he confronted

Robertson about why the State Department had attempted to stop the project. The assistant secretary explained that US officials feared that the visit would rally support for outlawing the bomb, which the government fervently opposed.[30] Acknowledging the State Department's concerns and recognizing that it could always choose to revoke the girls' visas, Cousins agreed to limit the media coverage of the Maidens. He ended the meeting by telling Robinson that all the poor publicity aside, the treatments could only serve to further the cause of international peace and goodwill.[31]

Since the US government banned the publication of photographs of atomic bomb victims until 1952, the arrival of the Maidens gave the American people their first real exposure to the human suffering caused by the bomb.[32] The physical presence of the disfigured girls in the United States had a much more potent impact than a photograph ever could. No matter how much the State Department tried to portray them as ordinary war victims, the American public saw what they really represented. Newspaper articles from across the country never failed to refer to the women as victims of the atomic bomb. The *New York Times* reported that this program sought to "repair some of the human wreckage left by the World War II atomic bombs."[33] The *Chicago Tribune* described them as the victims of "scars and disfigurements suffered in the first atomic bombing of their homeland."[34] The *Los Angeles Times* referred to them as "survivors of the first atomic bomb burst over a city."[35] One particularly poignant article, which must have especially irked the State Department, began, "Last year the same Air Force that dropped the bomb flew 25 terribly scarred and burned Hiroshima girls to the U.S."[36] The *New York Times* also published a critical article that juxtaposed the joy these women felt at the generosity of the Americans who donated to the project to the "deep sense of gloom" over the saber rattling that punctuated the United States' conduct of international diplomacy.[37]

Although Cousins upheld his end of the agreement to keep the girls out of the spotlight, the State Department kept a close eye on how the Japanese were reacting to the project. What officials found allayed their fears of negative publicity and indicated that Cousins's private diplomacy to improve US-Japanese relations through this project was getting some traction. In a letter to the editor of the *New York Times*, four members of the Japanese Diet expressed their concern about the suffering of the atomic bomb victims but spoke in glowing terms about the Hiroshima Maidens project. "As members of the National Diet of Japan," they stated, "we wish to express our profound gratitude to the American people."[38]

International mail also poured into Cousins's New York office, demonstrating his growing influence on international relations. "I am now writing this letter because I believe you are a sincere friend of new Japan, and also a very influential person to contribute to a lasting friendship of the States and Japan," wrote the director of the Research Institute of Comparative Educational Culture.[39] Even Japan's first ambassador to the United States, Toshikazu Kase, wrote to ask if he could pay a visit to Cousins at his home in Connecticut in order to express his personal gratitude for Cousins's efforts.[40] Cousins received some twenty-five thousand letters from individual Americans expressing their support for the project.[41]

Recognizing the positive public response to the Hiroshima Maidens project within Japan, the US ambassador to Japan, John Allison, dispatched a lengthy cable to Washington. Calling the use of the bomb a "catastrophic display of American military power," he claimed that the reluctance of the United States to treat the victims had "greatly damaged the reputation of Americans as a humanitarian people." Encouraged by the positive coverage given to Cousins's efforts, he requested funds to help build a university treatment hospital for the bomb victims, writing that it was "still not too late to make a gesture towards the survivors of Hiroshima and Nagasaki which would allow the United States to regain a little lost stature."[42]

Robert Holmes, director of the ABCC, wrote in support of the ambassador's request, arguing that "it would provide a very convenient loop-hole in our alleged policy of 'no treatment' . . . thus relieving the political pressure ever upon ABCC."[43] Internal State Department memos reveal that while the possibility of building a US-sponsored treatment hospital was debated, the department feared that "the patients now being examined at the Atomic Bomb Casualty Commission will be diverted. Should this occur it would be impossible effectively to continue the research work of the ABCC."[44] The Japanese critics were largely correct in their assertion that they were being used as guinea pigs. Internally, the US government admitted as much in its desire to continue to use the Japanese victims as research subjects.

Encouraged by the story of the Hiroshima Maidens, and knowing that there was an additional city that undoubtedly had its own atomic bomb victims, a hospital in Mobile, Alabama, offered pro bono services to the victims of Nagasaki.[45] The issue of what to do about these additional programs (hospitals in San Francisco and Philadelphia also expressed interest) was discussed at the highest levels of government, with the Department of Defense, the Central Intelligence Agency, and the United States Information Agency weighing in. State Department officials eventually decided that these additional initiatives were of an "undesirable nature," and approval of them would be put on hold.[46]

The power of Cousins's private diplomacy efforts to improve relations was ultimately confirmed by President Eisenhower. Writing on behalf of the president, presidential assistant Sherman Adams congratulated Cousins and noted that everyone involved in the Hiroshima Maidens project "should take satisfaction in their contribution toward strengthening the bonds of friendship between our two countries."[47] Upon receipt of the letter, Cousins responded directly to the president, thanking him as well as requesting a meeting. On his trip back to Japan, Cousins explained, it had been "apparent that America is winning new respect and prestige among the majority of the world's people because of the working demonstration of your determination to seek peace through clearly defined principle." Cousins noted that he was very eager to talk to the president on this issue.[48] Eisenhower replied that he was "going away for a rest" and would not be able to meet.[49] With the approaching 1956 election campaign, which saw Eisenhower once again battling Adlai Stevenson, who attacked him over the issue of nuclear testing, the White House did not want Eisenhower anywhere near the Maidens for fear of how it might play in the press. Administration officials even banned the taking of photographs when the Maidens visited the White House.[50]

In America, the lasting effect of the Maidens' presence was minimal, but in Japan they had a much stronger impact on policy, forcing the Japanese government into action after years of effectively ignoring atomic bomb victims' need for effective treatment. After learning of the Maidens' successful treatment, the *Japan Times* reported, some fifteen thousand in Japan applied for similar treatment.[51] The *Times* pointed out the embarrassing fact that the Japanese government spent only seventy-five thousand dollars annually on treatment of *all* atomic victims—just one-fifth of what was spent treating the twenty-five Hiroshima Maidens.[52] Japanese doctors sprang into action, with Cousins telling the media that in Hiroshima "doctors have asked for a plan to be set up for the care of other survivors for treatment and surgery."[53]

Hiroshima's mayor, Tadao Watanabe, established and chaired the Atomic Bomb Patients Treatment Council, a group of local surgeons who were willing to treat victims on an ongoing basis. Cousins and the Hiroshima Peace Council Associates agreed to immediately underwrite the council's activities with the money left over from the Maidens project.[54] It was through all of this international exposure that the Hiroshima Maidens project resulted in two of the biggest changes of all. First, Dr. Robert Holmes, the director of the ABCC, endorsed the idea of building a local treatment hospital and became a vocal supporter of providing active treatment. Cousins later stated that one of the most heartening developments that grew out of the Maidens project was Holmes's unqualified offer of cooperation. Cousins called the offer "a towering asset."[55]

Perhaps the greatest achievement of all came in 1957, a year after the project ended, when the Japanese government enacted a law providing free lifetime medical treatment to all atomic bomb victims. It was largely the political pressure marshaled by Cousins and Tanimoto through the Hiroshima Maidens project that proved to be the catalyst for this new law. To show their appreciation for Cousins's hard work to raise awareness of the need for such medical care, the Japanese government colloquially named it the "Norman Cousins Law."[56]

Further recognizing Cousins's tireless efforts to improve U.S.-Japanese relations and his achievements in getting treatment for the atomic bomb victims, Cousins was awarded the very first honorary citizenship for the City of Hiroshima in 1964. For decades to come, Cousins would remain a notable personality in Japan.[57] As the Hiroshima Maidens project wound down and the 1956 election heated up, Cousins would vastly increase his participation in civic life, blending both his anti-nuclear activities and his diplomatic initiatives into a potent force for change, soon becoming the country's premiere anti-nuclear activist.

CHAPTER 15

THE ANTI-NUCLEAR AGENDA

By the 1950s the American people had largely come to accept the perils inherent in a defense policy reliant on nuclear weapons. "The destroyer of 1945," historian Paul Boyer contends, "had become the shield of the republic."[1] Starting in 1954, though, a series of events began to expose the first cracks in the nuclear shield. The *Lucky Dragon* incident pierced through the claims of the Federal Civil Defense Administration that radioactive fallout was not a health danger. A few months later the fact that nuclear radiation *was* dangerous to human health was first supported by scientific evidence in November 1954, when nuclear physicist Ralph Lapp published an article in the *Bulletin of Atomic Scientists*.[2] Disturbed by this article and the growing numbers of other such reports, the British philosopher Bertrand Russell joined with Albert Einstein and nine others to issue, in July 1955, the Russell-Einstein Manifesto, an appeal to governments to acknowledge the suicidal nature of nuclear war.[3]

Norman Cousins also contributed extensively to the effort to help both the American people and the president himself comprehend the problem and then act on it. Cousins used his access to leading scientists and his position at the *Saturday Review* to undermine the US government's claim that nuclear testing posed no health risk. Clearly, increasing numbers of Americans were drawn to the magazine's international perspective and foreign policy analysis, which went beyond a simple critique to offer inspirational ideas and concrete proposals for the use of American power.

In his editorials and activism Cousins skillfully deployed his expertise to persuade the public to act on a moral imperative. His growing credibility in the public and political spheres made Cousins a crucial actor in the rapidly expanding field of anti-nuclear activism. Ever since the publication of "Modern Man Is Obsolete," Cousins had editorialized about the dangers of nuclear weapons. While his editorials had attracted increasing numbers of readers to the *Saturday Review*, and the occasional article had been noticed and praised in political circles, it was not until 1956 that Cousins had his first immediate and direct impact on the thinking of the American president.

In August 1956, to mark the eleventh anniversary of the Hiroshima bombing, Cousins penned a lengthy editorial, "Think of a Man," which he hoped would "break through to a new awareness of the crisis of man."[4] In eloquent prose, Cousins outlined the history of some of humankind's most notable achievements in medicine, science, literature, the arts, and political thought. The leaders who drove these advances, Cousins wrote, had sought to continuously enlarge the cause of human achievement, thought, and freedom, frequently at the cost of their own lives. "These were the leaders who believed that the act of being born carried with it a long list of natural and basic rights—political, spiritual, social," he wrote. In the nuclear age, though, the world now stood on the edge of a precipice that imperiled all that man had achieved because "when excessive radiation enters this world it changes it and condemns it," Cousins contended. "How much more radioactivity can be pumped into the upper atmosphere before the fallout of strontium becomes menacing to life?"[5]

Before the atomic bomb, Cousins explained, individuals and governments could do all manner of things to cheapen, debase, cripple, and kill others, but radiation was different. It attacked the very nature of life itself and persisted in its attack long after the fight was over.

Worst of all, nuclear weapons tests were attacking humans during what was supposed to be peacetime. In continuing to develop and test atomic weapons, governments were piercing the physical integrity of the human race, violating its genetic structure far outside their own national borders. Radiation respected neither national sovereignty nor borders drawn on a map. American and Soviet nuclear tests poisoned everyone equally. While earlier generations of leaders might have had the power merely to affect history, the current generation required only seconds to expunge it. Are we not living in a society that champions justice and respects the rights of the individual, Cousins asked? Should something not be done about the poisoning of our earth and bodies through radiation caused by nuclear tests?[6] The August 1956 editorial "Think of a Man" immediately garnered national attention and high-level praise.

Two days after the article's publication, Cousins received a letter from President Eisenhower. Praising the editorial for its "meaningful character," Eisenhower stated that Cousins "expressed in powerful and persuasive terms some of the great dangers facing the individual—which means civilization—and the need for the individual to do something about it." Eisenhower lamented that he was finding it difficult to reach the American people "with an idea that requires them to think of unpleasant possibilities or to undertake the work and effort required to eliminate such possibilities." Eisenhower went on to detail how, through his disarmament proposals, he was working hard to achieve the sort of change Cousins called for in his article. The president concluded by telling Cousins, "To me it is especially encouraging to see that intelligent people are studying this problem so seriously. . . . I am going to circulate [your article] among some of my close associates here."[7] One of those close associates was Eisenhower advisor Arthur Larson. Larson later wrote that the president "pulled out a copy of a recent editorial Cousins had written on the hydrogen bomb," which, Larson saw, "had made a deep impression on [Eisenhower]."[8]

Eisenhower's letter made an equally powerful impression on Cousins, who would later write to a friend that in all the correspondence he received in reference to "Think of a Man," "what astounded me was a warmly appreciative letter from the man in the White House, whose speechwriters apparently do not agree with him, judging from his pronouncements on the hydrogen bomb."[9] The underlying problem was that despite what Eisenhower's words told the American people about his desire for nuclear disarmament, his actions did little to move the issue forward.

Cousins had many misgivings about both Eisenhower's pronouncements and his actions (or failure to act) in the realm of nuclear disarmament. In a private letter to Lewis Mumford, he expressed his opinion that "what Dulles and Eisenhower have done is bad enough but it represents, to my mind, a hideous consistency with the kind of insanity that led Truman to drop the first atomic bomb on a live target."[10] Despite Cousins's position on the government's "insane" nuclear policies, Eisenhower's response to "Think of a Man" provided Cousins with a ray of hope and formed the first real connection between the two men, a connection that would become increasingly important in Eisenhower's second term, when he began to turn to Cousins on occasion for advice in nuclear matters. Eisenhower historian James Ledbetter argues that "through persistence, diplomacy, and moral reasoning, Cousins functioned as a kind of nuclear conscience for the president, the representative of a set of principles that would become increasingly important as Eisenhower aged."[11] Cousins's daughter Sarah too recalls that at first her father was not impressed with Eisenhower, but by the end of Eisenhower's time in office he had come to be "pleasantly surprised with President Eisenhower. [My father] felt he was a good man."[12]

Eisenhower was not the only high-level government official to express his praise for "Think of a Man." Senator (and future vice president) Hubert Humphrey (D-MN) wrote Cousins a note that reveals how the editorial swept through the halls of power. "So many people had already mentioned this editorial to me that I made a special note to read it," the senator wrote. Humphrey concluded by congratulating Cousins "on the depth of insight which you have demonstrated so often in the past and which you repeat with such eloquence in this editorial."[13]

Not all the responses were positive, however. Alfred Gray Reid, of San Francisco, took the time to write to Cousins that he "found the editorial pompous and windy, smug and self-righteous, platitudinous and pseudo-profound." He asked if he was the only one who was "less than ecstatic about 'Think of a Man.'"[14] Cousins responded that Reid's letter was one of only three critical letters he received out of more than three hundred letters and twenty-one thousand requests for reprints. Still, Cousins replied, "the fact of the matter is that you are right. I do have the fault of being windy and platitudinous in my writing. I have tried in recent years, especially in articles that concern questions of human destiny or moral justice, to sound less preachy and more informal and uninvolved. Prodding such as yours will help me to try even harder."[15]

The three negative letters aside, "Think of a Man" was a major contribution to the change in the national mind-set about atomic weapons and a direct challenge to Eisenhower's Atoms for Peace program and his contention that a nuclear weapon was no different than a bullet. Cousins was helping to expose the fact that nuclear weapons *were* in fact different—they had the power to expunge all human life—and people needed to come to truly understand what that meant. What Eisenhower's response to Cousins reflects is that by 1956 Eisenhower was beginning to take the issue of radiation seriously. In March 1955, he appointed Harold Stassen as his special assistant on disarmament in order to reinvigorate the test ban issue, and advisors were discussing options for a nuclear testing moratorium.[16]

The national attention that "Think of a Man" focused on Cousins happened to coincide with the newest research findings produced by a group of scientists from Washington University in St. Louis headed by biologist Barry Commoner. The scientists invited Cousins to their lab, where they showed him the latest evidence on the human costs of radioactive fallout.[17] The scientists presented him with the results of examinations of the teeth of one thousand students in St. Louis: every single student showed evidence of radioactive strontium 90 as a direct result of nuclear testing. They showed him the results of tests on an area of farmland near Chicago that was positive for traces of strontium and explained that this posed a threat of contamination to vegetables grown on that land. Another survey revealed to Cousins showed that radioactive elements were present in cow's milk.[18]

During every bomb test the radiation released was like a dust that drifted through the air. Eventually it would rain down on a pasture, for example. As the radioactive elements soaked into the soil, they would be absorbed by the grass. When a cow came along and ate that grass, the radiation would be transferred to the cow and eventually end up in the cow's milk, which then ended up on a grocery store shelf. Worst of all, these radioactive elements mimicked calcium, bonding to bone and teeth in the human body to create an ongoing radiation assault from within.

Cousins later wrote that he "came away from that meeting with an enlarged understanding of the need to bring nuclear testing under control." This meeting began what Cousins later referred to as his "intense concern with this question" of outright ending nuclear tests.[19] No longer was international control of nuclear weapons enough. These scientific revelations persuaded Cousins that the continued development of nuclear weapons—whether or not they were deployed in a war—imperiled humanity. Spurred on by both the shocking scientific revelations and the public response to "Think of a Man," Cousins used this new momentum to making a lasting mark on national politics.

CHAPTER 16

1956

The Anti-Nuclear Election Campaign

The 1956 presidential election saw Adlai Stevenson once again challenging Dwight Eisenhower for the Oval Office. Stevenson had kept in touch with Cousins over the past four years and wrote him in June 1956 to lament that he had "been reflecting in my misery over all the last minute improvisation of four years ago." Employing some flattery to recruit Cousins to his 1956 campaign, Stevenson wrote, "I am sure your soaring spirit, fertile brain and eloquent pen will produce much of what I need if I can enlist it. Can't I?"[1] With the issue of nuclear testing gaining more widespread recognition, Stevenson would become the first national leader to take a clear public position in favor of ending or at least limiting nuclear testing.[2] Stevenson first introduced the nuclear issue to his campaign on April 21, which drew sharp retorts from both the national press and President Eisenhower.[3] Stevenson demurred for a few months before he returned the testing issue to the spotlight with a proposal on September 5 that called for an end to the testing of hydrogen bombs. Eisenhower responded that he would not endorse any end to testing without a reliable system of inspection.[4] From this point forward Stevenson, who felt a strong moral commitment to speak out on the issue of nuclear testing, turned to Cousins to help him make the case.

On September 25, in consultation with his longtime friend the former governor of Connecticut and Stevenson campaign speechwriter Chester Bowles, Cousins submitted a major speech draft covering the issues of both hydrogen bombs and nuclear testing.[5] Stevenson told Cousins that his speeches and information were a "splendid contribution." Stevenson would later say that Cousins had been his "constant counselor and conscience" during the campaign.[6] Backed by Cousins, Stevenson pushed forward with his anti-nuclear platform. On September 29 he challenged Eisenhower to debate the issue of a testing moratorium, and on October 15 Stevenson appeared on television with a promise to make a nuclear test ban his "first order of business as president."[7] Eisenhower stood firm, responding that it was "foolish for us to make any . . . unilateral [moratorium] announcement."[8] Although Eisenhower may have been against a unilateral moratorium, he remained committed to the goal of a test ban.

As political scientist Barry Steiner notes, though, Stevenson's favoring adoption of a test ban actually made it a politically unviable position for Eisenhower to take. Having to contrast himself to the "weak" Stevenson, Eisenhower was forced to reject a moratorium—one that his own advisors had recommended. The issue ran deeper than just campaign politics. Eisenhower thought that a unilateral moratorium would allow the Russians to make "tremendous advances where we would be standing still."[9] Eisenhower believed that suspending tests without a bilateral, verifiable agreement would prevent the United States from developing important new weapons with which to deter Soviet aggression.[10]

Cousins, however, saw Eisenhower's response as an intransigent position on testing, especially given the president's comments regarding "Think of a Man." Cousins seemed to believe that Eisenhower personally supported a test ban, a position Cousins reflected on when he later wrote to Indian prime minister Jawaharlal Nehru. Cousins first became acquainted with the prime minister in 1950, when he was touring India and conducted an extensive interview with Nehru, which he later published in a book, *Talks with Nehru: India's Prime Minister Speaks Out on the Crisis of Our Time.*[11]

The two men continued their correspondence over the years, occasionally exchanging ideas on international issues. This time Cousins vented about the election. "What is most ironic," Cousins wrote to Nehru, "is that the President may have been forced through the pressure of political circumstances to alter a decision [to propose a test ban] he may have made privately before the question erupted in political debate." Cousins lamented that raising the issue too early might have forced Eisenhower to entrench. He told Nehru, "It was unfortunate . . . that the question of hydrogen bomb testing became a political issue. This caused many people . . . to react in terms of political opposites rather than in terms of the problem itself."[12]

While the nuclear testing issue certainly did not cost Stevenson the 1956 election, it did not win it for him either. The result was a rout. Stevenson lost by an even greater margin than he had in 1952, with 73 Electoral College votes to Eisenhower's 457 and 9.5 million fewer votes in the popular vote. While the nuclear testing issue neither defined nor derailed the campaign, it did something much more important. The national exposure the issue got during the election campaign provided Americans with their first opportunity to hear the two sides debated in a national forum.

In November 1956, 56 percent of Americans polled by Gallup opposed a test ban. Just six months later, however, the same question put to Americans showed that 63 percent now agreed that the United States should stop such tests. More than half agreed with the statement that there was "real danger" in test fallout.[13] That rapid shift in American public opinion can be traced, in large part, to Cousins. Six days after the election Cousins published an editorial titled "It's Only Moral," in which he argued, "The air around the earth doesn't belong to us alone or to the Soviet Union alone. It belongs to all the people who inhabit the planet. If that air is to be robbed of its purity, if it is to be infected by harmful substances that will last for years, contaminating grasses and vegetation, affecting the water supply, weakening or poisoning the livestock, then this becomes very much a moral issue to other peoples."[14] Cousins believed that the United States did not have any right to take military measures, especially in peacetime, that were dangerous to others without their consent. He wrote that "the principle argument against Nazism, and more recently against communism, was that they were scornful of the rights of others and did harm to innocent people in their pursuit of military advantage."[15] By his contention, the United States was doing a similar thing with its ongoing peacetime nuclear tests.

Eisenhower contended that relying on nuclear weapons was a defense posture that could be sustained over the long run without bankrupting the country, but in order to deter the Soviet Union the most advanced weapons were necessary. "That is why we conduct our tests—to prove that our advanced weapon designs will work," claimed Eisenhower.[16] Supporting Eisenhower's position on testing were publications like *U.S. News & World Report,* which claimed that all charges of nuclear fallout were bogus.[17]

To help counter this narrative, Cousins again turned to the Indian prime minister, asking whether Nehru might make a public statement denouncing nuclear testing. During the US presidential campaign Nehru had publicly demanded an end to all nuclear tests, fearing that they "might put an end to human life as we see it."[18] In response to Cousins's request, though, the prime minister declined on the grounds that he did not think anyone would listen to him a second time. "I don't think my stock in public opinion," Nehru replied, "especially in the West, at this particular moment is very high. Why don't you try Albert Schweitzer?"[19]

Dr. Albert Schweitzer, a highly respected humanitarian and the 1952 Nobel Peace Prize winner, ran a hospital in Africa. Cousins thought that Schweitzer would make an excellent spokesman: "There was no one in the world whose voice would have greater carrying power than [Schweitzer's]." Thus, in January 1957 Cousins departed for Africa on a perilous journey to reach the remote village of Lambaréné (in present-day Gabon), the final leg of which included a flight across the jungle that he described as "probably the most hazardous regularly scheduled flight in the world."[20] Cousins spent more than a week at the hospital with Dr. Schweitzer attempting to persuade him to speak out on the dangers of nuclear fallout and the need to bring an end to the tests.

To bolster his case, Cousins showed Schweitzer the evidence of radioactive contamination that he had obtained from the scientists in St. Louis. He implored Schweitzer to make a statement to the world. Schweitzer replied, "No one will listen to an old man stuck away somewhere in a corner of Africa. You are making a great mistake if you think that my saying something on this issue will make any difference."[21] Schweitzer explained that he had spent his life carefully staying away from making pronouncements on public matters or supporting one political group over another because he had no interest in getting involved in world affairs or politics. Schweitzer was definitely not a member of the Cousins "fan club." He remarked that he tended to think Cousins's proclamations that the planet could be made unfit for life through radioactive contamination were "absurdly melodramatic."[22]

The two men chatted more about the issue over the next couple of days to little avail. When it came time to depart, Cousins noted that he was leaving "not without some heartbreak, because I felt I had failed in my purpose in going to Lambaréné." But Cousins's heartbreak did not last long. Two weeks after he returned to New York, he received a letter from Schweitzer saying that he had looked into what Cousins told him about the dangers of radiation. Cousins had him convinced; the radioactive fallout issue was now of grave concern to him. Schweitzer had decided to write an appeal to the world to be issued in his name, but he said that it would take some time to draft.[23] In the meantime, Cousins attempted to schedule a meeting with President Eisenhower in order to discuss his conversations with Schweitzer. The president's appointments secretary replied that although Eisenhower "would like very much to hear of your visit with Dr. Schweitzer," his schedule was simply too crowded.[24]

Shortly thereafter, Cousins wrote again to Prime Minister Nehru both to thank him for suggesting that Cousins contact Schweitzer and to inform him that Schweitzer had agreed to "give himself fully to the present crisis, feeling as he does that all men and the generations to come are in grave danger."[25] Nehru responded that he was pleased to hear that Schweitzer was working on a statement. "Whatever he says," Nehru responded, "[it] will at least command world attention."[26] This much was true.

On April 23, 1957, Schweitzer's "Declaration of Conscience" was broadcast by radio from Oslo, Norway, to some fifty nations. His address focused on the danger that nuclear fallout posed to life on earth. Reprinted by newspapers worldwide the following day, it attracted widespread public attention around the globe. Historian Lawrence Wittner writes that "Schweitzer's message had a substantial impact on world opinion" and confirms that "Cousins was the catalyst in recruiting Schweitzer into the nuclear disarmament movement."[27]

In the United States however, the impact of Schweitzer's "Declaration of Conscience" was muted. Not a single radio station carried his message. Cousins, attempting to explain away this glaring silence, claimed that it was simply the result of some confusion over the timing of the release. But this claim that it was simply a miscommunication is undermined by the fact that the printed statement was also largely ignored by US newspapers.[28] The *New York Times* was the only notable paper to run a short column on the declaration, which it did alongside a statement from Secretary of State John Foster Dulles that the United States would continue its tests because the government maintained that the tests were not a danger to human health.[29]

The *Saturday Review*, in fact, was the only US publication to run the full text of Schweitzer's declaration, along with four pages of editorial comment from Cousins.[30] American readers clearly thirsted for the knowledge they had been largely denied; the following week Cousins noted that "more requests for reprints of the Schweitzer Declaration have been received in the first week following publication than for any article in the history of *Saturday Review*."[31] The more widespread initial reaction in the United States, however, was mostly negative. *U.S. News & World Report* claimed that the whole episode was "Communist inspired."[32] Congressman Lawrence H. Smith (R-WI) called Cousins "a Communist dupe" for having solicited the statement from Schweitzer; he claimed that Cousins was "stirring up a national hysteria."[33] The issue might have died on the vine, largely ignored by the US. media and openly panned by those in power who did take notice. Instead, in a clear example of the growing clout Cousins had in shaping opinion and driving American political debate, the *Saturday Review* itself became the principal forum for the public airing of this issue.

The week after the publication of the Schweitzer Declaration, the chairman of the Atomic Energy Commission felt that it was necessary to respond. Dr. Willard Libby drafted a letter aimed at assuring Dr. Schweitzer (and the public) that "the risk [of radiation] is extremely small [compared with the] far greater risk . . . of not maintaining our defenses against the totalitarian forces."[34] Cousins was all too happy to publish Libby's letter in the *Saturday Review* alongside a response from nuclear chemist Dr. Harrison Brown, who argued that the US government seemed to have backtracked and changed its position recently. "For a long time," Dr. Brown wrote, "Dr. Libby contended that there were no dangers of any consequence from bomb fallout. . . . Recently, however, there has been a change of tone."[35] With this exchange Cousins declared, "The Great Debate Opens."[36] Historian Robert Divine points out that Schweitzer's message might have gone completely unnoticed in the United States had it not been for Libby's response sparking this continued debate in the pages of the *Saturday Review*, a debate the *New York Times* and *Time* magazine quickly joined.[37]

Many members of the public certainly recognized Cousins's central role in bringing the issue to light and not relenting in the face of public criticism and government pushback. *Saturday Review* reader Percy Ludlow wrote that "[Americans] have a great debt of gratitude to pay you and your associates at the Saturday Review. We find your articles and, most of all, your editorials of tremendous importance."[38] Vincent Glason wrote that there was a "desperate need . . . for a press with the power and principle of thought to bring logic to our society. My congratulations to you for your efforts in this behalf."[39] One correspondent even recognized what Cousins was attempting to do by pointing out that "you have a certain power in molding public opinion; keep it up, please, for Mankinde's [*sic*] sake."[40] Despite recognizing that the odds were against him in this mission, Cousins revealed his motivation when he responded that "I can think of nothing more rewarding in the world than to take the odds as they are and attempt to reduce them so that we may eventually at least have an even chance to justify our existence and preserve it meaningfully."[41]

But building public awareness was only part of Cousins's approach. Off the record too Cousins was engaged in a heated exchange with the president himself. Eisenhower fired the first salvo when, during a June 5, 1957, press conference, he commented in reference to Cousins and the growing push for a test ban, "It looks almost like an organized affair."[42] Everyone at the time recognized this as a loosely veiled hint that test ban proponents might be under the direction of Communists. Eisenhower's (false) claim drew an aggressive response from Cousins. Writing the president directly two days later, Cousins charged that he had "detected a note in your press conference this week that was not characteristic of the breadth and generosity of spirit you brought with you to the White House. Certainly I have never before known you to reflect on the good faith and integrity or intelligence of those who held views different from that of the Administration."[43]

Cousins continued with a long letter explaining his position on the testing issue and imploring the president to recognize it as a matter of global importance. In the White House, the task of drafting a response was passed off to the AEC chairman, Lewis Strauss. Strauss first cautioned Eisenhower about "the fate of an exchange of correspondence with the publisher of a magazine" before crafting a five-page response.[44] Eisenhower did not use Strauss's long draft, choosing instead to reply personally in a letter that chastised Cousins for making "a very personal interpretation of press conference statements."[45]

The issue did not end there. Cousins grew more concerned after learning of Eisenhower's June 24 meeting with three physicists from the Livermore nuclear lab who had come to persuade the president of the necessity to continue testing.[46] Firing off another letter to Eisenhower, Cousins expressed his concern that "the impression has been created that only scientists connected with the A.E.C. have had a chance to present their evidence to you."[47] Cousins proposed to the president that it would only be fair to allow a small group of scientists with an opposing view to meet with him to present their own evidence. Cousins offered to arrange such a group. A note attached to this letter (most likely from Eisenhower's secretary, Ann Whitman) explained, "Far from [your last letter] discouraging Mr. Cousins, he wants to bring a group of scientists in to see you."[48] This time Eisenhower thought Cousins's proposal was actually a good idea. Forwarding the letter to Strauss for his advice, Eisenhower wrote, "I rather think it might be a good idea for me to pick two or three scientists who represent a contrary view and ask them in for a visit."[49]

Strauss, however, was less than impressed, both with the idea and with Cousins himself. "I have read and return your latest letter from Norman Cousins," Strauss wrote. "He is certainly an energetic correspondent. Several of my friends have received letters from him, urging them to take part in the fallout propaganda." Strauss recommended that Eisenhower decline the invitation lest people begin to question "your confidence in the competence of the very eminent men who are devoting their talents and reputations to a vital, though presently unpopular service to the Government."[50] Although Eisenhower seemed to have initially felt the need to hear the viewpoint Cousins's scientists might present, in his response declining the offer he claimed, "I assure you that I have frequently heard scientific dissertations dealing with every phase of the atomic question, and from diverse viewpoints."[51]

Cousins remained unconvinced and later published an editorial claiming that this visit of pro-testing scientists "is believed to have undercut whatever plans may have been in the making for a genuine effort to seek workable agreements on the cessation of testing."[52] On the other hand, Eisenhower's reply also gave Cousins an issue to latch on to. Eisenhower stressed that although he was declining the meeting, he still believed in peace, he referred Cousins to his April 1953 "A Chance for Peace" speech, which Cousins had publicly praised.[53]

Buoyed by Eisenhower's mention of the speech and urging him to take the initiative in doing more, Cousins replied on July 15, writing, "I hope you will agree that the time may be at hand for another major speech . . . an historic speech which is directed to all peoples in their status as fellow human beings." Cousins indicated that he would be happy to write the speech if Eisenhower so desired.[54] This letter did not even make it to Eisenhower's desk. It was intercepted by Whitman and forwarded to Strauss with the comment, "I do not think the President should acknowledge, do you?"[55] Strauss dryly replied, "Mr. Cousins seems determined to have the last word. I would be inclined to humor him in this regard and file his letter. Otherwise your correspondence looks like it will be endless. He writes to me too. What a busy man!"[56]

Cousins was indeed a busy man when it came to the testing issue, both in sparking the debate and in pursuing every possible means of getting his message across. Within a month of the Schweitzer Declaration, the US Congress launched a special subcommittee to study the nature of radioactive fallout and its effects on man.[57] Cousins, incidentally, upon learning that Congress was holding hearings, wrote the chairman of the subcommittee with a request to appear as a witness. Although his request was rejected because he did not have a "competent scientific background," Chairman Chet Holifield's (D-CA) reply included praise for Cousins that illustrates his success in bringing the issue to widespread attention: "I would like to compliment you and the Saturday Review for the great public service you are rendering in keeping the public informed on the problem of radiation, and particularly for your efforts to present varied points of view on the major issues involved."[58]

Three weeks later an invitation arrived indicating that Cousins not only was having an impact on American debate over nuclear issues but was seen as a credible voice on the international stage as well. Cousins received an official invitation from Radio Moscow to draft a statement on nuclear testing that would be broadcast in the Soviet Union. Although the message actually broadcast was a greatly shortened and edited version of the full written statement he submitted (and subsequently published in the *Saturday Review*), Radio Moscow kept one of his most prescient points: "The Soviet Union can act on the basis of its stated conviction that the nuclear tests are contaminating the atmosphere. There is nothing to keep the Soviet Union from announcing to the world that consistent with the health and safety of the world's peoples it is suspending its nuclear tests and it can call upon the rest of the world to do likewise."[59]

This was exactly what the Soviet Union did the following year when it announced that it would be unilaterally halting its nuclear tests at the end of March 1958. In response to this announcement, Cousins publicly praised the Soviet government for its "imaginative thrust" and claimed that this had "given dramatic momentum to [the Soviet's] claim for leadership." The initially negative US response to the Soviet proposal that it was simply an act of propaganda was, in Cousins's mind, "puny, petulant, unimaginative."[60] The very fact that it was the Soviet Union that first responded to the growing calls for an end to testing was, Cousins proclaimed, "a moral disaster for the United States."[61]

This point is raised here not to claim that there was a direct link between Cousins's 1957 radio address suggesting that it would be possible for the Soviet Union to unilaterally end its tests and the 1958 Soviet decision to do so but simply to show how much of a danger Cousins believed radiation was and how committed he was to ending the nuclear tests that caused it. It did not matter to him who took the lead in ending nuclear testing, as long as someone did, even if that someone was the Soviet Union.

The announcement of the Soviet moratorium focused world pressure on the United States to reverse its stand on testing as well, which it did when Eisenhower ultimately agreed to participate in the moratorium.[62] Domestically, one of the main sources of public pressure on the United States to join the moratorium came from one of Cousins's other initiatives, the Committee for a Sane Nuclear Policy (SANE).

CHAPTER 17

SANE *and the* ANTI-TESTING CAMPAIGN

Cousins's publication of the Schweitzer Declaration and his sparking of "the great debate" over radiation not only pushed Americans to think deeply about the issue but also revealed that many were ready to take action. A man from Illinois wrote, "It was not until I read Schweitzer's simple and eloquent words that I realized the extent of the threat to mankind."[1] "I have been waiting for someone to say something that might lead to action," Lynn Brooks wrote to Cousins. "If only the leaders (political) could possess the intelligence to call upon you and men like you to show them the way."[2] Expressing exactly what Cousins was hoping to spark, a letter from a New Yorker claimed, "I am convinced that nothing is going to stop the bomb tests until a far more general protest from the public takes place. I am pretty sure that there is enough knowledge now to produce the beginnings of such a protest."[3] What they needed, though, was a leader for the movement. One letter in particular urged Cousins to form a "committee of the ordinary well-intentioned citizenry" who would work to foment "strong and concious [*sic*] protest."[4] Just months after this letter was written, an anti-nuclear protest committee would indeed form, with Cousins at the helm.

In April 1957, the same month the Schweitzer Declaration was published, Lawrence Scott, the peace secretary of the American Friends Service Committee, began to establish a group that would work to stop the bomb tests. Scott turned to Cousins and peace activist Clarence Pickett for help in putting a selection of leading activists together. Cousins agreed to help, but only on the condition that the issue of nuclear tests be taken out of the context of political polarization (as had occurred during the presidential campaign) and that it be approached as a moral issue on which international leaders of moral thought (like Schweitzer) would take the lead.[5]

Most importantly, Cousins strongly believed that the scientific facts and moral question needed to be driven into the consciousness of all Americans and people of other countries. By October 1957 this group had launched a new organization called the National Committee for a Sane Nuclear Policy (SANE), with Cousins and Pickett serving as co-chairmen. Under Cousins's direction, SANE ran a full-page advertisement in the *New York Times* on November 15. It proclaimed that "we are facing a danger unlike any danger that has ever existed." Going on to explain the dangers that radioactive fallout posed to humans, the advertisement was largely written by Cousins, with themes pulled from his previous editorials.[6]

Historian Milton Katz wrote the seminal study of the history of SANE in his 1986 book *Ban the Bomb*. Katz argues that the organization was an important reflection of American Cold War liberalism in its belief that mistaken US policies could be remedied and set right because the government was willing to change in the face of new facts and public pressure. Katz points out that SANE ended up being effective because it had one specific goal—an end to nuclear testing—which it pursued through direct persuasion and advocacy rather than through civil disobedience and noncooperation. For this reason, Katz writes, "SANE offered a retreat bunker for liberals who couldn't find a place to take a stand in the structure of political parties." It also "filled a gap that had opened among nuclear pacifists following the decline of the world government cause in the early 1950s."[7]

Through SANE, Cousins essentially created a movement specifically tailored to people like himself, a movement that embodied his own Cold War liberalism. Cousins had come to believe deeply in the idea that the individual need not be helpless in the face of seemingly intractable government policies. When the policies of the US (or any) government failed to serve humanity's best interest, it was up to the individual to identify and challenge these policies. In these cases non-government actors, Cousins believed, had a responsibility to lay the groundwork by building public support for more moral and humanitarian government policies and positions. In doing so, they could show policymakers that there was enough support for an issue to make it politically advantageous to pursue.

Cousins wrote personally to President Eisenhower two days before SANE went public with its first advertisement and boldly stated that SANE's challenge to the US government's position on nuclear testing was, in effect, for the president's own good. "Several times before, in our correspondence," Cousins wrote, "you have expressed the view that it was not enough for an American President to advocate large ideas. It was important for the American people to be prepared to receive such ideas and to act on them." Cousins continued to explain that a new lobby group (SANE) had formed and said that "we hope you will feel that what we propose to do is of service to you . . . [and] we hope you will welcome this effort to strengthen your hand in coming before the world with specific recommendations [to end nuclear testing]."[8]

Eisenhower responded to Cousins's letter with a short note of thanks, but an internal memo the following day reveals his true feelings about the activities of SANE. Robert Sprague, a consultant for the National Security Council, wrote a memo about how to improve the United States' ability to defend against nuclear attack. The memo contained some ideas that caught Eisenhower's attention. One such idea was that the country could engage in a nationwide fallout shelter program to protect the civilian population. Eisenhower wrote to John Foster Dulles, "Here's an interesting idea from Mr. Sprague. . . . It strikes me that it might possibly be an antidote to the free-wheeling things such as Norman Cousins and his group will be doing."[9]

The "free-wheeling" Cousins and "his group" proved to be exceptionally effective despite the administration's hope for an "antidote" to them. The anti-nuclear advertisement that SANE ran in the *New York Times* on November 15 garnered an overwhelming response. Within six weeks some twenty-five hundred enthusiastic letters arrived, along with $12,000 in donations. The $4,700 cost of the *New York Times* ad was quickly recovered.[10] Cousins later wrote that "the response to our public appeal was an inspiring example. . . . If any of us had any doubts about the effectiveness of citizen organizations in the shaping of great decisions, the record of SANE should provide dramatic reassurance."[11]

Cousins, of course, was only a small contributor to Eisenhower's evolving views on nuclear testing. For one, Harold Stassen, special assistant to the president for disarmament, had succeeded in persuading Eisenhower to de-link the disarmament issue from the resolution of other Cold War issues. He recommended that as long as the United States could be assured of being able to conduct reasonable inspections within the Soviet Union, Eisenhower should push ahead with a test ban. Concurrently, the National Security Council concluded that the United States possessed sufficient nuclear superiority over Russia to justify a test ban agreement. Finally, the evidence that strontium 90 was contaminating food and causing a grave health risk became overwhelming and persuaded Eisenhower that aboveground testing had to end.[12]

October 1957 proved to be a fortuitous month. On October 4, 1957, news that the Soviet Union had successfully launched the world's first space satellite sent the American public into fits of anxiety and measured hysteria. Eisenhower biographer William Hitchcock writes that "after a decade of intense anti-Soviet propaganda, Americans had come to believe that the USSR was a brutish, backward, and totalitarian society in which individual creativity had been extinguished." Yet, Sputnik demonstrated that this nation had just outperformed America in scientific achievement.[13]

Five days after the Sputnik announcement, Eisenhower endured a press conference that biographer Stephen Ambrose describes as "one of the most hostile of his career." Inundated with questions about the Soviet achievement and the state of American national security as a result, Eisenhower attempted to calm an anxious public. "[Sputnik] does not raise my apprehensions, not one iota," the president stated. "I see nothing at this moment . . . that is significant in that development as far as security is concerned." He proclaimed that the country was just as safe as the day before the launch and that American military technology was certainly not obsolete and destined for the scrapyard, as Soviet premier Nikita Khrushchev had mockingly maintained.[14] Norman Cousins, however, saw things differently than did the majority of Americans, neither succumbing to hysteria nor stolidly expressing that nothing had changed.

In an editorial on October 19, 1957, Cousins told Americans that the Sputnik launch provided an opportunity to reflect on American mistakes and gain a better understanding of the Soviet Union. Cousins claimed that America was *not* inadequate in its science and technology, as many were claiming, but "our failure—and it is a critical one—has been in our reasoning, in our judgement, in our moral imagination. The failure is a continuing one."[15] Cousins charged that Americans had long suffered from a national delusion fueled by government propaganda that theirs was the richest, most powerful, and most technologically advanced nation in the world. Cousins recalled that the United States had "made the even greater mistake of assuming indefinite superiority." "And now a Russian earth satellite spins around the globe, sending out signals which mock our delusions of superiority," Cousins concluded.[16] Most of all, though, Sputnik represented a grave acceleration in the nuclear arms race. The atomic age had suddenly become the space age.

Although still years off, it was recognized that the same rockets that sent satellites into space could also be loaded with a nuclear warhead and used to attack. Intercontinental ballistic missiles (ICBMs) would eventually offer the ability to launch a nuclear attack on the United States with just minutes of warning instead of the hours previously provided by slow-flying bombers coming over the Arctic. Sputnik made it especially imperative that nuclear weapons be brought under control, but to Cousins it also made it equally important to pursue friendlier relations with the Soviet Union—the "backward" adversary that had just proven itself to be more technologically advanced than previously thought.

Already a vocal opponent of the arms race, Cousins now feared that Sputnik would soon spark a space race as well. In his initial Sputnik editorial he implored politicians to "make sure that the launching-sites for satellites or space-ships will not be used for intercontinental hydrogen-bomb carriers, but for carrying out the great adventures of tomorrow."[17] Cousins's hopeful message apparently stuck with President Eisenhower as well. The following month, the president called Secretary of State John Foster Dulles to say that he was unhappy with a speech that had been written for him on the topic of space. Referring directly to Norman Cousins, Eisenhower stated that he "thinks a little of [Cousins's] idealism ought to go in this speech."[18] Cousins, however, was unaware of the impact he had had on Eisenhower in this regard. Instead he set his sights wider and attempted to use a new international humanitarian project to connect with the world's people and also, if all went well, ingratiate himself with the Soviet Union.

CHAPTER 18

THE RAVENSBRÜCK LAPINS *and the* COMMUNIST CONNECTION

The waning months of 1957 saw Cousins engaged in constant activity. After inaugurating SANE and responding to the launch of Sputnik, in December 1957, Cousins later recalled, he caught "a glimpse into the bowels of an imaginary hell [that] was part of our age and part of our world."[1] This glimpse was provided by a visit to his Midtown Manhattan office from Caroline Ferriday.

Ferriday was an international activist who got her start during World War II working as a volunteer at the French Embassy in New York, where she helped to raise money for the French Resistance.[2] After the war she began to work closely with the Association Nationale des Anciennes Deportées et Internées de la Résistance (ADIR). One of ADIR's mandates was to help secure compensation for the victims of Nazi medical experiments.[3] In 1951, the Federal Republic of Germany (FRG) passed a law stating that all victims must receive "effective aid" regardless of their current place of residence.[4] In response to the new law, Związek Bojowników o Wolność i Demokrację, or ZBOWID (Society of Fighters for Freedom and Democracy), a veterans' organization for Polish resistance fighters, submitted claims for Polish nationals who had been subject to Nazi medical experiments at the women's concentration camp at Ravensbrück. The German Foreign Ministry claimed that since the FRG did not recognize the political legitimacy of the Communist government in Poland, there was no provision in German law for paying the claims.[5] Through her work at ADIR, Ferriday came in contact with a group of Polish women with outstanding claims, and she decided to try and help them.

After years of unsuccessfully pressing the issue, in early 1957, Ferriday retained the services of the American attorney Benjamin Ferencz. Ferencz had made a name for himself as a young man prosecuting Nazi war criminals at the Nuremberg Trials. When he learned of the plight of the Polish victims, he thought there was a moral argument to be made. He thought "these victims of Nazi medical experiments" might be used as an example "to establish that Germany has not been quite as generous in their compensation programs as she would have the American public believe."[6] With Ferencz's legal guidance, ADIR presented the case to the Human Rights Division of the United Nations, which forwarded it to West Germany. Bonn soon replied, stating once again that "because of the legal and practical difficulties it does not consider itself at present able to act upon requests submitted by persons who live in a country with which it does not maintain diplomatic relations."[7] Stonewalled by the Germans, Ferencz had another idea about how to get their attention.

Ferencz remembered that a few years earlier the Hiroshima Maidens had made "quite a good stir in the press as a demonstration of American sympathy to victims of the nuclear bombings."[8] He recognized that Cousins had successfully redefined an intransigent political position as a moral one, ultimately forcing a change in government policy, and he told Ferriday that perhaps Cousins could do the same for the Ravensbrück women. Ferriday arranged a meeting with Cousins, who, after hearing from Ferriday the story of the women's plight, wrote, "What I had seen in these records was enough to convince me."[9]

Hoping to emulate the successful methods of the Hiroshima Maidens project, Cousins set off for Warsaw, Poland, two weeks later with the goal of selecting a number of victims who could be brought on a publicity tour of the United States. Cousins had some initial difficulty persuading both the Communist authorities and the women themselves that this offer of treatment was not some sort of trick. After a week in Warsaw and many meetings with the concerned parties, Cousins received a cable from the Polish authorities that made him believe that the Polish government would be cooperative and that the prospects were excellent.[10]

The Ravensbrück Lapins program was modeled entirely on the Hiroshima Maidens. Dr. Bill Hitzig, a prominent doctor at Mt. Sinai Hospital and a longtime close friend of Cousins's, also traveled to Warsaw to help select thirty-five women whose lives he thought could be improved through American medical treatment. *Saturday Review* readers were asked to donate, and more than three hundred heeded the call, contributing a total of six thousand dollars. Fresh off the experience of the Hiroshima Maidens, Cousins had a clear plan about how best to achieve his political goals, while also pitching the project to the public as a benevolent humanitarian initiative. He believed that "if what was needed was a hot poker to prod some consciences, we could at least attempt to heat up the coals."[11] And a heating of the coals was exactly what Cousins provided. While the public side of the campaign sold the story of Americans generously helping to treat the victims of Nazi crimes and get them the monetary restitution they deserved, the prodding of German consciences was done through Cousins's private diplomacy.

Cousins formed (and chaired) a private committee to pursue the group's diplomatic goals. He left the actual diplomatic negotiations to the much more experienced (and German-speaking) Ferencz, while he built a public pressure campaign to strengthen Ferencz's political overtures. The group hired a Madison Avenue advertising agency, which, according to Ferencz, "arranged a high pressure publicity campaign."[12]

But before unleashing the full public onslaught against the West German government, the group first chose to engage diplomatically with the Germans, to give them a chance to do the right thing and head off the negative publicity. "The silk glove must precede the mailed fist," as Ferencz explained.[13]

Cousins called a press conference in New York. He had brought with him the Polish ambassador to the United States, as well as a declaration from the Polish government in Warsaw saying that it would welcome an initiation of redress procedures for the Lapins. Cousins also told the West German Press Office (members of which were in attendance) that he was asking the FRG to support his actions in whatever form they could as early as possible. The West German authorities, Cousins assured those gathered, could be confident in the benevolent nature of his humanitarian mission.[14]

This press conference sparked a flurry of diplomatic activity within the West German government. Documents from the Bundesarchiv reveal that the Press Office, foreseeing trouble, requested that someone immediately be sent to New York to speak with Cousins and acquaint themselves with the position of the Polish government.[15] The following day, December 20, 1958, the West German Embassy in Washington asked the Finance Ministry to set aside one thousand dollars per woman for medical costs while the women were in the United States. This would only be a contingency fund, whose existence would be kept secret, and nothing would be paid until West Germany saw how the situation played out in the United States.[16] Things did not play out well for West Germany from the start.

The Germans coordinated their response out of their consulate in Detroit, hiring the Julius Klein public relations firm to monitor the US and international press.[17] (In 1963 Julius Klein would be forced to testify before the Senate Foreign Relations Committee in response to accusations that he was an agent of the West German government.)[18] Evidently, the Germans assumed that the issue and the accompanying press coverage would quickly dissipate, but as the months wore on the bad press kept coming. In February, two months after Cousins's initial press conference, the tipping point was reached, and the FRG felt that it could no longer ignore the issue hoping it would fade on its own. *Look* magazine published a scathing article on February 3 eviscerating the West Germans over their inaction on the reparations issue. On February 17 the embassy in Washington cabled the Press and Information Office to say that it could no longer hope to influence the issue and that the *Look* article had had a major and damaging impact.[19]

Bonn, hoping to generate some good publicity, announced that it would release the money that had initially been set aside. Cousins soon received a telegram from the Press and Information Office of the German Embassy saying that thirty of the thirty-four women had been approved to receive one thousand dollars each. Cousins thanked Germany for the offer but stated that a one-time lump sum was unacceptable. The women would accept only ongoing pensions.[20]

When weeks went by without any response from the FRG, Ferencz set off for the West German capital, Bonn, to press the women's case. Ferencz met with Dr. Berger, of the Foreign Ministry, who, he reported, was not moved by the argument that "it did not pay financially or politically to incite strong American public reaction against Germany on an issue of this kind." Ferencz reported back to Cousins that the Germans had shut him out. "Only the highest level in the Foreign Office could even bring about a serious reconsideration," he wrote, "and I must therefore throw the ball back to you for action on the other side."[21] Cousins and Ferencz then engaged in a game of good cop, bad cop. With Ferencz in Bonn threatening strong public action, Cousins informed the German Press and Information Office that his moderating influence on the Lapins Committee was on the wane. He warned that several members were going to urge US Senator Jacob Javits (D-NY) to raise the matter in a Senate speech. In reporting this message to Bonn, the German Embassy in Washington, apparently unconvinced of Cousins's power, noted that "it will be determined whether Cousins's messages are true."[22]

The embassy warned that if no satisfactory solution could be found, the FRG could expect to receive more bad publicity, which was a situation the embassy was extremely worried about.[23] The German Press and Information Office also recognized that the threatened campaign could seriously harm the reputation of the FRG in the eyes of the American public. It considered hitting back and generating some anti-Cousins publicity of its own. "It should be noted," they advised, "that the announcement of the payment and its subsequent rejection by Cousins in connection with a demonstration of the behaviour of the Communist Polish government could provide a measure of counteraction to the matter."[24] The Cousins committee, however, was quickly moving forward with its campaign. On May 19, 1959, Cousins's "warning" that Senator Javits might become involved came to fruition. Javits organized a special dinner in honor of the Lapins in the Senate dining room. Congressman Thaddeus M. Machrowicz (D-MI) also chaired a meeting with the women.[25]

On the floor of the Senate, Edward Muskie (D-ME) entered into the record that "for nearly 10 years, various groups and individuals have attempted to persuade the Government of West Germany that it has an obligation to these courageous women." He concluded by asking that the visit of the Lapins "serve to dramatize the necessity for a prompt and just settlement of their claims against the Federal Republic of West Germany." Demonstrating Cousins's influence in bringing the issue to the attention of the US government after it had languished for nearly ten years, Muskie opened his statement to the Senate by "paying particular tribute to Mr. Norman Cousins . . . without [whom] it would never have materialized."[26]

The stories of the Lapins that Cousins published in the *Saturday Review* sparked debate throughout America and around the world, garnering comment across a wide range of media channels. After learning of the project, *New York Times* reader Samuel Weiss wrote in a letter to the editor that "the Germans perpetrated these inhuman acts. Wouldn't you think they would come forward freely and provide any funds necessary to ameliorate the agony which these Lapins live with?"[27] The *Washington Post* editorialized that "justice for the 'Lapins' is still a major obligation." The *Post* noted that the "visit served to bring public opinion pressure upon the West German government, with some success."[28]

American citizens also expressed their concerns directly to the FRG. Albert Shaft, a Philadelphia doctor, wrote to the German ambassador that "it is disgusting to learn that the present German government has taken [this] position. . . . [It is] an insult to individuals of any intelligence and good will."[29] The embassy relayed all such messages to Bonn. Even the West German press took notice, with the *Frankfurter Allgemeine* reporting that when "these Polish women went to the United States the American public opinion was intensely occupied with their complaints. . . . [The West German Embassy] was acutely aware of the political and psychological nature of this matter."[30]

Both Cousins and Ferencz added to the pressure. Ferencz recalls being on the phone with the German ambassador nearly every day, and every day the ambassador demurred. "We'll keep on marching," Ferencz told the ambassador at one point, "and we're going to continue to hammer the hell out of you until you take a more moral position."[31] Cousins sent a telegram directly to German chancellor Conrad Adenauer that read, "All efforts through official channels to obtain equitable compensation for Ravensbrueck Lapins and other victims of Nazi medical experiments unproductive after more than a year. Urgently request you in light of your statement at Belson yesterday to advise us how to proceed to obtain justice for these women."[32] Finally recognizing that the publicity campaign was negatively affecting American's opinions of West Germany and that Cousins would not relent, the ambassador cabled Bonn saying that it needed to find a way to settle the matter.[33]

Shortly after the Lapins' departure from the United States, Cousins received a letter from the West German Embassy saying that it was working to remove the obstacles to a settlement. The Germans included a check for twenty-seven thousand dollars to cover medicals costs incurred during the US treatment.[34] While Cousins reported this to his *Saturday Review* readers as a positive development, he left out the fact that the Lapins had rejected the payment as being "wholly unacceptable." The West German Embassy assured the committee that "urgent consideration was being given to further relief measures by the Federal authorities."[35] While they had made measurable steps toward their goal, at this point the public pressure campaign had some unintended consequences. Ferencz, who was in Bonn to negotiate a permanent settlement, wrote to Cousins with the distressing news that he had been "unable to withstand the opposition of the Finance Ministry" to more funding. In fact, Ferencz was told by a German member of Parliament that "I was getting a reputation as a Communist sympathizer because of my intervention on behalf of people behind the iron curtain and he further suggested that I keep my hands off."[36]

Many members of Parliament supported the Finance Ministry's line of reasoning and argued that no money should be paid because it would be used for nefarious Communist purposes. In response to this, Ferencz immediately offered to recuse himself and have the International Red Cross handle all the money. This solution seemed to satisfy some of the skeptics, but the money never came.[37] An increasingly agitated Cousins dispatched an angry telegram to the German Embassy in Washington that read, "We do not want to believe that these were merely empty phrases yet cannot understand unexplained delay. . . . [We will] take necessary steps in our unrelenting determination to see justice done."[38]

Not wanting to endure another round of public outcry, the German cabinet called a special meeting to debate the issue. A statement was read into the record that shows the impact that Cousins's pressure campaign had in Germany. "A short while ago," the statement read, "the women were in the American senate and received a big reception as victims of Hitlerism. America is today still deeply aroused about this matter. We have not only a political but also a moral duty to help in this instance." That very day the Bundestag voted unanimously to approve payment to the Ravensbrück Lapins.[39] This marked the first time that the Federal Republic of Germany had paid reparations to victims in Communist regimes. In the wake of this decision the *Frankfurter Allgemeine* reported that "only when an American publisher [Cousins] took it up again was the Bonn Government shamed into action."[40]

Back in the United States, the *New York Times* praised this historic development in a front-page article, where it noted that "a key role in the negotiations was played by Norman Cousins."[41] In announcing the deal, the *Polish Review* wrote that "this settlement was achieved through the persistent efforts of Norman Cousins."[42] Even Caroline Ferriday, who had personally championed this issue since 1951, gave much credit to Cousins for the success. She wrote that "our committee had the great good fortune to find Norman Cousins who took up the cudgels on behalf of our Polish friends. . . . Public outrage helping, after a resonant *Nein*, the Bonn Government was forced to change its attitude."[43] Although the Polish government had almost no direct involvement in this project or in the negotiations, it too sent a letter of thanks. "As I am sure you realize, all of us . . . are deeply indebted to you personally and to the Cousins Committee for the unstinting time and effort you have devoted," a counselor at the Polish Embassy wrote.[44] The Polish government even extended a warm invitation to Cousins and his wife to return to Poland as guests of the government in order to be properly thanked for their efforts.

Cousins took the Polish government up on its offer, traveling to Warsaw to accept his accolades. This trip ultimately represents the biggest benefit Cousins derived from his involvement with the Ravensbrück Lapins project: it gained him a good deal of prestige in the Communist world that he otherwise might have struggled to earn on his own. Cousins had made multiple attempts in the years since 1945 to obtain a visa to visit the Soviet Union on a reporting trip, all of which were met with rejections.[45] But after his success with the Lapins and his positive reporting on Poland in general, the Soviets rolled out the veritable red carpet for him in the coming years.

Both Cousins and Hitzig saw the Lapins program as an opportunity to foster better East-West relations, and Cousins did much work on that front. During his first trip to Warsaw in 1958, to select the Lapins, he published a *Saturday Review* editorial titled "The Toast of Warsaw." On his first night in Warsaw he attended a performance of the touring American Ballet Theater, which was in the country on a cultural exchange. His editorial not only lauded the performance but also praised the Polish people for their resilience in the face of the many tragedies they had faced during the war. In a conversation after the ballet performance with a Polish music critic, Cousins observed that the Polish critic "found himself changing his mind about the United States." It was, Cousins proclaimed, "the result of the successes scored by our cultural ambassadors."[46]

Upon his return to the United States, Cousins referenced this experience during a commencement speech he delivered at Mount Holyoke College. He cited foreign tours by orchestras and dancing groups, praising America's "cultural ambassadors," whom he credited with being a "potent influence for good will and understanding among all people."[47] This was a shining example of what Cousins had called for just months earlier when he wrote that "there can be no security for America unless we can establish and keep vital connections with the world's peoples."[48] Those words he wrote in 1957 would soon have meaning in his own life.

CHAPTER 19

A CULTURAL EXCHANGE *of* HIS OWN

Cousins had long called for more cultural contacts between nations both in his editorials and in his lobbying. As early as 1946, Cousins lent his support to the State Department's attempt to create a program for international information and cultural exchanges.[1] After World War II the United States did, in fact, establish exchange programs with Germany and Japan, but these "exchanges" were mostly one-way funneling of American culture in the form of Hollywood movies, comic books, or convenience items flooding into the occupied zones.[2] Cousins spilled much ink over the years, annoyed that citizens of other countries got a skewed view of America mostly through the Hollywood movies that were exported, while Americans learned little to nothing about other cultures except through the lens of negative Cold War propaganda.

President Eisenhower himself had also advocated direct exchanges between peoples, which he described as "one fine, progressive step toward peace in the world." Thus, in September 1956 the president launched the People-to-People Program.[3] This came on the heels of Khrushchev's 1956 "Secret Speech," in which the Soviet leader signaled changes in Soviet policy that called for peaceful coexistence and increased contacts with the West.[4] Both leaders got their wish on January 27, 1958, when a US-Soviet agreement on cultural exchanges was signed.[5] As a result of both this new agreement and Cousins's recent Ravensbrück Lapins success, which garnered him much recognition in the Communist world, Norman Cousins was among the first American citizens, perhaps even *the* first, to be invited to Russia under the auspices of this new program. In fact, Cousins was specifically invited separately from, and in advance of, the official US delegation being planned for the following year.[6]

Alice Bobrysheva, a Russian interpreter who later worked with Cousins, recalls in her memoir that in June 1959 she was asked to "organize a meeting . . . for a prominent American, Norman Cousins." Cousins would soon have such an impact on Bobrysheva's life—she writes that "meeting with Norman Cousins was like opening a window into a wider world. . . . [He] left me enriched by his ideas, his energy, and his dedication to improving life on our planet"—that she vividly remembers his file: "Besides biographical data and a listing of his various positions and numerous activities, his resume stated that he had actively protested against the Soviet suppression of the Hungarian revolt in 1956, criticized the Soviet Peace Committee for being a propaganda tool of the Soviet government. . . . In our eyes he was a typical 'anti-Sovietchik.' This did not sound like a very desirable guest."[7] Clearly, Cousins had won over someone much higher up the Soviet chain of command, likely as a result of the Ravensbrück Lapins project. As Bobrysheva recounts, "Nevertheless, it had been decided (as I see it now) at a high level of the Communist Party that the meeting should take place. There may have been mention of President Eisenhower's support for Cousins's visit, and that probably influenced the decision."[8]

Having long wished to visit Russia, Cousins graciously accepted the invitation. The Soviet Cultural Relations Societies would be his host as well as his benefactor, covering all expenses save for transportation to and from the Soviet Union. Incredibly, they claimed that they were going to give Cousins complete freedom to travel wherever he pleased in the Soviet Union, speak to whomever he wanted, and deliver "a small number of lectures on subjects of [his] own choosing."[9] Cousins was granted an unprecedented level of freedom in a time when even visiting

US congressmen were frequently denied the opportunity to meet with Soviet officials.[10]

With the trip scheduled for June 1959, word of Cousins's imminent departure spread. Forty-three separate television stations in the United States requested that he undertake some reporting on their behalf while in the Soviet Union. Cousins contacted Moscow with his proposal. He wished to do (1) "a filmed interview with Premier Khrushchev"; (2) "interviews with leading philosophers, writers and cultural figures in the Soviet Union"; and (3) "short films having to do with education, village life and sports activities."[11] While the Soviets said they would allow him to photograph whatever he pleased, they did not respond to his request to film an interview with Khrushchev.

Capitalizing on this new climate of increased cultural contacts with the Eastern Bloc, and bolstered by the increase in his own stature provided by the nature of his prestigious and groundbreaking trip, Cousins wrote to Eisenhower for the first time in a year to offer him some bold advice. Cousins told Eisenhower:

> People are ready for a bold new approach on the large problems of war and peace. . . . They are ready, I believe, for a new vision and a new approach. . . . All this sets the stage for one of the grand moments of human history—far greater, even, than Athens knew at the time of Pericles' Funeral Oration or that Britain knew when Winston Churchill rallied the free world after the fall of France. In short, I believe that the great idea you voiced in the closing pages of "Crusade in Europe" [Eisenhower's 1948 memoir] on the need for world law, and about which you have written to me earlier, may now serve as the great theme and rallying call for the creation of peace with justice on earth.

Cousins informed Eisenhower that he had read all his previous writings and speeches and used them to draft a speech that he believed "may speak to the historic needs of the times." Cousins hoped Eisen-

Cousins in Europe, ca. 1959.

(PHOTO COURTESY OF CANDIS COUSINS KERNS)

hower would accept the speech and "consider it as the basis for a major Presidential Address."[12]

Within days Eisenhower responded with a very affirmative letter. "As you know, I have had the 'Rule of Law' concept on my mind for many years," the president wrote. "Perhaps now is the time to devote an entire talk to the subject. . . . I gladly accept [your speech draft]."[13] Eisenhower wrote Cousins on the day of his departure for the Soviet Union to thank him again for the speech as well as to wish him "the hope that your assignment is interesting and that you will be able to incorporate in it a little fun."[14] While Cousins's trip to Russia was indeed interesting, he may not have described it as "fun," certainly not after he got heckled during one of his speeches.

Nine days after arriving in Russia, Cousins delivered his most high-profile lecture to date: an address to the Presidium of the Soviet Peace Committee in Moscow. This was a groundbreaking invitation: Cousins was the first American ever invited to address the committee. The committee, however, was hardly an independent body. As historian Lawrence Wittner points out, its purpose was to "illustrate abroad that the Soviet people supported their government's foreign policy; and to ensure support of Soviet foreign policy from the public abroad."[15]

Beginning his speech by commending the genuine spirit of friendliness he had encountered in Moscow and praising the Russians for their concern about peace, he thanked his Russian hosts for allowing him the opportunity to speak "in absolute candor," and then he did just that. Shocking his Russian audience, Cousins—recycling the rhetoric of his 1949 speech at the Cultural and Scientific Conference for World Peace—charged that the Communist Party of the United States was "a party without honor." He proclaimed that the thousands who fled East Berlin each year were escaping from "an intolerable situation." He described how he had reacted with "shock and revulsion . . . when the Hungarian revolt was violently put down when Soviet tanks and guns went into action." Finally, he informed his increasingly agitated listeners that in Poland, which he had just visited, "a terrible wall of resentment exists . . . against the Soviet Union."[16] Bobrysheva, who was interpreting for Cousins, recalls that she "could see the audience was shocked by his candor. Some people started to protest."[17]

Cousins himself notes that the audience "was polite and attentive, except for several minutes during that part of my talk when I spoke about the American Communist Party and the situation in Central Europe. . . . I stopped my talk for perhaps thirty seconds, the chairman called for order, and the talk was uninterrupted until it was completed."[18] The speech was important because, as Cousins later wrote to famed reporter Walter Lippmann, according to his contacts at the US Embassy in Moscow "this was the first time that a talk critical of Soviet policy has been given by an outsider from a public platform in Moscow."[19] Thus it is unsurprising that Cousins's message did not make it out of the room. Much to his chagrin, even though the speech was well attended by members of the Soviet press, not a single outlet published the text of his speech or even mentioned it.[20] Cousins later found out that it was not simply overlooked; it was officially censored. "Four correspondents . . . informed me that their detailed stories had not been cleared [by the censor's office]," Cousins wrote.[21]

Despite his critique of Soviet policy, Cousins also spoke positively in his speech about ending the arms race and nuclear testing and proclaimed that "the peace of the world is much too important to be left to governments. If the peace is to be real, people everywhere will have to speak up."[22] Cousins notes that during the discussions after the speech he continued to stress "the importance of individual participation in the shaping of important foreign policy decisions. To this end, he urged that prominent individuals from the Soviet Union meet with prominent Americans to consider the problem of an enduring peace."[23] Cousins himself noted that the speech was not a success in terms of reaching large numbers of people. Philip Stewart, a close associate of Cousins's, remembers that Cousins "was pretty discouraged. But somehow, because bureaucrats will do that, they sent the report [of Cousins's speech] upward . . . to Khrushchev."[24] Cousins must have impressed the Soviet leader, because the seed he planted during the speech with his proposal to bring both Soviets and Americans together for informal talks would soon sprout into one of his most lasting achievements.

Much has been made of the great Kitchen Debate at the 1959 Moscow Exhibition, which saw Vice President Richard Nixon debating Khrushchev over the merits of capitalism while visiting a model American home. American observers at the time, of course, were convinced that capitalism was superior. Cousins attended the fair himself while in Moscow and came away with a different impression. He had long criticized the one-way view that the best thing the United States had to offer the world was consumerism, and he especially wanted to counter the dearth of objective reporting about life inside the Soviet Union. Instead of following Nixon's lead and championing American superiority and material plenty, Cousins attempted to introduce *Saturday Review* readers to daily life in the Soviet Union as he saw it.

Cousins returned from his month-long trip to the Soviet Union with changed attitudes. He published a series of articles that attempted to show Americans that the Soviet Union was not a nation to be feared because of its alleged desire to destroy the West or mocked because of its poverty and backwardness. "The situation in the Soviet Union is far from being as glorious as the diehard supporters had advertised at a distance; but neither is it as dismal as the American public has come to believe," Cousins wrote.[25] The Soviets," he explained, were focusing all their energy on building an economy that produced internal prosperity, competed on the global stage, and provided economic aid for other nations.[26] He reported that the Soviet people "liked their government and were genuinely enthusiastic about their national prospects," and he warned that in five to ten years the United States could find itself engaged in a serious, worldwide, nonmilitary showdown with the Soviets, especially in Africa and Asia.[27]

Having caught a glimpse of where the Soviets might be headed, Cousins was eager to share his thoughts with members of the US government. He wrote to Senator Richard Neuberger (D-OR): "There is no doubt in my mind that the Soviet leaders are sincere when they say they want peace. The reason for it is they realize, even if we don't, that it is no longer possible to conceive of victory in connection with modern war. And they also realize, while we do not, that they can win in the world on the non-military level."[28] Cousins even wrote to CIA director Allen Dulles to relay the "clear and emphatic impression I had, in talking to various Soviet officials, that the Russians were ready to give ground on a wide variety of issues, including the Middle East and nuclear testing." He attempted to persuade Dulles that "the Soviet is willing to make peace, real peace, with the United States."[29] Cousins would get a chance to relay these thoughts, and more, directly to Eisenhower when he was summoned to meet with the president on August 6, 1959.

Eisenhower administration officials recognized that Cousins had enjoyed privileges considered rare for American tourists during his visit to Russia, and they were eager to get his opinions. Cousins arrived for the 8:40 a.m. private meeting with Eisenhower and Eisenhower's son, Major John Eisenhower, who took notes. Cousins explained that any hope the United States still held that disenchanted Soviets would rise up and overthrow their government was unrealistic. As a result of discussions during his trip with prominent Soviets (civilians, academics, and officials alike), he "visualized the Soviet Union now, not as an iron curtain, but as a red magnet." Russia is now ready to be showcased and would attempt to attract converts from around the world.[30] To make his point more clearly, Cousins presented Eisenhower with a fifteen-page report detailing his impressions and his recommendations for dealing with the Soviet Union going forward.[31]

Cousins's trip opened his eyes to a major opportunity. Russia, he later noted in a speech at Mills College, "was not what I expected. . . . I had a vision of a country totally run down at the heels, a country where people wore rags, and perhaps spent a great deal of their time on bread lines."[32] Instead, it was now a "have" nation, and its newfound pride and power under Khrushchev would pose a grave challenge to the United States unless some way could be found to reduce the tensions between the two nations. In his discussions with a wide spectrum of Soviet citizens, from politicians to taxi drivers, he had become convinced "that the Soviet Union's desire for peace is genuine."[33] Achieving disarmament and peaceful coexistence with the United States had been a Soviet priority, albeit a somewhat cynical one, since 1956. With the benefit of distance and a more robust understanding, we can now see that at the time the Soviets were far behind in the arms race and thus were all too happy to get rid of nuclear weapons and achieve "peace," especially if it meant the United States would have to disarm as well.

Cousins's contacts with Eisenhower had persuaded him that while leaders might like to pursue peace, they were constrained by political circumstances. "Government itself cannot do the job," Cousins believed.[34] He wrote to a Soviet journalist whom he had met on his trip, "This is why it becomes all the more important for men who have access to the public . . . to recognize that we have an important role to fill in helping to create a basis for mutual survival."[35]

Cousins was beginning to see that the basis for mutual survival might be as simple as opening a dialogue between the two nations—a point he raised when he proposed to the Presidium of the Soviet Peace Committee that prominent individuals from the Soviet Union meet with prominent Americans to consider how to achieve an enduring peace.[36] Cousins was moved by how much the Soviet Union exceeded his expectations, especially how receptive Soviet citizens were to his peace overtures, and he believed that if he could just get the leaders of both sides to see past the stereotypes and have a genuine conversation, they could solve their underlying differences. He especially believed that in this age of potential pushbutton nuclear destruction it was crucial to open a second channel for dialogue in case official relations turned sour.[37] Cousins's determination for Americans to talk to Soviets sparked the creation of the Dartmouth Conferences, the first citizen-to-citizen dialogue between the United States and the Soviet Union.

On November 10, 1959, Cousins received a letter from the Soviet Peace Committee. The chairman and the executive secretary of the committee wrote to thank him for "the very proper view you expressed in Moscow that direct friendly contacts should be established between public representatives of our countries in the interest of rapprochement between the USA and the Soviet Union." They explained that "our view fully coincides with yours: the time has come to take the first important step. . . . Why not arrange a Soviet-American meeting as soon as possible?"[38] Bobrysheva would later recount that the approval for this proposed meeting came directly from Khrushchev himself.[39]

Upon receiving this letter, Cousins immediately set to work liaising with Eisenhower advisor Arthur Larson to arrange the conference. This idea to bring leading Soviet and American thinkers together for informal conversations was "strongly encouraged" by the State Department, with whom Cousins was in close touch for planning purposes.[40] Cousins put together a list of eminent Americans, including George Kennan, a former US ambassador to the Soviet Union. Kennan was a questionable choice. During his time as ambassador to the Soviet Union he had compared the Soviet Union to Nazi Germany, angering the Soviets and undermining his ambassadorship. Kennan certainly was *the* American expert on the Soviet Union, but his inclusion had the potential to put a damper on any discussions. Also on the list were Arthur Larson; Averell Harriman, former US ambassador to the Soviet Union; Walt Rostow, advisor to Senator John F. Kennedy (D-MA); and William Benton, former Democratic senator from Connecticut.[41]

Keeping Eisenhower informed as plans came together, Cousins wrote to the president that "we are eager to expose some of their leading non-governmental people to the thinking of prominent Americans on the needs of the human community rather than the usual ideological or political kind of discussion."[42] This claim that the discussion would not be the "usual ideological or political kind" is somewhat laughable since the majority of American attendees that Cousins recruited were in fact politicians, former politicians, or ideologues themselves. In any case, former assistant secretary of state for Near Eastern affairs Harold Saunders, who participated in later Dartmouth Conferences, contends that Cousins quickly gained a good deal of credibility with the State Department because he involved so many credible, high-level people in what was seen as a unique and important initiative.[43] Perhaps this was Cousins's plan. Later Dartmouth Conferences would still include many politicians, but they would be rounded out with businessman, artists, writers, and thinkers.

The first conference took place from October 29 to November 4, 1960, and the agenda shows that what Cousins was really eager to expose the Soviets to was his long-standing personal views. The discussion topics were all culled from the central themes of Cousins's previous editorials:

1) Disarmament
2) A Structured Peace
3) The Psychological Gap in Understanding [the other nation]
4) Economic Aid to the Hungry World
5) The Role of the Citizen in Foreign Policy[44]

Despite the conference being a close reflection of Cousins's personal views (he *was* told by the Soviets to pick the topics after all), it was an immediate success. Former ambassador Kennan later privately reported that in the more than two decades he had served in the Soviet Union, "during all that time he had sought every opportunity for a frank exchange of views with Russians of genuine intellectual substance. But he had had to wait until he came to Hanover, New Hampshire [the site of the conference] to fulfill this aim."[45] Bobrysheva, who attended the conference as one of the Soviet interpreters, observed that "[Dartmouth] brought tremendous changes in the minds of the 25 Russian and American participants."[46]

In order to foster the freest possible exchange of ideas, Cousins ordered that the conference take place behind closed doors and be completely off the record, so we lack a written record of how the discussions actually unfolded. Despite this, Cousins did report to the State Department about the conference, which provided a valuable source of intelligence. In a presentation attended by Ambassador Bohlen, as well as twenty-eight other State Department officers, Cousins told them of insights about the Soviets that he had gleaned from the discussions. The deputy director of the Soviet and Eastern European exchanges staff later wrote Cousins to thank him for "the insight you gave us into the thinking of the Soviet group with which you met," and he asked for any other documents or information that "would fill out our understanding of the subjects discussed and the points of view expressed by the Soviet participants."[47] Philip Stewart, an organizer of subsequent conferences, notes that the CIA was often debriefed as well and was especially interested in the thinking of the top Soviet citizens who attended the conference, whom the agency previously had not been able to gather intelligence on.[48] If that was truly the case, then far from Cousins's ideal of free and open off-the-record discussion, Dartmouth, at least in the later years, morphed into a more typical Cold War intelligence-gathering operation.

Publicly, Dartmouth received much praise. Impressed with what the conference had achieved, the *New York Times* editorialized:

> Thoughtful persons in all countries are searching for ways to improve the situation and to lessen the tensions which might explode in a thermonuclear holocaust that would destroy us all. In this dark setting a small—but potentially important—gleam of light has now appeared. It is the fact that these past two weeks . . . a group of distinguished Americans and of distinguished Soviet citizens was able to meet amicably and to discuss vigorously the outstanding issues between our two countries. . . . It is a measure of the straits we are in that a mere civilized discussion of issues must be

> counted an appreciable advance . . . [but] their initiative might lead to a new tone and a new atmosphere in Soviet-American relations, and thus help achieve [a] "just and lasting peace."[49]

The conference also garnered attention in Moscow. *Pravda* published an interview with one of the participants on November 13.[50] The biggest moment came after the Soviet participants returned home and four of them hosted a well-attended public lecture in Moscow in which they praised the achievements of the conference.[51] Leslie S. Brady, the counselor for cultural affairs at the US Embassy in Moscow, attended the lecture and wrote to Cousins, "You would have been glad to hear your name repeated again and again in a large Moscow auditorium packed with people last night. . . . You got full credit for your personal role in the whole project, which the speakers seemed to feel was indeed worthwhile."[52]

Even months after the conference the State Department noted that "Radio Moscow seems to have become rather active in reviving comment on the Dartmouth Conferences."[53] The conference was worthwhile not just for helping to establish open dialogue between the two nations. It was especially helpful for Cousins's network-building among the many prominent individuals who would be part of the incoming Kennedy administration, such as Harriman and Rostow (who attended the conference), as well as for forging ties on the Soviet side with those who were close to Premier Khrushchev. Cousins's growing top-tier network of contacts in both countries and his strong record of international success would prove to be immensely important going forward. This venue for Soviet-American discussion was especially important given the events of the previous May.

Having become convinced by early 1960 that nuclear testing needed to end, Eisenhower announced on February 11, 1960, that he was willing to accept a test ban treaty, contingent upon reasonable inspections. On March 19, Khrushchev responded positively, and the leaders agreed to meet in Paris that May to discuss the deal.[54] When word got out that a test ban was on the agenda at Paris, many of Eisenhower's advisors, as well as the American media, immediately went on the offensive against any test ban agreement.[55] British prime minister Harold Macmillan was quite upset at the hostile reaction to the plan in the United States, as he had long been advocating for a test ban and wanted to accept the Soviet offer. He arranged, in haste, to travel to the United States and consult with Eisenhower about the situation.[56]

Cousins had remained publicly silent about the Paris Summit proposals, but when he got wind of the Macmillan visit, he sent Eisenhower a telegram. "Everything you stand for and your place in human history," he wrote, "are now directly involved in the decision confronting you on nuclear arms control." Cousins continued: "I think I know how great are the counter arguments and pressures but the American Presidency offers a man no higher privilege than to be able to count on the good sense of the American people to support courageous decisions.... People everywhere look to you as the soldier who will win history's great fight for peace with justice."[57] Cousins need not have worried. Eisenhower was committed to pursuing a test ban and disarmament talks with Khrushchev in Paris, but he also made a grave error. The hoped-for historic breakthrough on nuclear testing that might have occurred at the Paris Summit came crashing down with the debris of a destroyed American U-2 reconnaissance plane.

The United States had been running secret flights over the Soviet Union in order to collect intelligence. Soviet anti-air defenses were thought to be unable to reach the high-flying U-2 spy planes, and Khrushchev had publicly kept quiet about the embarrassing intrusions he could do little to stop. Worried about the diplomatic ramifications should he be exposed, Eisenhower fretted about approving one final flight before the Paris Summit, but assured that there was little to no risk, he signed off on an April 9 flight. This time the Soviets managed to shoot the spy plane down and capture the pilot alive. Khrushchev responded by setting a trap to catch Eisenhower in a lie about the nature of the illegal flight. Unaware that the pilot had been captured and that the Soviets knew that he had been on a spy mission, Eisenhower blundered into the trap and refused to admit US wrongdoing, claiming that it had been simply a weather plane that had accidentally strayed off course. Khrushchev used the failed flight as a pretext to walk away from the summit.

The collapse of the Paris Summit had devastating consequences for the Cold War. The arms race accelerated, suspicions increased, and the prospect for disarmament negotiations virtually disappeared.[58] Cousins reacted with nearly as much fury as Khrushchev had, expressing his anger across three separate editorials. Cousins wrote that "a mountain-sized assortment of hopes and plans about peace has been knocked down and sent sprawling all over the historical landscape by what happened at Paris."[59] He lamented that "the general standing and prestige of the United States, its persuasive power, and its role as a prime source of stability had been severely and tragically diminished."[60] He slammed President Eisenhower, claiming that because of his attempted cover-up, "we are now calling on our soldiers to give their lives, not to serve our honor or our freedom, but to spare us the indignity of being caught in a lie."[61]

Cousins later wrote that he actually crossed paths with Eisenhower that September at the United Nations, where he took the opportunity to ask the president about the U-2 incident. He claimed that Eisenhower responded that few events in his career had troubled him more deeply. The president also revealed to Cousins that he was looking forward to his retirement "so that he could devote himself to the cause of world peace."[62]

Knowing that Eisenhower's days in the Oval Office were numbered and seizing on this revelation about Eisenhower's hopes for the future, Cousins made one final attempt to influence the departing president. On December 14, a note from Eisenhower's secretary, Ann Whitman, told him that Cousins had called that day. The note read, "His suggestions: that you give a 'farewell' address to the country . . . reviewing your Administration, telling of your hopes for the future. A great, sweeping document."[63] According to Cousins, the two men did discuss this issue and "the opportunity presented by [Eisenhower's] Farewell Address, not far off, to talk some sense into the American people, and he invited me to send him some notes for that occasion."[64] Cousins submitted a speech draft in which Eisenhower would emphasize his goal "of a world made safer for mankind. By this I mean a world in which man can be at peace and yet be free. . . . There is nothing contradictory between the cause of peace and freedom." [65] While Cousins's draft was not directly used in the speech Eisenhower ultimately delivered, Whitman did notify Cousins in advance that "the content of the talk [Eisenhower] will give on Tuesday night is also in line with your thinking."[66] Eisenhower's final words to the country were contained in his now iconic Military-Industrial Complex speech.

Eisenhower advisor Arthur Larson expressed his opinion that by the late 1950s "[*Saturday Review*] was becoming an important periodical on public affairs, especially through [Norman Cousins's] editorials."[67] By Eisenhower's second term Cousins was directly influencing public opinion and engaging with Eisenhower administration policies. His persuasive arguments about the dangers of nuclear radiation caused by weapons testing garnered concern from notable world figures like Dr. Albert Schweitzer, whom Cousins directly influenced. His editorial on the subject, "Think of a Man," forced even the president himself to take stock. Historian James Ledbetter writes that "[Eisenhower's] meditations about the moral, military, and scientific complexities of nuclear weapons were often prompted by his correspondence with Norman Cousins."[68]

But to Cousins, the goal of ending nuclear testing was so important that it trumped both politics and national allegiances; it needed to be a global priority. For all his success, though, Cousins's coup de grace—ending nuclear testing—remained unachieved as the Eisenhower administration left office.

CHAPTER 20

THE DAWN *of the* KENNEDY ADMINISTRATION

John F. Kennedy won the 1960 election without any help from Norman Cousins. Having established himself in the presidential campaign world by working on both of Stevenson's campaigns, Cousins was quickly asked to join Kennedy's campaign team as well. Surprisingly, though, he declined. In an illuminating letter to his old friend Adlai Stevenson, Cousins revealed his true feelings: "They've asked me to join the writing team for Kennedy. This is something a fellow ought to do only if he has his heart in it. I don't—at least not now. Oh, I'll vote for him all right; but it would help if I could think of a good reason for becoming enthusiastic. What I mean is, does Kennedy really have stature?"[1]

Candis recalled her father being cool on Kennedy. "I think that my father knew about the Kennedy family, he knew about Joseph Kennedy." Joe Kennedy had been the US ambassador to the United Kingdom at the outbreak of World War II. He had been recalled after espousing anti-British sentiment and arguing against US aid during the war. He soon lost most of his political standing after opposing the reelection of Franklin Roosevelt and cozying up to Senator Joseph McCarthy (R-WI). "I can see why my father, knowing about Joe Kennedy, would not be very excited about a Kennedy being in the White House," Candis noted.[2] Sarah too remembers her parents' coolness toward Kennedy's run. "When

Kennedy was running for office," she explained, "I remember my mother and father were worried that he was too young to become President, and were concerned that it was the Kennedy family's wealth that was primarily responsible for his political ascendancy."[3]

Cousins's lack of enthusiasm for Kennedy extended to the pages of the *Saturday Review*. In past elections, his editorials had often discussed the nature of the election campaign and offered aspirations for the candidates to live up to, but now Cousins was nearly silent about the campaign. When Kennedy ended up winning the election, although no record has been found to show that Cousins sent the president-elect a note of congratulations, he certainly sent Nixon a consolation letter, to which Nixon responded that "nothing could have meant more to us than to receive such a warm and thoughtful letter after losing."[4]

The new president would tell Americans in his revered inaugural address to "ask not what your country can do for you but what you can do for your country." Cousins too had a clear idea of what he could do for his country under Kennedy. Cousins had scored a number of public successes throughout the 1950s in which he was able to bring public opinion to bear on moral questions, forcing both the United States and foreign governments to change the policies that Cousins had in his crosshairs. But while small-scale humanitarian missions like the Hiroshima Maidens and the Ravensbrück Lapins had helped a small number of specific individuals, Cousins knew he had to make a bigger impact if he was to achieve lasting change on a large scale.

As the calendar advanced from 1960 to January 1961, it brought with it a major announcement from Cousins to his *Saturday Review* readers. Speaking personally, Cousins wrote that "nothing in my life, next to my family, has meant more to me than the *Saturday Review*." To that point the magazine had been wholly owned by its staff, with Cousins as a majority shareholder, but in February 1961 he revealed that he had recently accepted an offer to sell the magazine to the McCall's Corporation, a major New York publisher.[5] Cousins explained that his majority ownership would complicate matters for the magazine should he die and, even more significantly, that with its now 250,000 subscribers the magazine had grown to the point where it no longer had the resources to maintain reliable printing and distribution services. Joining McCall's would bring all the *Saturday Review*'s operations in-house, while allowing Cousins to maintain full control over content. While all these reasons for selling the magazine made reasonable business and practical sense, it appears that Cousins had a powerful additional motive for signing the deal: he would receive a substantial financial windfall. Still, he described the sale as "the toughest [decision] of my life."[6]

What Cousins neglected to tell his readers but soon shared in a personal letter to the recently retired President Eisenhower was that "with the amount paid to me for my stock in the *Saturday Review*, I shall now be able to put a million dollars into the fight for a durable peace." With this substantial windfall in his hands, Cousins explained to Eisenhower, "Naturally, I am eager to use this sum as effectively and wisely as possible. In order to do this, I shall need the best advice I can find. Nothing would please me more than to be able to include you in a small group of advisors."[7] Ann Whitman, Eisenhower's personal secretary, responded that Eisenhower was "much interested in your new project.... He would be glad to consult with you personally, at any time you choose.... I do know he would always welcome an opportunity to see you."[8]

While Cousins did meet with Eisenhower for one hour later that year, on October 23, he wasted no time in putting his newfound wealth to use. He partnered with the notable American poet and peace activist Lenore Marshall to create the Cousins-Marshall Fund. In a series of letters to Marshall, Cousins outlined his vision for how they would operate. For starters, he did not want to engage in or encourage street-level protest action. "I am not sure that demonstrations, however orderly can achieve or advance the kind of support or consensus that we need," Cousins wrote. "They fit too easily into a stereotype; they produce all sorts of opposing conditioned reflexes; they harden opposition and stiffen resistance."[9]

Instead, Cousins's mission statement read: "Our purpose is to use our personal resources and our energies in helping to stop the drift to war." He noted that their new fund would approach the problem in three ways: through direct contributions, to SANE, for example (which, interestingly, *did* engage in the types of "demonstrations" that Cousins frowned upon); through institutional giving to places like Columbia University, which might (hypothetically) carry out a disarmament study; and through creation of "a company which, in effect, would be a RAND Corporation for peace."[10]

Cousins also sought to do things like encouraging the production of "a motion picture similar to 'On the Beach' [a widely praised 1959 film that depicted the aftermath of a nuclear war] for the purpose of dramatizing the drift to thermonuclear war and the consequences of such a war."[11] He would fund a national committee of scientists, men like Harrison Brown, Hans Bethe, Jerome Wiesner, and Glenn Seaborg. (The latter two had joined the Kennedy administration.) His hope was that these men would publish articles to educate the general public as well as put pressure on the administration.

Finally, he wanted to create a "world perspective group" of the globe's leading thinkers. His proposed members included Lewis Mumford, Paul Tillich, Erich Fromm, Robert Hutchins, and Norman Thomas. Cousins concluded, "What I am trying to suggest here is that any attempt to shape public opinion in a decisive way requires the fullest possible participation of leadership people from various areas of American life."[12] This last point, however, shows the myopia of many of the liberal Cold Warriors of the era. The proposed members of Cousins's "world perspective group" were all Americans. Cousins himself did maintain a wide network of people from around the world, including since 1960 Soviet citizens, whom he asked for advice and who helped to inform his thinking. But looking closely, one can see that

Cousins is at the center of the network. Dartmouth was focused on *his* issues. *Americans* made up his "world perspective group."

Convinced since the Dartmouth Conference that the Soviets wanted peace (or at least willing to believe the Soviet *claims* that they wanted peace), and with substantial new financial resources at hand, Cousins was going to let nothing get in the way of his goal of pushing American public opinion away from the Cold War arms race and toward disarmament. "Our fundamental objectives ought to be," he wrote, "to achieve specific and important new directions in foreign policy and public opinion."[13] Cousins's first act was to write another book that aimed to provide a thorough exploration of the facts surrounding nuclear war. *In Place of Folly* (1961) explained in vivid detail exactly the type of unthinkable destruction that a nuclear war would entail. Cousins knew that he and his writing typically reached the urban, educated, left-leaning middle class. But Cousins the self-proclaimed gradualist knew that if he truly wanted to influence a long-term and lasting shift in US public thought, he had to reach an audience he had not previously targeted: the young, impressionable high school students.

Through SANE, Cousins established a program to distribute twelve hundred free copies of his new book to social science teachers nationwide. Cousins covered the costs himself. SANE ordered an additional ten thousand copies to distribute through its own offices and events.[14] The book-distribution project proved to be an overwhelming success. Copies were requested by 1,912 teachers, and the letters of praise poured in from teachers nationwide. Ernest Hacly wrote, "It is an event of public importance that a man of Norman Cousins's ability and authority has taken time out to master the curriculum of the atomic age. . . . It is the act of a notably responsible citizen, and will be received with wide public respect."[15] Edward Meyerding wrote to say that his wife "had the experience of hearing the head of the social science department say that his life would never be the same since reading your book."[16]

With the success of the book boosting his public image, on May 20, 1961, Cousins appeared on an NBC television program in which he debated economist and public policy expert Leo Cherne in an hour-long show titled "Is Co-Existence Between the US and USSR Now Possible?" Cousins, drawing from his experiences at the recent Dartmouth Conference and his travels in Russia, took the "yes" position, while Cherne took the "no" side.[17] Two years earlier, in fact, Cousins had been approached by a production company about hosting a television show of his own "centered around provocative subjects in current events, interpretation of events, interviews with well-known authorities and men of note in various fields." The company had told Cousins that his job as host of this new show "will be speaking for man . . . and bring[ing] to the television audience greater understanding of world events and their effect on man."[18] Seeking some legal advice on the matter, Cousins was told to recognize his growing national fame and urged to ask for more than the contract was offering.[19] Ultimately convinced that it was in his best interest to maintain his flexibility and authority, Cousins declined the offer.[20]

This is not to say that he did not stay in the public eye. The same week as the NBC debate with Cherne, Cousins produced a series of weekly syndicated radio broadcasts covering a wide variety of topics. The series came at an opportune time. On April 12, 1961, the Soviet Union succeeded in launching the first human into space, Yuri Gagarin. Three weeks later Cousins broadcast his assessment that although the Soviets clearly had proved their supremacy in space technology, this was nothing to fear. Cousins assured his radio audience that the Russians were not ideological fanatics. Khrushchev did not share Marx's belief that world revolution was necessary to achieve socialism. Cousins pointed out that "Khrushchev declared, in the interests of the Soviet Union, it is now possible to seek and achieve peaceful relations with Capitalist nations."[21]

Perhaps Cousins's most poignant radio broadcast came just weeks after the failed US-backed attempt to invade Cuba during the Bay of Pigs episode. In the *Saturday Review,* Cousins made no editorial mention of the incident at the time, although the magazine did run a feature penned by former Eisenhower advisor Arthur Larson arguing that not only had the botched coup had a terrible effect on American prestige but "the whole affair was a flagrant violation of law."[22] Cousins echoed this sentiment in his radio broadcast when he pointed out that "four years ago, we dissociated the U.S. from the action of Great Britain and France in the attack on Suez. Eisenhower declared that we could not approve in our friends that which we denounced in our foes. World law, we stressed, was binding on all nations."[23] Of course, Cousins conveniently overlooked the fact that the Bay of Pigs operation had been initiated while Eisenhower was still in office, so the implication that Eisenhower was somehow wiser than Kennedy simply does not hold up.

The *Saturday Review* was one of many US publications that battered the Kennedy administration for its actions in Cuba. The *Chicago Tribune* wrote that "the main results of the supposed Cuban 'invasion' are that . . . the United States has taken a dreadful kick in the teeth."[24] The *Wall Street Journal* described the whole episode as a "sorry mess."[25] But before President Kennedy could even fully recover from the Bay of Pigs fiasco, he would be kicked yet again.

CHAPTER 21

FLASHPOINTS

Berlin and the Congo

Shortly after Kennedy's election, Soviet premier Nikita Khrushchev began putting out feelers to the new administration. He was hoping for a summit meeting with the new leader that might allow them to reach an accord on nuclear testing, but the Bay of Pigs incident made the situation difficult. Surprisingly, though, even in his compromised state Kennedy agreed to meet Khrushchev in Vienna in early June 1961. Kennedy had prepared meticulously for the summit but proved to be no match for Khrushchev, who, believing that the Bay of Pigs episode showed Kennedy to be weak, inexperienced, and indecisive, berated him at every meeting.[1]

Tensions peaked when Khrushchev informed Kennedy that by the end of the year he was going to sign a separate peace treaty with East Germany that would end all occupation rights and cut off Western access to Berlin. The city had been a thorn in Khrushchev's side, and the time had come to remedy the problem at any cost, including, Khrushchev boasted, war.[2] Kennedy channeled his own inaugural speech in his resolve to bear any cost to defend Berlin, including nuclear war.[3] The summit ended on this ominous note. Sitting down with journalist James Reston, Kennedy described his encounters with Khrushchev as "[the] roughest thing in my life."[4] He told the reporter, "I've got a terrible problem. If [Khrushchev] thinks I'm inexperienced and have no guts, until we remove those ideas we won't get anywhere with him. So we have to act."[5]

Act, Kennedy did. On July 25, 1961, he delivered an aggressive speech in which he told the world that the United States would stand firm in its defense of Berlin. It would oppose the Soviet Union's threat to conclude a separate peace and force the Allies to withdraw even if that meant resorting to nuclear war.[6] Kennedy followed up his speech with more aggressive action meant to show Khrushchev just how serious he was. He requested an additional $3.45 billion in defense spending, increased the draft calls to allow a major expansion in the size of the army, and allocated more than $200 million to fund a civil defense initiative that would "identify and mark space in existing structures—public and private—that could be used for fall-out shelters in case of attack."[7] Khrushchev was livid when he read the speech, calling it a "preliminary declaration of war."[8] Cousins was also livid, but for a different reason.

Two weeks after Kennedy's speech Cousins declared, "Berlin: No Extermination Without Representation." Cousins viewed Kennedy's response to the Berlin crisis as going beyond just upholding American interests. He argued that neither Kennedy nor Khrushchev had the right to "engage in a war against the human race in the pursuit of [their] national aims or needs."[9] American citizens, though, were thinking less about the human race and more about their own survival. Historian Kenneth Rose points out that "nothing previously had brought nuclear war into the homes of Americans in such a literal sense as Kennedy's speech."[10] Debate erupted immediately after Kennedy's speech about how or even whether families should build bomb shelters in their homes.

The September 15, 1961, issue of *Life* magazine featured numerous designs for the average citizen's fallout shelter. It began with a message from President Kennedy imploring readers to "read and consider seriously the contents of this issue." Because they were living in "dangerous days" and because the nation was under threat of nuclear war, "we must prepare for all eventualities," he said.[11] Fifteen days later, Cousins noted that the United States and the Soviet Union were "on a collision course. . . . Each has warned the other it is prepared to use nuclear force rather than retreat." He used the current situation as a perfect example of what he had been arguing since 1945: the fallacy of nuclear deterrence. "If the deterrent idea held any water," Cousins wrote, "the Soviet [Union] would not have acted as it did in Berlin or elsewhere. Similarly, the existence of a heavy Soviet nuclear stockpile has not deterred the United States."[12]

The Kennedy administration was not interested in hearing about the possible flaw in its strategy, though. It continued to breathlessly push the idea of widespread shelter construction. Kennedy's goal was to have shelters constructed in one-quarter of all public buildings.[13] The debate over whether to build fallout shelters dominated public discussion. Between Kennedy's June speech and the end of October 1961, the *New York Times* alone published 149 articles or ads on the topic of fallout shelters, 35 in October alone.

As the crisis continued into the fall and Americans flocked to stores to stock up on canned goods and shelter supplies, people began to take a more cynical view. "Examples of apathy and fatalism were found everywhere," the *New York Times* reported in September. A young father in Detroit described fallout shelters as "utterly useless."[14] The *Saturday Review* was a key driver in fomenting this cynical—or as Cousins would claim, realistic—attitude. Beginning on October 21, 1961, Cousins published a four-part editorial series systematically dismantling the Kennedy administration's claims about both fallout shelters and the strength of the US nuclear deterrent.

To undermine the government's cheery claim that nuclear war was survivable, Cousins countered,

> Life will not be resumed as usual. Those who survive will embark upon an ordeal unlike anything the human race as a race has ever known. The supply of uncontaminated food will run out; even the rain will be poisoned. When the survivors crawl out of their holes they will not be looking at the world they knew. The crust of the earth will be burned and clotted; anything that stands,

> whether a tree or a structure, will be charred and skeletonized. There will be no communications, there will be no hospitals, there will be no institutions to attend to the needs of human society. This is what nuclear war is. No deodorizing can change that fact.[15]

Cousins was nearly unique in his ability to write about nuclear war with such evocative imagery. He had personally witnessed nuclear tests, walked the streets of a destroyed Hiroshima, and worked directly with its maimed victims. He had welcomed top atomic scientists into his home for conversations. He had been worrying about the atomic bomb and giving the issue sustained thought for the better part of fifteen years.

Time added to the furious debate when it printed an article in which a Chicago suburbanite claimed, "When I get my shelter finished I'm going to mount a machine gun at the hatch to keep the neighbors out if the bombs fall. I'm deadly serious about this."[16] The "Gun Thy Neighbor Debate" was born as Americans grappled with the moral implications of keeping their own family safe by potentially killing their friends and neighbors who had not built shelters of their own and tried to break in. In his second article in the series Cousins stated his position on the issue: "Some are now preparing their children psychologically to accept the murder of their playmates. All this goes under the heading of civil defense.... People speculate on the horrors that would be let loose by nuclear war. It is not necessary to speculate on such horrors. Some of the worst horrors are already here ... the moral insolence of those who presume to prescribe the circumstances under which it is spiritually permissible to kill one's neighbors."[17]

In the third article in the series, Cousins argued against the claim that building shelters would persuade the Soviets that the United States was not afraid to fight a nuclear war because the country was preparing to survive it. Cousins asked, "Would United States policy makers change their position on Berlin or any other vital issue if the Russians began to build underground shelters? ... Certainly not."[18] In fact, the

Russians already had a robust civil defense regime, including fallout shelters deep under Moscow.

Finally, at the end of November Cousins charged, "It is, we repeat, an act of prime irresponsibility to lead the American people to believe that 95 per cent of them can be saved in their shelters." One of the government's prime responsibilities was to keep its citizens safe from attack. But in this crisis the US government was not only marching toward war with its aggressive nuclear threats but shirking its key responsibility. "The idea that each citizen should be individually responsible for his own shelter," Cousins argued, "is as absurd and unworkable as expecting him to be responsible for his own electric supply or his own roads. Safety from attack is a government function."[19] But by the time Cousins's final installment hit the newsstands, the crisis had largely abated.

Deciding to take decisive action, Khrushchev allowed the East Germans to construct a wall cutting East Berlin off from the West. Early the morning of August 13, 1961, East German police began to seal the border. Although the building of the Berlin Wall did not end the crisis in Berlin, it did provide a relief valve for the growing tensions. Kennedy called the wall "illegal, immoral and inhumane," but he did not believe, as he told his advisors, that it was a cause for war. In a way, the wall even proved to be "a godsend" to Kennedy, according to biographer Robert Dallek.[20] It removed the pressure to act on Berlin.

While Cousins never directly commented on the wall at the time, or on the dissipation of the Berlin Crisis that followed shortly thereafter, he did, the following year, apologize to his readers. "I have become increasingly troubled," Cousins wrote, "about the extent to which I have allowed *SR* to reflect my personal interests and concerns. I have wondered whether I have gone far beyond reasonable limits in using this page as a combination reflector and magnifying system for my obsessions and preoccupations, particularly in the areas of nuclear problems and peace."[21] To help change the subject, as 1962 dawned Cousins set off on a tour of Africa, specifically to report from the Congo, which was then in the throes of a decolonization crisis and civil war.

The Congo Crisis, which broke out in 1960, shortly after the country was granted independence from Belgium, quickly descended into a civil war. This conflict also coincided with a fiscal crisis at the United Nations owing largely to unpaid assessments from France and the Soviet Union. The United Nations was in such dire financial straits that there was little support for the continuation of its peacekeeping operations in the Congo.[22] To help alleviate these money problems, in late 1961 the United States proposed getting the United Nations to issue bonds that would help finance its continued peacekeeping operations. In January 1962, Kennedy urged Congress to approve the US purchase of $200 million worth of these bonds.[23]

Cousins had maintained a special interest in the Congo after traveling there in 1957 to meet with Dr. Albert Schweitzer. With the war in the Congo showing no signs of abating, Cousins decided to build public support for the continued UN mission by informing his readers firsthand about the situation on the ground. Keeping to his word to write less about nuclear issues, while also remaining true to his own belief that the most important cause in the world was peace, in January 1962 he flew to the Congo to report on UN peacekeeping operations there. Cousins sent Kennedy an advance copy of the article he generated from this trip one month before it appeared in the *Saturday Review.* Kennedy responded a week later thanking him. "The article on the Congo was excellent," the president noted.[24]

Cousins's Congo article clearly established him as one of the few people who had on-the-ground knowledge of the situation, and his long-standing support of the United Nations made him especially valuable to the administration, which was in the midst of trying to pass the UN bond issue. Kennedy confirmed as much when he invited Cousins to join him at an Oval Office meeting to hear firsthand from Cousins about the situation in the Congo and his thoughts about the role of the United Nations there.

When Cousins arrived at the White House on March 13, he was warmly greeted by Kennedy. Cousins recalled him saying, "Hello Norman. It was very good of you to send that [Congo] letter a few weeks ago. It was much appreciated." During the meeting Cousins proceeded to give Kennedy advice on how to persuade official Washington to recognize that there was already significant public support for the United Nations. Cousins recalled telling Kennedy "that what was needed was for the President to create an affirmative, confident attitude about the U.N."[25] Cousins did his part in this regard a few months later when he published a UN-boosting editorial.[26] Cousins also wrote, at Kennedy's request, a memo containing specific recommendations on how to engage with the public on this point.[27] Kennedy was clearly impressed with both Cousins's ideas and his company, because he asked Cousins to return to the White House six weeks later—with his wife this time—to dine with him and the First Lady privately.

Cousins, laughing (*right, behind President Kennedy*), at a White House meeting, March 1962.

(PHOTO COURTESY OF CANDIS COUSINS KERNS)

The Cousins Papers at UCLA contain many boxes of green spiral-bound notebooks filled with Cousins's handwritten notes about all manner of meetings he had with prominent people. But this time, unfortunately, Cousins, normally a copious recorder of private meetings—typically even vividly describing not just what he ate and drank but the mood, the way the light came in through the windows, how the other person looked—took no notes on his dinner with the Kennedys.

McGeorge Bundy would later reveal that Kennedy was deeply pleased by his budding friendship with Cousins. "Their relationship was unusually direct and personal for a notable editor and a modern President. But I came to know that the president liked and respected Norman." Bundy also states that "whenever the president did not know Norman's current view of pressing questions at the U.N. or next steps on arms control or relations with Khrushchev, he would want to know about it."[28]

Cousins was not entirely unfamiliar with having a close working relationship with those in power. Since his first meeting with President Truman in 1946, Cousins had met with every American president and maintained close personal friendships with a number of US senators and congressmen. He was also no stranger to international political power. He won the praise of the prime minister of Japan and the premier of Poland; he personally interviewed Jawaharlal Nehru and Nikita Khrushchev and had access to the top advisors to the pope. Cousins hobnobbed with prominent Americans like Walter Lippmann, Norman Thomas, and Leo Cherne; he met and corresponded with public intellectuals like Bertrand Russell and Albert Einstein. All these connections fostered over the years made him comfortable around eminent people, but until 1962 he had never had such an intimate and sustained connection with someone as powerful as Kennedy. Nor had a US president so quickly embraced Cousins and his ideas, welcoming him into the "inner circle." Bundy notes that Cousins and Kennedy "shared a deep common concern about the search for peace. I knew also that each understood and respected the calling of the other, as not enough publicists and politicians do."[29] But despite this brief interlude in the Congo, Cousins could not resist the pull of disarmament and peace for more than a few months.

By mid-1962, with the Dartmouth Conferences continuing to build on their initial success (a second successful conference was held in the Soviet Union in 1961, and a third was scheduled in the United States for fall 1962), Cousins was certainly one of the most well informed American citizens regarding life and issues in the Soviet world. He wrote of having "had a substantial number of private discussions with Soviet citizens—professors, scientists, writers, churchmen, artists, and everyday people."[30]

Located on West 45th Street just a few blocks from Times Square in one direction and Grand Central Terminal in the other, Cousins's New York City office became a veritable pilgrimage stop for Soviet citizens passing through the United States. "The other day," Cousins noted in June 1962, "a small delegation of Soviet writers visited the offices of *Saturday Review*. . . . We chatted pleasantly about sundry matters, literary and otherwise, then got around to the number one topic: the relationship between the U.S. and the USSR in particular and the problem of peace in general."[31]

As Philip Stewart, a longtime associate of Cousins's, noted, "His primary motivation in talking to the Russians was to prevent a nuclear war, because he saw firsthand in Japan what the consequences of it were and he felt that the most important thing he could do in his life was to do whatever he could to make that less likely."[32] But despite Cousins's hard work in this field and his rapidly growing network of Soviet contacts who were also interested in working for peace, Cousins's fears of nuclear war would become very real when the Cuban Missile Crisis broke out in October 1962.

CHAPTER 22

COUSINS, *the* VATICAN, *and the* CUBAN MISSILE CRISIS

At first it might seem puzzling why Norman Cousins, a man who had spent most of his professional career as a vocal anti-nuclear campaigner, did not rush to publish an editorial in the weeks after the Cuban Missile Crisis. The crisis was a perfectly tailored example of Cousins's argument that nuclear deterrence was a fallacy, and it even reflected his 1945 prediction that with nuclear weapons in a nation's arsenal "the slightest suspicion could start all the push-buttons going."[1] Unlike many other commentators of the day, Cousins never mused about how close the world came to destruction; he never praised Kennedy's tough stance; he never admonished Khrushchev for his (according to the United States) dangerously aggressive behavior. As the world teetered on the brink of a potential nuclear showdown, Cousins remained silent. For most, the Cuban Missile Crisis was a time of grave danger. For Cousins, who was personally involved at the highest levels in ameliorating the crisis, it was a time of incredible opportunity.

Cousins was well aware of and even foresaw the dangers of nuclear weapons ever being located in Cuba. In 1960, Cousins wrote a personal letter to the editor of the *Omaha World Herald* in which he noted, "If Cuba should obtain a nuclear weapon, the security problem for the United States becomes magnified a thousand-fold."[2] While this may have been conventional thinking at the time, and while it may have been what Cousins himself believed, it was not actually true. Even Defense Secretary Robert McNamara believed that nuclear weapons stationed in Cuba did not really change the strategic balance. This was Khrushchev's thinking as well. The United States had placed nuclear weapons near the Soviet border in Europe, so placing nuclear weapons in Cuba near the American border was simply a rational response. Whether a nuclear missile had to fly for eight minutes from Cuba or thirty minutes from Russia before it hit its target in the United States, they were equally unstoppable, and the end result would be the same.[3]

The discovery of Soviet nuclear weapons on Cuban soil in October 1962 provided Cousins with a moment when he could reap the rewards of decades of hard work building a stellar reputation as a proponent of peace and anti-nuclear activism, and it gave him an opportunity to advance his peace agenda in the international realm. The crisis happened to coincide with the third Dartmouth meeting, attended not just by prominent Soviet citizens but by a top Vatican advisor as well. At a pivotal moment during the crisis Cousins used this conduit to persuade Pope John XXIII to publicly implore both Kennedy and Khrushchev to focus on peace, thus offering them a face-saving way out of the tense nuclear stalemate. In doing so, Cousins not only played a small role in helping to bring the Cuban Missile Crisis to its peaceful conclusion but also set the stage for bigger opportunities to come.

Cousins's involving the Vatican also helped to change their perception of their role in international diplomacy while also furthering his own peace agenda. Embracing Cousins's stance, the Vatican recognized that direct person-to-person dialogue *could* help reduce international tensions. The Vatican's growing trust of Cousins was reflected in an internal memo written by a top Vatican advisor informing Pope

John that Norman Cousins was "worthy of special confidence of our headquarters. He is seen by K[hrushchev] . . . as a typical leader of a new peace loving generation. . . . I have proofs that he is a very conscientious American citizen and will also be dependable for coordination of all policies."[4]

Cousins's actions during the missile crisis further cemented his reputation with both American and Soviet leaders as a man who maintained valuable political connections on both sides of the Iron Curtain. He was also seen as a man of discretion who could be trusted and relied on to handle and pass along sensitive information. It helped that he had such widespread and constructive political connections throughout the Soviet world, along with an address book full of notable Soviet friends and correspondents.

From the moment he was elected in October 1958, Pope John XXIII charted a new and unexpected course for the church he had inherited. Pope John would break from the tradition of his vocally anti-Communist predecessor, Pope Pius XII, and pursue an unexpected sort of detente with the Communist world.[5] In a report they hoped would further establish the Vatican's credibility with Khrushchev, Vatican officials stressed that "in the more than four years that have elapsed since the election of Pope John XXIII, there has been not one official statement of the Catholic Church in which the word 'communism' has been used."[6] This lack of condemnation of the Communist world was more than just a matter of political expediency or appeasement of Khrushchev. Pope John believed that the church should play a larger role in world affairs, and he recognized that antagonizing the Soviet Union as his predecessor had done would be counterproductive.

Within days of his election it was clear that John would be a new sort of pope, one who intended to position the church to address the great demands of history. "The world is starved for peace," he explained to a close advisor.[7] The pope's fresh outlook and focus on humanistic political and economic interpretations certainly would have resonated with Khrushchev's notions of peaceful coexistence. In fact, the rumor had already begun to swirl through Moscow that Pope John might be a very different kind of pope.[8]

A Belgian-born Dominican friar high in the Vatican leadership, Father Felix Morlion, was inspired by the new path the pope seemed to be pursuing. By early 1962, it was clear to Morlion that Pope John's vision could be applied to help ease the superpower conflict. "Why not investigate," he thought, "through some recognized humanitarian pacifist, if minds could be prepared on the two sides of the special political curtain to accept Pope John's mediations." [9] Morlion soon found a perfect candidate in Norman Cousins, and he traveled to New York to meet with him in March 1962.[10]

Cousins and Morlion discovered that they shared a philosophical and intellectual outlook on the world. As Morlion recalled their conversation, "[Cousins] began by expressing his preoccupation about the drift towards war. He explained that political leaders cannot stop this drift because they are too conscious of pressures. [So I asked the question,] If the men in power cannot stop the war, who can? His answer: There is Pope John."[11] Cousins recalled that "when Father Morlion began to talk about the Pope's ideas and hopes, I could feel the excitement of profound changes in the making."[12]

What most drew Morlion to Cousins was that his thinking was quite compatible with the pope's on the issues of global peace and reconciliation. Many of the pope's early encyclicals dealt with the subject of peace and gave the strong impression that Pope John was duly aware of the dangers that nuclear weapons posed to humanity. Cousins and Pope John shared the belief that the troubling dangers of nuclear weapons went beyond just physical catastrophe should a new war break out. A common theme in Cousins's writing and speeches was that since the atomic age had begun, "now man has the power to war against the uniqueness of human life.... In this sense, nuclear war will not be a war of nation against nation, but a war of man against God."[13] Pope John too understood that a nuclear war would destroy religion as well as human society.[14] In his view, those who threatened nuclear war were the enemies of God, "striving to smother and crush the seed of God's work."[15]

It was this shared moral and spiritual invocation of the need for peace that endeared Cousins to Morlion, and vice versa. During their first meeting Morlion commented to Cousins that Pope John wanted to be useful and relevant but was uncertain about how best to achieve that goal.[16] As fall 1962 approached, Cousins and Morlion continued to discuss the possibilities of both the book project and ways for the pope to get more involved in the push for world peace. They agreed to undertake a long-range program to initiate private contacts between Kennedy, Khrushchev, and Pope John. "To do this," Morlion writes, "we formed a small group of friends who shared the same convictions on the urgent need for new approaches to peace. . . . Monsignor Igino Cardinale, then head of Protocol of the Secretariat of State of His Holiness, and Cardinal Dell'Acqua, then Pro-Secretary of State, soon started giving personal advice and cooperation." Through them, Pope John was regularly informed.[17]

On October 11, some 2,240 bishops descended on Rome and gathered in St. Peter's Basilica to open the Second Vatican Council. The pope welcomed the representatives of seventy-nine nations by telling them that although this was a religious event, he hoped that it would contribute toward world peace. This notion would soon be put to the test. Since August 1962, the United States had been monitoring, with mounting concern, the increasing number of Soviet freighters steaming toward Cuba with military supplies.[18] On October 16, U-2 spy planes detected Soviet missile installations in Cuba. Kennedy waited until Monday, October 22, to announce the discovery of the missiles to the world. In a televised address to the nation that evening, Kennedy announced that there was unmistakable evidence that nuclear missiles were being prepared on the island of Cuba. Ordering a full naval quarantine of the island, Kennedy demanded that the Soviets dismantle and remove all the missiles. So important was this objective that Kennedy told the world that the United States was willing to risk a major war and would attack any Soviet ships that attempted to run the quarantine. Referring to it as a "quarantine" rather than a naval blockade (which it was) was a semantic choice to avoid the charge that the United States was committing an act of war.[19]

Kennedy's announcement of the missile discovery and his decision to quarantine shipping to Cuba reverberated around the world, not least in the halls of St. Peter's Basilica. Vatican authorities debated whether it might be prudent to call an end to the Vatican council in order to allow the delegates to return to their parishes should the unthinkable happen.[20] They decided to continue with the council. It just so happened that the third Dartmouth Conference was also under way in Andover, Massachusetts, when the news arrived. It was an extremely fruitful coincidence that Cousins found himself presiding over a meeting attended by some of Khrushchev's confidants. Cousins recalled the tension in the room as both Soviets and Americans crowded around a small television to watch the president's address to the nation. A member of the Soviet delegation denounced Kennedy's actions as aggressive, arrogant, and illegal. The Soviet delegates retreated to a private room to discuss whether they should immediately return to the Soviet Union lest they find themselves in an enemy nation if a war broke out, but ultimately they decided to stay and continue the conference.[21]

In this moment it was Norman Cousins who took the first concrete step toward involving the pope and spurring Vatican diplomacy into action. Through a previous arrangement, Father Morlion had arrived at Andover a few days earlier to observe the Dartmouth Conference, and on Wednesday, October 24, his presence proved to be a stroke of luck. Knowing that the father maintained close ties with the Vatican, Cousins telephoned Morlion early that morning to ask if he thought there might be any possibility of Pope John making "a very special appeal for restraint on all sides."[22] Morlion placed a call to Rome at 4:00 p.m. (Rome time) and put his Vatican "brain trust" into action by getting in touch with Monsignor Cardinale, who immediately informed Morlion that the pope had already taken a first step on his own.[23]

That very day, at the end of his weekly audience, the pope added a thinly veiled appeal to the "good will of statesmen." Immediately following this he delivered an expanded message containing the same sentiment to the Soviet Embassy in Rome for transmission to Moscow.[24] Cardinale informed Morlion of these initial measures during their phone call, in addition to telling him that the pope was "planning a most solemn and energetic appeal for diplomacy, restraint, and peace to be made the next day."[25]

Members of the pope's brain trust, Morlion, Cousins, Cardinale, and Dell'Acqua, began to discuss what specifically the pope's message should say. The group recognized that "it would be better for both powers, and for the whole world, if a face-saving procedure were found to make it easier for the Soviets to call back the missile-laden ships." Hoping that the pope's long-standing avoidance of anti-Communist statements had gained the Vatican some credit with the Kremlin, they considered whether taking a sympathetic tone toward Khrushchev's predicament might have a positive effect. "What if the universally heard voice from the Vatican," Morlion asked, "were to change its tune and invite others to understand and esteem the new kind of Soviet leadership? [After all,] they had dared to dissociate themselves from the madly criminal leadership of Stalin." Morlion argued that the Soviets would respond positively if Pope John used his power of persuasion to "call on all people of goodwill to break the circle of distrust and contempt."[26]

After debating this point, the brain trust decided that the "evil image" the world held of the Soviet Union could not be so easily changed. Not helping the situation was the fact that Khrushchev, by trying to sneak the missiles into Cuba, had already created a new phase of distrust and isolation. Cardinale, who was the resident expert in diplomatic issues, confided to Morlion that while the pope was in favor of taking some sort of public action, he was also quite concerned about the political consequences in the United States should he make an independent call for peace. Cardinale explained that Pope John did not want to offend President Kennedy.[27]

Pope John's concerns about offending the US president were more than reasonable. During John F. Kennedy's campaign for president much had been made of his Catholicism and his possible susceptibility to Vatican influence. To combat any misconceptions, he had devoted an entire campaign speech to the issue of papal influence on his decision making should he be elected president. He made it clear that no Catholic prelate would ever tell him how to act. "I believe in an America," Kennedy said, "where no public official either requests or accepts instructions on public policy from the Pope . . . where no religious body seeks to impose its will directly or indirectly upon the general populace or the public acts of its officials."[28] Despite this, as president Kennedy still needed to tread lightly whenever the Vatican was involved.

With Kennedy's politically sensitive religion issue in mind, Morlion asked if it might help the pope's work if they could gain Kennedy's support for a papal statement. Cardinale gave permission for Morlion to inform the White House, as a matter of courtesy, of a forthcoming appeal from the Vatican.[29] Morlion waited as Cousins telephoned the White House and spoke to Kennedy's special counsel and primary speechwriter Theodore Sorensen, informing him of the pope's intentions. Meanwhile, Cousins recognized that many of the prominent Soviet figures attending the Dartmouth Conference had close ties with the Kremlin, most notably the leading Soviet journalist and friend of Nikita Khrushchev, Yuri Zhukov. Cousins noticed that Zhukov, who was described by Kennedy's press secretary, Pierre Salinger, as a "rather hard line cooperator of [Khrushchev]," was in constant contact with Moscow during the week.[30]

It is unclear how Zhukov was able to maintain this alleged "constant contact" with Moscow. Placing telephone calls from the United States to the Soviet Union was extremely difficult. Not even the White House got a direct phone line to the Kremlin until the following year.

As late as the 1980s, the Soviets used a slow, primitive, manual telephone switching system allegedly with only six operators in Moscow Central, who handled all US phone traffic manually.[31] Regardless, Cousins claims that it was through this channel that he learned that Premier Khrushchev would be open to a public message of restraint from the pope.[32]

Back at the White House, Sorensen confirmed to Cousins that the president would welcome any initiative that might help prevent an escalation of the crisis, but upon hearing that the pope intended to call for an immediate withdrawal of the Soviet shipping and the American blockade, Sorensen could not be encouraging about Pope John's specific proposal. Sorensen, attempting to shape the pope's statement, claimed that "the issue was not so much the shipping but the presence of Russian missiles on Cuban soil. Those missiles had to be removed—and soon—if the consequences of the crisis were to be averted."[33]

With this new information from the White House, Morlion telephoned the Vatican at 10:00 p.m. Rome time that same day. Mindful of Kennedy's request, the pope was asked to "delete any reference to any immediate abandonment by the United States of its blockade; to confine himself to a general plea for peace."[34] After relaying the message about the White House's concern, Cardinale explained to Morlion that the matter had been discussed and the pope would not, in fact, make any concrete proposals for peace, but he might agree to arbitrate between the two countries if asked, even if asked secretly, as long as it was an official request.[35]

After Morlion ended the call, the pope worked late into the evening with his advisor Angelo Dell'Acqua to prepare his statement, retreating from time to time to his private chapel to pray. Pope John's message was broadcast over Vatican Radio the afternoon of Thursday, October 25. In his message he asked "heads of state not to remain insensitive to the cry of humanity. . . . Let them do all that is in their power to have peace. . . . Let them continue to negotiate."[36] To the Vatican, the biggest indicator that the message was positively received was that the pope's statement appeared in the international news section of *Pravda*.[37] This was seen as a very significant development, indicating that the pope's message had had at least some effect on Khrushchev.[38] Although both Kennedy and Khrushchev welcomed the pope's message, neither leader made an attempt to respond directly to the Vatican at the time.

Pope John's major involvement in world affairs during the missile crisis did, in fact, have a deep impact on both Khrushchev and Kennedy despite their reluctance to say so publicly. That December, Cousins would have a rare personal meeting with Khrushchev in Moscow (detailed in the next chapter), during which, according to Cousins, Khrushchev "volunteered the remark that Pope John's appeal during the missile crisis had carried considerable weight in his thinking. In fact, he said, it was the first ray of light in the fast-developing darkness."[39] Going beyond just the missile crisis, Khrushchev gave the pope much credit for his tireless work for peace. Cousins claimed that Khrushchev had remarked that "if by a miracle the world could be spared a nuclear war the Pope would deserve much credit."[40] Cousins was later told by Secretary of State Dean Rusk "that [President Kennedy] had informed him about the importance and success of [Pope John's] action for peace."[41] An internal White House memo confirms that the Kennedy administration recognized that "Pope John was making serious attempts to appeal to all the leaders of the world to settle their problems peacefully."[42]

It is clear that to this point the Vatican's entry into public diplomacy during the crisis had been initiated largely by Cousins's request that the pope make a public statement. Although the pope's message itself was crafted within the confines of the Vatican, the scaffolding to support this diplomatic initiative had been constructed in the United States by Cousins and Morlion, with Vatican authorities reacting to information relayed to them through this channel. The contact Cousins opened to the White House helped put the pope more at ease about getting directly involved after receiving the positive response from the Kennedy administration.

As the crisis continued into Friday morning, aside from the publication of the pope's radio address in *Pravda*, whether or not the pope's message had any deeper effect on the situation was still unknown. Back in Andover, however, as the Dartmouth Conference convened for another day of meetings, Zhukov pulled Cousins aside and asked, "If Khrushchev should make an offer to withdraw the [missiles], wouldn't President Kennedy crow about this victory and be tempted to take more aggressive action against the Soviet Union?" Cousins replied that "he felt confident the President would not crow about such a victory or would he do anything to humiliate the Soviet Union; that the President was always a firm but reasonable man."[43]

Either a very prescient Zhukov raised these concerns on his own initiative or in his many contacts with Moscow he was prompted by higher-ups to gauge the Americans' openness to this gambit. Khrushchev's son Sergei explained regarding these types of "back-door channels" during the missile crisis that it had not mattered whether they were back- or front-door channels; Khrushchev had been behind all the doors.[44] Since Zhukov's concerns closely mirror the proposal Khrushchev was then working on, it is reasonable to assume that the questions he posed to Cousins (whom the Soviets knew was in direct contact with the White House) had been planted by the Kremlin to gauge the US reaction. Cousins himself certainly saw this as a direct message from the Kremlin, later saying that Andover had become a sort of clearinghouse between the two sides.[45]

Back in Moscow, Khrushchev had already discussed his conciliatory proposal with the Soviet leadership and was in the midst of penning an offer to Kennedy that signaled a shift in the Soviet position on the crisis. The letter in which he offered to withdraw Soviet military forces from Cuba in exchange for a US non-invasion pledge was sent to the American Embassy in Moscow on Friday at 5:00 p.m. Moscow time, 10:00 a.m. in Washington.[46] This letter marked the first step back from the thirteen days of highest tensions. But just as the Kennedy administration was gathering to discuss the US reply to Khrushchev's first letter, a second one arrived changing the terms and requiring the United States to also remove its nuclear missiles from Turkey. Some in the Kennedy administration suspected that a coup had just taken place, ousting Khrushchev and replacing him with advocates of a harder line.[47] The Executive Committee decided, publicly at least, to ignore the second letter and send a positive reply to the terms outlined in Khrushchev's first letter. Privately, Kennedy also accepted the terms to remove the missiles from Turkey in exchange for Khrushchev's silence and a delay so that the two issues did not appear to be linked. While it was not all that Khrushchev had asked for in his second letter, it met the minimum terms he was willing to accept, and he replied positively on October 28, agreeing to remove the Soviet missiles.[48] Although the world breathed a sigh of relief at this news, the crisis actually continued for three more weeks, until Khrushchev removed the Soviets' nuclear-capable IL-28 bombers from the island as well, which he did on November 20, thus fully ending the crisis.[49]

But in addition to marking the end of the most dangerous part of the crisis, the contents of the letter further reveal the impact of Pope John's involvement.[50] During a private meeting with Zhukov, Morlion made clear that if any future cooperation with the Vatican was to be fruitful, the Soviet government needed to make some gesture to show that it recognized and respected the *spiritual* basis of life. This request clearly made its way directly to Khrushchev. On the third page of his letter to Kennedy, Khrushchev wrote, "Our people are enjoying the fruits of their peaceful labor. They have achieved tremendous success since the October Revolution, and created the greatest material, *spiritual*, and cultural values."[51] That the word *spiritual* appeared in the letter prompted the Vatican to consider this a clear indication of the Kremlin's willingness to pursue further discussions.[52]

Although the active crisis ended with a Radio Moscow announcement that the Soviet Union had accepted a negotiated end to the situation in Cuba, Morlion requested a private meeting with Zhukov and another delegate, journalist Grigory Shumeiko. Morlion, thinking beyond just the crisis of the moment, wanted to use this opportunity to spark an era of stronger contacts between the Soviet Union and the Vatican. Morlion pressed the Soviets to ask Khrushchev to meet privately with Cousins at a future date "to inform him further on what he would know through private contacts with [Pope John]." Evasive at first, Zhukov and Shumeiko soon admitted that they genuinely trusted Cousins, but they requested more details about sending Cousins to meet with Khrushchev, asking how Morlion expected to get Cousins into the country in an apolitical manner. Morlion explained that Cousins was widely known as a "literary man, editor of a cultural review, and that it would not be difficult to have him invited by some literary circle or review." Shumeiko agreed that this could be arranged.[53]

Ultimately, it was Cousins's actions during the Cuban Missile Crisis that won him notice at the highest levels of the Kennedy administration as someone who had deep and effective connections in Moscow. It would also bring him to the attention of the Soviet leadership, a fact that would pay dividends going forward.

CHAPTER 23

THE CRISIS ABATES *but* CONTACTS CONTINUE

Although Pope John was not needed to arbitrate a peaceful end to the Cuban Missile Crisis, following its resolution he was informed of Father Morlion's secret conversations with the Soviets and the positive opening they seemed to provide, leading to Khrushchev's inclusion of *spiritual* in his letter to Kennedy.[1] The pope had already been briefed on Cousins's role in connecting with the White House, and he was impressed with Cousins's verve.[2] Seeing that both the Vatican's official and unofficial attempts to resolve the conflict were met with at least some success, Pope John authorized further explorations of this sort. He told Morlion, "If the Heads of the Great Powers should again come to face a situation where it is difficult for them politically to avoid the use of military instruments, they can be informed that the Holy See would agree to be intermediary for such means of peaceful coexistence that would be required by common sense and sound reason."[3] Cousins later wrote that "this approach was consistent with Pope John's determination, in light of the horror of the Cuban crisis, to do what he could toward helping to free the world's people from the threat of a nuclear holocaust."[4]

The larger impact of this episode, however, was that it opened a door to the Kremlin that many within the Vatican were anxious to exploit. During the private meetings at Dartmouth, Zhukov had "elicited the hope that it might be possible to make a step forward with Khrushchev."[5] Not wanting to squander this opportunity, on October 30 Cousins called the White House to offer a debriefing of what had transpired in Andover. He spoke to Pierre Salinger and informed the press secretary of some of the other pieces of information he had gleaned from the Russians during the week, including that the Russians had a strong positive impression of Kennedy advisor and chief disarmament negotiator John McCloy. They were "willing to put anything McCloy says in the bank," he told Salinger.[6]

Five days later, on November 5, Cousins received Soviet journalist Grigory Shumeiko at his home in Connecticut to discuss at length the details of arranging a personal meeting with Khrushchev.[7] As it turned out, Khrushchev was also eager to meet with Cousins. Khrushchev was quite familiar with Cousins's efforts at improving Soviet-American relations. According to historians Aleksandr Fursenko and Tim Naftali, "[Khrushchev] had received, through the KGB, direct reports from Soviet participants at transnational conferences that Cousins had sponsored."[8] In addition, Khrushchev had previously written Cousins in February 1961 in support of SANE's activities. "I hope that the activity of your committee directed toward the strengthening of the world peace, will bring real fruits," he had written encouragingly.[9] This was not out of character for Khrushchev, who had a habit of embracing peace activists from the non-Communist world, a fact that would soon work greatly in Cousins's favor.[10]

Just days after this meeting, Cousins received a telephone call from Soviet ambassador Anatoly Dobrynin informing him that the proposed meeting had been approved and that December 14 was the date that he suggested Cousins plan on being in Moscow to meet with Khrushchev. Cousins quickly booked a flight to Moscow via Rome. Meanwhile, informed that the proposed Khrushchev meeting had been approved, Morlion told Cousins that members of the Vatican Council had "unanimously confirmed" that they would explore the benefits of private contacts with the Soviet Union.[11]

Keeping the White House in the loop regarding these developments, Cousins had lunch on November 16 with Salinger, who told him that the administration considered this a "very sensitive" matter.[12] Cousins was asked back to the White House the following week to meet personally with Kennedy before his trip. During their Oval Office meeting, Kennedy explained what he hoped Cousins would relay to Khrushchev on his behalf. Cousins recalls Kennedy telling him,

> I don't know if the matter of American-Soviet relationships will come up. But if it does, [Khrushchev] will probably say something about his desire to reduce tensions, but will make it appear there's no reciprocal interest by the United States. It is important that he be corrected on this score. I'm not sure Khrushchev knows this, but I don't think there's any man in American politics who's more eager than I am to put Cold War animosities behind us and get down to the hard business of building friendly relations.[13]

Although Cousins by this point in his life was extremely well traveled and had much experience working with prominent civilian and government figures, he admitted that he could not help but feel a little humbled and apprehensive about the mission he was about to embark on. He was being asked to be the personal liaison to three of the most powerful men in the world.

Cousins's self-proclaimed humility obscures the fact that he had spent the past two decades slowly building his credentials with successive US administrations; ingratiating himself with foreign governments and peoples through his humanitarian missions; building the *Saturday Review* into a respected voice in international affairs; working tirelessly to establish prominent foreign contacts; leading international peace campaigns such as SANE; recruiting prominent figures like Albert Schweitzer and Dwight Eisenhower to advise him and spread his ideas; and intending to put $1 million of his own money into buying influence in the realm of peace education and promotion. In fact, Cousins's close connection to the Cuban Missile Crisis would continue into 1968. A twenty-five-thousand-word article was found in Robert Kennedy's personal effects after his assassination. It was a manuscript he was working on based on his detailed notes of the crisis. Cousins, through his position at the McCall Corporation, purchased the manuscript for $1 million—the largest amount ever paid for such material.[14] In October 1968, the *Saturday Review* ran excerpts under the title "Lessons of the Cuban Missile Crisis," and later McCall would publish the bestselling book *Thirteen Days: A Memoir of the Cuban Missile Crisis.*[15]

It was no accident that Cousins now sat in the Oval Office briefing the most powerful man in the world about his upcoming trip to see the second most powerful man in the world. All his previous groundwork had put him in this situation. His being there was a direct manifestation of his belief that if statesmen were failing to lead the world to peace and moral justice, then it was up to the private citizen to lead the statesmen. Cousins saw his and other citizens' role as "helping to fashion a foreign policy consistent with the larger needs of the human community."[16] To Cousins, the cause of establishing open and effective dialogue with the Soviet Union was the most meaningful cause of all because it would lead, he hoped, to a lessening of dangerous tensions.

With Kennedy briefed, Cousins departed for Rome on December 1 on a rather tedious journey with multiple layovers. On arriving in Italy, he was greeted by Father Morlion and taken to the Vatican for the first time. The pope had sent over (through Morlion) a seven-point agenda, which the Vatican expected Cousins to propose to Khrushchev. The ambitious program included complete disarmament; having the Soviet Union recognize religious rights and allow the distribution of religious texts; releasing all religious prisoners; establishing a permanent Soviet contact in Rome; hosting a conference recognizing peaceful coexistence in the ideological (and religious) realms, and, finally, having Khrushchev agree to declare 1963 the International

Geo-Spiritual Year, in which all countries would focus on humanistic efforts to assist underdeveloped nations. Most importantly, capitalizing on the pope's successful intervention during the Cuban Missile Crisis, the Vatican hoped to greatly increase its own importance in international affairs. Pope John wanted Cousins to stress with Khrushchev the fact that "if the Heads of the Great Powers should again come to face a situation where it is difficult for them politically to avoid the use of military instruments . . . the Holy See would agree to be intermediary for such means of peaceful coexistence."[17]

While Cousins agreed to discuss the Vatican's ambitious agenda with Khrushchev, he also advised that the Vatican needed to ask Khrushchev for a specific thing that would serve as a gesture of his genuine interest in better relations. In debating what to ask for, Cardinal Bea complained that many members of the religious community had been imprisoned inside the Soviet Union. "It would be a most favorable augury if at least one of them could be released," he stated. Bea posited that the Ukrainian bishop Josyf Slipyj would be the best candidate because of his advanced age and his eighteen-year imprisonment. The council agreed. Carrying the name of Bishop Slipyj as his "ask," Cousins departed early the next morning for Moscow.[18]

As soon as Cousins arrived in Moscow, he got together with his new friends Zhukov and Shumeiko, both of whom helped prepare him for his meeting with the premier. They warned Cousins that when meeting with Khrushchev everything depended on the first two minutes. "If I was not able to raise his interest immediately," Cousins wrote, "he would soon find an opportunity to send me away."[19] He also spent hours practicing with his Russian translator to ensure that no part of his meaning would be lost in translation.[20]

The next morning Cousins received an unprecedented invitation to attend the meeting of the Supreme Soviet at which Khrushchev was to discuss the Cuban Missile Crisis.[21] Cousins took his seat in the chamber, one of the few American civilians ever welcomed as a guest of the Supreme Soviet. Khrushchev, who was being accused of appeasing the United States, took to the podium and spoke of the tremendous pressure on him. There was considerable conflict between Khrushchev and high-ranking Soviet officials over a number of issues at the time. He had alienated some with his post-Stalinist reforms and what some saw as his erratic form of leadership. He made countless efforts, not universally accepted by the Council of Ministers, to support peaceful coexistence with capitalist countries.

Since the beginning of the year the Chinese had levied withering attacks against Khrushchev. China was ideologically opposed to making agreements with the United States, especially nuclear agreements, not least because it was pursuing a nuclear device of its own at the time. Khrushchev was intent on proving to the Chinese that his policy of peaceful coexistence would bring benefits, but the Chinese continued to point to his missile crisis reversals as a sign of weakness.[22] In speaking to the Presidium, Khrushchev defended himself by saying, according to Cousins, that "he and Kennedy had a special responsibility whatever anyone else might say—to anticipate what the consequences of a war would be—and he was grateful that he had been able to work it out with President Kennedy and looked forward to taking those measures that would lessen world tensions."[23] Khrushchev clearly had invited Cousins to witness this speech in order to set the tone for their subsequent discussion and to illustrate that he was, in fact, under siege from all sides.

The following day, December 14, Cousins got his chance to sit down with Khrushchev in his Kremlin office. As the meeting began, Cousins noted that Khrushchev was "relaxed, optimistic, confident."[24] Cousins used Zhukov's warning to his advantage and reported that upon entering the room "I told him immediately that his friends warned me that I would have to tremble if I did not give a good impression within the first two minutes. Khrushchev laughed."[25] Cousins opened the conversation by stressing that he was simply a private citizen not traveling under any official auspices but that he had come to certain conclusions that he wished to share with Khrushchev. Khrushchev jokingly chided that he knew exactly who Norman Cousins was: every Soviet who had had any contact with him (through the Dartmouth Conferences) "speaks now well to me about America. Do you know what you have done? You have subverted my nation!" But Khrushchev also admitted that through Dartmouth he could "see that real work is done for peace."[26]

The conversation soon shifted to the topic of the Vatican, which was what Cousins had come to discuss. Khrushchev stressed that while he and the pope might have divergent views on many questions, they were united by their wish for peace. Cousins raised the point that Vatican leaders were looking for a gesture of goodwill that would prove that the Soviet Union was truly serious about improved relations. In that vein, the pope hoped Khrushchev might consider releasing Bishop Slipyj. Khrushchev claimed that he was quite familiar with Bishop Slipyj's case—he remembered his arrest—and he promised to look into the matter. Khrushchev also agreed to send an ambassador to the Vatican for further discussions about opening official communications between the Vatican and the Soviet Union.

Cousins need not have worried about not impressing Khrushchev within the first two minutes. Their meeting, originally scheduled for two hours, stretched to three hours and fifteen minutes. Before Cousins left the Kremlin, Khrushchev gave him handwritten cards to both Kennedy and the pope and instructed Cousins to deliver them personally upon his return. The note to Pope John wished him "good health and strength for your abiding quest for the peace and happiness and well-being of all mankind." Concluding the meeting, Cousins rushed to send back to Rome an "open" telegram (not in code) that he hoped the Soviet monitors would intercept and pass along to Khrushchev. It read, "Mission Completely Accomplished."[27]

Cousins flew back to Rome on December 17 to debrief the Vatican on what had ensued in Moscow. Pope John welcomed him into his private quarters for a personal meeting. Cousins observed that despite the pope's clearly failing health (he would die of stomach cancer six months later), he was determined to see this unique opportunity to engage with the Soviet Union through in whatever time he had remaining. "World peace is mankind's greatest need," Pope John told Cousins. "I am old but I will do what I can in the time I have. . . . Much depends now on keeping open and strengthening all possible lines of communication." Pope John also revealed that he was pleased that his missile crisis appeal had been given prominent attention inside the Soviet Union. Concluding the meeting, the grateful pope presented Cousins with his personal medallion in recognition of what Cousins had attempted to do for Bishop Slipyj, along with an ancient icon for him to personally carry back to America and present to President Kennedy with the pope's blessing.[28]

After the fortuitous events of the past days and weeks, as Cousins flew back across the Atlantic he wondered what he would have thought many years earlier if he had been told that in due course he would have met with both the chairman of the Soviet Union and the pope and now would be on his way back to the White House to deliver to the president of the United States his analysis of the international political situation as well as the ancient icon from the pope.[29]

Immediately upon his return to New York, Cousins penned a letter to Khrushchev on behalf of Pope John, thanking him for the opportunity to meet, as well as recognizing his kind words about the pope.[30] A few weeks passed before Cousins received an unexpected phone call from the Soviet Embassy in Washington on January 18, 1963. An aide to Ambassador Dobrynin explained to Cousins that the ambassador was desirous of making his personal acquaintance, and he invited Cousins to come down to Washington to have lunch at the Soviet Embassy. Traveling to the capital on January 24, Cousins arrived for lunch at the embassy, where he soon joined Dobrynin in his private dining room at a table set for two. Given that this was his first time meeting the ambassador, the ever-observant Cousins made sure to note that "the Ambassador is a tall, well-built man who appears to be in his mid-fifties. He is informal and pleasant of countenance. He speaks idiomatic English; he has the relaxed, friendly manner that is associated with Americans."[31]

Dobrynin unfolded handwritten notes that he had made during a recent conversation with Khrushchev. The ambassador soon confirmed what Cousins had hoped to hear: Khrushchev had agreed to release Bishop Slipyj. "The Chairman has undertaken this action," Dobrynin explained, "in the spirit of his conversation with you, in which the importance of strengthening the peace was recognized." Adding to Khrushchev's message, Dobrynin went on to explain that he personally was also pleased with these developments that Cousins set in motion because they opened the door for a future widening of the possibilities of peace. The ambassador stressed his convictions that "while the world was still a long way from a firm peace, positive things were now in motion." Dobrynin asked Cousins what his next steps would be now that the lines of communications were open. Cousins replied that he hoped to use these lines to explore other constructive new possibilities.[32] The Soviets were not the only ones who took notice of Cousins's activities. The highest levels of the Kennedy administration were paying attention too. Cousins made sure that his trip to talk to Khrushchev had a dual purpose. The Vatican's request to explore freedom of religion and the opening of relations was secondary to serving his primary goal of pressing Khrushchev on the issue of a nuclear test ban treaty that had been in the works since the Eisenhower administration. To Cousins, the missile crisis made it all the more imperative that some form of nuclear treaty be signed even if a test ban served just as a first step. Cousins was serious when he told Ambassador Dobrynin that he intended to use the newly opened channel to pursue constructive new possibilities. Within a month, Cousins was asked to undertake a much more crucial citizen diplomacy mission on behalf of the Kennedy administration.

CHAPTER 24

THE BREAKTHROUGH *to the* LIMITED NUCLEAR TEST BAN TREATY

The experience of the Cuban Missile Crisis deeply affected both US president John F. Kennedy and Soviet premier Nikita Khrushchev by illustrating in no uncertain terms how rapidly a nuclear crisis could escalate beyond their ability to control it. Both men privately acknowledged how close they had come to war and resolved to take steps to reduce the Cold War tensions. The eight-month period between the Cuban Missile Crisis in October 1962 and the signing of the Limited Nuclear Test Ban Treaty (LTBT) in July 1963 witnessed one of the largest pendulum swings in attitudes of the entire Cold War period. Kennedy and Khrushchev went from proverbially staring each other down—fingers on the nuclear button, poised to launch the world into nuclear war—to coming together to sign what historian and political scientist Matthew Evangelista calls "the first significant agreement of the nuclear age."[1]

The narrative of how the test ban was achieved is one of the most studied episodes in Cold War diplomacy. It is clear that Kennedy was a key driving force behind the treaty and that without his determination the treaty would never have succeeded. However, Norman Cousins intervened at a pivotal moment to reenergize both leaders. His actions almost certainly kept the treaty from collapsing. Cousins was not a direct participant in the negotiations, but he served as a courier, meeting with the two leaders and delivering messages from one to the other. Cousins used his unique position and direct access to both Kennedy and Khrushchev to influence their thinking and thus the outcome of the LTBT, but both leaders also used Cousins to quietly further their own agendas through "unofficial channels." Most dramatically, it was Cousins who persuaded Kennedy to deliver the now-famous American University speech, and then he wrote the first draft.

Cousins revealed some details of his participation in the LTBT discussions in his 1972 memoir of the events, *The Improbable Triumvirate.*[2] However, with the benefit of hindsight, objective distance, and newly declassified government documents, we can now see that Cousins's memoir of his participation in these events understates his own significance. Cousins humbly referred to his involvement as "hardly more than an asterisk in history."[3] It was much more than that.

For anti-nuclear activists like Cousins, who were pushing for a nuclear test ban, Kennedy's election was a mixed sign. As a young senator Kennedy had strongly advocated for a nuclear test ban.[4] Yet, during the election campaign he had excoriated President Eisenhower over the (nonexistent) "missile gap," charging that the United States was falling behind in the production of nuclear missiles. While many of Kennedy's top advisors (including Dean Rusk, Jerome Wiesner, and Arthur Schlesinger) favored disarmament, which was what the Soviets were calling for, Kennedy himself had little interest in the topic and dismissed the idea as impossible to achieve.[5] Still, Kennedy believed that nuclear war was a grave threat, and he especially disagreed with Eisenhower's New Look defense policy, which relied on massive nuclear retaliation to deter Soviet aggression. Kennedy thought that a hair-trigger nuclear response to *any* Soviet aggression was irresponsible and dangerous, and he sought a more appropriate and flexible policy.[6] However,

Kennedy's personal beliefs did not necessarily correlate with his public belligerence and aggressive international actions.

The ill-fated Bay of Pigs invasion cast a pall over Kennedy's first summit meeting with Khrushchev, in Vienna in April 1961. The heated discussions that ensued in Vienna led to one of the tensest summers of the Cold War. Khrushchev, already under pressure from his military advisors to respond to the US provocations, chose to break the three-year-old nuclear testing moratorium by launching a Soviet nuclear test series on September 1, 1961. Contributing to Khrushchev's decision to test was the fact that France had recently tested a nuclear bomb of its own. In Khrushchev's view, "the West" had broken the pact first.[7] Under immense pressure from Congress, the Pentagon, and the American public, Kennedy ordered the resumption of US nuclear testing two weeks later. In order to capitalize on the negative propaganda directed toward the Soviet Union, the United States stopped short of atmospheric testing at first, authorizing only the type of underground tests that limited the amount of radiation entering the atmosphere.

Perhaps hoping to foster goodwill with the new administration, Cousins waited two months to respond to this turn of events. In an uncharacteristically subdued editorial, he wrote that Americans should be grateful "that our government so far has abstained from following the monstrous example of the Soviet Union in testing atmospherically." But Cousins also issued an open warning that he would "split the sky" with his indignation should the Kennedy administration decide to launch atmospheric tests.[8]

The majority of the American people reacted to the resumption of US nuclear tests with support rather than indignation. A July Gallup poll found that Americans supported Kennedy's decision by more than two to one.[9] The Soviets only increased tensions when they detonated the most powerful nuclear explosion in history on October 30, 1961. In the face of mounting military pressure against falling behind the Soviets in nuclear technology, Kennedy ordered the resumption of atmospheric testing in April 1962. In this climate of rapidly accelerating nuclear tests the prospect for achieving a test ban seemed dim.

Throughout the fall of 1961 and the spring of 1962, SANE was extremely active in campaigning against nuclear tests, but Cousins himself was beginning to withdraw from the scene. He did not "split the sky with his indignation" as he had warned. Compared with his editorials of earlier years, the current ones were mostly silent on the issue of the test resumption, and in March 1962 Cousins informed his readers why when he wrote about his concern that the *Saturday Review* was devoting too much space to his own interest in nuclear issues.[10]

This was becoming a running theme with Cousins. He would become fixated on an issue, "flooding the zone" with editorials and public talks, and then becoming self-conscious about the extent to which the *Saturday Review* was an extension of his own beliefs. His retreats, though, do not seem to have been in response to an outpouring of reader annoyance. The "angry" letters arriving at his office were always few and far between. In fact, Cousins seemed to enjoy crafting thoughtful responses to readers who had a bone to pick with him. Positive notes typically received a response of just a few lines typed by his secretary, if they got one at all. But over the years Cousins frequently replied personally to readers who took him to task. He seemed to relish it. Candis remembers that her "father really liked to have friendships with people who disagreed with him." "I believe," she noted, "that my father knew that if he only spoke to the choir, he would be missing the chance to further develop his rhetorical flourishes. After all, he spent his adult life crafting a single message: rather than responding with force or violence, it is serious, committed dialogue between people of conflicting ideas and interests that holds the promise of saving this world from nuclear disaster."[11]

But in March 1962, deeply dismayed by the resumption of nuclear testing and his apparent inability to have an effect on stopping it despite his decade-long campaign, Cousins appeared to be giving up. Four days after writing that he would refrain from discussing nuclear issues on the editorial page, he resigned as the cochairman of SANE. In a letter to the board, he wrote that the cochairman "should be in a position to represent the organization effectively and speak for it before official bodies." Cousins believed this was something he could no longer do without also giving up the *Saturday Review*. Paradoxically, although he had just publicly announced his intentions to temper his anti-nuclear position in the magazine, he also told SANE that "there is something to be said for having a national journal which takes a strong position on questions related to effective disarmament and an organized peace under law. In any event, it becomes important for each of us to maximize his efforts. This I believe I can best do through the Saturday Review and through my writing. . . . I am resigning, therefore, as co-chairman."[12]

On the surface it appears that dismayed by what seemed to be the receding prospects for a nuclear test ban, Cousins had decided to pull back on his efforts to vocally promote the anti-nuclear agenda. The test ban that he had been advocating for more than a decade seemed to be dissolving before his eyes as both nations ratcheted up the tensions by engaging in a near call and response of nuclear tests. But there was more to it than that. Behind the scenes Cousins was also juggling other important developments.

Cousins had recently been invited to meet with and advise Kennedy, a meeting that was scheduled for just days after he dated his resignation from SANE. Perhaps he felt that with direct presidential access he did not need to rely as heavily on the lobby organization to attempt to influence government policy. In fact, being associated with it could be a liability. Cousins's resignation letter hinted that being a cochairman of SANE made him less effective in his other endeavors.[13] Cousins also recognized the impact that his private behind-the-scenes diplomacy had had during the missile crisis. Given his recent experiences and his growing political connections, it is possible that Cousins made the calculation to focus more on engaging directly with those who held political power instead of levying pressure on policymakers from the outside by fomenting public-opinion pressures as he had successfully done in the past.

To succeed with this new approach, he would have to tame his voice on the editorial page and disassociate himself from the politically divisive single-issue campaign that SANE was running. This reorientation of his efforts proved to be a prescient decision. Kennedy's national security advisor, McGeorge Bundy, would later remark, "The kind of persuasion we need now has to come from people who are not readily identified with causes."[14] Regardless of his motivations, it is clear that for the first time in his career, in order to further a cause he felt strongly about, Cousins chose to be quiet rather than go public. The choice paid dividends.

In the summer of 1962, Soviet, British, and American negotiators were hard at work in Geneva hammering out the specific terms of a possible nuclear test ban treaty. What was holding them back was the question of how many on-site inspections to allow. Should a country decide to cheat on the treaty, atmospheric tests would be easily detectable through radiation monitors around the globe, but detecting underground tests was difficult. A small-scale nuclear test was indistinguishable from a small earthquake without visual inspection. If instruments detected something, the country under suspicion could nefariously claim that a suspected test had actually been an earthquake. The United States might risk wasting one of its limited number of inspections only to discover that it really had been just an earthquake. During the Eisenhower administration the number of inspections demanded started off at one hundred per year. According to science advisor James Killian, this number would provide a "high probability of catching any violations."[15] One hundred inspections was a complete nonstarter for Khrushchev, who was convinced that the United States would use inspections as a cover for espionage.[16]

By 1962 the United States had reduced its demand to twenty on-site inspections per year. Khrushchev had vacillated on the issue of inspections over the preceding months, at times agreeing to a small number of inspections, while at other times refusing any inspections at all, such as when he stated that "we shall not accept inspection, this I say to you unequivocally and frankly."[17] Although he was concerned about US espionage, Khrushchev had another reason to reject inspections. He would later write in his memoirs that if he had let inspectors in, "they would have discovered that we were in a relatively weak position."[18] With both sides unable or unwilling to move on this point, the negotiations stalled.

The Cuban Missile Crisis erupted in October 1962, before any further progress could be made on inspections. The magnitude of the crisis was felt at Geneva, where all disarmament negotiations came to a full stop as the crisis unfolded.[19] And yet, even at the peak of the crisis Kennedy never turned his back on the possibility of a test ban. In a letter to Khrushchev on October 28, Kennedy apologized for a US reconnaissance plane's accidentally straying into Soviet airspace and used the opportunity to propose resuming the test ban negotiations. Khrushchev replied two days later and suggested that "we now have conditions ripe for finalizing the agreement on signing a treaty."[20] On the same day, US disarmament negotiator Arthur Dean allegedly hinted to Soviet first deputy foreign minister Vasilii Kuznestov that Kennedy might be willing to even go as low as three or four inspections a year. Dean would quickly claim that the Soviet minister simply misunderstood him, but to Khrushchev it was evidence that Kennedy was ready to bend on the inspections issue. When Kennedy continued to insist on ten to twenty inspections, though, Khrushchev accused him of negotiating in bad faith.[21] From Kennedy's perspective, ten inspections was the absolute minimum number he could get if the treaty had any hope of passing a Senate vote. The test ban negotiations deadlocked over the inspections issue. It was Cousins who emerged to unjam the diplomatic gears.

During his first meeting with Khrushchev, in December 1962, Cousins also looked for a way to raise the nuclear test ban issue. After already exceeding their allotted time discussing Vatican matters Cousins stood up to leave. He would recall being "mindful of the fact that we hadn't even discussed the matters of concern to President Kennedy. But I was also mindful that the Chairman hadn't eaten his lunch, even though we had been talking for nearly three hours and it was now almost 2:00pm. The Chairman was reading my mind. 'Please sit down,' he said. 'How is President Kennedy?'" As the discussion continued, Khrushchev expressed his desire to meet Kennedy "more than halfway" in reducing tensions between their two nations. He told Cousins that "one thing the President and I should do right away is to conclude a treaty outlawing testing."[22] This was exactly what Cousins was hoping to hear. He thanked Khrushchev for his hospitality and departed the Soviet Union in good spirits. Subsequent actions by Khrushchev make it clear that the first Cousins meeting at least helped to break the impasse that had stopped the LTBT negotiations since the outbreak of the missile crisis.

On December 19, just a few days after Cousins left Moscow, Khrushchev sent Kennedy a lengthy letter devoted entirely to the test ban issue. Kennedy was surprised and "exhilarated" upon receiving Khrushchev's letter.[23] In the letter, Khrushchev stated that the Soviet government was ready to meet the United States halfway on the question of inspection and agreed to two to three inspections per year.[24]

Immediately upon his return from the Soviet Union, Cousins wrote a three-page letter to the White House outlining the intelligence he had gleaned from his meeting with Khrushchev. Having recently dined privately with Kennedy, he had reason to believe that he now had special access to the president, and he was expecting to personally inform him about the meeting. Cousins presumptuously ended his letter by saying that "all these items will be covered in my conversation with the President."[25] Cousins would only get as far as meeting with Kennedy advisor Ralph Dungan, who said to the president that "as you can see [Cousins] is pressing very hard for some time with you." Despite Cousins's growing personal relationship with the president, he still did not enjoy unfettered access. Dungan served as a screen, telling Kennedy, "My own feeling is, after having talked to [Cousins] at length, that it would not be a very useful conversation."[26] Growing increasingly impatient, Cousins wrote to Dungan, blistering him over "the lack of an appointment even though more than a month has elapsed since my return."[27]

Kennedy's initial exhilaration over the breakthrough December letter did not last long. He replied to Khrushchev on December 28, quashing his hopes for a test ban by writing that the United States continued to insist on eight to ten inspections.[28] Khrushchev was absolutely livid because Kennedy's rejection of this offer embarrassed him in front of his Presidium. He had gone out on a limb and fought hard to get his Council of Ministers to approve accepting even three inspections. From Khrushchev's perspective, Eisenhower had first betrayed him regarding the U-2 incident, and now Kennedy's intransigence on the inspections issue "was a deeply humiliating experience." He later told Cousins, "I put the full weight of my prestige before the Council of Ministers and got them to accept, and the next thing I knew, things changed. . . . I tried to accommodate the President, I carried my part and I got slapped in the face."[29]

Khrushchev encountered considerable opposition from the Council of Ministers in pushing them to accept even three inspections. He had now been humiliated yet again because they had been correct in warning him not to compromise with the United States. Khrushchev withdrew his offer, broke off talks in February, and nearly six years of working toward the test ban agreement seemed to be quickly falling apart. Soviet ambassador Anatoly Dobrynin would write in his memoirs that AEC chairman Glenn Seaborg had later told him with regret that it had been he who pushed Kennedy to bargain for more inspections, thinking they would settle somewhere in the middle. Had he known that Khrushchev would withdraw the offer, he would have pushed Kennedy to accept the proposal.[30] The reality was different, however. No matter what bargaining took place, Kennedy would still have needed more inspections than the Soviets were willing to accept in order to build confidence in the Senate that there would be no cheating on the treaty. The fear was that with just three inspections the Soviets might stage a few "false alarms" in order to trigger American inspections and thus exhaust the US quota early in the year, leaving the Soviets free to conduct unmonitored tests.[31]

Cousins was particularly dejected at the collapse of the talks, but he was determined not to lose hope. In early February he had lunch with Dungan in Washington. Given the renewed tensions, Cousins asked if there might be any useful purpose for him to take a return trip to the Soviet Union on behalf of the United States.[32] Secretary of State Dean Rusk invited Cousins to lunch to discuss the idea on February 19, 1963. By the conclusion of the lunch, Cousins had resolved to return to the Soviet Union, and he asked Rusk to get in touch if he had anything that he wished to say before he left.[33]

Concurrently, recognizing that Khrushchev "may be the best type of Russian leader we are likely to get," British prime minister Harold Macmillan decided to redouble his efforts in the hope that taking the initiative in the test ban could help bolster Britain's status as a great power as well as his own waning political fortunes. In a series of long letters to Kennedy, Macmillan encouraged the president to approach Khrushchev again. Most importantly, he implored Kennedy to recognize that the test ban was really about a personal duty to human survival.[34] Macmillan would leave his indelible mark by helping to persuade Kennedy that positive rhetoric could play an immeasurable role in winning support for the treaty.

Meanwhile, Cousins finally secured the private meeting with Kennedy that he had long been asking for. He was invited to the White House on March 12 for an eighty-minute discussion during which the president mused that he felt the Russians had been most eager to have a treaty until there was a sudden change in January. Cousins suggested that in mid-January Khrushchev had become convinced that the United States was backing away from its own proposals—proposals that he thought he had accepted by agreeing to three inspections—and was therefore turning, under pressure, to a hard-line posture.[35] Despite having told his readers that he would refrain from writing about nuclear issues, Cousins, willing to help amplify Kennedy's message, mentioned that he was prepared to use the *Saturday Review* to launch a major publicity campaign in support of the test ban treaty. Kennedy, however, asked him to hold back until a signed treaty was actually presented to the Senate.[36]

After meeting with Kennedy, on his own initiative Cousins contacted Ambassador Dobrynin and asked whether Khrushchev might accept a second meeting. The answer was in the affirmative, and the meeting was scheduled for April 12, 1963. However, on April 3 Dobrynin delivered to Robert Kennedy a twenty-five-page letter that would come to be known as the "rude letter." Ostensibly from the ambassador to Robert Kennedy, the letter clearly had been written by Khrushchev and was directed at the president.[37] In the letter, Khrushchev berated the president for not standing up to aggressive circles in Washington and instead demanding Soviet concessions because he was too afraid to confront hawkish senators.[38]

Incidentally, for the better part of a month Macmillan had pushed the president to send someone (Robert Kennedy was his recommendation) to meet Khrushchev in the belief that sending a personal emissary to Moscow would demonstrate Kennedy's seriousness.[39] Rusk instead recommended that Cousins be the one to carry a message since he had already made arrangements to see Khrushchev again. Kennedy agreed to use Cousins to "unofficially" help overcome the most recent setback.[40] To his credit, Kennedy also chose (in consultation with Macmillan) to reply calmly and constructively to the "rude letter."[41] The day before his departure, Cousins received a telephone call from Kennedy, who impressed upon him the importance of "support[ing] the fact [with Khrushchev] that I am acting in good faith and that I genuinely want a test-ban treaty." He also asked Cousins to "see if you can't get Premier Khrushchev to accept the fact of an honest misunderstanding . . . [so that] the way can be cleared for a fresh start."[42]

With his talking points in hand, Cousins departed for Moscow via Rome, as he had planned a stop to consult with the Vatican as well. While meeting with his Vatican confidants, Cousins was presented with a copy of the ailing pope's final encyclical, *Pacem in Terris* (Peace on Earth). This encyclical was Pope John's response to the international political conditions that had created the Cuban Missile Crisis. The Vatican wanted Cousins to deliver an advance copy to Khrushchev.

CHAPTER 25

A SOJOURN *with* KHRUSHCHEV

After arriving in Moscow, Cousins was informed that his meeting with Khrushchev would actually take place at the chairman's dacha in the small resort town of Gagra, in southern Russia, on the shores of the Black Sea. The next morning Cousins would have to follow him the sixteen hundred kilometers, and this time he was not traveling alone. When Cousins had first visited Khrushchev back in December, the Soviet leader had reprimanded him for leaving his children at home. When Cousins answered that he couldn't bring his daughters because they were in school, Khrushchev said that he should know that his children would learn much more on such a visit than they would by remaining in school.[1] Correcting the mistake, this time Cousins brought twenty-one-year-old Andrea and eighteen-year-old Candis along on the trip.

After the two-hour flight from Moscow, they landed at the airport in the nearby city of Sochi, where they were ushered into two black Volgas, the Russian government's favored vehicle, for the thirty-mile drive to Khrushchev's private resort. The road from Sochi to Gagra hugged the shore of the Black Sea, climbing and diving through the rugged and verdant hills that dropped down to the water. The cars proceeded cautiously (ultimately making them a half hour late), not only because of the blind curves but because the road was a haven for cyclists.

The vast estate was ensconced behind a painted concrete wall. The car carrying Cousins and his daughters was waved through the gate by a lone guard (Cousins was surprised at how lightly guarded the compound was) and headed up a driveway that wound through a pine forest before finally approaching a large, attractive house beautifully situated on a knoll overlooking the Black Sea. Andrea noticed a heavy-set man wearing a green tweed cape and a wide fedora hat standing in the front doorway. It was Khrushchev, whom Andrea described as "dogged, sturdy, and curiously gracious." Alice Bobrysheva, Cousins's longtime Russian translator, had traveled with them, and Khrushchev warmly took her hand upon opening the car door, quickly ushering them inside the house, where he said their lunch was getting cold.

Andrea and Candis were directed to sit on Khrushchev's side of the table, while their father was placed opposite. For five minutes the two men held court over which wine, brandy, and mineral water should be

From left, Alice Bobrysheva (Russian translator), Candis, and Nikita Khrushchev.

(PHOTO COURTESY OF CANDIS COUSINS KERNS)

distributed to whom. Andrea asked for a glass of Georgian wine, while Khrushchev urged a glass of brandy on her father. Khrushchev himself served his guests, filling their plates with local fish, smoked salmon, and a type of rare fish that Khrushchev said was his favorite. He persuaded the girls to try the fresh crabmeat and then pointed proudly to a golden cheese pie that he said was made by the locals. Khrushchev joked that had his wife been with them for lunch, she—determined that her husband should lose weight—would have attempted to keep him from eating and drinking so much.

Once everyone was served, Khrushchev started in with the toasts: to their health; to the American guests; to the Armenians, who made such fine wine, far better than the French. Of course, each toast came with a hefty pour of vodka. Cousins, who did not drink alcohol, brought the glass to his lips and took only the tiniest of sips. That launched Khrushchev into a story about how he had once found himself in a similar situation, expected to hold his own with a bunch of heavy drinkers. He had tried to keep up and was sick for a week.

Andrea paid keen attention to the lunch banter, which mostly consisted of her father peppering Khrushchev with questions. How did Khrushchev like to spend his leisure time? Yes, he did like to walk along the beach. Every morning he played a vigorous game of badminton and then took a long walk through the forest. His afternoons brought another round of exercise followed by a massage. He enjoyed his vacation spot especially because it afforded him time to read and think. It was a place where the burdens of his office usually didn't follow him. In fact, Khrushchev frequently unplugged the phone and told his staff in Moscow not to bother him. (One can imagine Cousins being envious. He frequently complained that the phone in his office never ceased ringing and that his work always seemed to catch up to him no matter where in the world he traveled.)

Following the questioning came joking. More than joking perhaps. Candis recalls that Khrushchev was funny and playful, a charming raconteur.[2] Khrushchev, with his love of folklore and (often crude) parables, told a few anecdotes. One was about the husband whose wife never allowed him to put sugar in his tea, which was counterproductive because it meant only that the husband overdosed on sugar whenever he was away from home. Another about how the key to longevity was to have sex five times a day. The laughing and joking continued through five more courses: soup, trout, veal, vegetables, pancakes and pudding. Candis recalls that "he was friendly and informal with that gap between his two front teeth and a relaxed, winning smile. He looked much more like my Russian Jewish grandfather than the monstrous autocrat who had crushed the Hungarian revolution."[3] Eventually the conversation turned more serious as Khrushchev spoke reverently about Yuri Gagarin's achievement in getting to space and the difficulties they foresaw in getting to the moon.

The lunch ended with coffee, after which Khrushchev suddenly said "Let's go" and walked outside. The party ambled down to the beach for a spell before walking back up to tour the "sport house," complete with gymnasium, massage room, and a heated pool. The Cousinses were especially impressed by the fact that it had electrically operated retractable glass walls that converted the building into an open-air pool. Cousins, tongue in cheek, told his host that *nowhere* in the capitalist world had he seen a private swimming pool as magnificent as this. Khrushchev, with an equally straight face, replied that American society was still very young and he was sure the country would have one in due course.

As they walked through the gym, Khrushchev challenged Cousins to a game of badminton. At first Cousins thought that etiquette required him to be easy on Khrushchev, playing as he did with his daughters. But Khrushchev was competitive, hitting the bird hard and fast and sending it whizzing right at Cousins's head. Andrea and Candis then got to have a round with the chairman. Khrushchev was a formidable opponent despite having consumed two glasses of wine and half a glass of brandy with lunch, along with all the vodka from the toasts.

Khrushchev and Andrea Cousins.

(PHOTO COURTESY OF CANDIS COUSINS KERNS)

But now the time had come to get down to business. Khrushchev told the girls that they were free to do as they wished while the men chatted, but he recommended they go for a swim. When they lamented that they had not brought their bathing suits, Khrushchev told them not to fret, they could use *his* swimming trunks. Candis recalls, "I don't doubt that K wanted us to enjoy ourselves by going for a swim. But, how is it that the Soviet premier at his luxurious hide-away, did not provide us with women's bathing suits? Perhaps he wanted the armed guards circling the property hour after hour to also enjoy themselves, provided with the welcome sight of young women cavorting in men's extra-large swimming trunks and their bras."[4]

While the girls swam, the men went up to Khrushchev's light-filled study, with its view of the Black Sea, to have their talk. When they finally sat down to chat after lunch, Cousins found Khrushchev "angry and suspicious" but also "weighted down, even withdrawn." But this frosty start soon gave way to the most fruitful of meetings.[5] Although the two men spoke frankly, covering a plethora of topics, the situation did not look promising. Khrushchev paid close attention to what Cousins was saying and claimed that he believed the president's plea that the current deadlock was just the result of a simple misunderstanding, but he was dejected. He told Cousins, "This is the end of the line for me. This [animosity between the two nations] has been going on for 40 years. If we can have it [the test ban treaty] we'll have to have it soon."[6]

In addition to having to deal with Chinese criticism, Khrushchev was encountering fierce opposition from within his own government to his push for the test ban. Most of Khrushchev's high-level Presidium colleagues had already succeeded in reimposing much of their military and heavy industry policy because of Khrushchev's weakened position after the missile crisis.[7] He explained that his advisors were pushing him to take the hard-line stance they had thought he should take all along. He might have to swallow a "bitter pill" and resume testing, Khrushchev lamented.[8]

With Khrushchev imploring Cousins to understand the difficulties he faced, and with the outcome of their discussion looking increasingly bleak, Cousins chose to try a risky bluff to win back control of the agenda: he packed his briefcase and stood up to leave. When Khrushchev asked what he was doing, Cousins explained, "I'm going home.... It's clear that I've failed and am going home and I'm going to have to confess my failure to the president. I had hoped to be able to convince you that he was acting in good faith.... Apparently I failed in that."[9] Khrushchev implored him to sit down, commending his "human touch," and said that he was willing to give the test ban treaty a second chance but that he had expended all of his political capital. In order for the treaty to move forward, it would be up to Kennedy to reach out and take the next step.[10] After spending nearly the entire day with Khrushchev, Cousins returned to Washington unsure of himself and fearing that he had tried the chairman's patience.

Cousins's lengthy meeting with Khrushchev revealed a side of the man that few Westerners had seen. Cousins later reflected, "He was a lonesome figure who gave the impression of being gregarious. He was a man who obviously managed to take time in his own life for sustained and sequential thought. . . . He was supposed to be crude, yet I had seen that he was capable of gentility, kindness, and great courtesy."[11]

After his return to the United States, Cousins met with Kennedy on April 22 in an Oval Office meeting that Kennedy secretly recorded. These tapes offer a unique insight and a rare unadulterated primary source from a president who was notorious for not keeping written records of his meetings. Since Kennedy himself controlled the recording device with a switch under his desk, it stands to reason that the existence of this tape indicates that Kennedy thought the Cousins meeting was important enough to record for history's sake.

During this meeting Cousins proposed some fresh thinking. Knowing that the negotiations were at an impasse and that the issue of inspections numbers was likely to be a political minefield, and mindful of Khrushchev's insistence that Kennedy be the man to take the next step, Cousins suggested a bold plan to President Kennedy: "Maybe what we ought to do is not to call now for a definite treaty but to propose a trial period of six months. [We] ought to have a six month trial go of this thing to see what the problems are. . . . This leaves us free at the end of six months, of course, to pick up and go our own way. But in the meantime it provides a basis or a one step really into something a little more consequential."[12]

Kennedy interrupted at this point and remarked that one of the negatives of this plan would be that it would cost millions to set up the required equipment that might only be used for six months. However, a few minutes later Kennedy remarked that he liked the idea of the trial period and wanted Cousins to write up a proposal of "a page or so" explaining how it would work. Kennedy opined, "I really want to put something different because we're at a dead end right now and I'm afraid the whole thing will collapse."[13] Kennedy held this pessimistic attitude even outside the Oval Office, remarking during a news conference on May 8, "I would say that I am not hopeful at all."[14]

This negative attitude toward the test ban marked quite a change in attitude for Kennedy, who just a month earlier had remarked to Cousins that he was not a defeatist. He expected a lively fight, but he was "genuinely eager to reach an agreement, and . . . prepared to do everything possible towards that end."[15] Khrushchev's comment that this was the end of the line for him and Kennedy's fear of the whole thing collapsing show that both men had little hope of reaching an agreement.

What Kennedy could not know at the time was that three days later Khrushchev would appear to have turned the corner. On April 25, Khrushchev secretly proposed to the Presidium that they forgo the comprehensive ban and move ahead with a limited treaty that allowed for continued underground testing.[16] This would eliminate the need for the on-site inspections that were holding up the treaty. But while Khrushchev may have made his mind up in principle, he was still holding out for Kennedy to, as he told Cousins, "reach out and take the next step" before he announced anything publicly. With his political capital largely expended and having already gone out on a limb once for Kennedy, he was not eager to do so a second time without assurances that the Americans would not change their position again.

Cousins made the rounds in Washington, dining next with Ambassador Dobrynin. Summarizing for the ambassador his meetings with both Kennedy and Khrushchev and listening to Dobrynin's response, Cousins ominously noted, "I thought it significant that he did not refute my view that the Chairman felt he had come to the end of the line in his attempt to show tangible results for his basic policies." The ambassador told Cousins that "the situation is not now very good and seems to be moving in the wrong direction. . . . I cannot just express an optimistic view about the President's intentions; they will want to know whether

I can point to anything specific that can support a feeling of optimism."[17] His dinner with Dobrynin can only have served to reinforce Cousins's sense that Kennedy needed to seize the moment to make a specific grand overture lest Khrushchev grow tired of waiting.

Not knowing that Khrushchev had already privately decided to move forward with a limited ban, American policymakers expressed growing concern that he might be pondering a major shift in Soviet policy aimed at unifying the Communist world and confronting the West from a position of strength.[18] Alarmed by his conversation with Dobrynin and growing apprehensive that their window of opportunity was quickly closing, Cousins wrote the president again on April 30. Arguably, this was the letter that changed everything. Imploring Kennedy to make a "determined fresh start," Cousins wrote, "The moment is now at hand for the most important single speech of your Presidency." He envisioned a speech that would take a friendly tone toward the Soviet Union, recognize the Soviet's tragic losses in World War II, and advocate for the human interest. He expected that such a speech would create a groundswell of support for American leadership, make it difficult for Khrushchev to disparage the United States, and head off some of the internal and external opposition to the test ban.[19]

A month passed before Kennedy telephoned Cousins. Kennedy told him that he had been thinking about the proposals in Cousins's letter and hoped that Cousins would work with his speechwriter, Theodore Sorensen, on crafting the speech that Cousins had recommended. Sorensen followed up with a phone call of his own, and the two men agreed to meet in a restaurant in Washington.[20] Over lunch, Sorensen told him that Kennedy had given him Cousins's letter and wanted to go ahead with the idea. According to Sorensen, although Kennedy had been pondering giving a speech on the general topic of peace, Cousins's letter had inspired him to fully embrace the idea.[21] Cousins's letter also made clear his belief that such a speech delivered now could help cinch the treaty.[22] Deputy national security advisor Carl Kaysen later said that Cousins "was the trigger, in a sense, to crystallize the speech."[23]

Sorensen also noted in his 1964 oral history interview that Cousins had been "one of the main sources of inspiration [for the speech]."[24]

The administration decided that Kennedy's upcoming American University commencement address would be the perfect moment for the bold fresh start that Cousins proposed. At this point the idea had been discussed with no one else. This was to be a speech written without interference, and Cousins was to have a central part in writing it.

Cousins fulfilled his task with vigor and submitted a sixteen-page draft on June 1.[25] Using Cousins's draft as a basis, a small group of advisors speedily crafted the speech, purposely bypassing the relevant departments despite this being a major foreign policy speech. Typically, major speeches would be circulated to all relevant departments for edits and input. However, Kennedy did not want this speech to be diluted by the usual threats of destruction and boasts about nuclear stockpiles.[26]

While Bundy and Kaysen had some input and Kennedy made some changes, Averell Harriman, who had been intimately involved in the test ban negotiations, liked it and encouraged Kennedy not to change it further.[27] Sorensen took Cousins's framework and polished it into the final draft on June 7, 1963, while on a flight back from Hawaii.[28] Only after he delivered the speech did Kennedy inform members of his administration that the policy outlined in the speech would be the new agenda.[29]

A substantial portion of this historic speech can be traced to language in the draft that Cousins submitted, with many phrases used verbatim. As just a few examples of major passages, Cousins wrote,

> . . . the most important matter in the world. I refer, of course, to peace. In speaking about peace, I want to make it clear that I speak about genuine peace—the kind of peace that makes life on earth worth living; the kind of peace that helps a man to come fully alive, to grow, to develop his abilities, to create a good life for his children. . . . To create a better life for the society of humans

> on this earth. . . . We seek a genuine peace not just for ourselves but for all men.[30]

And Kennedy said,

> . . . that is the most important topic on earth: peace. . . . I am talking about a genuine peace, the kind of peace that makes life on earth worth living, and the kind that enables men and nations to grow, and to hope, and build a better life for their children—not merely peace for Americans but peace for all men and women.[31]

Cousins wrote,

> Radioactive poisons produced by a nuclear war will be carried by winds to nearby and faraway lands alike, invading the bones and germplasm of people, infecting their food supply and reservoirs, condemning their future.[32]

And Kennedy said,

> It makes no sense in an age when the deadly poisons produced by a nuclear exchange would be carried by wind and water and soil and seed to the far corners of the globe and to generations yet unborn.[33]

Cousins's influence can even be seen in some of the most frequently quoted passages. For example, he wrote,

> There is no political or economic system so evil that their people must be considered without virtue or achievement. Our view of governments or systems must not be allowed to distort or poison our view of peoples. As Americans we find communism

> profoundly repugnant, but we can hail the Russian people for their many achievements.[34]

And Kennedy said,

> No government or social system is so evil that its people must be considered as lacking in virtue. As Americans, we find communism profoundly repugnant as a negation of personal freedom and dignity. But we can still hail the Russian people for their many achievements.[35]

Cousins himself later said, "I felt that the spirit of [my] draft was beautifully reflected in the speech that the president gave. And I thought that Sorensen's way of dealing with it was very poetic."[36] In turn, Sorensen noted that "Norman Cousins, the innovative *Saturday Review* editor and peace activist [informed us] that the Soviet leadership was ready for a breakthrough if Kennedy could make the first move."[37] Cousins had the intimate firsthand knowledge necessary to intuit what would spur Khrushchev to act.

Although it would later be called "the most remarkable speech by a U.S. president in the Cold War era," the speech received surprisingly little attention in the United States at the time.[38] Overseas the reaction was immediately positive. The United States Information Agency reported that "the press of India hailed the speech as 'significant,' 'dramatic,' and a triumph of statesmanship."[39] The West Germans welcomed the speech "with satisfaction and vigorous approval."[40] The US Embassy in Belgrade reported that to the Yugoslav leaders and public it was apparent that the "speech represents [a] major departure in US policy, perhaps [the] most significant in years, and one that can hardly fail to have enormous and beneficial effects."[41] Although the White House did not know it at the time, even Khrushchev told his staff that the speech was the best given by an American president since

Roosevelt.[42] The CIA reported that "the atmosphere created by this speech is now such that the possibilities of agreeing on a test ban treaty are very good."[43] Just as Cousins had hoped.

The Kennedy administration waited with bated breath for the response from Moscow. A tense ten hours passed before the news finally arrived. At 6:14 a.m. on June 11, a "priority" cable from the US Embassy in Moscow arrived in Washington announcing that a Russian translation of the speech had been broadcast in Moscow on multiple radio stations. The embassy reported that "jammers were obviously deliberately ordered silenced in Moscow area in spite of frank language of speech and Russian listeners had unusual chance to hear major US policy statement."[44] The White House viewed this as a positive sign. Days later, Cousins wrote Khrushchev congratulating him on publishing the speech in full, telling him that it had been a "friendly act and will have a positive bearing on our relations."[45] The CIA's assessment mirrored Cousins's when it reported that "the Soviets were favorably surprised. . . . Kennedy's speech has gone a long way toward assuaging Soviet doubts of United States sincerity."[46]

The speech had an impact on individual Soviet citizens as well. Mr. Grigori Vasilevich Nikiforov took a risk in writing to the American Embassy in Moscow, "I wish very much to transmit . . . our heartfelt gratitude for [Kennedy's] wise and truthful words. . . . Those to whom peace is dear and who are against war and poverty want to repeat those words because they speak about peace and justice." The surprised Moscow Embassy informed Washington about this letter, stating that "it is very rare that Soviet citizens corresponding on consular matters discuss political matters in their letters. All mail to the Embassy is assumed to be opened [by the Soviets]."[47]

Cousins's influence in this matter is apparent. His second meeting "warmed" Khrushchev to the point that he was willing to break the impasse if Kennedy was willing to make a direct overture. With his sophisticated and realistic view of Russian policy and having had private, direct conversations with both Khrushchev and Dobrynin, Cousins possessed a thoroughly informed opinion of what needed to be done to elicit an agreement from Khrushchev. Drawing on this experience, he proposed the conciliatory "peace speech" idea that ended up being the signal he knew Khrushchev was waiting for. Not only did the speech indicate to Khrushchev that Kennedy was serious about the treaty but Kennedy also used the speech opportunity to do an end run around his internal opposition and propose a whole new approach to the Soviet Union, an approach that recognized it as an equal partner. Through his intimate personal discussions with Khrushchev, Cousins was able to get a feel for his psyche. He empathized with his position and thus knew that this rhetoric would be immensely appealing to Khrushchev.

Concurrently, Khrushchev was doing an end run of his own. Khrushchev complained to Cousins during his April visit that American leaders did not understand his predicament. He was not some all-powerful tyrant who could dictate his terms and get whatever he wanted. He had to lobby, petition, and persuade just as Kennedy did, which was difficult given his precarious political standing.[48] In a deft political move Khrushchev had invited Cousins during his initial visit in December to witness this firsthand at the meeting of the Supreme Soviet. The tactic paid off, as Cousins later tried to explain Khrushchev's delicate political position to Kennedy.

Khrushchev received a bit of luck too. On April 11, 1963, the powerful party hard-liner Frol Kozlov was incapacitated by a stroke, which gave Khrushchev some new room to maneuver.[49] Whether coincidental or on purpose, on the exact same day the party's theoretical journal "uncovered" and printed a Lenin document on the utility of supporting realistic elements in the West through concessions.[50] It was only after Kennedy's speech "reset" the tone of US-Soviet relations that the first ray of light was seen after nearly ten years of futile negotiations on this issue.

The fact that Cousins was not linked to the official negotiations helped his cause. His role as a direct liaison to both leaders allowed him to foster communication and understanding, helping to clear the air at a pivotal moment. His mission was not an alternative to negotiation but a parallel track to supplement what the negotiators to that point had been unable to achieve. Although the official negotiations were uniquely resilient, even continuing after the Soviets resumed testing, they made little progress because neither side was ready to trust the other or to offer the concessions necessary to allow a deal to happen.[51]

It should be noted that citizen diplomacy cannot function without a political atmosphere conducive to attempts to solve the problems encountered. Kennedy, Khrushchev, and Macmillan all had strong personal and political reasons to see the treaty successfully completed. Spurred on in part by Macmillan's urging, Kennedy was open to using Cousins as his emissary to Khrushchev, a gesture that the chairman did indeed welcome and take seriously.

The fact of the matter is that Cousins had only one small part in a multifaceted, years-long negotiation effort to end nuclear testing. However, the evidence is strong that Cousins intervened at a pivotal crossroads. His direct private access to Khrushchev allowed him to fully understand the precarious position the chairman was in and to relay this back to Kennedy. Sorensen noted that the speech provided the signal Khrushchev had been waiting for, a signal the White House was only aware it needed to provide in the first place thanks to Cousins. But the decision by both Kennedy and Khrushchev to pursue the treaty was only the first hurdle; the real test would be persuading the US Senate to ratify it.

CHAPTER 26

THE FIGHT *to* RATIFY

Although the White House considered it an unprecedented positive sign that Kennedy's American University speech was broadcast unjammed in Moscow, it remained unclear how Khrushchev would officially respond. For weeks the treaty's fate was uncertain. On June 24, Cousins wrote Khrushchev to offer a positive reminder. Enclosing a *Wall Street Journal* article that expressed support for the treaty, he wrote, "There has been a profound change in public opinion in the U.S. President Kennedy's leadership on this issue has been most effective. There can be no doubt of the sincerity of the U.S. in seeking a test-ban treaty."[1]

Khrushchev's official reply finally came during a speech in East Berlin on July 2. Within two days, Averell Harriman had his instructions to return to Moscow and begin a new round of discussions. By late July the American, British, and Soviet negotiators had reached an agreement on the text of the LTBT.[2] Cousins happened to be attending a White House strategy meeting on July 23 when the news arrived that an agreement had been reached.[3] President Kennedy clearly recognized that Cousins had played a major supporting role in getting the treaty to this point, and to show his gratitude, the president signed the original UPI report of the agreement and gave it to Cousins as a keepsake.

More important, Kennedy also offered Cousins a job in the White House, asking if he might be willing to come down to Washington to pursue these sorts of initiatives on a full-time basis. Cousins replied that he would not be able to extricate himself from the *Saturday Review* for at least six months, but a job at the White House was something he would seriously consider.[4] Since he could not join the administration immediately, Cousins told Kennedy that in the meantime he would like to lead a citizens committee that would work in concert with the White House to help build public support of the test ban ratification. Kennedy approved of the idea, and Cousins soon recruited former UN ambassador James Wadsworth to chair what became the Citizens Committee for a Nuclear Test Ban. Wadsworth was a Republican who commanded great respect and lent bipartisan credibility to the committee.[5]

Basking in the remarkable success of the citizen diplomacy mission that had gotten him this far, Cousins made plans to return to the Soviet Union to continue his discussions with Khrushchev. He wrote to Khrushchev, "I should of course be most pleased and privileged to undertake the trip if you would welcome it. I am holding the latter part of September open in my calendar in the event my visit is agreeable."[6]

On July 26, the day after it was publicly announced that the treaty had been agreed to, Kennedy went on national television to advocate in its favor and begin the campaign to build public support. He called the treaty "the finest concrete result of eighteen years of effort by the United States to impose limits on the nuclear arms race."[7] Dishearteningly, after the announcement the bags of mail arriving at the White House indicated that the American people were heavily against the treaty.[8] This was precisely what Cousins's committee was tasked with countering.

On August 2, Cousins returned to Washington to meet with Kennedy's deputy national security advisor, Carl Kaysen, who had recently returned from Moscow, where he had been part of the Harriman mission. During their lunch meeting Kaysen explained that the White House was going to do everything possible to create an atmosphere for success in the ratification fight. He told Cousins that generating an outpouring of letters would be of the utmost importance, especially letters from businessmen in support of the treaty.

Cousins had to rush away from this meeting to make a 2:30 p.m. appointment with Senator Hubert Humphrey (D-MN). Humphrey told Cousins that he was "profoundly impressed by what [Kennedy] had told him [about Cousins's activities]." Continuing his barnstorming through the capital, Cousins then went to a 4:30 p.m. meeting with Rusk and Harriman. Rusk, who was set to depart for Moscow the following day for the treaty signing, wanted to impress upon Cousins the "disaster that would be represented by the failure of ratification." He told Cousins that "we had to make a world impact. . . . This meant we ought to try for upwards of 85 [yes] votes."[9] Kennedy himself was pessimistic that this could be achieved.[10]

Cousins returned to Washington once again the following week to meet with Kennedy and Wadsworth to discuss how the Citizens Committee could be useful to the White House in supporting ratification.[11] During the meeting, Kennedy expressed his pessimism about the treaty's chances for ratification, complaining that most senators had yet to announce their support. Mail to Congress and the White House had been overwhelmingly negative. Kennedy thought that persuading two-thirds of the senators to ratify a treaty so controversial would be a miracle. If the vote were held that day, he thought, the treaty would certainly fail. In his estimate, this would be a catastrophe comparable to America's failure to ratify the League of Nations.

Kennedy admitted that he was unsure he could even hold his own administration in line. Several influential Democratic senators were threatening to propose reservations to the treaty that would sink it. Cousins, however, buoyed the president when he presented a list of forty-eight prominent national individuals who had agreed to serve on the committee to support ratification.[12] Using his past experience with SANE, he also commissioned protreaty advertisements to run in newspapers nationwide. Cousins kept in daily contact with the assistant secretary of state for congressional relations, Frederick G. Dutton, who reported to McGeorge Bundy that in just a week Cousins had been able to persuade a "significant" number of establishment businessmen and scientists to come out in support of the treaty.[13] According to Cousins, because of his ability to get the backing of businessmen, the Citizens Committee was able to "show much more clout" and "make more of a dent on the Senate of the United States."[14]

The Citizens Committee also provided support to protreaty senators by being on call to answer their questions, and Cousins specifically wrote a number of speeches for senators to use in their public appearances.[15] Cousins notes that "we were giving [senators] nutrients that they needed to justify their position, nutrients in terms of effective public support for their position."[16] Kennedy was willing to stake his entire career on this treaty. He told Sorensen that he would "gladly forfeit reelection to win the sixty-seven votes needed to ratify it in the Senate."[17] Fortunately, this was a trade-off he did not have to make. Gradually, over the course of August and September, support grew for the treaty, and it passed the Senate on September 24, 1963, with a landslide vote of 80 to 19.

It wasn't all positive persuasion. The Kennedy administration assuaged concerns by attacking the Soviets during the Senate hearings and promising to increase funding for underground nuclear tests. Ultimately, Atomic Energy Commission spending on nuclear tests skyrocketed from $133.2 million in 1963 to $314.6 million in 1969.[18] In fact, by some arguments the LTBT did little to stop the arms race. The allowance of underground testing meant that nations could continue to test their weapons without raising public ire over fallout contamination. It was, to be sure, a significant environmental victory, but when it came to true arms control, although the nuclear test ban treaty seemed like a major accomplishment at the time, it was really an insignificant victory.[19]

Cousins too recognized the treaty's limitations. He later reflected, "I do think, however, that we missed an opportunity in the months following the test ban treaty to come back with a wider ban, a complete ban."[20] But he maintained that it did do *some* good in changing public perception: "The very fact that it was done enabled people to believe that we were not altogether at the mercy of an irreversible tide. The very fact that it could be done indicated to many people that more could be done. It's too easy to be a scoffer or a cynic and say, 'Well, what good did it do? After all, look where we are.'"[21]

Working on the LTBT was the embodiment of Cousins's worldview that the *individual* had to take a stand and do what was morally right. The *individual* could inspire the human spirit toward a safer and more peaceful world even if the government did not. Cousins was that individual who, through his citizen diplomacy efforts undertaken at his own personal expense, was able to help move the world slightly closer to peace in 1963. Former Kennedy advisor and chairman of the Atomic Energy Commission Glenn Seaborg acknowledged that Cousins "helped to create history."[22]

Kennedy too saw an opening to ease the Cold War in the summer of 1963, a time that his brother Bobby described as "the happiest time of his administration."[23] Cousins claimed that a "new spirit of hopefulness" was washing over the world that summer.[24] Just before the beginning of the Kennedy administration, Cousins had written that "nothing is more powerful than individual action out of his conscience, thus helping to bring the collective conscience to life."[25] And while the test ban treaty brought the American collective conscience to life in pursuing the moral imperative to end atmospheric nuclear testing, in November 1963 the American people would learn that individuals acting alone could also spark national tragedies.

In September 1963 the future looked bright. Cousins had decided to accept Kennedy's offer to work at the White House. As of January 1, 1964, he would resign from the *Saturday Review* and become a full-time advisor to Kennedy on peace and disarmament initiatives.[26] In the meantime, though, Cousins planned to travel to Hiroshima on November 24, 1963, to accept an honorary citizenship from the city for his work on behalf of the victims of the atomic bomb.[27] But Cousins would have to cancel once again. As he was preparing to depart for Japan, tragedy struck.

At 12:30 p.m. on November 22, 1963, President Kennedy was killed by a gunman in Dallas. Cousins, like much of America and the world, was shocked. He immediately cabled his contacts in Japan and notified them that he would not be traveling on account of the "national tragedy."[28] In addition to its being a tragedy on the national level, a letter Cousins sent to a friend four days later illustrates how deeply the loss of Kennedy affected him personally:

> What an unspeakable, incomprehensible event. . . . I suppose the rational mind is conditioned so completely to its own schooling that it cannot take anything as random and wanton as this. Even war seems to be much more within the range of comprehensible events than a bullet through the brain. . . . It is now four days since the killing and the bereft feeling is deeper than it was the first day. I suppose the mind can take in only so much shock at one time; so little by little the horror has been growing inside.[29]

Cousins later admitted that "there were millions of Americans, I think, who felt that bullet. . . . I don't think that any bullet in history traveled as far, or in so many directions, as that bullet." The bullet that killed Kennedy clearly traveled into Cousins's life as well and caused havoc. Sarah remembers that "when Kennedy was assassinated it was dark days for my father."[30] His doctor noticed that for some time after the assassination Cousins was losing weight, walking around in a daze, and unable to think sequentially. Cousins later recalled that

> it was hard for me to adjust again; I'd just about made the adjustment to the decision to accept the president's invitation to work with him on matters concerned with an imaginative approach to peace. It had permeated my subconscious, these were

> the things I was dreaming about, writing speeches about in my sleep, trips that would be taken, living them before they happened many times. Then this grotesque discontinuity, as though I'd walked off a cliff.[31]

On December 7, 1963, Cousins used his editorial space in the *Saturday Review* to publish an eight-page tribute to Kennedy. He concluded it by stating that "there is nothing to stop the American people from giving life to the ideas and purposes of the man whose memory they now cherish. The loss of John Kennedy becomes a total one only if our understanding of what he tried to do is emptied from our minds."[32] J. Wayne Fredericks, the deputy assistant secretary of state, wrote Cousins to "express to you my profound appreciation for your tribute. . . . You were able to give expression to the feelings shared by many of us who knew this great man."[33] Sorensen also wrote to say that "eleven years of serving the greatest man of our time obviously could not be termed wasted if so many understand so well the tragic meaning of his loss."[34]

Cousins's understanding of the loss spoke to his own long-standing worldview, a worldview that had solidified when humanity was thrust into the atomic age on August 6, 1945. To Cousins, the use of the atomic bomb was a violence that unhinged history, and eighteen years later history was unhinged once again by violence. In Cousins's mind, the assassination of Kennedy represented the ultimate significance of the atomic age. His editorial asked whether civilization itself could be assassinated. "Not just a President but all civilization is now vulnerable to weird turnings of a disturbed mind," Cousins wrote.

The Kennedy assassination illustrated to Cousins the insanity of nuclear deterrence. Hundreds of men on each side of the Iron Curtain had access to nuclear weapons, and although only a few men had *authorization* to use the weapons, any unstable commander could start a war on his own regardless of how fervently those in charge argued there were many safeguards that ensured such a thing could not happen. The Kennedy assassination proved, to Cousins at least, that that notion was false. "The chances that a deranged assassin could penetrate the protective mechanism set up to safeguard the life of an American President were very small," Cousins wrote, "but it still happened. It was irrational. It was remote. It was most improbable. But it happened."[35] And with that editorial published just three days before Christmas, Cousins closed out 1963—a year that only recently had appeared so hopeful—on a rather ominous note.

CHAPTER 27

1964

Near Death and Rebirth

Nineteen sixty-four was a life-changing year for Norman Cousins. In the days and weeks following John F. Kennedy's assassination, Cousins struggled to adapt to the constitutional reality. The president might be dead, but the presidency marched on. Lyndon Baines Johnson, sworn into office aboard Air Force One just hours after Kennedy's death, was also adjusting to the new reality while vowing to continue Kennedy's legacy. Cousins had hoped to be a part of that legacy. The problem was that Cousins had been so focused on Kennedy that he had not built a relationship with Lyndon Johnson. He had some catching up to do.

Less than a month after Johnson took office, Senator Joseph Clark (D-PA) wrote to Cousins to tell him that "[Grenville] Clark called me the other day about your efforts to bring President Johnson behind us on disarmament . . . but I would hate to hit him too hard, too soon." Cousins had come to know Clark, the famed international lawyer and peace activist, through their work on the Dublin Committee back in 1945. Clark told Cousins that he thought the best approach would be to go through Johnson's principal advisors (many of whom had stayed on from the Kennedy administration, so Cousins knew them well) rather than to make a bold direct attack on his thinking. Clark pointed out that Johnson was "an intelligent man and I believe, in due course, he will move away from his quite natural Texas belligerence."[1]

Cousins, however, was not quite ready to embrace Johnson, and he shared his solemn feelings with the nation in a subsequent editorial. "[The White House is] still possessed by the spirit and color of a man no longer there. . . . The echoes of the last three years still race through the air in the big house," he wrote longingly. Cousins noted that the true depth of the tragedy could be read on the faces of the Kennedy advisors who had stayed on to serve LBJ. But three months had passed, and now, with the transition nearing completion, he would not blame most of them for slowly trickling out one by one. Cousins called Johnson "a man substantial and able in his own right," but he noted that "there is a sense in the house of a persisting presence—inescapable, palpable, pervasive."[2]

It would be July 1964 before Cousins returned to the White House again, for a twelve-minute Oval Office meeting. While there is no evidence that Johnson rescinded Kennedy's job offer, he also did not extend an invitation of his own. Perhaps wanting to get some distance from the tragedy of Kennedy's death, Cousins left for Japan to accept his Honorary Citizenship of Hiroshima for the work he had done to help atomic bomb victims. From Japan he traveled through the Philippines and Australia, visiting Fiji on his return trip.

Mostly, he was eager to focus on planning for the long-delayed fourth Dartmouth Conference, to be held that year in Leningrad. The preparations would be a special burden that year since his partner from the beginning, a scholar of the Soviet Union, Dr. Philip Mosley, had returned to Columbia University to serve as an associate dean and the head of the European Institute. He could not spare the time to attend, much less to help organize the conference.[3] Still, Cousins was hopeful. Fresh off the signing of the test ban treaty the previous fall, he felt that the United States and the Soviet Union could achieve even more in 1964. Perhaps the momentum and positive spirit engendered by the first three Dartmouth meetings could overcome the malaise caused by Kennedy's death.

By 1964, there was a close relationship between the Dartmouth Conference participants and their respective governments, certainly on the US side.[4] In fact, shortly before Cousins was set to depart for Russia, he met with former Kennedy, now Johnson advisor McGeorge Bundy. Knowing that Cousins would essentially have a direct line to Soviet premier Nikita Khrushchev while in Leningrad, the White House had a number of messages for him to pass along. First, Bundy asked Cousins to emphasize that while the United States would stand by its commitments in Vietnam, it would do everything possible to "keep the lid on." Second, he asked Cousins to discreetly convey to Khrushchev that he ought to refrain from publicly taking sides in the upcoming American presidential election.[5] For Cousins, the fourth Dartmouth Conference, which began on July 25, 1964, was clouded by his "very deep sense of lost opportunity because of Kennedy's death."[6] Indeed, only Cousins and two other Americans were veterans of the conference, compared with almost half of the Soviet attendees.[7]

Dark political clouds notwithstanding, the participants, buoyed by the success of the LTBT, proposed further disarmament measures. The discussions got bogged down on the thorny issue (which the Soviets had raised in previous meetings) of why so few Soviet authors were being published in the United States. This discussion arose when one of the Soviet participants asked how Americans could shake hands with a man like Hermann Kahn, a military strategist at the Air Force think tank RAND, who had recently published *On Thermonuclear War*, a widely read book about how a country could "win" a nuclear war. Cousins may have considered this a personal attack. He had indeed shaken hands with Kahn, he told the participants, even after the *Saturday Review* had severely criticized Kahn's book. Despite his personal view that the message of the book was reprehensible, he still would have urged its publication because "public opinion in America is created by an exchange of views. These views are often abrasive, often distasteful—but we consider it essential that *all* views are aired."[8]

It was a tough meeting in general for Cousins. The implications of Kennedy's death were still very raw, and tense moments such as the Kahn discussion were daily reminders of lost ground. To make matters worse, word came in the midst of the conference that Khrushchev wanted to see Cousins in Moscow. Without Mosley there as cochair, Cousins did not think it was right to simply abandon the meeting for a personal visit with the Soviet leader. He declined and instead asked Chase Manhattan Bank president David Rockefeller, who was also attending the conference, to travel to Moscow and meet with Khrushchev in his place.[9]

Perhaps this decision can be chalked up to Cousins being off his game, still reeling from the assassination, or maybe he had been influenced by the idea circulating at the end of the Eisenhower administration that it would be a good idea to expose Khrushchev to American businessmen, but sending Rockefeller was a major misstep by Cousins. *Pravda* had previously painted the Rockefeller family as "capitalist enemy number one."[10] Rockefeller traveled to Moscow and met with Khrushchev across a large wooden table in a sparsely furnished room in the Kremlin, a portrait of Lenin glaring down on them. Rockefeller's twenty-year-old daughter, Neva, accompanied him and took notes.

Their two-hour meeting began ominously when Khrushchev referred to the Rockefeller family as warmongers. It only got worse. Khrushchev was testy throughout the meeting, which Rockefeller later described as "tough, at times combative, even hostile."[11] Cousins had asked Rockefeller to pass along Bundy's two requests about Vietnam and the election, but the timing could not have been worse. Tensions between North Vietnam and the United States had been growing. In the days before their early August meeting, during the early hours of August 2, North Vietnamese torpedo boats had allegedly attacked a US destroyer off the coast of North Vietnam. Johnson, with the unanimous consent of his advisors, chose to respond with retaliatory airstrikes that ultimately destroyed twenty-five North Vietnamese boats and an oil storage facility.[12]

In a case of terrible timing, news of the American retaliation reached Moscow at the exact moment when Khrushchev and Rockefeller were meeting, just after Rockefeller had explained Bundy's assertion that the US position was to limit the war in Vietnam. A Khrushchev aide burst into the room and handed the premier a note. Khrushchev looked up and said, "You say the President doesn't want to widen the war? They just handed me a dispatch saying that the United States has bombed the Gulf of Tonkin, bombed ships. What kind of assurance are you trying to give me?" The meeting ended on an even more sour note than it began.[13]

One can only imagine how Cousins must have felt when he learned this. He knew how much progress he had made with Khrushchev on the LTBT in just one meeting. When Rockefeller returned, he could only tell Cousins, "I'm not sure I was able to convince the old man."[14] This was a missed opportunity. It was also a poor choice on Cousins's part to decline Khrushchev's personal invitation and send instead the "enemy number one" in the Soviet's eyes to meet with Khrushchev. Little did Cousins know that it would be the last opportunity he would ever have. Khrushchev was overthrown and removed from power in October, and Cousins himself was about to fall deathly ill.

The months of stress and sadness that followed Kennedy's death finally broke Cousins. In Leningrad, paperwork had kept him up late into the night, and he felt that he had been relegated to a ceremonial role instead of actively participating, which he relished. He later described the final sessions of the conference as "an exercise in almost total frustration."[15] The chairman of the Soviet delegation was hosting a final reception at his dacha outside Moscow. Cousins had been asked to arrive early to help prepare. A car from the Soviet government motor pool arrived at his hotel to pick him up with plenty of time to spare and then promptly got lost. At 6:00 p.m., the time when the dinner was set to begin, Cousins found himself in open country on the wrong side of Moscow, some eighty miles from where he was supposed to be. Apparently, there had been a miscommunication with the driver about directions. Cousins finally arrived three hours late and found, to his horror, that the guests had not yet eaten; they were waiting for his arrival. The soup had been reheated multiple times; the veal had dried out. The dinner was a disaster.[16]

His hotel that night provided no refuge. Cousins was staying in the VIP Sovietskaya Hotel, located just outside the city center adjacent to a major road. Across the street an apartment project was under construction, with work taking place around the clock. Cousins's room was on the second floor of the hotel, at the exact height of the elevated exhaust pipes from the endless stream of construction trucks that roared up and down the street, day and night. In the August heat he had no choice but to keep his windows open, thus filling the room with the acrid exhaust from the heavy trucks. Cousins woke up each morning feeling nauseated from the fumes.[17]

The morning after the disastrous dinner, he was set to return to the United States. At the airport, while he was waiting on the tarmac to board the plane, a Soviet jet turned around and blasted him with the full force of the jet spew. Breathing in the toxic exhaust gasses deepened his nausea. Candis and Sarah, who had accompanied their father to Russia on this trip along with their mother, were on this flight home. They remember seeing their father, a robustly athletic man, suddenly become incapacitated after their plane took off. On the first leg of his flight from Moscow to Copenhagen he developed a high fever, and by the time the flight landed he almost had to be carried off the plane.[18] His doctor wrote later that when he arrived in New York, Cousins "was in a very precarious clinical state."[19] His fever had reached 106 degrees Fahrenheit. Admitted to the hospital, by all accounts he should have been in a coma.[20]

Cousins's health deteriorated rapidly while the doctors scrambled to make a diagnosis. Cousins himself wrote it off as simply being a bout of heavy metal poisoning caused by inhaling exhaust fumes for a week.[21] His doctors, though, suspected that it was a toxic reaction to some mysterious poisoning. In fact, at the hospital they found a bolus filled with streptococci, which doctors told him was what you would typically see in cases of deliberate poisoning. Since this suspected "poisoning" would have occurred in the Soviet Union, Cousins later privately noted to an aide of President Johnson that it left open a rather wide field of speculation.[22] Was it possible that the same anti-Khrushchev forces who were planning to soon depose the premier and move the Soviet Union in a harder-line direction also wanted to eliminate one of his strongest connections to the West, host of a conference bringing Soviets and Americans together in pursuit of peace? His wife certainly thought it was a possibility. Later in life she wondered aloud to a friend whether Norman could have been poisoned in the Soviet Union because he was so closely associated with Khrushchev and the push to reduce Cold War tensions.[23]

Cousins himself would never publicly voice his suspicions that he had been poisoned while in Russia. According to Candis, her father had considered it a possibility since it was a common Russian practice to poison enemies. "But he would never talk about this in public," she says. "He was the *last* person to say something bad about Russia," because that would have undermined everything he was doing. Sarah notes, "I think it was my mother who told me that she and Daddy considered it possible that he had been poisoned by the Soviet military. But Daddy would not make an unverifiable suspicion public."[24] While Cousins himself would never publicly state that he suspected that he had been poisoned while in Russia, he did not hesitate to write to close friends and colleagues about his suspicions.

In any case, there was no time for wild speculation; the pain that began in his spine soon led to almost total paralysis. Cousins could only move from the neck up. With no easy diagnosis at hand, the doctors ultimately concluded that Cousins was suffering from a form of ankylosing spondylitis (AS), an incurable long-term inflammation of the spine and joints. He was rapidly losing weight, and he was unable to sleep because of the pain. At one point the doctors doubted he would survive; one specialist gave him a one in five hundred chance of recovery.[25]

Cousins was treated with the anti-inflammatory drug Butazolidin. He immediately noted a marked relief of his symptoms. The improvement was so dramatic that he soon felt "almost perfect."[26] But this began a pattern of worsening, recovering, and then worsening again that would continue for nearly a month. On the last day of the treatment course, Cousins had a massive toxic reaction to the drug, resulting in an intensification of the original symptoms.[27] Even though he had been in the hospital or nearly two months and was in "considerable pain," Cousins insisted that they discontinue the course of drugs. The reaction had led him to believe that the cure might be worse than the disease.

The weeks of immobilization in the hospital at least afforded Cousins ample time to think, and especially to criticize the hospital's procedures. This would be a topic he would return to and write about later in life in what would become his most widely read book when it was published in 1979, *Anatomy of an Illness*. He wrote, "I was astounded when four technicians from four different departments took four separate and substantial blood samples on the same day. That the hospital didn't take the trouble to coordinate the tests. . . . Seemed to me inexplicable and irresponsible." Cousins, the man who had devoted his life to correcting what he thought were government failings, now directed his fight toward the hospital's shortcomings. He posted a note on his door stating that he would give only *one* blood sample per day and it was up to the hospital's departments to coordinate their testing. Cousins had even more to say about the food: "Perhaps the hospital's most serious failure was in the area of nutrition. . . . What seemed inexcusable to me was the profusion of processed foods, some of which contained preservatives or harmful dyes. White bread, with its chemical softeners and bleached flour, was offered with every meal."[28]

Fortunately, his wife stepped in. At home Ellen had a robust garden that she obsessed over. She once told a friend, "I get so involved in it. It ties me up in knots. It ruins my hands, it makes me hate animals, but I'm addicted to it."[29] Norman clearly thought she was a great gardener since he boasted that each one of Ellen's beans was worth five dollars. Ellen took pride in cooking wholesome, healthful meals for the family. She would bake fresh bread almost daily, and when Norman came home late from work she would take a flashlight out to the garden and pick fresh vegetables for his dinner.[30] Sarah remembers her mother as being "cutting edge" for the 1950s, growing an organic garden and raising her own chickens, which the family ate.[31] Reared on Ellen's wholesome food, Norman refused to eat the hospital food, and instead Ellen brought in fresh home-cooked meals every day. They both believed that better nutrition would aid his recovery.

After his toxic reaction to the drug treatment, Cousins resolved to take matters into his own hands. His longtime friend and personal physician, William Hitzig, once wrote that Cousins "masked the inner cravings to have been reborn as a physician." In earlier years Cousins would often join Hitzig on his medical rounds late in the evening at the hospital. "He would listen to their stories and return his own," with a knack for making patients laugh, Hitzig wrote, "He would listen to their complaints and before they could realize it, they were laughing and smiling without a trace of their earlier state."[32] Over their long friendship Cousins and Hitzig would also often discuss articles in medical journals. Cousins's interest in health and medicine was likely why his humanitarian missions over the years focused primarily on medical treatments. It was also what drove him to take charge of his own health in 1964. It became clear to Cousins that if he was to improve his chance of recovery, he needed to become more than just a passive observer lying in a hospital bed.

Cousins called Hitzig to his bedside and told him, "Bill, I appreciate your efforts but I have just made a new resolution to treat myself. . . . I want to be treated with Vitamin C intravenously, daily, and I will add to it positive emotions of fun and laughter."[33] Vitamin C deficiency, Cousins had read, was common among people suffering from collagen diseases. Thus, Cousins proposed that large infusions of vitamin C could combat his inflammation by serving as a starter for his endocrine system because it helped to oxygenate the blood.

It was Ellen, in fact, who brought this to Norman's attention. Sarah remembers that her mother had long before "discovered" vitamin C and taught her husband and children all about it. "She made sure that we all took our Vitamin C (along with a whole host of other vitamins) with our breakfast of organic eggs from her chicken coop, one or preferably two slices of her own homemade whole wheat bread, and freshly-squeezed organic orange juice." Ellen had always devoured books on medicine and nutrition, and "as far as health goes, she was the source," says Sarah. Her interest in vitamin C began with the 1950s groundbreaking books on nutrition and natural foods *Let's Eat Right to Keep Fit* and *Let's Cook It Right,* by Adelle Davis. It could also be that Ellen's passionate belief in vitamin C as a cure was sparked (or corroborated) by Cousins's close friend Linus Pauling.

The two men had come to know each other during their antinuclear work in the 1950s. (In fact, Pauling suggested to Cousins that he [Pauling] become cochair of SANE, an idea that the board rejected.)[34] It was Pauling's belief that high doses of vitamin C could not only prevent the common cold but help to cure cancer as well that most intrigued Cousins.[35] Pauling's assertions were controversial, but Hitzig fully embraced the vitamin C treatment. Perhaps at first, Hitzig thought it would serve at the very least as a placebo. He told Cousins that the most important thing was that Cousins continued to believe in everything he had just said.[36]

The second front in Cousins's plan was to enhance his body chemistry through positive emotions. He had observed during his hospital rounds with Hitzig years earlier that a few jokes could calm and soothe the pain of previously distraught patients.[37] Long before his own illness he had become convinced that creativity, hope, faith, and love had biochemical significance and could contribute strongly to healing and well-being.[38] Thus, he embarked on a self-prescribed treatment course of remaining positive and happy. He had a film projector brought into his hospital room and watched old Marx Brothers comedies. Hitzig even contacted Alan Funt, the producer of *Candid Camera*, a show Cousins especially enjoyed. Hitzig wrote, "Medicine has been known for many centuries as one of the best forms of therapy. What is new, I believe, is the fact that Candid Camera is being used as a prescription." Funt sent over eight tins of film, which Hitzig described as "a most potent medicine for Norman Cousins."[39]

Astonishingly, it worked. Cousins discovered that ten minutes of genuine laughter would give him at least two hours of pain-free sleep. However, his stream of visitors and his bouts of laughter were disturbing the other hospital patients.[40] Hitzig discharged him from the hospital and moved him into the same hotel in which he was living, where Hitzig continued to administer the doses of vitamin C in increasing amounts and Cousins's friends visited to provide jokes and positive emotions.[41]

For the first time since his illness had begun, he was able to flex his fingers. "I observed this phenomenon," Cousins wrote, "staring at the hand in stark wonder; repeating the process a few weeks later with the right hand."[42] His recovery was still difficult, with relapses and remissions, but Cousins's spirits seemed to be buoyed by the miraculous results of his unconventional treatments. As he recovered mobility in his hands, he was able to write again for a few hours each day, which further improved his mood. Catching up on his correspondence, he described his situation to a friend:

> Although I'm still cooped up in this improvised medical tent here at the hotel, I'm actually quite comfortable. In fact, the situation is so pleasant that I'm not sure I'm going to let the medicos know when I'm better. I have a room overlooking the Park with round-the-clock nursing, good books, repose, and the chance to think in sequence and develop perspective. I have two hours a day for writing which has enabled me to maintain my schedule on the editorial page. And I now get weekend passes to New Canaan [his home], which is the best tonic of all.[43]

His home was a refuge, set among trees along a winding road. The property had a barn, one part of which was Cousins's study, which he rarely used (and into which squirrels had made inroads). With all his globe-trotting and editing and side projects and government liaising, Cousins had barely had a moment's rest since 1945. He was frequently away from home, and while that did have an impact on his family, it was also a reality that his wife did not seem to mind. She would later tell Cousins's archivist that "Norman was gone a lot. [He] feels sorry for me being here alone but I love it. Of course I love it more when he's here but it's quiet and peaceful. . . . I have the dogs and the chickens and I have things to do."[44]

Now, his forced convalescence gave him ample time to consider the state of his life. He had pondered leaving the *Saturday Review* at least twice before, only to be persuaded to stay; by 1963 he had been ready to check out. The magazine was approaching its twenty-fifth anniversary. Before Kennedy's death Cousins had accepted the offer to work for the White House. After that had fallen through, he had received a lucrative offer in early 1964 to become the chancellor of the East-West Center at the University of Hawaii.

But his illness threw everything into a new light. He wrote that being sick had "given me more than time for reflection. It's given me a new context in which to consider where I go from here. . . . I've been able to do some long-overdue ruminating."[45] The first thing he decided was to decline the chancellorship in Hawaii. "I ain't agonna do it," he wrote his archivist Fran Thompson. "What bothers me is not the hard work but being peppered with exhausting interruptions."[46] In that same vein, he resolved not to go back to the kind of professional lecturing that he had been doing for almost thirty years. Nor was he going to take on as many projects on different fronts. He hoped to be more focused and to "bring greater concentration and preparation to whatever I decide I will do."[47]

By November 1964, he had recovered enough to be discharged from his hotel convalescence room in order to accept the inaugural

Publius Award. Bestowed by the United World Federalists, of which Cousins was the honorary president, the Publius Award was named after the pseudonym under which Alexander Hamilton, James Madison, and John Jay had published the Federalist Papers. The UWF conceived of the award to recognize those who worked to promote world peace. Some six hundred guests gathered at the Waldorf-Astoria Hotel in New York to honor Cousins. It was an especially poignant moment since the organizers had almost called it off due to Cousins's illness. One of the committee members had written, "I don't think we'd better go too far with this dinner; I don't know whether you've heard the news about Norman, but I just hate posthumous awards."[48]

If Cousins thought positivity was central to his recovery, this dinner must have contributed much to his good health. The six-hundred-person guest list included a who's who of American political society: Vice President–elect Hubert Humphrey; Ambassador Adlai Stevenson; former New Jersey governor Robert Meyner; Assistant Director of the US Arms Control and Disarmament Agency C. Maxwell Stanley; and C. V. Narasimhan, chef de cabinet to the UN secretary general, among many others.[49] Stevenson started the ceremony with a praise-filled introduction of Cousins. Humphrey too lauded Cousins, saying that "the world needs the wisdom of Norman Cousins in these careless times. . . . All of us have appreciated his tremendous fund of knowledge about the world in which we live. [He expresses his views] fearlessly and objectively, courageously, eloquently and wisely."[50]

The Publius Award was the perfect end to a year of negativity for Cousins. Although he was gleeful to have recovered and to be able to venture out into the world again, the illness would leave him with long-term scars. He had to wear steel braces on his knees for more than ten years afterward. It wasn't until 1979 that he could lift his arm above his head again.[51] Ultimately, though, his illness would make him far more aware of the environment around him. Even before he fully recovered, he would launch himself into a new crusade.

CHAPTER 28

CRUSADE *against* DIRTY AIR

Norman Cousins came out the other side of his illness grateful to have survived what was supposed to have killed him. After grappling with many possible causes of his illness, Cousins claimed (publicly at least) that the heavy air pollution he was exposed to in the Soviet Union had been to blame. Whether or not that was true, it was abundantly clear that pollution led to negative health effects. Now, everywhere he looked he saw human life being debased and degraded by things much less insidious but much more common than nuclear radiation. Cousins suddenly became aware of a particularly menacing public problem.

After he recovered from his illness, Cousins decided to rent an apartment in Manhattan so that during the week he could avoid the stress of the nearly one-hundred-mile round-trip commute between Connecticut and Manhattan each day. He never enjoyed the long drive, so he often took the train. But the miles would still rack up on their cars since Ellen would frequently drive into the city to see him during the week. Perhaps the long drive was the reason for her many speeding tickets. The writer and social commentator Cleveland Amory once introduced her as "the woman who has the most speeding tickets in Connecticut." It was not far from the truth; she apparently once came close to having her license revoked.[1]

Cousins settled on a ninth-floor apartment at 10 Park Avenue, just two blocks from the Empire State Building. When he looked out his window, the vista that greeted him in the distance was four red-and-white smokestacks that belched thick yellow smoke from the Consolidated Edison (Con Ed) steam and power plant on the shore of the East River. Watching the great and seemingly endless exhaust slowly curl from the smokestacks so perturbed Cousins that he wrote a letter to the president of Con Ed, C. E. Eble. "From my apartment at 10 Park Avenue," Cousins wrote, "I can observe the smokestacks of your East Side power plants. . . . There literally has not been a single day when these plants have not been in violation of the city Ordinance."[2]

In 1955, New York City created the Department of Air Pollution Control to put in place some environmental regulations, and inspectors were employed to ensure that factories and power plants did not emit excessive amounts of smoke. There was, however, no way the city's thirty-five inspectors could cover the 320 square miles of land and 570 miles of waterfront to adequately monitor violations.[3] In discussing this issue with commissioner Arthur Benline of the Department of Air Pollution Control, Cousins learned that Con Ed had "been found guilty of violations at least forty times and that the number could easily have been four or more times that figure." Cousins revealed to Eble that his conversations with the commissioner had "turned up information of a profoundly disquieting nature." "Whether as a citizen or an editor, I feel an obligation here to address myself to the problem," he informed Con Ed's president. He also levied an explicit threat, writing that "considerable resources are at my disposal for pursuing this matter publicly, whether in the magazines or in prominent newspaper advertisements or in a general campaign."[4]

One can imagine Cousins's mind turning out ideas on how to weaponize his previously successful public pressure campaigns and turn them against Con Ed's smokestacks. No level of response from Con Ed could have influenced him, for Cousins had already made up his mind to excoriate Con Ed and other polluters in the *Saturday Review.* Cousins did what he had been doing for two decades: he decided to take action himself to force the government to do more to address a problem.

On May 22, 1965, just weeks after Cousins wrote to Elbe, the *Saturday Review* published a major, multipart exposé titled "The Fouling of the American Environment." Cousins introduced the section by writing that there was more than enough evidence to "persuade even the most skeptical citizen that the American environment is being subjected to a vast debasement from which literally no one can escape." The section brought together thirteen experts in the environmental field, including Secretary of the Interior Stewart L. Udall, who wrote a special guest editorial. In introducing the problem, Cousins argued that "in the end, only an informed and aroused public outcry will summon up the resources, the research, and the coordinated legislative effort that is required if we ever hope to restore America the beautiful."[5]

Cousins was undoubtedly a master at arousing public outcry on these very sorts of issues, but while in the past he had been a groundbreaking pioneer, bringing to public attention a pressing issue of moral standing that few had thought deeply about, on the topic of air pollution he was a bit behind the times. Air pollution in the form of industrial exhaust (rather than radiation) had been an issue in the public eye for over a decade. Comfortably ensconced in his bucolic Connecticut surroundings, Cousins seems to have become acutely aware of the problem only after his illness caused him to spend more time living in the city.

The menace originated not only from the Con Ed power plants that Cousins had noted in his letter but from other major sources as well. The City of New York operated thirty-two garbage incineration plants in the city, none of which had any pollution controls. In fact, Commissioner Benline described twelve of them as "in bad shape."[6] The city incinerators and the Con Ed plants were the most recognizable sources of air pollution simply because of their size, but adding a great deal more to the smog were the seventeen thousand smaller garbage incinerators located inside apartment buildings. It was quite common at the time in privately owned buildings for the owners to burn their residents' trash on-site rather than pay to have it picked up by a private company. Throw into the mix some 2 million cars, trucks, and buses, and it was a recipe for noxious air; the result was that sixty-eight tons of oily black soot per square mile fell from the sky over New York City each month.[7]

Not only could residents of the city see the yellowish haze on the horizon but they could wipe black soot off their windowsills. Children who lived near the incinerators were known to stop whatever outdoor games they were playing when it began "snowing" ash from incinerated garbage and instead chase the tiny scraps of partly burned paper that floated on the air. In 1964, New York City had the worst air pollution among big cities in the United States.[8] The problem was so overwhelming that Senator Edmund S. Muskie (D-ME) commented that it "far outstretches our efforts to do anything about it."[9] The *New York Times* reported in the fall of 1963 that "for the first time within memory, citizen interest in reduction of air pollution in the New York metropolitan area is being organized on a basis that promises steady and lasting effectiveness."[10] There was a very specific reason why citizens' interest in this issue had peaked.

"Every once in a while in the history of mankind," explained Senator Ernest Gruening (D-AK), "a book has appeared which has substantially altered the course of history."[11] Gruening was speaking to Rachel Carson, who was testifying before a Senate subcommittee on pesticides. The book that "altered the course of history" was Carson's *Silent Spring*, which was first serialized by the *New Yorker* in the spring of 1962. Concerned about the effect of pesticides on the environment, Carson made a strong case against the use of a powerful industrial pesticide called DDT. She discovered that it entered the food chain and accumulated in the fatty tissues of animals (including humans) and caused genetic damage. A single application of the chemical continued to kill for weeks and months, and it remained toxic in the environment even after it was diluted by rainwater.[12]

Carson advocated for grassroots movements led by concerned citizens who would form nongovernmental groups that she called "citizen's-brigades."[13] Carson, though, would never get a chance to put her call into action herself because she died of breast cancer in April 1964. After her death, the *Saturday Review* opined that "we owe much to her and to those who still work for the cause of a safer and healthier America."[14] Perhaps Carson owed Cousins a debt in turn. The Rachel Carson Council notes that Carson may have actually been influenced in her thinking by Cousins's *Modern Man Is Obsolete.*[15]

Like Carson, Cousins believed that a flood of dangerous chemicals was being let loose, but his target was the smokestacks and tailpipes of the city instead of pesticides. Riding the wave of growing public awareness, a year after Carson's death came the *Saturday Review* exposé "The Fouling of the American Environment," in which C. W. Griffin's article "America's Airborne Garbage," excoriated both New York City and the automotive industry in general for ignoring the issue as pollutants rose to alarming levels.[16] Other articles in the series highlighted the blight of water pollution, including the fact that each year the raw sewage of 82 million Americans was being dumped into local rivers, lakes, and oceans completely untreated.[17] Specific cities like Los Angeles and Pittsburgh were singled out for opprobrium in stand-alone articles. The little being done to combat New York's pollution was likened to "fighting a five-alarm fire in the Empire State Building with a single hand extinguisher."[18]

Scrambling to respond to the charge that the government was ignoring the problem, politicians insisted that they were in fact taking action. New York governor Nelson Rockefeller wrote to congratulate Cousins, claiming that New York State was undertaking a "multitude" of effort to remedy the problem of local sewage treatment.[19] Senator Joseph Clark (D-PA) called the series "splendid" and entered it into the *Congressional Record.* Congressman Richard McCarthy (D-NY) wrote to tell Cousins that he was "hopeful that this series will have its impact on elected officials."[20]

In New York City, the 1965 mayoral race was entering its final stretch. The contest pitted the "liberal Republican" state senator John Lindsay against the flamboyant editor of the conservative *National Re-*

view, William F. Buckley Jr. As the unofficial leader of the postwar conservative movement, Buckley had received much criticism from the Left. Despite being contemporaries in the relatively small and intimate world of New York magazine editors, Cousins and Buckley do not appear to have corresponded much. However, in 1990 Buckley did interview Cousins on his show *Firing Line*, when he commented that he and Cousins had "been friends for about 30 years."[21]

It was John Lindsay who took advantage of the pollution controversy Cousins helped to stir up when, just a month after the *Saturday Review* series, Lindsay accused the then mayor of not spending enough city money for antipollution controls and offered to institute a program of immediate measures to curb pollution if elected.[22] Although he won a narrow victory in November, before he even took office Lindsay contacted Cousins and offered him a job advising the administration on air-pollution issues. The *New York Times* announced that Norman Cousins, "a leading commentator on the problems of air pollution," would become the chairman of Mayor Lindsay's new ten-person Antipollution Task Force. The article highlighted the fact that the *Saturday Review* was "among the first publications to concern itself with air pollution" and credited Cousins's "Fouling of the American Environment" as a major contributor to the creation of the new task force.[23]

Once again, the Cousins model of identifying a public problem that the government was ignoring, bringing attention to it through editorials, and ultimately working on behalf of the government to help change policies and laws had proven effective. As the chair of the task force, Cousins did not waste a moment before getting to work. Just over a month later, the executives at Con Ed, who had ignored his letter of ten months earlier, had been summoned to be interrogated by Cousins, who now had political in addition to editorial power. Accompanying the two Con Ed vice presidents were the president of the National Coal Association and its director of research.

The group had come to the *Saturday Review* offices for their 11:00 a.m. meeting in response to Cousins's insistence that they report to him about current research their organizations were conducting in the field of pollution reduction and whether they could step up their efforts. "We have looked into the matter rather thoroughly," the group stated, "and we feel that a great deal of research is already being done in this area. . . . We are certain you agree there's no point in getting into another research program with so much going on already." Cousins blasted back, "I'm somewhat astounded, apart from my disappointment. . . . Since there's been so little in the way of tangible progress, I should suppose the need for additional research is clear." He asked how much Con Ed had spent on research and development the previous year. "Thirty thousand," was the reply. "Thirty Thousand against a profit of $140 million!!! . . . The disparity between profit and research is a rather remarkable one, considering the fact that Con Ed has so many unsolved problem[s] in areas that concern the public welfare." Cousins wrote in his notes, "None of the men present showed the slightest interest."[24]

Clearly frustrated, Cousins told the group that he had always wondered why Con Ed would allow itself to be regarded as everybody's villain and get such a black eye in public. Now he understood the answer: The men in front of him had absolutely no sense of creative imagination. No sense of public relations. No sense of how to make vital connections that might solve this grave problem. After this dressing-down, Cousins's notes read, "that was the end of the meeting."[25] Whether he recognized it at the time or not, Cousins was beginning to get an education into why, despite federal action since 1953, the pollution problem was so difficult to solve. Major industries launched token "anti-pollution" research divisions that produced little in the way of actionable science but whose existence allowed the companies to say that they were taking the issue seriously.

Cousins and his task force moved extremely quickly. Within four months they had a report ready for the mayor. An exhaustive survey of the multitude of pollution sources in the city had found that "New York pumps more poisons per square mile into its air than any major city in the United States."[26] When the report was released to the public the following day, that finding got front-page treatment above the fold in the *New York Times*, followed by a full-page summary of the report.[27] Cousins's report was damning. It charged the city with hypocritically violating its own laws, with its own municipal operations being a major source of pollution. [28]

But in his typical manner, Cousins called for the thing he knew best: citizen engagement. "Nothing effective was done, nor could have been done," he wrote later, "until citizen action created a groundswell of support for official measures." Despite his optimism, he included the ominous warning that "all the ingredients exist for an air-pollution disaster of major proportions."[29] That warning would become reality just six months later when a temperature inversion (of the exact type Cousins warned about in his report) settled over New York during Thanksgiving 1966. As the blanket of warm air that rolled in over the city trapped pollutants near the ground, it sent the air-pollution index up to the danger point. The city shut down its incinerators, and officials warned people with health issues to stay indoors.[30]

But even without the Thanksgiving smog event, the publication of the task force's report in May had immediate effects. Just eight days later Con Ed, which had previously refused to consider Cousins's suggestions, now came hat in hand. Mayor Lindsay praised Cousins for his success in negotiating a deal with the electric utility company according to which it would take "immediate measures that will have a substantial effect in combating air pollution." The company would close four of its generating plants in the city and replace them with new, cleaner plants outside the city.[31] Cousins was praised by the Citizens for Clean Air group, who invited him to join a roundtable discussion on further issues.[32]

The task force's impact kept rippling across the city. Five months later Mayor Lindsay announced an aggressive anti-pollution plan that the *New York Times* called "the hardest hitting, most aggressive campaign to clean up the air in New York City in history."[33] Cousins would later tell his archivist that serving on the Antipollution Task Force had been one of the best things he had done in his life.[34] The programs launched in 1966 as a result of Cousins's task force would be simply the first in a long line of effective anti-pollution measures. New York's efforts would spark a nationwide commitment to clean air and water and lead to the creation in 1970 of the federal-level Environmental Protection Agency.

CHAPTER 29

DAYS *of* APPREHENSION *and* CONFUSION

The early to middle 1960s was a time of great upheaval in American society. The civil rights movement and the protests against the Vietnam War added stress points to a fracturing nation. While Cousins had enjoyed great success with his international projects to this point, he seemed mostly oblivious of other prominent issues of his day, especially on the domestic front. The *Saturday Review* itself covered domestic issues quite thoroughly, but Cousins's editorials skewed heavily toward the international. Issues like the civil rights movement in the United States were not his primary focus.

On a personal level, says his daughter Sarah, it was utterly taken for granted that race had absolutely zero bearing on a person's worth, that it was a person's deeds that mattered. The Cousins family hosted children in their home from the Fresh Air Fund, a program that brought mostly black children from the inner city out to the countryside for the summer. "But this wasn't done with do-gooder condescension," says Sarah. "It was just fun having them. I was the youngest one and I liked having temporary siblings my own age." Theirs was an open and accepting home. Sarah recalls learning from her mother the fervent belief that to demean or look down upon someone because of his or her race was indicative only of one's own lowness and stupidity. The absurd notion that you would discriminate against someone because of race was absolutely rejected.[1]

While Cousins himself was not directly involved in the civil rights movement, his daughters Andrea and Candis were. Andrea moved into Harlem in 1963 to work with the Harlem Education Project. At first her father was not excited about this. "It was still a new idea at the time, black and white working together on these projects in these neighborhoods," Andrea recalls. But her father soon warmed to the idea, giving money to the project and helping with contacts and networking. Andrea must have blazed the path, because Candis remembers that by the time she headed south to work on voter registration and school desegregation initiatives, her father was very proud and supportive. "My other friend's parents wouldn't allow it," Candis noted, but her parents were fully supportive.[2]

In one instance, Cousins did join his daughter at a civil rights meeting that disturbed him. Two black activists talked about blowing up the Liberty Bell. "My father was very upset about this," Andrea said. Perhaps this was related to a concern Cousins had expressed in a meeting of the *Saturday Review* editorial committee. Cousins had noted that "the race relations problem was becoming explosive in the North" and he feared a "blood bath in Harlem before too long." The American novelist John Steinbeck, who occasionally wrote for the *Saturday Review* and had been invited to attend the meeting, responded, "There's got to be violence. In fact I think some violence is necessary, indeed useful. We all have it in us. You can't deny this. A man needs to be violent at times."[3]

Three weeks later, Cousins wrote a rare editorial on the civil rights movement. In "Black Wind Rising," he expressed his fear that the civil rights movement was entering "a new, explosive, and tragic phase." He penned a long list of injustices that African Americans faced and indicated who the perpetrators of these injustices were: the landlords who overcharged and violated the laws; housing inspectors who ignored the violations; white merchants who short-weighted; education officials; white employers who instituted racist practices; union leaders who drew color lines. At the same time, he also raised the alarm that the movement's leadership was "passing into the hands of haters," thus making it impossible for the more "responsible Negro leaders like Roy Wilkins, Martin Luther King, Bayard Rustin . . . [t]o be heard above the battle cries of the showdown-minded partisans." He implored his white readers to "listen more to, and strengthen the position of men like [King]. . . . They may seem like radicals to the uninitiated, but within the civil rights movement they represent the best hope against the . . . inciters of violence." Cousins also advocated the passage of the civil rights bill as "the least, not the most, that is required."[4] Opposite his editorial, the *Saturday Review* gave civil rights leader Martin Luther King space to publish a long article examining the status of the civil rights struggle and race relations in America.

Andrea remembers that her father never got directly involved in the civil rights movement, partly because of the big generational gap (Cousins was fifty years old in 1965) but mostly because of a difference in worldview. "Someone like my father who was working from the top down had a very different view of the world and what was needed, what we should do. . . . The Northern Students (a civil rights group formed in 1961) was all about grassroots, bottom-up."[5]

Despite the critical illness that struck him in mid-August and would keep him largely out of commission for five months, Cousins managed to publish twenty-five editorials that year. But his final editorial of the year foreshadowed the fact that the rapidly growing war in Vietnam would soon envelop the United States. During the 1964 election campaign, Johnson had portrayed himself as the peace candidate against his far more aggressive opponent, Barry Goldwater. As the situation in Vietnam deteriorated throughout 1964, it became quite clear to the White House that the United States would need to significantly increase its presence in Vietnam in order to stave off a possible defeat. Although there was fierce debate within the White House over how to limit US involvement, President Johnson never wavered from his determination not to let Vietnam "fall" to Communism on his watch.[6]

Over the course of his first full year in the Oval Office, President Lyndon Johnson would authorize covert operations, approve a massive ongoing aerial bombing campaign against North Vietnam, and prepare to introduce American ground troops into the conflict. Johnson's justification for these actions was the pledge he had made to honor John F. Kennedy's legacy. To Johnson, part of that "meant seeing things through in Vietnam." But Johnson believed that much more was at stake than Kennedy's policies. American credibility was on the line, as were Johnson's own political fortunes. He was determined not to be "the President who saw Southeast Asia go the way China went."[7] (President Truman had endured withering criticism for "losing" China to Communism.)

Johnson got his chance to "see things through" in the early days of August 1964. The US destroyer *Maddox* was "innocently" sailing (or so the administration claimed) in international waters off the coast of North Vietnam when it was attacked without provocation by North Vietnamese boats. The *Maddox* returned fire. Two days later, the North Vietnamese launched a second unprovoked attack.[8] At least according to the White House. In reality, though, whether the second attack actually occurred has been the source of much controversy. Historian Frederik Logevall writes that after a detailed study, the deputy director of the CIA concluded that "no second attack had occurred." This was a war that Johnson *chose.* According to National Security Advisor McGeorge Bundy, Johnson had decided possibly even before the shooting started to use the incident as a means to get a congressional resolution passed.[9] It would take until 2003, but even Defense Secretary Robert McNamara admitted that it was simply the product of "confusion" and that the second attack "never happened." "We were wrong," McNamara would state in a rare mea culpa.[10]

In response to this "unprovoked" attack against American ships, on August 7, 1964, the US Congress passed the Gulf of Tonkin Resolution, authorizing President Johnson to take military action to assist any nation in the Southeast Asia Treaty Organization. The resolution was decidedly not a declaration of war, but it did provide the president with the ability to rapidly escalate US military involvement in Vietnam if he so chose. Two months after the passage of the resolution, Norman Cousins was growing increasingly alarmed by his assessment that the Soviet Union's recent decision to send military aid to Hanoi had been sparked by its belief that full-scale US military action in Vietnam was imminent. Cousins called the Soviet moves "an action which in itself brooks the serious risk of causing the conflict to erupt far beyond Vietnam as a whole." But Cousins also levied a biting critique against Johnson's policy, arguing that "shoring up the Vietnamese government and supporting the military actions against the guerillas—has bogged down in a costly and futile holding operation." Cousins, along with many others, feared that Johnson might attempt to force a military solution, which would "almost certainly precipitate a mushrooming conflict."[11]

As it turned out, Johnson indeed did rely on a military solution, and it did mushroom into a nearly decade-long conflict that not only would consume the United States but would command an inordinate amount of Cousins's time and energy to little result; it was a time in his life that Cousins would later describe as punctuated by much "confusion and apprehension." Cousins would attempt to help negotiate a settlement with Hanoi, but the model he had previously deployed to astounding success in Japan and Germany—of public pressure coupled with private diplomacy—failed completely in this case.

On November 23, 1964, the front page of the *New York Times* carried an alarming report. General Maxwell Taylor, then ambassador to South Vietnam, was due to return to Washington to brief President Johnson after traveling through Vietnam "studying the Vietnam situation intensely for two weeks." It was widely reported that Taylor was going to urge Johnson to expand the war. While in Vietnam, Taylor apparently had advocated for conducting air strikes in North Vietnam.[12] That report came out on Sunday, and by the following Friday Cousins, despite still being laid up in the hospital battling his illness, put through a phone call to White House press secretary Bill Moyers to discuss US actions in Vietnam and how they were being interpreted in the Communist world. Two days later he sent a written memo emphasizing his concern that "the Russians' big difficulty is that they don't know how to read our newspapers. They have made serious miscalculations based on American news reports attributed to unnamed 'authoritative' sources. . . . The Russians interpreted this [Taylor] story as an attempt to prepare American public opinion for a large-scale attack on North Vietnam." Cousins implored Moyers to consider the advantages and disadvantages of "referring" the Vietnam situation to the United Nations for a mediated solution, claiming that "we have come to a dead end on the military front."[13]

Using his connections to the White House, Cousins initiated a private influence campaign. He drafted a letter directly to President Johnson that read, "All the news from Saigon and Washington indicates that you are faced with a very hard and immediate decision. The situation in Vietnam further deteriorates. To pull out of Vietnam as a surrender would be unthinkable. To carry the war northward might be catastrophic."[14] Signing off, he assured the president that should he choose to respond, Cousins would not release the letter to the press without Johnson's approval.

Cousins's claims about the privacy of their correspondence did not stop him from publishing an editorial in the *Saturday Review* two weeks later imploring Johnson to refer the Vietnam conflict to the United Nations (which he had advised in the private letter as well). Whether Johnson even read Cousins's letter is unclear, but the publication of this editorial was simply "phase two" in the standard Cousins playbook. First, try to reach out directly and persuade the policymakers; second, inform the public in the hopes of sparking constituent pressure; then third, keep up the pressure through frequent editorials that stoke people's moral outrage. In this case, though, Cousins could not prevent the continuing deterioration of the security situation in Vietnam from superseding his peacemaking efforts.

In February 1965, Cousins penned his first of what would soon become many editorials that year criticizing US actions in Vietnam. Cousins pointed out that it was clear that the "United States today does not have the backing of the Vietnamese people in whose name it went into Vietnam in the first place. . . . Military forces have had to cope not just with secret agents from North Vietnam but [with] the growing opposition of the populace as a whole." He went on to criticize the American retaliatory bombings, while also praising Johnson, likely hoping to stay in his good graces if he was to have any effect on the president's thinking. Cousins wrote that "President Johnson has genuinely tried to keep the military lid on Vietnam, recognizing the ease with which the hostilities could mushroom into a general war." He expressed his concern, however, that Americans did not seem as alarmed about this as he thought they should be. Cousins complained that there had been all too little public pressure in support of a policy of restraint, a failing, he said, "that the American people have it within their means to change whenever they wish to do so."[15] The American people did not seem to want to remedy that "problem." At that point, according to a Gallup poll, only 24 percent of Americans thought it was a mistake to send troops to Vietnam.

No matter how much Cousins praised Johnson's restraint, it would ultimately be for naught. By the time that editorial went to press, Johnson had already made up his mind and given the order to initiate Operation Rolling Thunder, a massive bombing campaign of targets in North Vietnam. According to historian Robert Buzzanco, "The immediate cause of the air war came on 7 February, when the VC mortared an army barracks in Pleiku, killing 9 and wounding 109 Americans."[16] But Johnson had made this decision to bomb well before February. The White House had pushed Taylor to request more ground troops, but the ambassador and even General William Westmoreland, commander of the United States forces in Vietnam, had quickly rejected the notion. Now, with the attack on Pleiku, the administration had all the political cover it needed to pursue the war it had chosen. Although the order had been given in February, Operation Rolling Thunder would not begin to pound its targets until March 2, delayed because of poor weather. As the B-52 Stratofortresses and the F-105 Thunderchiefs unleashed their bombs over Vietnam, Cousins was crafting another editorial.

Two weeks after the bombing started, Cousins marked his position as what now might be recognized as a fairly mainstream Cold War liberal one. He posited that the original problem in Vietnam had been "an unremitting Communist campaign of terror, assassination, and brutality against the South Vietnamese people and government."[17] If he had wanted to, Cousins could have laid some of the blame at the feet of the US-backed South Vietnamese president Ngo Dinh Diem, a nepotistic authoritarian whose administration was rife with corruption and who had killed about twelve thousand suspected opponents to his regime and imprisoned forty thousand more.[18] Instead he claimed that "whether that government was good or bad or in-between is irrelevant."[19]

It is clear that Cousins bought into the prevailing American mindset that the spread of Communism had to be stopped at all costs, and he even stated that "our presence in Vietnam is in our national interest." Cousins, like many others at the time, took America's "greatness" for granted. He had long argued that the nation should be a force for good in the world. That it should build, not bomb. Even though he believed that Communism needed to be driven out of Vietnam, his main concern was that the way in which the United States was approaching Vietnam was not working, and further violence was not the solution. He asked, "What lies beyond the bombings in North Vietnam? . . . What about the large majority of the Vietnamese who by this time have become bitterly opposed to the United States? . . . The big and bulging fact about Vietnam is that our policy there has not worked."[20]

Mirroring the fury of the bombs falling over North Vietnam, Cousins wrote at a ferocious pace. Beginning on March 13, he penned six consecutive editorials on the topic of the war, each growing more despondent, with a crescendo after the *New York Times* reported on March 23 that the United States had deployed chemical gases in Vietnam.[21] One can imagine that Cousins, upon learning of this fact, felt much the same rage he had felt after first reading about the use of the atomic bomb. His reaction was immediate. At the *Saturday Review*, Cousins's editorials would frequently sit in the queue for a few weeks before publication. In any given year, Cousins would typically write fewer than half the editorials, the rest being written by other staff members or guests. In fact, sometimes there was a delay of a few months before Cousins weighed in on a given event. Thus, one can get a sense of how strongly Cousins felt about an issue from how rapidly he published on it. His editorial on the bombing of Hiroshima was published twelve days later; that on the use of chemical gas in Vietnam, eighteen days after the report was made public.

"Whatever the military argument," Cousins wrote, "[the use of gas was] wicked, incompetent, and prejudicial to the vital interests of the United States. . . . What is most menacing of all is the lack of respect for the moral principles that affect our station in the world."[22] Interestingly, Cousins again let the president himself off the hook, claiming that the decision to use the gas had been made without Johnson's knowledge. He praised Johnson for not defending the decision. Perhaps he did not want to openly antagonize Johnson at that moment because Cousins was also engaged in some back-channel efforts with the Russians. He hoped to soon bring the results to Johnson.

Two days before his editorial "How to Lose the World" hit the newsstands, Cousins himself was trying to save the world. On April 8, 1965, Cousins was in Washington for a private appointment with Soviet ambassador Anatoly Dobrynin. Cousins intended to discuss two matters: one, making arrangements for the next Dartmouth Conference; and two, a request to interview the new Soviet premier, Leonid Brezhnev. Cousins hoped to establish a relationship with the new leader similar to the one he had had with Khrushchev. But before they could get to any of Cousins's agenda items, the ambassador opened the meeting by expressing that he was very concerned about Vietnam. Cousins responded, "Didn't you think the President made himself [and the US position] clear in his talk at Johns Hopkins last night?"

The previous evening Johnson had given an address titled "Peace Without Conquest." In it, he had outlined the US position in Vietnam and stated that "we have no territory there, nor do we seek any." Continuing to outline US objectives in this war, Johnson had stated that the United States' only goal was to ensure that South Vietnam had the opportunity to shape its own destiny. "We want nothing for ourselves," he had claimed, "only that the people of South Viet-Nam be allowed to guide their own country in their own way."[23] Cousins told Dobrynin that he thought it had been a magnificent speech that made clear that the United States "had no military purposes or objectives beyond Vietnam and that we were genuinely interested in stabilizing the area."[24]

"But this bombing is a terrible thing. It can change our relationship with you," Dobrynin responded. "There are many people in my government . . . who are thinking it might not be possible to have peace with your country." The more Cousins conversed with the ambassador, the more he sounded like a White House spokesman. Cousins fully backed the president and said that the speech represented Johnson "speaking his true feelings." He continued to argue that the US. position on the bombings was sound and necessary, that they had been directed only at military and not civilian targets, and that their only aim had been to "dampen the fire, not intensify it." (Has bombing *ever* "dampened" a conflict?)

Dobrynin immediately criticized Cousins's assertion that the United States had sought to dampen the conflict by bombing. "I would like to believe this," the ambassador said, "but I honestly cannot understand the bombings. It is doing nothing except making the people there more determined to resist." Incidentally, Cousins had made precisely that same argument in an editorial a few weeks earlier when he pointed out that the increased US involvement was only leading to more and more South Vietnamese becoming opposed to the US presence.[25]

Dobrynin also pointed out that the continued bombing was rallying citizens across the Communist world to openly protest the United States. Clearly, this point stuck with Cousins. A month later he repeated Dobrynin's claim in an editorial when he wrote, "The bombings have not only stiffened resistance but have intensified the popular opposition and hostility to the United States. . . . Arrayed against the U.S. today are not only Communists but a broad cross-section of the people . . . [who have been] heavily involved in these protests." Still, even in this editorial Cousins openly defended Johnson, saying that "we are convinced the President arrived at his decision to bomb Vietnam honestly and conscientiously."[26] Cousins's position of opposing the growing war while also wanting to remain in the good graces of the Johnson administration by not criticizing them directly was increasingly untenable.

Back in the Soviet Embassy, the conversation continued to devolve, with neither side giving ground. Finally, an exasperated Dobrynin told Cousins, "Please don't think I am trying to argue with you. We have known each other a long time. I know you are sincere; I hope you feel I am sincere." Then, appealing to Cousins's signature project and the real purpose of his visit, the ambassador continued, "What worries me is that a great deal of work that has been done by people on both sides who believe in friendship between our two countries is being torn down."[27]

This conversation had gone off the rails. Cousins was meeting with Dobrynin specifically to discuss arrangements for the fifth Dartmouth Conference, which was to take place later in 1965, and now the ambassador was hinting that it might not happen. During their discussion that day, so focused on the Vietnam War, the two men did not get a chance to discuss the Dartmouth plans. In fact, as the US involvement in Vietnam deepened over the summer and the US-Soviet relationship continued to decline, the Soviets would postpone the conference. In both 1966 and 1967, Cousins would renew the invitation to no effect. Because of the Vietnam War, the fifth Dartmouth would not take place until 1969.[28]

Still, Cousins fought the ambassador in the waning minutes of their meeting. He told Dobrynin that an indication by Hanoi that it wanted to negotiate might have a specific effect on the bombings. Dobrynin replied that the US government had already indicated that it would not ease the bombings in order to negotiate, and Hanoi would not negotiate while there was continued bombing. Dobrynin concluded by saying that he felt a great sadness; he said the situation was dark. Attempting to salvage the mood by oozing his typical optimism, Cousins responded to the contrary. "The President's talk had made things much lighter," he said. "Even if the Ambassador couldn't yet discern the light, [Cousins] begged him to believe that the black was less black as a result of the President's [Johns Hopkins] talk. And there was some room to maneuver in the new opening."[29] Their meeting ended without covering the agenda items they had intended to discuss. Vietnam had consumed all the air in the room.

During their discussion Dobrynin mentioned something that alarmed Cousins enough that he felt the need to report it to the White House. "I believe that we are moving into military action ourselves in Vietnam. I don't see how we can avoid it," Dobrynin revealed. "A Socialist country—a very small country—is being bombed by you. We have to respond. . . . We know how dangerous this can be, but we have to do it."[30]

Cousins ruminated on this alarming revelation for four days before drafting a memo to inform Vice President Hubert Humphrey of what he had learned from Dobrynin. "Far more consequential, I know you would regard it as of the highest importance that an assessment be made concerning the implications of a large Soviet involvement in Vietnam," Cousins wrote. "I was confident you would want me to give you a full account of my meeting with the Ambassador." He chose to send this directly to Humphrey, not only to capitalize on their long-standing friendship but because he thought the vice president was "in the best possible position to act on the information contained." More ominously, in a personal note to Humphrey, separate from the memo, he shared his private thoughts. "I would prayerfully urge you," Cousins wrote, "not to appear on the same platform with and in close proximity to the President. . . . There is a real and specific danger of retaliatory action growing out of the Vietnam situation."[31] Here we see the first instance of what would become increasingly common as the war dragged on: Cousins being used by forces far above him to pursue their own agendas through his connections. Dobrynin clearly knew that Cousins had proven to be an effective conduit for passing information through to the White House. And in December 1965 it was the White House's turn to try to use Cousins for its own purposes.

On December 1, 1965, Cousins was in Washington for a conference when he received a phone call from presidential assistant Jack Valenti asking him to stop by the White House. Johnson was to give his State of the Union address the following month, and they wanted Cousins to help write it. The ulterior motive of this meeting appears to have been to influence the tone of Cousins's editorials. Under the guise of bringing Cousins up to speed on the State of the Union, Valenti gave a briefing on the president's ideas on domestic and foreign policy, with special attention paid to Vietnam. Cousins recalls that he "was impressed by Valenti's careful and detailed recital of the President's position on Vietnam. . . . Basically he said, President Johnson's policy in Vietnam was to fight a limited war, and to get to the negotiating table as sonn [*sic*] as possible."[32]

As the bombing dragged on into the end of 1965 to little effect—Hanoi still had not come to the negotiating table—and armed with this newly acquired information, Cousins launched a private diplomatic mission of his own. Because of the Ravensbrück Lapins initiative of 1958, Cousins had established a good degree of rapport with officials from the Polish government. On December 13, Cousins put those connections to use when he invited Polish ambassador Bohdan Lewandowski to dine at his Park Avenue apartment in New York. Many times Cousins hosted private meals like this, most likely prepared by Ellen.

Cousins would often call home and ask his wife to prepare a meal for whomever he happened to be inviting over. Sometimes it was one person for a private chat, as in this case; other times he would bring a (literal) busload of visitors home for lunch, as he did once with a visiting delegation from India. "My mother would make these banquets for people," Candis remembers. "She loved it." Cousins's archivist would also recall that Ellen "was happiest when she was in her own kitchen."[33]

As the two men shared their meal, Lewandowski explained that his government, like many others, was seriously concerned about the direction events were taking in Vietnam. "His government feared," he explained to Cousins, "that unless something were done soon to halt or moderate the war, it would mushroom beyond control." The ambassador hoped to get Cousins's deeper thoughts on this prospect that Johnson might be open to negotiations.

Revealing (correctly) that he believed Cousins was in close contact with the White House, the ambassador asked how he knew for sure that Johnson wanted negotiations (a claim Cousins had made in a recent editorial), and if he did, would the United States seriously conduct them in a way that could produce a successful outcome? Cousins recorded in his notes that, "for the next hour, I put before Lewandowski the substantial first-hand evidence I had to support my view." "I drew heavily upon Valenti's bruefing [*sic*] to provide substantial evidence of U.S. sincerity in seeking a negotiated peace." The ambassador responded that he found Cousins's points quite convincing and only wished that the government in Hanoi could have heard the briefing too.

In Cousins's own recollection of the discussion, "Presumptuously, perhaps, I said I would be willing to attest to the same things I said to him in Hanoi or anywhere else." Lewandowski responded that Poland was prepared to serve as something of a bridge between both worlds and he would explore, privately of course, whether such a trip could be arranged.[34] The very next day, Cousins called the State Department and reported this conversation to William P. Bundy, assistant secretary of state for East Asian and Pacific affairs. Cousins wrote that Bundy "encouraged me to take advantage of other similar openings to put across the idea that the United States was . . . genuinely eager to end the war through a political rather than a military settlement."[35]

Four days later, Cousins received a phone call from Lewandowski, who asked whether Cousins could meet with him at the United Nations. They arranged a 3:00 p.m. meeting in the corner of the Delegates Lounge, where Lewandowski explained that he had good news: the initial response by Hanoi to the suggestion of Cousins's visit was promising. That was all he could say at the moment. That same day, Cousins telephoned Secretary of State Dean Rusk directly and relayed the news of the development. The following day, William Bundy called back to ask for further details.[36] Clearly, Cousins's machinations were getting some high-level attention.

The rush of the impending Christmas holidays kept Cousins busy with last-minute preparations and family meals. Two days before Christmas, Cousins was having lunch with his wife's sister at the Hotel Roosevelt in New York City when the headwaiter informed him that there was a telephone call for him. To his surprise, he learned that it was the White House operator on the line with not just one but three incoming calls for him—one from Bill Moyers, one from Jack Valenti, and the third from the president himself. When the president's call was put through, President Johnson came on the line and asked Cousins if he would represent him at the inauguration of President Ferdinand Marcos of the Philippines. Vice President Humphrey would lead the delegation, and Cousins would be officially designated as a "special Presidential representative." Moyers then got on the phone and told Cousins that the *real* reason they wanted to go was so that he could ply his international contacts to pick up information that might be useful in connection with the attempt to end the war in Vietnam.[37] After the inaugural ceremonies, he would proceed with Humphrey on a tour of Asia, where he would have ample time to meet with people. This was just the moment that Cousins had been waiting for. He understood that his presence on the trip would be little more than cover so he could work his way up to Vietnam and get word to Ho Chi Minh about Johnson's desire for negotiations.[38]

But Cousins (as well as the US government) was targeting the wrong person. Historian Lien-Hang T. Nguyen's book *Hanoi's War* highlights that by this point Ho Chi Minh was increasingly marginalized within the government. In fact, the North Vietnamese leadership was pulled between a "peace" faction, calling for negotiations, and more militant members, who easily outmaneuvered them.[39]

Cousins would not have much time to decide whether to give up his Christmas holidays to accept the assignment. The delegation was scheduled to leave just five days later, on December 27. Of course he said yes.

CHAPTER 30

THE "HUMPHREY MISSION"

Departing for the Philippines, Cousins arrived at Washington's National Airport at 1:12 p.m. He was met by a State Department officer, who escorted him to a car. In twenty-two minutes they were at Andrews Air Force Base, where they were driven right out onto the tarmac and boarded Air Force Two. Much of the newspaper coverage leading up to the trip emphasized that the so-called Humphrey Mission was part of a sizable "peace offensive" during the Christmas holiday bombing pause. Cousins's role in this endeavor, as he understood it, was to "prowl around the fringes, picking up information that might be useful."[1]

Overall, Cousins thought that the presence of the second highest elected officer in the United States representing his country at an event of prime importance to the Filipinos was "dramatic proof to the peoples of Asia and Africa that the United States was paying high tribute to the emergence of once-colonial nations as equal members in the community of nations."[2] Ultimately, though, the trip was a disappointment for Cousins. In his private notes he wrote, "Not much eventuated during the trip to justify my unannounced assignment."[3] He failed to make any direct contact with the North Vietnamese. The closest he came was meeting a businessman friend in Tokyo who had been a school chum of Ho Chi Minh's. Cousins attempted to persuade the man to pass along the message of Johnson's good faith.[4]

After a long flight back from Asia—a trip Cousins had taken many times before but never in the storied confines of Air Force Two—they arrived back at Andrews Air Force Base at 11:30 a.m. Apparently, even the most exclusive airline in the world has luggage issues, and a loading problem had delayed their arrival by fifteen minutes. A "fretting" Lyndon Johnson paced at the White House awaiting their arrival. The delegation was not even given time to freshen up; they were whisked by motorcade from the air base straight to the White House to debrief with the president.[5]

In the Oval Office, Johnson settled into the rocking chair. Kennedy's rocking chair, Cousins noted, which had since been recovered in a different color. Johnson opened the meeting by stating that the reports he had received from the trip were positive. Vice President Humphrey explained that he had stressed with Asian leaders the need for them to support the American military effort in Vietnam. Cousins weighed in to explain to Johnson that while he had failed to make direct contact with the North Vietnamese, "the fact that the Vice-President was taking a direct part in the U.S. peace initiatives was having an impact."

As the meeting wound down, Johnson thanked the men and told them that the press was waiting to hear about the trip, about which they were authorized to give an uncensored account. The president instructed Humphrey to go first but suggested that Cousins also give an account to the press. They were ushered into the adjoining room, where Humphrey spoke for about twenty minutes, took some questions about the Vietnam situation, and then ended the press conference. Cousins was annoyed that he was not given a chance to speak to the reporters.[6] Still, he later said that he had been "tremendously impressed with the way the President spoke at our meeting and there is no doubt in my mind about his sincerity in saying that we had to find some way to crack through to negotiate."[7]

Three days after he returned to New York, Cousins did what he had done following trips for presidents in the past (and to much effect in the case of Kennedy): he drafted a memo offering his unsolicited advice. "I now venture a few thoughts," he presumptuously wrote, "on the matter of negotiations with Hanoi." Acknowledging that it seemed as though Hanoi was unwilling to accept Johnson's sincerity (or, as Nguyen points out, had already decided not to negotiate with the Americans at this point), Cousins proposed that "there are other possibilities tantamount to negotiations that may be possible. I'm thinking specifically of a step-by-step reciprocal de-escalation. If an initiative in one sector meets with a reciprocal response, then the way is cleared for a larger step." Cousins even proposed that the upcoming Buddhist holidays would be a perfect time to try such an initiative.[8] Cousins concluded his letter by putting himself at Johnson's disposal to further develop any of these ideas if the president so wished.

While Cousins did not receive a direct response to his memo from the White House, a few days later he again invited Polish ambassador Lewandowski to dinner. The ambassador was eager to hear whether anything had happened on Cousins's trip to change his view about the United States' readiness to negotiate. Far from it, Cousins replied; in fact, his conviction had been strengthened as a result of the trip and his meeting with the president.[9] After Cousins described his trip and how he had reached his conclusion about Johnson's sincerity, Lewandowski said, "It's just too bad that what you've just told me—and I'm convinced—could not also be told to Hanoi." Cousins responded, "Mr. Ambassador, if this is an invitation, I accept." He explained that as a private citizen he would not hesitate to testify to the good faith of President Johnson.[10]

A few days after that, on January 11, Lewandowski stopped by Cousins's *Saturday Review* office at 9:30 a.m. and declared that he had good news. After their dinner he had been in touch with the Polish Foreign Ministry. The ambassador had just received word that Hanoi was willing to send a representative to meet directly with Cousins just as soon as they could work out the details. Immediately after the ambassador left, Cousins telephoned the White House and reported the development. Jack Valenti, astonished, asked that Cousins come to Washington right away.

During the background check the FBI had conducted before clearing Cousins to join the Humphrey trip to Asia, Dr. Arthur Larson, former special assistant to President Eisenhower, had described Norman Cousins as "a brilliant and tremendously able individual who has an uncanny capacity for sensitivity as to what 'is in the air internationally.'"[11] This assessment was born out by the fact that the more Cousins thought about the situation, the more he put together a sophisticated understanding of the larger dynamics at play inside Vietnam. Or rather, what he *thought* was a sophisticated understanding. He came to believe that privately and secretly Hanoi would discuss negotiations but that publicly they would only discuss the hard conditions, the cessation of bombing. Cousins thought that the North Vietnamese, like Khrushchev in 1963, were playing to the Chinese, but he was wrong about this.[12]

Le Duan had risen to the position of general secretary of the Communist Party, becoming the top decision maker in North Vietnam. He had drawn a significant lesson from the First Indochina War with the French: that diplomacy without military superiority should be avoided at all costs. Le Duan was convinced that peace talks with the Americans were futile until the Communist forces had secured a major victory. On his other point too Cousins was wrong. The North Vietnamese were not playing to the Chinese. It was, in fact, the Chinese who had urged the Vietnamese to continue to fight, while it was Moscow that wanted negotiations, which the Chinese would try to foil at every turn.[13]

On January 12, Cousins arrived at the White House and Valenti took him directly to McGeorge Bundy's office. While Cousins was clearly eager to explore this opening, Bundy evidently was not. Cousins wrote that he "questioned me rather severely. It was difficult to get him to understand or accept the fact that the idea for the trip had grown out of a conversation with Lewandowski" and was not any sort of formal "official" proposal by either side. Cousins found Bundy's line of questioning to be "most distasteful and even humiliating." "He had somewhat the manner of a college dean questioning a freshmen about whether he had been honest in an examination paper." Cousins managed to rein in his frustrated responses, especially after Bundy leaned forward and glowered at Cousins, sharply stating, "But it's true, isn't it—that you *want* to go to Vietnam?"[14] Clearly Bundy was implying that Cousins had concocted this "peace opening" simply to give himself a reason to travel to Vietnam and thrust himself into US-Vietnamese diplomacy.

Cousins admitted that yes, he did want to go, but his reason for going out of his way to inform the White House of this development had been that he didn't think he would feel confident in going if those closest to the president felt that this was intrusive or presumptuous. Bundy replied that he hoped that Cousins understood that "peripheral efforts such as this could be most distracting and confusing." Bundy pointed out that he had to be absolutely certain about how this idea had originated. It would have one meaning if Cousins had initially suggested it and another meaning entirely if it had first come from the Poles. Cousins assured Bundy that it simply had been a "natural development" in his talk with Lewandowski. On that point, though, Cousins was being disingenuous. It was Cousins himself who had suggested the idea, explaining to the Polish ambassador that he, as a private citizen, would have no hesitation about testifying to the good faith of President Johnson if Lewandowski could set up a meeting with Hanoi.

Cousins pushed back against Bundy's suggestion that his efforts might be "distracting and confusing." He argued that perhaps this sort of peripheral effort would make more direct efforts possible because clearly the White House had failed to that point in bringing Hanoi to the negotiating table. That argument seemed to sink in. Cousins writes, "Mac became considerably more gracious at this point and said he had not intended in his questioning to be critical."[15] Ultimately, though, the

White House could take no action until they had confirmation from the Poles, so Bundy asked Cousins to keep them informed.

Two weeks later, on January 27 at 5:00 p.m., Cousins was in the midst of a meeting at his *Saturday Review* office when he was called out to take a phone call from the Polish Consulate. The news he was awaiting had arrived. Cousins dropped what he was doing and rushed back to his Park Avenue apartment, where he had been asked to meet immediately with Deputy Ambassador Eugeniusz Wyzner. The tall, pleasant, soft-spoken deputy arrived at 6:30 p.m. and informed Cousins that Hanoi was now ready to send someone to meet at his earliest convenience anywhere in the world *except* Hanoi. Wanting to honor the Poles, Cousins suggested they convene in Warsaw.

Immediately after his hour-long meeting with Wyzner, Cousins telephoned the White House and spoke to Valenti, who said he needed some time to run this development up the chain. An hour and a half later (9:15 p.m.) he called back and told Cousins that it was imperative that he immediately depart for Washington. Valenti had already made reservations at the Hay-Adams Hotel, one block from the White House, and they would expect him for a meeting at 9:00 the next morning. Cousins was instructed to pack a bag with enough clothing for a couple of days.[16] "I took this to mean that I was to leave the next day for Warsaw," he noted.[17] Given his wide international connections, his reputation as a straight dealer, and his efforts at citizen diplomacy, Cousins seemed poised to succeed again. But a single day can make all the difference.

By the time Cousins arrived at the White House the following morning, the mood had changed. He first spoke with Valenti for more than an hour and became somewhat confused because "[Valenti] kept referring to the fact that the President was waiting for some sign, however remote or obscure, even 'a finger beckoning somewhere.'" On the other hand, Valenti said that there had been numerous efforts to begin negotiations but that "it seemed clear to him that what was happening was that Hanoi was trying to vibrate the President's policy, first holding up the promise of talks, then pulling back, then starting up again, etc."[18] At that point Bundy arrived to say that on the matter of Cousins's visit it might be "too little too late." Frankly, he explained, "there was a strong feeling inside the government that the string had run out and that Hanoi should not be encouraged to believe that the United States could be manipulated into extending the bombing halt indefinitely."[19] (The Christmas bombing halt was ongoing in the hope that it would encourage an approach to the negotiating table.)

Pleading his case, Cousins asked if this was not the sign Johnson had publicly announced he was looking for. Sure, Hanoi's secret meeting with a private citizen was not the same as an open declaration, but Cousins knew from his long history of dealing with Communist nations that private approaches exactly like this one frequently opened the way to more consequential exchanges. On this matter his own record of success spoke for itself. But Cousins was failing to recognize a massive blind spot in his own reasoning. His own experiences with the Soviets were ultimately misleading: just because Moscow negotiated in one way by no means meant that the North Vietnamese would act in that same way. He was falling into the same trap that marred so much of US policy thinking during the Cold War: assuming that all Communist states were alike.

Valenti replied, "Norman, you've just got to understand that we've been through this before. We've had two leads in just the past 10 days, both of which led to nowhere. Each time they came up the President was advised to delay resumption and he agreed, but nothing happened.... Hanoi has had 36 days to come up with something definite, and they've failed." Cousins fought back. "True," he said,

> the suspension of the bombing has gone on for a month without getting us any closer to the conference table. But what about the bombing? That went on for 9 months. We were pretty patient then while we were bombing, which didn't produce any results either. I would just hope that the President wouldn't throw

> everything overboard now when a few more days might give us the chance to find out whether this is in fact the sign we've been waiting for.[20]

Bundy asked whether Cousins could get in and out of Warsaw within forty-eight hours. "It might be useful," Bundy said, "to register with Hanoi that the President desired to hold negotiations even though he had decided to resume bombing." It was now abundantly clear to Cousins that the decision to resume bombing had been made and would start on Monday morning. He argued with Bundy that it would be very difficult for him to operate under those circumstances. How could he possibly persuade Hanoi that the purpose of the bombing halt was to probe for peace if the bombing was resumed just after it indicated a desire to undertake preliminary conversations? "I don't think we have the slightest chance for getting negotiations with Hanoi for a long, long time to come if we should bomb," Cousins told Bundy. "You and I may differ on that," Bundy replied.

Cousins writes that "I'd a sense that the whole world was turning inside out. Could Bundy actually believe that Hanoi could be persuaded that the President was sincere about peace talks just after the bombers went into action?" The two men kept talking in circles. Valenti said that he did not think it was a good idea for Cousins to personally talk to the North Vietnamese ambassador about how sincere Johnson was just as the bombs were starting to fall.

Cousins later noted that he "had a sense of despair, bordering on desperation." Cousins implored Valenti, "Jack, I'll go to Warsaw but I beg you to persuade the President to hold off making the final decision until I can report to him on what was said. . . . Just let me talk to the Ambassador from North Vietnam." Cousins, sensing that perhaps the White House did not trust him, even offered to have the American ambassador with him in the room. "If you don't trust me to carry out the assignment successfully, for heavens [*sic*] sake, you can trust your own ambassador." Valenti replied, "Norman, it isn't that we don't trust you. It's just that . . . [w]e can't afford to make a mistake."

Cousins, not backing down from the fight, retorted that the mistake was in not checking out this opening. "[Hanoi has] said that [Johnson's] peace initiatives are phony. He's now in a position to show that he's won everything he's wanted."[21] Cousins continued, "It was tragic that the President should be deprived of what might well be the success of his policy. . . . How could anyone take the responsibility for saying the President's strategy had not been successful until every possibility had been checked out?"[22]

As Valenti leaned back in his chair, then picked up the cigar that had been smoldering in the ashtray and puffed on it, Cousins sensed that his tenacity had created an opening. Valenti stood up and told Cousins to wait; he would be back in a few minutes. Valenti presumably took the case directly to the president. Clearly there were fierce internal fractures among Johnson's staff over this issue of resuming the bombing. Johnson had decided to resume bombing but was willing to explore possibilities right up until the moment the bombs started to fall. Bundy was more pessimistic and believed the negotiations were a ploy. Valenti maybe just then had sided with Cousins. Still, as historian Fredrik Logevall points out in his book *Choosing War*, overall Johnson was the ultimate decision maker.[23]

Left alone, Cousins distracted himself during those anxious moments by walking around the room looking at the Remington paintings depicting the opening of the West. Suddenly the door burst open and Valenti returned. His argument had won the day. Cousins was instructed to telephone the Poles and tell them that he would be leaving that very night for Warsaw and would be prepared to meet with the representative from Hanoi the following afternoon. "Does that mean that the decision to resume bombing hasn't been made?" Cousins asked. "I can only tell you that the Executive Order has not yet been signed," Valenti replied.

Valenti left Cousins alone in the office again to make the arrangements. Elated that he had prevailed in the internal struggle, Cousins called his office in New York and had his secretary book a flight to Warsaw with a brief layover in London. Then, not wanting to use an "official" White House phone to call the Polish Consulate, Cousins walked to a phone booth in the basement to call and inform Wyzner that he would be departing the following day as long as Hanoi was ready.

After the call Cousins walked back up to Valenti's office. "Now, Norman," Valenti said, "there's one thing I've got to be very frank about. You're about to start off on a very delicate and important mission. I want you to give me a written statement that you will never write about or refer to anything that has happened during this episode. . . . You've got to understand, the sort of knowledge you know you have, if used the wrong way, could have very serious consequences. I want a written statement that you will never refer to this in any way." Cousins, however, refused Valenti's request. "Jack, if you think about what you've just asked me to do," he replied, "I think you will realize this is nothing you want to have on the record. . . . I think I've tried to be reasonably discreet in my life, and I think the President will just have to trust me not to exploit any knowledge I have for the wrong purposes. I'm afraid I can't sign the statement."[24] Valenti apologized for even asking and dropped the matter.

Cousins would stay true to his word for a while, but he eventually did start publishing after he became convinced that the Johnson administration had acted in bad faith on this issue. Perhaps they did. Historian James Hershberg thinks that the Johnson administration was likely "using" Cousins the whole time, stringing him along in order to keep him engaged, feeling important and on "their side" and thus less likely to rail against Johnson and the war in his editorials.[25]

At that point there was little to do but wait. Valenti told Cousins to go back to his hotel and wait for further instruction. Cousins had already checked out of the hotel, so instead he wandered two blocks east to the National Press Club. where he told the switchboard operator that he could be found in the library in case the White House called.

At 3:10 p.m. he was summoned back to the White House, where he was told that he needed to have a briefing with UN ambassador Arthur Goldberg, to whom Johnson had given a central role on the Vietnam issue. It became immediately clear that Goldberg had been called in to talk Cousins out of going. "First of all," he said, "I just hope you won't go to Warsaw. I would advise against it. It would hurt you personally."[26] He then told Cousins that President Johnson had asked him to give Cousins a full briefing. The ambassador explained that this was not the only time that Hanoi had "reached out" only to have it come to nothing. This time, he claimed, before the bombing halt could be extended the United States needed something far more definite than a statement of willingness to meet with a private citizen. If Hanoi were serious, it would get in touch with an official representative of the US government. "You can't blame the President for being reluctant to go through the same business again," Goldberg said, "You can understand that he doesn't want to be put in a position where his decisions will be made by Hanoi."

Ultimately, Cousins realized how little leverage he had. "[Goldberg] and [Averell] Harriman had just come back from a long journey which had failed to produce a single genuine lead, whereas I was trying to convince them that a real lead now existed that completely short-cut all the elaborate steps involved in the peace offensive."[27] Despite this, Cousins still tried to get his point across and proceeded to explain that in his experience, Communist nations were skittish about going through official channels. Cousins was fully convinced that that was why the North Vietnamese were willing to meet specifically with him. Here again, Cousins did not know as much about Hanoi as he thought he did. After all, he had no actual experience with the North Vietnamese. His single success with Khrushchev seems to have gone to his head and made him think he had discovered the secret to negotiating with all Communist governments.

Refusing to give up, Cousins asked Goldberg whether anything could be done to forestall the bombing decision. "Only a specific word direct from Hanoi unmistakably indicating a desire to get into talks could change the present course," Goldberg replied. "See if you can't get your friends to give you. . . . Some other sign outside of Warsaw so we know whether the Poles are just acting out of their own eagerness to avoid the resumption of the bombing."[28] Cousins realized that there was no point in pressing the matter further. It was moot anyway because Valenti's secretary interrupted to say Valenti needed to see him.

As soon as Cousins returned to the office, Valenti put his arm over his shoulder and said, "We sure appreciate everything you've done. The President has asked that Goldberg take over from now on in. . . . I know you've had a very tough time. I'm sorry we've kept you here all day." Then, probably hoping to get Cousins not just out of the White House but out of the city itself before he could interfere further, Valenti told him, "I know you're eager to get to the airport. I've got a White House car waiting outside."[29]

It was rush hour on a Friday night, and even though the drive from the White House to National Airport was only five miles, the city's infamous gridlocked traffic was impossible that night. Adding to his already horrible day, Cousins missed his flight by three minutes. Asking someone to hold him a spot in the long line of end-of-week business fliers returning to New York, he found a pay phone and called Wyzner. He explained that he would not, in fact, be leaving for Warsaw. Instead, he urgently needed to meet Wyzner back at his apartment in New York. Wyzner had news that made Cousins feel even worse: Hanoi was prepared to receive him Saturday in Warsaw. "Perhaps we had better speak first," Cousins said. The two men agreed to meet at 8:45 p.m. at his apartment in New York.

Cousins inserted another nickel into the pay phone, dialed Valenti, and explained that the North Vietnamese ambassador had just confirmed that he was ready to receive him immediately. "I just don't understand it," Valenti replied. "I don't know why he would want to see you rather than our own ambassador. We've got people all over the world he could talk to." An exasperated and frustrated Cousins told him once again what he had been trying to say all afternoon: "Jack, if you go back to all the important breakthroughs over the years in our dealings with the communists, you'll find the approaches sometimes came in obscure ways."[30] Valenti said that he would relay this development to the president.

Cousins normally loved flying. He found that it gave him perspective and uninterrupted time to clear his mind. On this flight, however, he felt eviscerated. He tried to write down what had happened to him that day, but his notes did not come easily. Cousins saw his place not just in the context of one negotiation during a war but in the larger scope of history. He admitted that it was difficult for him "to realize that one of history's great dramas was now being played out. I was somewhat close to the center but it had a dream-like quality."[31] Although Cousins strongly believed that he held in his hands a possibility that could have ended the war, he was giving himself too much credit. If the meeting had gone ahead, perhaps it would have led to *something*. But a complete end to the war? Almost certainly not.

By the time Cousins finally made it back to his apartment around 9:00 p.m., Wyzner was waiting in the lobby. The two men got a table at a nearby street-level restaurant to talk. Cousins notes, "I tried to be as diplomatic as possible in telling him of Washington's feeling that in view of the fact that the bombing pause had already been extended several times, a more direct and substantial indication of Hanoi's willingness to enter into or explore negotiations was now in order." Wyzner was upset. "Everyone knew," he vented, "that Hanoi felt it had been tricked before, and that it feared Washington had declared the bombing pause only because of rising clamor of world public opinion, and that [the] United States was more concerned about propaganda strategy than a genuine strategy of peace."[32]

Cousins could see that he and Wyzner were both working toward the same goal. He admitted that he found himself "filled with great admiration and liking for this man." Cousins ended their meeting by telling Wyzner, "I think both of us have reason to feel we're the luckiest men in the world being in a position to stop something terrible from happening. Until it does, I think we've got to try."[33] With that, Cousins went up to his apartment, where his wife had been waiting for him for the past two hours. He went to bed, setting his alarm for 5:00 a.m. He had much to do the next day if he was going to try to stop the United States from resuming the bombing and (in his estimate) destroying the chance for negotiations.

CHAPTER 31

THE SCRAMBLE *to* PREVENT *a* BOMBING

After a night of fitful sleep Cousins awoke to his clanging alarm. He telephoned Valenti to report on his previous evening's talk with Eugeniusz Wyzner. Evidently, at some point overnight Valenti had had a change of heart. "Maybe you ought to go, after all," he said. "I'll talk to the President and get back to you."[1] Clearly the White House was being pulled in two different directions and could not decide what to do. Cousins, both annoyed and overjoyed, called his secretary to rebook the flights.

Then another call came through that enlivened Cousins. It was Wyzner: the Poles had just received word that Ho Chi Minh had drafted a letter. This letter, if read correctly, was in direct response to the questions the White House had raised the previous day. The letter would be published the following morning in the *New York Times*. Wyzner said that he had an official message from the Polish foreign minister that he hoped Cousins would take down and transmit to the White House word for word. Cousins reached for his pen and recorded, "Foreign Minister Rapacki wishes to call attention to the letter from Ho Chi Minh. . . . He understands there may be a disposition by Washington to interpret the letter as containing nothing essentially new. . . . Read properly [the letter] provides the key to something essentially new in Hanoi's position." The minister went on to explain that the letter stated that for the negotiations to take place the United States must show "actual deeds," which meant that the resumption of the bombing would destroy the possibility of talks, while a continued suspension would lead to talks.[2]

Suddenly a ray of light in the fast-approaching darkness! But there was a problem: the letter contained the phrase that the United States *must accept* a number of terms that Hanoi had outlined before negotiations could begin. Cousins immediately pointed out that he was "deeply concerned" by the use of that term. It could easily be interpreted as an ultimatum. "The purpose of negotiations was," he argued, "to arrive at agreements, not endorse fixed positions."[3] Regardless, Cousins assured Wyzner that he would transmit the message to the White House.

As soon as he hung up the phone, Cousins picked it up again and dialed the White House. Jack Valenti took the message down word for word. He too was dismayed by the words *must accept*. An hour later he called Cousins back to report that the "official" message had now been received in the State Department and was identical in every respect to the notes Cousins had dictated. "Our government was studying the matter," he told Cousins, "but there was [a] serious problem, as he had anticipated in [their] earlier conversation."[4]

Cousins was stuck in his apartment waiting for the machinations to play out in Washington. One can readily assume that Cousins picked up a copy of the Saturday *New York Times* to see what the press reaction to the Ho Chi Minh letter was when it reached the public on January 29. He must have been irritated. The *Times* highlighted Ho's description of the peace talk offers as "an effort to fool public opinion."[5] The following day, Wyzner called to say he had an urgent message to deliver. Cousins suggested he come immediately to the apartment. The message was that clarification had arrived from North Vietnam that the letter had been mistranslated from the French. Instead of the implication of the letter being that the United States "must accept" the Vietnamese conditions, the wording in French should have been translated as "should consider" or "should recognize." Ho Chi Minh had intended his letter to say that the United States ought to consider certain positions as a basis for negotiations, not that there was an ultimatum.[6]

Cousins's hope was restored. He got on the phone, desperate to inform the White House of this new opening. He tried Valenti: no answer. Bundy: no answer. Goldberg: no answer. Ambassador Harriman: no answer. It was Sunday afternoon, and all four were out of the office. Cousins was able to track down Vice President Humphrey, who was spending the weekend in West Virginia. Humphrey said he would telephone the White House to urge them to consider this development. Finally, later that afternoon Bundy and Valenti both returned his calls. According to Cousins, "I told them about the corrected translation and the importance attached to it by the Poles. They said the information would be passed along."

Cousins could not just sit by and wait for someone to return his calls. He knew that the bombing was scheduled to resume on Monday morning. He went through his impressive list of prominent contacts he had made over the years, scouring it for anyone he thought might have influence with President Johnson. He settled on the secretary-general of the United Nations, U Thant. Cousins telephoned the UN operator and was told that the secretary-general was hosting a dinner party at his home. Since Cousins had a strong relationship with Thant, he thought he would have more of an impact if he met with him in person.

On that cold January evening New York's streets were laden with snow and ice. Cousins called for a private car service. He had Thant's address but no directions, so while they got to the area relatively easily, they wasted a good deal of time circling the neighborhood before they finally located the house. Telling the driver to wait for him, Cousins trudged up the snowy driveway. One can imagine that he pulled his coat tight against the cold as he looked into the brightly lit dining room and noticed a dozen or so people who "seemed to be in a rather gay mood." Thant came to the door and immediately took Cousins into his study.

Cousins, apologizing for the intrusion, told Thant that he had good reason to believe that the order had already gone out for the resumption of bombing. According to Cousins, "U Thant leaned forward and shook his head. 'I really don't think so. . . . My information is that if the bombing is resumed it will not be for four or five days.'" Cousins implored Thant to trust his own information that they were in a fight against time. It was imperative that Thant telephone the president immediately and ask him to rescind the bombing order.

As if to disabuse Cousins of the notion that he was somehow "special" for being tapped for a meeting with the North Vietnamese, Thant then reviewed for Cousins, much as the White House had done, the many times he had thought negotiations were at hand, including some that at first had seemed extremely promising, only to have them ultimately turned down. Thant asked Cousins what he thought he ought to do. Cousins again told him that "he ought to telephone the President immediately." Thant, finally giving some ground to Cousins, replied that he would call the President in the morning. Once again, Cousins "begged him to believe that the morning would be too late, and that any communication ought to be done immediately." "If [the bombing order] was to be rescinded," he said, "extraordinary measures were necessary." Thant agreed that a resumption in bombing would be a disaster, but he felt as though Cousins "might have been misinformed and that there were at least four days."[7]

They were talking in circles at this point, and it was clear Thant would not bend. Cousins left. On the trip back to his apartment, Cousins had his driver stop at a sidewalk telephone booth. He called Wyzner to check in. The conversation must have put Cousins in an even worse mood, because Wyzner said that "he'd been asked to convey the indignation of his government. . . . [The Polish] government had taken valid and responsible action and had received the long-awaited signal. Now that this signal had been provided, the [United States] kept asking for additional assurances. . . . The situation at the moment was that Hanoi was willing to talk and Washington was not. Under the circumstances, they had every reason to be indignant." Cousins tried to assuage the Polish diplomat. "You must believe," he said, "that there is only the greatest respect for and confidence in your government. The situation is such that, as I pointed out to you several times earlier, 36 days have passed [since the start of the bombing pause]."[8]

Cousins returned to his apartment around 8:00 p.m. At close to midnight Ambassador Goldberg called. He told Cousins that he did not think the information about the correct translation had changed Washington's decision. Then the ambassador confirmed Cousins's worst fear: the order to resume the bombing had already gone out, and it would recommence by the morning. Cousins relates that this was "shattering news." He begged Goldberg to call the president directly and ask him to rescind the bombing order, explaining that the pause had been meant to explore the chance for negotiations, and now there was an opening. The North Vietnamese desire to meet with Cousins—a mere private citizen—might not be taken as substantive, but surely the letter from Ho Chi Minh meant something. Moreover, of even greater significance was the special effort to meet the US objection to the implications of the phrase *must accept*. "Late though it was," Cousins implored the ambassador to understand, "it did represent a definite sign."[9]

Goldberg asked Cousins to please believe that he had done everything he could do personally but that the decision had been made and was only a few away hours from being put into effect. Asking the president to rescind the bombing decision was out of the question. Utterly refusing to take no for an answer, Cousins asked what he *could* do. Goldberg wearily replied that "if the Poles can say *definitely* that they're conveying an offer from North Vietnam to start talks immediately—that might make a difference."[10] However distant the possibility, it was enough to keep the hope alive in Cousins. He hung up and immediately telephoned Wyzner. The understandably annoyed Polish deputy ambassador told Cousins that he thought this request was repetitious but said that if that was what it would take, he would send the message through.

Cousins waited anxiously by the phone until Wyzner called back thirty minutes later and told him, incredibly, "You may say that North Vietnam is willing to talk to the United States immediately on the understanding that the bombing is not resumed." Cousins was overjoyed, but it was now well close to 1:00 a.m. on Monday. He knew there was no way of getting in touch with any of his White House contacts at that hour. He wondered whether he should call the president directly, telling the operator that it was a national emergency. Instead, he decided that he should try Bundy first.

Cousins called the White House switchboard. The operator told him Bundy was at home and they would not put the call through at that time of night. Cousins, gambling, deployed a line straight from a Hollywood action movie, saying that he "was calling on a matter of national emergency." The call was put through. Bundy answered. Cousins notes, "I could tell he had been sound asleep." Cousins apologized briefly and then "said I was certain he would want to hear about a new development."

Bundy's voice was cold, controlled.

"Norman," he replied, "I'm just afraid this will have to wait until the morning."

"It may be too late in the morning," Cousins said. "I have a message from the Poles that says North Vietnam is willing to start talks immediately."

"Please call me about it in the morning," Bundy replied.

"But in the morning they won't want to start talks for by that time the bombing is on again."

"Sorry, Norman, call me in the morning, if you wish. Good night."[11]

Bundy hung up.

Cousins admits that he did not sleep very much that night. At 7:00 a.m. he turned on the news. The first report was about the resumption of the bombing.

With the news playing in the background Cousins called Wyzner. The deputy ambassador also had not slept that night. He had been sitting at his desk all through the night hoping for news. Apparently, he had not yet heard about the bombings. Cousins broke the news to him. Wyzner responded in a flat voice, "I don't know what anyone can do now."[12]

CHAPTER 32

CAMPAIGNING AGAINST *(and during)* a WAR

Cousins's aggressive push to open a line of negotiation with North Vietnam did not seem to diminish his reputation within the Johnson administration. In fact, Cousins's star had risen to the point where the vice president invited Cousins to join him, his wife, and some friends for a boat trip on the Potomac.[1] One can hope that he enjoyed that trip, because there would be no more once he finally turned against the Johnson administration over its conduct of the war.

On April 1, 1967, Cousins published an editorial titled "Vietnam and the Fourth Group," in which he accused President Johnson of lying to the American people about his desire for a negotiated settlement of the war. Cousins pointed out at least three instances he knew of in which Hanoi had indicated its willingness to participate in talks, only to have Johnson ignore the overtures and continue bombing. Cousins wrote that citizens of the United States were slowly discovering that "the declared policy may not be the real policy. . . . Whatever the vagrancies of American public opinion, there are finite limits to its capacity to be manipulated."[2]

During the Johnson administration, Cousins's editorials circulated frequently through White House offices—at least ten of Johnson's top advisors received free copies of the *Saturday Review*.[3] In fact, Eric Goldman, a special consultant to the president, often placed Cousins's editorials on the Resolute Desk to make sure that the president "can have the full benefit of the thinking of men like [Cousins]."[4] Cousins himself frequently sent prepublication rough drafts of his editorials to Jack Valenti for comment.[5] Thus, it is unsurprising that Cousins's opinions had become a sort of bellwether for the Johnson administration. By the mid-1960s the *Saturday Review* was at the peak of its national influence. In 1967 it reached five hundred thousand subscribers.[6] "Losing" Cousins was a problem for the administration, and his April 1 editorial accusing Johnson of lying caused a scramble in the White House to conduct damage control.

The same day the issue arrived in the mail, John Roach, a presidential aide, called Cousins from the White House. "The President's attention has been called to the editorial of April 1st," he told Cousins. He expressed the White House's annoyance that the *Saturday Review* would publish such an incorrect assertion. (Not to mention that Valenti had earlier asked Cousins not to publish what he knew about the possibilities for negotiations.) Roach noted in particular a paragraph about an instance in which Hanoi had told the Indian government that it was willing to stop its military operations completely and have a ceasefire. Cousins contended in the editorial that the secretary of state had publicly denied receiving such a message, which Cousins knew to be a lie. Mr. Roach told Cousins that he was sorry the *Saturday Review* had published the editorial, because it was completely false: no such message from India had ever been received.

The White House insisted that the episode Cousins wrote about had never happened. But Cousins himself had seen the evidence. The document containing the negotiation request from the Indian government had been leaked to Cousins, apparently (according to Cousins's private notes) by the deputy secretary of state. Upon being informed that Cousins had proof, Roach said he'd have to look into it and call back.[7] The following day, Secretary of State Dean Rusk called Cousins and told him the same thing, that his editorial was "totally wrong." Cousins responded by reading him some key passages from the leaked document. According to Cousins, "It was clear at least that I had not written about a phantom message. The Secretary told me the State Department *did* have a record of it." Rusk then switched tactics and insisted that the incident had been blown out of proportion. Rusk invited Cousins to Washington to clear the matter up in person.

On April 6, Cousins traveled to the capital to meet Rusk. According to Cousins, the secretary told him that "he knew me to be interested in objective appraisal and felt that unlike most liberals on the subject of Vietnam I had been willing to examine the evidence per se. The President had every reason to end the war and no reason to prolong it. The key word in the President's policy was restraint. He was not giving in to the prodigious pressures around him for using drastic military measures to end the war.[8]

After his State Department meeting, Cousins went over to the National Press Club for a hamburger lunch and a game of chess. Thus fortified, he met with Senator William Fulbright (D-AR)—one of the loudest opponents of the Vietnam War—who gave him the opposing take on the situation. "I am absolutely certain," Fulbright said, "that the President doesn't want negotiation. There have been too many documented opportunities. Secretary Rusk just isn't telling the truth. The fact in which the ease of those in government take up lying and deceit is one of the saddest aspects of what is happening now."[9] Ultimately, Fulbright would be proven right when Daniel Ellsberg leaked the Pentagon Papers in 1971 and exposed the lengths to which the Johnson administration had gone to lie about the progress of the war. The Pentagon Papers, which Cousins read in June 1971, confirmed what he had written in his 1967 editorial, that "most of [the government's] deliberations were directed to ways in which they could carry out one set of policies while making it appear that they were carrying out another."[10]

Vietnam remained front and center in Cousins's mind. Between April and the end of 1967 he would publish seven more biting editorials on the war. Moreover, he stepped up his pressure. Just days after his White House meeting, Cousins doubled down on his stance for negotiation by launching a high-visibility national campaign to elicit public support for a negotiated political settlement. He began writing personal letters to prominent businessmen, influential newsmakers, and university presidents, asking them to come out publicly in support of negotiations.[11]

Outside the White House, others also took notice of Cousins's claims of proof that the US government was ignoring negotiation attempts. Stuart Loory, the White House correspondent for the *Los Angeles Times*, visited Cousins in New York to interview him for a book he was writing. Ultimately titled *The Secret Search for Peace in Vietnam* (1968), Loory's book explored the "missed opportunities" to end the war. On September 27, 1967, Loory met Cousins at his New York office, where a nervous Cousins ushered him into a conference room rather than speaking in his private office. He admitted to Loory that someone at the White House had warned him that his communications were likely being bugged.[12] The FBI records on Cousins do not contain any documented evidence that he was being surveilled (by the FBI at least). Either way, perhaps sparked by delusions of grandeur, Cousins *believed* that he was being monitored, which spooked him enough that for a time he took most of his meetings outside his apartment or office, usually preferring to meet in restaurants.

According to Loory, Cousins admitted to him that he only knew "5 percent of what's going on and not 90 percent." Still, Cousins did not think the United States was acting honorably in its approach to Hanoi. He (still) did not blame President Johnson, however. He thought that either the president was not always being informed or his hands were tied by the military.[13] (Neither claim was entirely accurate.)

Despite Cousins keeping the blame away from the president, by March 1968 Cousins's continued push against the war alarmed the White House enough that it called him in for another meeting to try to persuade him that Johnson was prosecuting the war in good faith. Cousins met one on one with Johnson in the Oval Office on March 15, 1968. During the meeting President Johnson insisted to Cousins that he had "incontrovertible evidence" that Hanoi would not be willing to negotiate because the North Vietnamese believed that the tide of battle had turned their way.[14]

Johnson implored Cousins to believe that he was doing everything possible to open negotiations. "Frankly, I think I would be impeached," Cousins writes that Johnson told him, "if people knew to what lengths I've gone to [*sic*] in trying to end the war through negotiations." He also admitted to Cousins that he didn't know how to end the war. Cousins gave Johnson a few ideas of his own. He suggested that the president handwrite a note to Ho Chi Minh saying that he was sending the vice president to Warsaw and would be open to any North Vietnamese emissary who wanted to meet him there. President Johnson responded positively (or, more likely, patronizingly) to the suggestion, telling Cousins that the idea was "a genuine service and [was] the first new idea he had heard in a long time."[15]

The fact that the president himself was calling Cousins in for a meeting to better inform him about policy and that other reporters were recognizing Cousins as a source for inside information was owing to the fact that on the issue of the war at least Cousins was truly a leading national voice. For the first time on a large scale, other news outlets made Cousins himself the story and reported on his positions regarding the Vietnam War. The *New York Times* wrote about Cousins "vigorously attack[ing]" the new Selective Service regulations to use college grades to determine which students would be drafted. CBS news interviewed him frequently.[16] While he was by no means a lone voice in the wilderness opposing the war, he had been consistent and vocal about it since before the war even began, and his position on this issue would have a wider impact on the election of 1968 as the campaign got under way in late 1967.

By early 1968 Johnson's presidency was in tatters. The war was going poorly. There was both growing dissent among American soldiers in the field and intense public protest and political pressure at home. Given the anger over the Vietnam War, the presidential election got under way early when Senator Eugene McCarthy announced in late 1967 that he would launch a primary challenge to Lyndon Johnson on an antiwar platform. In March 1968 McCarthy won 42 percent of the vote in New Hampshire's primary to Johnson's 49 percent. Buoyed by the prospect that a primary challenge against a sitting president might actually succeed, four days later Robert Kennedy entered the race as well.

There were some who thought the growing slate of challengers could use one more name: Norman Cousins. A group of supporters formed the Cousins for President Committee and began fundraising on the basis that "if this nation, and this planet, are going to get out of the hole they are in, it will take a man with the ability, orientation, and dedication of a Norman Cousins."[17] Some were enthusiastic about the prospect of Cousins as president, with many offering their efforts and money to support the candidacy. Most, however, had reservations despite their belief that Cousins would be an excellent candidate. The president of the Travis Oil Company wrote, "Without question Mr. Cousins stands head and shoulders above any potential candidates . . . [but] Norman Cousins has no power base; Norman Cousins is, in the very best sense of the word, an 'egg-head'; Norman Cousins is also realistic and knows full well that he doesn't have a ghost of a chance."[18] Another man who thought that Norman Cousins didn't stand a chance of getting elected was Norman Cousins himself.

The committee began their recruitment attempts without informing Cousins; they wanted to build momentum before bringing him into the loop. When Cousins found out about the effort a few months later, he expressed his gratitude at the committee's confidence but told them, "[I] believe I can best serve their purpose by urging upon you and them that the support they have so generously offered me now be transferred to Senator Eugene McCarthy."[19] This wasn't the first career move into elected office that Cousins had considered. In 1949, following the resignation of Senator Raymond Baldwin (R-CT), Governor Chester Bowles had asked Cousins if he would like to be appointed to fill the year remaining of Baldwin's term. Cousins thought hard about it, later saying that "I had always felt that the United States Senate was probably one of the finest jobs in the world." But his main concern was that he would have to campaign to keep the job. "I never had any taste for that," he said. "Having to sling abuse and having to take it. . . . I had no taste for the battle."[20]

Despite initially supporting McCarthy, Cousins would soon shift to supporting a new candidate. In November 1967, General Westmoreland told the American people that the North Vietnamese enemy was nearly defeated and unable to launch a major offensive. His words soon came back to haunt him when, on the night of January 29–30, 1968, the Tet Offensive began. A widespread series of attacks in South Vietnam shocked the American people and signaled to many that the war effort was doomed. With the offensive still ongoing a month later, on February 27 CBS news anchor Walter Cronkite—once a supporter of the war—urged disengagement during the evening news broadcast, saying, "To say that we are mired in stalemate seems the only realistic, if unsatisfactory conclusion. . . . It is increasingly clear to this reporter that the only rational way out then will be to negotiate, not as victors."[21]

After being informed of Cronkite's assessment, Johnson purportedly said, "If I've lost Cronkite, I've lost middle America."[22] And presumably, if he had lost middle America, he had also lost any hope of reelection. With opponents stacking up against him on all fronts, and increasingly consumed by the war, on March 31 Johnson shocked the American people by announcing that he would not be running for reelection.

With the nomination now an open contest, Vice President Hubert Humphrey decided to get into the race. Cousins, who immediately joined his campaign as a speechwriter and advisor, wrote Humphrey's announcement speech.[23] Cousins also proved to be a prodigious fundraiser, plying his wealthy contacts in the publishing industry. He wrote to Humphrey, "I have a hunch [publishing magnate Norton Simon] can be a $50,000-plus contributor to your campaign. He is very eager to talk to you."[24] More notably, Cousins, who previously had always sought to remain nonpartisan, allowed the *Saturday Review* to openly endorse Humphrey. His longtime friend and former senator from Connecticut William Benton (who, incidentally, had been appointed to fill the Senate seat offered to Cousins in 1949) wrote to White House aide Douglass Cater to express his surprise that "this is the first time Norman has endorsed a presidential candidate. I like him for it."[25] This break with his earlier policy was the result of reevaluating his life after his 1964 illness. He wrote to his archivist Fran Thompson describing how the illness had changed him: "I am not as careful perhaps as I used to be on the editorial page about not criticizing the people in government I have to work with."[26] Not only did he endorse Humphrey but he openly criticized Republican nominee Richard Nixon, claiming that he was jeopardizing the national interest with his aggressive stances.[27]

Interestingly, until 1968 Cousins had remained rather close to Nixon, maintaining a robust correspondence with him over the years. In fact, he had even dined with the former vice president in 1964. Speaking freely after a few drinks, Nixon had shared his thoughts on the then ongoing election campaign. He thought that there was an enormous amount of pressure building to give Robert Kennedy the vice-presidential nomination but that Johnson *hated* Bobby, so Nixon did not see that happening. Instead, Nixon said, "the man Johnson wants as a running mate is Hubert Humphrey."[28] Four years later, Humphrey was battling Nixon. Cousins advised Humphrey on political issues and wrote numerous speeches, including an election victory speech. Ultimately, Humphrey wouldn't get to use the victory speech, losing to Nixon by more than one hundred Electoral College votes. Perhaps Cousins's political instincts were not as good as he thought they were. He was 0 for 3 in presidential campaigns.

On the eve of the election Cousins sent Humphrey a consolation telegram. "What you stand for," he wrote, "has registered profoundly on the American consciousness and conscience. I will never cease being proud of you."[29] Proud as he was, Cousins had moved on to other things before the campaign even ended.

CHAPTER 33

THE BIAFRAN WAR

In 1960, Nigeria became independent of the United Kingdom, but the borders of the new country did not reflect the ethnic divisions on the ground that separated the country into three conflicting major ethnic groups. The Muslim majority concentrated in the North, and predominantly Christian groups in the Southwest and the Southeast. With the economy in decline in the new nation, ethnic violence increased. In early 1966, Nigerian military officers launched a coup. Six months later, a coalition of western and northern military officers staged a countercoup and took power. The ensuing violence only deepened the ethnic tensions.[1]

On May 30, 1967, C. Odumegwu Ojukwu, the military governor of the southeastern region, citing the fact that some thirty thousand Nigerians of southeastern origin who lived in the North had been targeted and killed in the postcoup violence, announced that the southeastern region would separate from Nigeria and form the Republic of Biafra. Because the southeastern region was home to most of Nigeria's oil industry, this declaration caused an immediate crisis in the northern Federal Military Government, led by Colonel Yakubu Gowon. His government imposed an economic blockade and ordered a full mobilization of the army, charging that the East had "committed an act of rebellion which must be crushed."[2]

The US government had seen this coming. Five days before the secession announcement, Johnson's national security advisor, Walt

Rostow, had warned that "events are about to take a nasty turn in Nigeria.... The dissolution of Nigeria is imminent."[3] Two months later, Colonel Gowon asked the United States to sell him fighter-bombers and anti-aircraft guns, a request the United States denied. The White House maintained that the problem in Nigeria was an internal one and it would be inappropriate to intervene on either side.[4] Three days later, Gowon declared war and attacked Biafra.

While the United States struggled to maintain its neutral stance, American public opinion strongly supported the Biafran cause. The US Embassy in Nigeria reported that "Americans admire Ojukwu.... [He] has panache, quick intelligence and an actor's voice and fluency." Moreover, as the war continued into 1968, Ojukwu launched what the US Embassy described as a "skillful and persistent effort to enlist American journalists and other potential publicists in the Biafran cause."[5] One of those journalists "enlisted" was Cousins.

Cousins had been following the escalation of the Biafran war and was especially horrified at the human consequences of the conflict. By December 1968 the war had claimed the lives of some 2.5 million people. Most perished as a result of the starvation caused by the economic blockade enacted by Nigerian forces, which had completely cut off food supplies. The Red Cross was flying in sixteen to twenty tons of food every night, but it had only a single aircraft, which wasn't nearly enough. The US National Security Council estimated that in August 1968 up to six hundred people were dying of starvation daily. By February 1969, four thousand adults and two thousand children were starving to death each day.[6]

In September 1968, Cousins decided to do what he could to improve the situation. Once again, his focus turned to the children impacted. His original plan was to try to evacuate Biafran children by air. The logistics of that proved impossible, so instead he arranged for American doctors to travel to Biafra to attend to the medical needs of children directly. Cousins thus introduced the *Saturday Review* readers to his latest humanitarian aid project, the Aid to Biafran Children

(ABC). American and Biafran doctors would set up mobile units to go directly to local villages and provide on-the-spot medical care primarily for children.[7]

As they had in the past, *Saturday Review* readers poured donations into Cousins's New York office. He also got a boost from the new Nixon administration. Whereas Johnson's White House had maintained a strict non-intervention policy in Biafra, Nixon was exploring taking a fresh approach. He asked his national security advisor, Henry Kissinger, for a report on the Biafran relief problem, which he was provided within eight days of taking office. In this report Kissinger laid out five "step-up" plans should Nixon want to take action. The key problem was that the Red Cross was only capable of delivering a tiny percentage of the thirty thousand to forty thousand tons of food needed each month. Kissinger estimated that without a large-scale relief program some 3.5 million Biafrans would be at risk of starvation within the next six months.[8]

Kissinger recommended to Nixon that he support Biafran relief operations, if only for the political benefits. The young administration could demonstrate its fresh thinking in a search for practical solutions, as well as the president's "serious concern for the suffering," and it could tamp down domestic pressure.[9] Convinced, Nixon appointed a "Special Coordinator for Nigerian-Biafra relief" and began to explore the use of American cargo aircraft to deliver food supplies.[10]

Just days before Nixon's appointment of the special coordinator, Cousins had announced his own relief efforts through ABC, but behind the scenes he was doing far more than just providing aid: he was attempting to end the war. By May 15, 1969, it was clear that the military offensive Nigeria had launched against Biafra had "ground to an indecisive and even perilous halt."[11] By July, the White House recognized that Nigeria couldn't win this war. In a telephone conversation with Kissinger, Nixon stated that he wanted "to use everything we have to get this over with." "The trouble is," Nixon opined, "that Nigeria can't win but whether they are ready to settle is a real question."[12] Nixon would soon have an answer to his question, as at that very moment Norman Cousins was in Nigeria trying to determine whether either side was willing to settle.

In July 1969, Cousins took it upon himself to travel to Nigeria, ostensibly to report on the relief effort for the *Saturday Review*. But as always, he had larger diplomatic goals in mind as well. Flying into Lagos, Nigeria, he managed to secure a meeting with General Gowon. The editor and the general discussed the progress of the war. Gowon showed Cousins a letter he had written to Ojukwu proposing talks without preconditions. More importantly, Gowon asked Cousins, whom he knew was traveling next to Biafra, to transmit to Ojukwu his desire for peace. Carrying this message, Cousins flew to an airstrip in the small town of Uli, then traveled overland to Owerri, the provisional capital of Biafra. While there, he somehow managed to secure a meeting with Ojukwu.[13]

The intelligence that Cousins ultimately brought back to the United States about the war was invaluable. He was one of the few people who had crossed the front lines and not only seen the situation on the ground but met with the leaders of both sides of the conflict. Once again, Cousins found himself in the rare position of having personal access to top leaders in a foreign country where the United States had few contacts, which was an asset that the US government recognized and coveted. Kissinger would later tell President Nixon that "Cousins has a shrewd and well-informed appreciation of the realities of the civil war," and he "strongly recommended" to Nixon that they use Cousins to "keep this dialogue going."[14] Cousins, in turn, reported to Kissinger his clear impression "that the President's good offices would be welcomed in the present situation."[15]

A month later, the White House was ready to act on Cousins's suggestion, their only caveat being that his activities "would have to be disavowable." Kissinger telephoned Cousins to explain that "the problem is that the President is willing to proceed but he doesn't want to put it in writing. . . . We [also] don't want to make an official move until we see some progress."[16] Nixon authorized Cousins to proceed "on his own to explore Gowon's and Ojukwu's position." Kissinger explained that if, and only if, both men responded positively, the United States would publicly commit to efforts to negotiate a settlement.[17]

As an indication of Cousins's worth to the White House, Kissinger expressed that both he and Nixon were deeply concerned "in case something should happen to Cousins." It was not a misplaced concern. In June, Nigeria shot down a Red Cross plane carrying relief into Biafra and threatened to shoot down *all* relief planes. The deputy leader of the Nigeria government stated, "All is fair in war and starvation is one of the weapons of war."[18]

Out of an abundance of caution, to avoid flying into Biafra on a relief plane as he had before (and perhaps to better obscure the nature of his travels), Cousins arranged to meet with a Biafran representative in Paris during a stopover on his way to Nigeria.[19] While no direct records have been found indicating what was discussed during his meetings, they proved fruitful, as evidenced by a debriefing he had with National Security Council member Roger Morris. Morris reports that "Cousins is convinced there is no doubt that the Biafrans want to negotiate, and quite possibly are looking toward some kind of reunified Nigeria." However, the Biafrans wanted one more secret meeting to hammer out some specific details about the terms of the negotiation before they even considered committing to it publicly.[20]

Internally, Kissinger strongly recommended to the president that they pursue the meeting. "We could ask Cousins to return to Paris," he noted, "but the Biafrans obviously want some proof they're in a serious conversation with the Administration." Kissinger then praised Cousins to the president, saying that he deserved prompt attention "for following our earlier request with both precision and discretion." Nixon approved plans for a "strictly quiet, informal meeting with a Biafran representative in the next few days."[21]

Four days later, the foreign minister of Biafra, G. A. Onyegbula, spoke to Cousins and asked him to set up a meeting. In a letter to

Kissinger delivered by Cousins, Onyegbula wrote, "I look forward most eagerly to an opportunity of a meeting with you. . . . I am confident that this can be arranged without embarrassment through the good offices of our mutual friend, Mr. Norman Cousins."[22] Cousins did more than just "arrange" the meeting; to keep it completely secret he hosted it at his apartment in New York the very next day.

For four and a half hours on September 25, the foreign minister of Biafra, one of his representatives, and two members of the US National Security Council discussed possible peace terms in Cousins's apartment. Their wide-ranging discussion clarified a number of issues and solidified the Biafran position on negotiations. Ultimately, Biafra was ready to welcome US mediation.[23] Cousins reported the news to Gowon shortly thereafter, delivering a letter to the United Nations to pass along to the foreign minister of Nigeria, who would deliver it to Gowon. "I have been informed," Cousins wrote, "[that] General Ojukwu is prepared to commence discussions with a view towards ending the war."[24] Nothing would come of the efforts, though. By the end of 1969 the tide of the war had shifted, and Biafra had lost much of its territory.[25] At the beginning of January 1970 it controlled only a small enclave measuring barely sixty by one hundred miles. It was clear that Biafra's continued existence was untenable. On January 10, 1970, Biafra's last remaining town fell to Nigerian forces as Ojukwu held what would be his final cabinet meeting.[26] The following day, Ojukwu and members of his entourage boarded one of the last planes leaving from the Uli airstrip and fled to the Ivory Coast. He left his chief justice behind to broker a peace. Three days later, a surrender was formally signed. On January 15, 1970, Biafra ceased to exist.[27]

That same afternoon, Cousins was on the phone with Kissinger. Even though his peace mission had come to naught, he was pleased that the war was over. He explained to Kissinger that the United States ought to immediately convene a conference that would work toward rebuilding Nigeria. Former Biafra still suffered from critical food shortages and ethnic violence. Cousins proposed a sort of postwar reparations plan, figuring that it would require about $50 million, which he thought he could help raise from public and private groups. Most notably, Cousins told Kissinger that he "would be willing to take a leave of absence [from the *Saturday Review*] to devote my full time to this." He reminded Kissinger of his success working with the Kennedy administration to ratify the Limited Nuclear Test Ban Treaty.[28] Cousins even outlined the domestic political benefits Nixon could reap by supporting such a plan. Specifically, it would improve his access to and standing with "certain groups" who didn't support the president.

Immediately after he got off the phone with Cousins, Kissinger telephoned Nixon. Kissinger's fixation was on the "certain groups" Cousins had mentioned—clearly a reference to African Americans. "I had a call from Norman Cousins about Biafra," Kissinger told the president. "He felt you could gain prestige with groups you do not generally have access [to]." Kissinger pitched Cousins's idea, which he said "would make a good impression [on black Americans]." Nixon replied, "I want to be sure we take leadership on humanitarian problems. They are savages."[29]

While Nixon did not think of himself as racist, he did harbor a deep prejudice toward the black community in America, and against Africans specifically. The following year he would refer to Africans as "cannibals." According to historian Tim Naftali, "Nixon believed in a hierarchy of races, with whites and Asians much higher up than people of African descent and Latinos. And he had convinced himself that it wasn't racist to think black people, as a group, were inferior to whites, so long as he held them in paternalistic regard."[30]

By January 20, it was clear that Kissinger had soured on one of Cousins's ideas for a conference. "I'm not sure we should have a White House conference," he told Nixon on the phone. The president too was unconvinced. "We've already shown enough interest [in Africa]," he replied. As to the pushback they expected from Cousins, Nixon remarked, "Let Norman Cousins take it up with the State Department. . . . The White House conference can go on the back burner."[31] Ultimately, that burner was turned off completely a few days later when the State Department decided that the extent of its program would be to provide cash to non-governmental aid agencies like the Nigerian Red Cross and UNICEF, some military transport aircraft and vehicles, and six thousand tons of food. The State Department's position was that the United States had to be mindful of Nigerian sensitivities and allow Nigerians to run relief programs themselves.[32]

It was during this same time—as national and international troubles weighed heavily on Cousins's heart and mind—that a gravely serious illness was first detected in one of his four daughters. A poet, artist, and musician, and named after Cousins's literary mentor, Amy, who as a teenager had won first prize in the National Scholastic Awards Writing Contest, was in her final year at Sarah Lawrence College at the onset of the illness.

The Cousins daughters choose not to delve, for the purposes of this book, into this chapter of the family's personal history. Sarah, who lived close to Amy in Jerusalem from 1976 until the latter's return to the United States in the late 1990s, writes as follows:

> It has always seemed to me that Amy's suffering occupied the undeclared center of our father's emotional life from the mid-1960s on, even as he kept going full-throttle as a writer and magazine editor, and in his varied impassioned roles in the diplomatic sphere. In a Biblical commentary by Rabbi Samson Raphael Hirsch about the Patriarch Abraham's mourning for his wife, a sparse one-liner can in my opinion serve as an accurate description of Norman Cousins as a father: "His grief was infinite, but the full extent of his pain was concealed in his heart and the privacy of his home."[33]

Amy Loveman Cousins died in 2005.

Both his torment over his daughter's illness and whatever irritation Cousins may have harbored regarding the White House rejection of his relief plan, he kept to himself. He held his anger even three months later after Nixon announced a major expansion of the war in Vietnam. On April 30, Nixon revealed that part of his "secret plan" to end the war was to conduct military operations in neighboring Cambodia. Cousins's uncharacteristically subdued editorial on the topic two weeks later simply fact-checked Nixon's national address justifying the decision, saying that it "call[s] for close examination," which he provided by claiming that parts of Nixon's statement were "misleading" or "correct, but incomplete."[34]

Four days after Nixon's announcement, protesting students gathered on the campus of Kent State University in Ohio. National Guard troops attempted to disperse the crowds. Clashes broke out, and the guardsmen opened fire on the students, killing four and wounding nine. In response, millions of students walked out on a nationwide strike, with hundreds of thousands descending on Washington to protest.

Two weeks later, Cousins wrote another subdued editorial. His typical moral indignation was muted. He took the rather mealy-mouthed approach of stating only that the students had the "historic right and ability to assert themselves as the framers of the Constitution intended." But he also admonished the students by reminding them that "they don't have to demolish the system in order to be heard or to have an effect. The system works if it is properly used. What doesn't work is the use of violence—whether by the government or by protestors."[35]

By 1970 the protests against the Vietnam War, led by America's youth, had reached a crescendo. Despite Cousins being against the Vietnam War, he was not all that supportive of the protestors in the streets. In fact, just months before the Kent State shootings he had published an editorial that planted him firmly in the older generation, who were often critical of those who engaged in street protest. His editorial reprimanded young adults for their "shortness of temper.... Accompanied by the kind of vocabulary that only a few years ago was considered borderline in male locker rooms." He stated that there was a "growing student disregard for what historically has gone by the name of rational discourse." He lamented that the protestors had no regard for the attributes of "restraint, sequential thought, the primacy of ideas, good will, good humor."[36]

His daughter Andrea, who was part of the anti-Vietnam movement, remembers that there were people of her father's generation, such as peace activist and Yale chaplain Bill Coffin, who were "really with us, but for the most part there was a big generational gap." Her father rarely talked about the anti-Vietnam movement of his own accord. "I'm sure he appreciated the anti-war movement, but he wasn't an activist," Andrea said.[37] A decade earlier, when writing to a colleague, Cousins had noted that he disliked street protests. He thought they were too easy to stereotype and produced all sorts of opposing reflexes that only served to harden opposition and stiffen resistance.[38] For Cousins, what mattered most was engaging in reasoned dialogue. After all, as Candis recalls, "he spent his adult life crafting a single message: rather than responding with force or violence, it is serious, committed dialogue between people of conflicting ideas and interests that holds the promise of saving this world."[39]

The decade that began as a hopeful "new frontier" under President John F. Kennedy ultimately was a tumultuous one. What opened with optimism closed in mass protests over a war that just kept expanding. It was a decade full of ups and downs for Cousins as well, and by the dawn of the 1970s he was looking for a change. He was approaching his thirtieth anniversary at the *Saturday Review*, and he had (again) begun thinking about leaving the magazine. He was starting to consider what else he wanted to do with the rest of his life.[40]

CHAPTER 34

THE *SATURDAY REVIEW*'S FINAL CRISIS

With a new decade dawning, Cousins decided to make a fresh start. For years he and his family had been taking trips to Arizona. It was a welcome escape from New York, and Cousins relished flying to the state whenever he found a chance to get away. Cousins noted that he found himself spending as much time there as he possibly could and that he always felt regenerated by the beauty and peace of the area.[1] Sarah recalls that her parents loved the desert landscape of Arizona. "They especially loved the astounding, star-studded night skies, which in Connecticut and New York were not visible because of light from human habitation. My father bought a telescope and they would set it up outside in the dark, and stand out there together looking through it, so excited. I remember them showing me Saturn with its rings. They were thrilled, and they communicated their jaw-dropping amazement and wonder to their daughter."[2]

They had become so enamored of their vacation spot that in 1968 the family began constructing a small home in the state.[3] Cousins commented that part of his recipe for relaxation was that "you should be located near the things you want to do."[4] Before they selected a town in which to build their vacation home, Cousins checked out all the local golf courses. But while Cousins mulled the possibility of stepping back from the *Saturday Review* on his thirtieth anniversary, the change was made for him sooner than he expected.

In 1969, the McCall Corporation, which had owned the *Saturday Review* for the previous ten years, was consolidated into a single corporate unit, Norton Simon Inc (NSI). The following year, Norton Simon himself (whom Cousins was close to) decided to retire. This development sparked somewhat of a crisis for Cousins and for the *Saturday Review.* Since McCall had acquired the magazine in 1960, the *Saturday Review* had been allowed to operate completely independently, while drawing from McCall's substantial resources. In the newly reorganized company, however, the publishing wing was dwarfed by NSI's primary businesses, canned foods and beverage production (NSI owned Hunt's tomato products and Canada Dry beverages). Cousins feared that the magazine would be left to wither in this arrangement. He decided to pursue taking the magazine private again, as it had been before 1960, and he approached NSI about buying it back. NSI recommended that Cousins wait three months, giving the merger some time to shake out. If after three months Cousins still wanted to purchase the magazine from NSI, David Mahoney, the new president of NSI, would make the acquisition possible.[5]

In early 1971, NSI informed Cousins that it was in a position to discuss a sale. To Cousins's shock, NSI presented a take-it-or-leave-it deal that was highly unfavorable. Cousins would be forced to also buy an unprofitable books division of the company. He was told that the deal was not negotiable. Cousins described it as "a nightmare."[6] Cousins informed NSI that if those were the terms, they would be unable to complete the deal, and three days later NSI sold the *Saturday Review* to Boise Cascade, another major conglomerate that dealt primarily in lumber products, for $5.5 million.[7]

Cousins was livid. He had approached NSI in good faith, and NSI had encouraged Cousins to wait, and then it had used the interim to strike its own deal behind Cousins's back. The reason Cousins had wanted to take the *Saturday Review* private was that he feared the effects of being a small part of a large and unfocused manufacturing company. Now the magazine had ended up in exactly that position, owned by a

Cousins in his *Saturday Review* office, 1971.

(UCLA SPECIAL COLLECTIONS / NORMAN COUSINS PAPERS)

lumber company that had little experience in publishing. In fact, during the negotiations many stockholders at Boise Cascade did not want to acquire the magazine for that very reason. Furthering the ownership turmoil, Boise Cascade, under pressure from the shareholders, quickly sold the *Saturday Review* to the owners of the small publisher C/R/M.

Publicly Cousins spoke positively of the sale; privately he fumed. He wrote to his longtime friend Hubert Humphrey, who had taught at a college after losing the 1968 election but then returned to the Senate in 1971, that "the sale could be consummated only if this was acceptable to those directly involved in that relationship. It was not."[8] Within months Cousins's simmering anger boiled over. At first he erupted over the fact that the new owners were using the list of subscribers to market other, unrelated goods, specifically Christmas fruitcakes. This rankled subscribers. One wrote, "By commercially exploiting the subscription list (and selling fruitcakes under the 'Saturday Review Industries'!!!!!) you are prostituting the magazine's name and reputation."[9] Cousins voiced his strong objections "to the commercial use of the *Saturday Review* subscription list for purposes that have nothing to do with the magazine."[10]

The real crisis came four months after the sale. The new owners informed the staff that they intended to split the *Saturday Review* into four separate monthlies, each with its own staff and identity. The magazines were to be rotated, so that each week subscribers would receive a different one. Cousins was staunchly against this idea. To put it lightly, he wrote that he was in "philosophical and professional disagreement."[11]

With Cousins refusing to budge and mired in deadlock, the owners tried for an end run, announcing the new four-magazine approach in a leak to the *New York Times* that implied Cousins's assent to the idea.[12] This was the last straw; Cousins resigned the next day. "The news release indicated that the plan had my support and that, indeed, I participated in its development," he wrote. "This, of course, was not true, and it became necessary for me to state my position immediately lest I be locked into a position just out of tacit acceptance."[13] In Cousins's words, the owners "went to extraordinary lengths to persuade me to stay," but he could not put his name to something he deeply disagreed with.[14] Although this was not the first time in his thirty-one-year career at the *Saturday Review* that he had tendered his resignation, it was the first time it stuck.

Cousins broke the news to his readers in a final editorial just after Thanksgiving, on November 27, 1971. "It is hard, very hard, to imagine myself without the *Saturday Review*," Cousins wrote. "The magazine has been more than just a career. It has been a way of life. I can't think of any job in the world I would have preferred."[15] Six months later, after some reflection, Cousins would tell a *New York Times* reporter that leaving the magazine had been "the low point of my life."[16]

News of Cousins's resignation swept across the country. Interviewed by the *New York Times*, Cousins described his feeling as "the kind of wrench that goes up your spine and right into your soul."[17] The *Los Angeles Times*, reporting on Cousins's resignation, described the *Saturday Review* as having been "one of the most influential [publications] in the literary world."[18] Two days later the *Times* mused over the fact that the newly appointed editor also shared the initials NC—with which Cousins had signed his work for the past thirty-one years. The initials were so well known that the new editor felt compelled to tell the *Times* that because he had "the highest respect and affection for Mr. Cousins . . . [h]e will forgo using the initials and sign his editorials with his full name—Nicolas H. Charney."[19]

The response from readers was visceral. "Shock and sorrow were my response to your [decision]," one reader wrote. "I cannot imagine SR without N.C., much as N.C. cannot imagine himself without SR."[20] Another reader praised Cousins for being "the last voice in the wilderness. At times I did not agree with you but it was comforting to know that someone really cared about the human race and took the time to say so and become concerned and involved."[21] And another wrote that "as a devoted reader of SATURDAY REVIEW since my teens, I want to tell you how very sorry I am that you will be leaving."[22]

Senator Hubert Humphrey went so far as to enshrine Cousins in the *Congressional Record*, going onto the floor of the Senate and saying,

> It was a result of Norman Cousins's wisdom and guidance that the *Saturday Review* became one of the most effective and wholesome influences on the American literary scene. More than that, however, the magazine and Mr. Cousins have played a crucial role in the strengthening of our society's democratic institutions.... No man in private life worked as hard to accomplish world peace and no man deserves greater appreciation for those efforts.[23]

Cousins thanked his old friend, writing, "All my life I've worked with words, yet now I find myself floundering for a way to tell you how deeply moved I was by your tribute published in the Congressional Record."[24] Cousins told Humphrey and other friends that at the age of fifty-six he found himself "a member of the army of the unemployed, finally a free man and not sure that I know how to make the most of it." He had finally reached a time in his life when he wanted to read and think and certainly have time for fun.[25] When the *New York Times* asked Cousins what he intended to do now, he spoke of golfing and playing tennis.[26]

Despite being unemployed, Cousins did not lack for job opportunities. Generous offers arrived for professorships, even some college presidencies.[27] Still, as he told a *New York Times* reporter, this newfound life of leisure "might last a couple of weeks. And then back into the arena again."[28] He confided to Humphrey that "there is every reason why I should not start a new magazine and every reason why it probably can't be done. But it is what I want to do and I have a hunch it may happen."[29]

There was no pressing need, no pressing *financial* need at least, for Cousins to rush into another job. He was quite well off. By 1961 his annual *Saturday Review* salary was around $324,000 (2020 dollars). He had income from his book royalties and speaking fees. Most of all, Cousins received a payout of about $19 million (2020 dollars) from the sale of his shares when McCall sold the *Saturday Review.* Certainly, maintaining two homes plus an apartment in Manhattan meant that his expenses were higher than the average person's, but he had a nest egg to tide him over for a while.

But Cousins could not sit still. He missed the magazine world too much and soon thrust himself back into it. With only his name, his expertise, and his reputation (and his money, of course), he launched another magazine. One of the offers Cousins received after his resignation was from the major broadcaster CBS, which offered to fund another magazine venture headed by Cousins. Despite that lucrative source of capital, perhaps burned by the corporate experience, this time Cousins did it himself. He risked his own fortune to launch a brand-new magazine at a time when other magazines were folding because of increased postage rates and printing expenses.[30]

Ten of the remaining *Saturday Review* employees resigned their positions and followed Cousins to the new magazine; the *Los Angeles Times* called it a "mass exodus."[31] Not everyone took the leap with Cousins, though. His longtime colleague William Patterson, managing editor of the *Saturday Review*, chose to stay with the new owners. This decision strained their relationship. Other staff members at the "old" *Saturday Review* claimed that Cousins was trying to strategically undermine their publication.[32]

Cousins's new venture, which he called *World*, launched in June 1972. It was essentially a facsimile of *Saturday Review*, billing itself as "a review of ideas, the arts, and the human condition." One reviewer wrote, "*World* looks very much like the old *Saturday Review.* It looks more like the old *Saturday Review*, in fact, than the new *Saturday Review* looks like the old *Saturday Review.*"[33] This was unsurprising since Cousins, in addition to absconding with much of the *Saturday Review*'s staff, also managed to poach about one hundred thousand former subscribers. In a testament to how much of a following Cousins himself drew, the *New York Times* wrote that for subscribers to *World* "the big attraction is simply Mr. Cousins himself."[34] Still, Cousins was nervous. He told his archivist, "At the very start it's like any pregnancy. You feel the new life stirring inside you. It's quite exciting. Then you get the morning sickness and the pains in the back."[35] At times he lamented not accepting one of the many job offers he had received from colleges instead.

World published biweekly, and in less than a year it almost doubled its subscriber base, to 187,000. It was clearly on an upward trajectory when Cousins received some news that would change his career once again. Less than a year after *World* launched, rumors appeared in the press that the *Saturday Review* was in financial trouble. The *New York Times* reported that the company was nearly $5 million in debt after a precipitous fall in subscription numbers and an enormous increase in expenditures to produce and mail four separate monthlies. Not helping their financial situation was the fact that the new management had uprooted the magazine from its longtime home in New York City and relocated the entire office to San Francisco—a major financial outlay that one industry insider said he never would have approved had it been his own company.[36] Despite the management's claim that "it's going quite well, and we're not even contemplating the chance of not succeeding," within a month the *Saturday Review* had ceased operations.[37]

Bankruptcy proceedings were filed in a San Francisco court on April 24, 1973. Asked by a reporter to comment, Cousins seemed gleeful at the news. The *Times* described him as "jubilant" and quoted him as saying "this has been something that has been in my dreams. . . . There's a feeling of the deepest possible gratification."[38] Granted, he wasn't exactly dancing on the grave of the *Saturday Review*; rather, he was jubilant at the prospect of regaining ownership. Forty-eight hours before the *Saturday Review* filed for bankruptcy, the managing directors called Cousins and told him that they "wanted to entrust the future of the magazine to [him]." They outlined an offer for Cousins to purchase it out of bankruptcy.[39]

Buying the magazine out of bankruptcy involved extreme financial risk, but Cousins was undeterred. He told friends that he "didn't spend 30 years to see it go down the drain."[40] Thus, he braced himself for spending the next eight weeks in contentious bankruptcy negotiations, frequently flying back and forth to San Francisco in order to deal with the claims. "The problem gave me nightmares," he admitted.[41] Ultimately the bankruptcy court approved of the deal Cousins proposed, which assured that some 380 creditors would get repaid more than 20 percent of the $6 million they were owed.[42] To come up with the money, Cousins put up a considerable amount of his personal savings and took out a "substantial" line of credit from Chase Manhattan Bank (perhaps it helped that David Rockefeller, Cousins's acquaintance from the Dartmouth Conferences, was still chairman), yet he still had to lean on some of his closest friends to scrape together another $750,000 (nearly $4.5 million in 2020 dollars).[43]

Cousins's intention was to merge the *Saturday Review* and *World* back into one publication that he claimed would be "stronger, brighter and more accessible than the design of the old Saturday Review in 1971."[44] As an example of how bloated the new *Saturday Review* had become, of the two hundred employees who lost their jobs, Cousins was only able to hire back eight.

Astonishingly, despite the complex challenges, Cousins was able to restore the new *Saturday Review* to profitability in even less time than it had taken the previous owners to run it into the ground. In less than a year Cousins announced that the magazine was operating in the black again. He was pleased to announce that by the magazine's fiftieth anniversary (1974) the circulation had edged back up to 550,000—only about 100,000 fewer than when Cousins had left it. This made it a near competitor to *Time* and *Life* magazines.

F. Scott Fitzgerald once declared that "there are no second acts in American lives." Norman Cousins might disagree, for his resurrection of the *Saturday Review* from the ashes could very well be seen as a successful second act. Even more improbable was his *third* act. At the end of the 1970s, right around the time he should have been contemplating retirement, he would move across the country and embark on an entirely new career.

CHAPTER 35

THE THIRD ACT

The experience of leaving the *Saturday Review* and then returning to resurrect it left Cousins wondering if this was really what he wanted to do with the rest of his life. He was ten years past his miraculous medical recovery. In the wake of his near death, his doctors had ordered him to cut back on his speaking engagements. This had left him ample time to devote to his growing fascination with medicine.

The Norman Cousins Papers at the University of California, Los Angeles, contain hundreds of boxes of medical research and clippings from medical journals that Cousins (and his *Saturday Review* assistants) began to gather during his 1964 illness. Ultimately, Cousins used this research to stake a groundbreaking but controversial claim. In 1976, he published an article in one of the most prestigious peer-reviewed medical journals in America, the *New England Journal of Medicine*. Titled "Anatomy of an Illness (As Perceived by the Patient)," the article's primary claim was that a patient could (and should) mobilize their own body's natural defenses to take charge of their health. He described his own (negative) experience in the hospital and the experiments with vitamin C doses that he and his personal physician, Dr. William Hitzig, had undertaken during his recovery. His ultimate argument was that positive thinking helped him overcome his illness because it helped unleash his body's own healing mechanisms.

The journal printed Cousins's article despite opposition from the journal's editorial board. Their main concern was that Cousins was decidedly *not* a doctor, and his "alternative" treatment seemed more anecdotal than scientific. The editor, Dr. Franz Ingelfinger, overruled the board and published anyway "to show the attitude of an intelligent layman who thought he could figure out a difficult medical question that none of his doctors had solved."[1] Ingelfinger noted that the article was not meant to be taken seriously by doctors as instructive for treatment approaches.

Indeed, many physicians were evidentially angered upon reading Cousins's claims, but a much larger number responded favorably. Cousins claimed that he had received more than three thousand personal letters from doctors praising him for taking an active role in his treatment. Two thousand additional letters came from civilians. It was the highest number of responses he had ever received to an article in his thirty-one years of publishing.[2] The positive response to this article allowed Cousins to think deeply about his career. Two things occurred at the end of 1976 that would change the trajectory of his career. His publication of "Anatomy of an Illness" would launch him on a new path, and an opportunity would arise for him to pull back from the day-to-day management of the magazine.

Weeks after he published the article, Cousins got a call from an old friend, former assistant administrator for aid to Africa in the US Agency for International Development R. Peter Straus. Straus was the president of Straus Broadcasting, a successful radio broadcasting group.[3] Plying the "old boys network," Straus was calling to see whether Cousins might have a job for his twenty-five-year-old son-in-law, Carll Tucker. The old editor and the young man had lunch, and Cousins was impressed. Rather than just helping Tucker out with a job, Cousins was thinking about what Tucker could do for *him.* The broadcasting industry had been financially lucrative for the Straus family. Cousins intended to take advantage of that. Carll Tucker came in looking for a writing job; instead, Cousins offered him and his father-in-law an ownership stake in the magazine.

Cousins was not exactly selling the magazine; he was still badly scarred by the events of 1971. Instead, Cousins would turn day-to-day responsibility for the business side of the magazine over to Tucker. Cousins admitted that he "had little inclination or temperament for the business side."[4] It was true. Cousins was clearly *not* cut out to be a business manager. According to Sarah, in all his time at the *Saturday Review* her father never fired anyone. The head of advertising told her, "Believe me, he's had his share of jerks on staff, but your father—he can't bring himself to do that to anyone."[5] Even if a person truly did not fit at the magazine, Cousins would make it a point to find that person a job somewhere else.

Cousins's inability to fire people even worked in reverse. When Cousins was at the Office of War Information during the war, he learned that someone he knew had been let go from his job and was despondent about it. Cousins invited him to be coeditor of *U.S.A.*[6] While Cousins's aversion to leaving anyone without a job may be considered noble on a human level, it did not make for the best business management practice. Cousins himself admitted that he "felt uneasy and inadequate every time people . . . came to me with problems or had differences among themselves."[7] Cousins had taken on the burden of office management after repurchasing the *Saturday Review*. Under the new arrangement Tucker would now handle that.

The Straus-Tucker investment allowed Cousins to fully repay friends who had lent him money two years earlier to relaunch the magazine. Cousins himself received some money for his equity, as well as a 10 percent share in the profits for a period of twelve years. Mostly, though, Cousins rejoiced at the prospect of his liberation from his management duties. He told his readers that he hoped "to do a better job in the editor's chair. I expect to write more for the magazine. I also hope to contribute articles from abroad, as I did years ago."[8] This deal was supposed to allow Cousins far more time to do what he wanted in terms of writing and traveling for the magazine. But this new arrangement would last just one year before he decided to resign from the *Saturday Review* for good on April 15, 1978. Cousins turned full editorial control of the magazine over to Tucker.

Cousins honored at a luncheon in 1978 to mark his retirement from the *Saturday Review.*

(PHOTO BY MARTY LEDERHANDLER / ASSOCIATED PRESS)

The impetus for Cousins finally to leave the *Saturday Review* for good came in early 1978, when he was invited to give a talk at the UCLA medical school. During the visit he had a discussion with the dean of the medical school about the fact that undergraduates who planned to enter the medical field tended to concentrate their studies in the sciences. Once they were admitted to medical school, much importance was placed on, and classroom time was focused on, diagnostics and textbook approaches to treatment. The result, Cousins argued, was that students were "superbly trained but poorly educated." Cousins mused, "Why shouldn't a broad cultural background be regarded as essential in the practice of medicine" so that practitioners can better understand the circumstances of a patient's life.[9] Cousins thought that literature, philosophy, and ethics also should be taught to medical students. He and the dean discussed, hypothetically, what might go into teaching a course on "medical humanities." Thoroughly impressed by their conversation, Dean Sherman Mellinkoff quickly invited Cousins to join the faculty and said he would put it to the board. It only took a few days for the board to approve bringing Cousins on as an adjunct lecturer who would also help to launch a new research center.

Although the timing could not have been better—Tucker was now adequately managing the daily operations of the magazine—Cousins was still unsure about the idea. It was Ellen who ultimately persuaded him to accept the position. Originally from Utah, she relished the idea of a lifestyle change and the challenge of a move back to the West. Once the decision was made, Cousins put their longtime Connecticut home up for sale the very same morning he accepted the job. On April 4, 1978, the *Los Angeles Times* announced that Cousins would be joining the UCLA faculty, and eleven days after that he resigned his position at the *Saturday Review*.[10] Traveling to Los Angeles to look for a house, they were taken to a beautiful home in Beverly Hills that had an unobstructed view all the way to the ocean. Even though Cousins said the house was selling for "an outrageous price," he claims that they made an offer within five minutes of setting foot in it.[11]

Cousins joined the UCLA faculty to help launch the Brain Research Institute along with a team of ten other researchers. Their goal was to study how emotions affected health outcomes. While it was an exciting time, the chief of UCLA's Department of Psychiatry, Dr. Milton Greenblatt, took Cousins aside as he was settling into his new office and gave him a friendly but ominous warning. "You're going to run into a great deal of opposition to your notions about laughter as therapy," he said. "A lot of my colleagues here think you are confusing hunches and anecdotes with medical science. . . . [The doctors] respect your work as a writer and editor, but now you're on their turf and must play by their rules. If you don't, they can cut you to pieces. You're the only layman on the medical faculty and you've got to recognize your vulnerability."[12] Even though he was wading into uncharted waters where he might find himself vulnerable, Cousins found this new job deeply rewarding. He wrote to a friend, "At the age of 63 I find myself with a new career. . . . I like the idea of giving my subconscious new things to chew on. I like the different sights and sounds of the University in contrast to the magazine office."[13]

Cousins also found himself getting swept up by the Hollywood glamour. Cousins soon joined a weekly golf round with three or four screenwriters, including the comedy writer Sid Ceasar. He played tennis with actor and gun-rights activist Charlton Heston, who lived nearby. He dined with feminist writer Betty Friedan. "Having all these things handy makes it very seductive," Cousins told his archivist.[14] As Candis recalls, "My father was sought out by researchers at UCLA as well as accomplished, politically liberal Hollywood writers. It was a far more creative, fun-loving atmosphere than what my parents experienced in Connecticut and New York. In addition, their dream of being able to play tennis the year round was fulfilled."[15]

At work, Cousins was buoyed by his immersion in a rapidly growing field. At the University of California medical school in San Francisco, new research had recently identified some of the biochemical changes that take place as the result of positive emotions. Johns Hopkins University hosted a conference on the subject of health and positive emotions and invited Cousins to be their keynote speaker.[16]

Not everyone was enthusiastic about having a layman as the keynote speaker at a medical conference. One attendee complained that Cousins "delivered as his keynote a scathing attack on the medical profession, replete with stale jokes. . . . The ensuing discussion was manipulated by Cousins so that it dealt with only matters of medical deficiency." The writer blamed Johns Hopkins for "inviting Norman Cousins to be something which he is not."[17] He was generally viewed with skepticism by medical experts, who perhaps (rightly) felt attacked by his blanket criticisms of the medical field.

Cousins was quick to point out that he was *not* pretending to be a trained physician who diagnosed and treated patients. His role at UCLA made use of his notable talents as an accomplished communicator. During a radio interview Cousins described his role as studying "the way the physician communicates with patients—how language can be translated into an environment conducive to recovery. And conversely, how inartistic language can impede recovery."[18]

Cousins's classes began with a discussion of literature and philosophy focused on the great doctors who were well rounded in their knowledge. He thought classic literature had a lot to teach medical students. After all, the impact of serious illness on people was a recurrent theme in many novels. Writers dealt with the universals of the human experience and with the struggle not just to stay alive but to get the most out of life. Almost every author had something to say about doctors.[19]

Outside of his teaching, Cousins's newly appointed task force at UCLA studied the effects of attitudes such as the will to live and laughter on the curative and restorative processes. His mandate was to find out whether the brain could affect the biochemistry of the body in positive ways. It was a quest he described as an "obsession." He needed to "find proof," he said, "or at least to help create it, that the human brain could bring about changes for the better in the way that human beings confront illness."[20]

While it may have been cutting edge, what Cousins was researching was by no means new. As his colleague Dr. L. J. West described, humans had known for two thousand years that negative feelings caused patients to fare worse. Cousins arrived at UCLA convinced that the opposite was also true. In 1975, psychologist Robert Adler and immunologist Nicholas Cohen used a number of experiments to demonstrate that the immune and nervous systems were linked. Cousins set out to prove, then, that you could use emotions to *improve* health outcomes.[21] While Cousins's work was controversial in the 1970s, since then there has been a plethora of research in this field. In 2008, Dr. Francisco Tausk at the University of Rochester Medical Center concluded that "there is no longer much question that the nervous and immune systems are tightly connected. . . . Important lines of evidence have converged over time to establish the connections as incontrovertible."[22]

Cousins was not the first to posit that positive emotions were influential in healing, but what Cousins did do was to popularize the concept and rally those scientists who saw some credibility in the idea. "I think Norman was the first one to really expound . . . on the fact that the individual could play an important part in the fight for recovery," wrote Harold Benjamin, who founded a nationwide network of wellness centers to provide support and counseling to cancer patients using Cousins's model.[23] The chairman of the Department of Community Health Sciences at UCLA told the *Los Angeles Times* that "in a certain way, [Cousins] legitimized it."[24] Cousins's great gift over his entire career was his ability to take a small, unknown issue of great consequence and bring it to public attention.

Buoyed by his work at the Brain Research Institute and encouraged by the popular response to his 1976 article drawing the links between positive emotions and successful recovery, Cousins published a book on the theme in 1979, also titled *Anatomy of an Illness: As Perceived by the Patient.* This book would quickly become the best-selling book of Cousins's entire career, appearing on the *New York Times* bestseller list soon after its publication. (It is the only one of Cousins's books that is still regularly in print today, four decades after its initial publication.) It brought him far more widespread name recognition than any of his previous books or even his anti-nuclear work had done. It was extremely financially lucrative for Cousins. He told his archivist, perhaps tongue in cheek, "My illness was the best thing that ever happened to me." He sold the paperback rights to the book for $180,000 ($670,000 in 2020 dollars).[25] The book was also the basis for a 1984 TV biopic by the same name starring Ed Asner, which dramatized Cousins's self-cure through laughter.

That nationwide exposure on a level that he hadn't experienced since 1945 brought Cousins more attention but also more criticism. Within months of the book's publication, Dr. Florence Ruderman, a sociologist of medicine, published a review that blasted it as an "illogical, deceptive, self-serving production which raises more questions than it answers."[26] She claimed that "instead of pursuing factually and logically any substantive issue, Cousins provides an uplifting sermonette, an inspirational (and scientifically worthless) ramble."[27]

Many readers and other doctors agreed with her criticism. Dr. Richard Selzer, of Connecticut, wrote a letter to the editor of *Commentary* magazine to express his outrage at "the shabbiness and lack of control that Norman Cousins exhibits in his presentation." He called it a "destructive and misleading book."[28] Dr. Martin Goldner criticized Cousins's book for its "underlying inaccuracies, intended or unintended omissions or distortions, and particularly the disservice Cousins's views could to do patients and physicians in general."[29] Most of the medical critics claimed that far from discovering a miraculous cure, Cousins had simply been misdiagnosed. His gradual drop in blood sedimentation rate and his recovery had been just natural remission. This backlash echoed what happened to Cousins's friend Linus Pauling, who also got roasted by the medical community over his staunch advocacy surrounding the health benefits of vitamin C.

Cousins, of course, was used to the occasional irate *Saturday Review* reader, and he was no stranger to criticism. This time was different though, and even some of his close friends fiercely disagreed with him. An old friend from Mount Sinai Hospital, Dr. Sidney Kahn, accused Cousins of "reckless use of scientific terminology and the citing of irrelevant references to substantiate arbitrary beliefs."[30] Cousins reacted with indignation to the criticism. He dispatched a number of letters to his most vocal critic, Dr. Ruderman, threatening to sue her for libel.[31] It did not come to that, however, as Cousins seems to have eventually dropped the matter. Ultimately, in a 2010 *New Yorker* article examining laughter as a prescription for better health, investigative journalist Raffi Khatchadourian concluded that "there is not enough evidence to conclude much of anything. . . . Much of the science on laughter and healing has not been convincingly replicated, or suffers from methodological problems or small sample sizes."[32]

Despite the criticism, Dean Mellinkoff's gamble in hiring Cousins paid off handsomely. He was ubiquitous on campus. He wrote prolifically. He lectured, assisted in clinical research, and poured enormous effort into fundraising. Another impressed colleague later said, "We thought [Cousins] would teach and write and would be a delightful and valuable scholarly person to have on the faculty. We never reckoned that he would also be a demon fund-raiser."[33]

Cousins also taught courses to medical students about the crucial relationship between patient and physician. What Cousins had observed during his research was that illness often took a sharp turn for the worse right after diagnosis. Patients went to the doctor because they felt that something was wrong, but it was a negative diagnosis making their ailment "real" that unleashed a wave of panic and depression that negatively affected their physical health as well. Cousins's courses taught physicians how to "lessen the blow," as it were, how to use language to frame negative results so that patients left the doctor's office with a sense of hope and challenge rather than devastation.[34]

Cousins shared these conclusions in a 1983 lecture that received such popular acclaim that it was broadcast over dozens of National Public Radio stations and as far away as Australia.[35] During this lecture, Cousins explained that thirty-four basic substances are produced in the brain, including substances that can help fight viruses, serve as natural morphines, and fortify the immune system. Essentially the brain can write prescriptions for the body, and his goal was to find out how the patient could get delivery of those prescriptions when needed.[36] In 1980, though, he would put his new research to the test on the most important patient of all—himself.

It was a Monday afternoon just days before Christmas 1980. Cousins was working from home that day, and just after enjoying his typical lunch of his wife's "special" salad and steamed fresh vegetables, he was hit by a wave of nausea and weakness. He felt a pressure in his chest and had some difficulty breathing. Included in the Cousins's home medical kit was a portable oxygen tank, which he had Ellen fetch and hook him up to. He called UCLA and had an ambulance dispatched. At the hospital the diagnosis was clear: he had suffered "significant" heart-muscle destruction and congestive heart failure. There was a good chance that he wouldn't make it through the next twenty-four hours. "I found myself wondering whether this would be my last night in this world," Cousins wrote later.[37]

Cousins thought back to the events leading up to the heart attack. For the past few months he had been extremely busy, enduring a hectic travel schedule with numerous stressful flights. He had had little time to engage in his favorite pastimes, golf and tennis. Just before the heart attack he had been dismayed to discover that he was scheduled to leave shortly for another trip. He unsuccessfully tried to postpone or cancel it, but his secretary told him that only the "most drastic event" would get him out of it.[38] His body was listening: he had the heart attack the next day. But even though he knew that 50 percent of heart attack victims don't survive the first twenty-four hours, Cousins had some cause for optimism.

Given his research into how emotions affect health outcomes, Cousins knew that it was crucial to reduce his feeling of panic. Panic leads to stress, and stress further constricts the blood flow. On his ride to the hospital he told the ambulance driver to shut off the siren and drive at a normal speed. He wanted to de-escalate the emergency mood in order to calm himself. He was wheeled into the emergency room to find some of his colleagues waiting for him. He looked up at them and told them "they were looking at what was probably the darndest healing machine that had ever been wheeled into the hospital."[39] And indeed he was. As during his 1964 illness, Cousins took an active role in his own recovery. His heart attack also provided the prime opportunity to further his own research into the impact of positive emotions. It is rare that a life-threatening health condition is welcomed by the victim, but Cousins leveraged this near-death experience into a work of scholarship.

In 1983, he published *The Healing Heart*, which outlined his experience and the effect of his "self-healing." At the time, doctors generally prescribed bedrest for heart attack victims. Cousins's own physician had instructed him, "You've got to settle down. . . . Stay flat on your back and just be a vegetable."[40] Cousins, however, defied the order. He writes, "I continued to do all the things that had worked so well for me earlier. . . . Things that nourished the spirit and were joyous."[41] Within a week he had recovered enough to be discharged from the hospital, but all was not well. His doctors recommended an angioplasty in preparation for a possible bypass operation because of blockages in his arteries. Cousins refused to even consider it. He wanted to see whether he could put his own research and beliefs to the test. Through diet, exercise, and positive emotion, could he adequately heal his own heart?

With his 1964 illness as his guide, Cousins overcame the objections of his doctor and began his new routine immediately. He found a running track near his home and proceeded to walk there. The first time he tried it, he was able to walk for only a minute before getting dizzy. But slowly, day by day, his capacity increased until he could keep going for an hour or so. He increased his other activities as well. He dove back into his writing, publishing yet another book in 1982, *The Physician in Literature*, an edited work that looked at the writings of classic authors to determine the role of the physician in literature as a symbol of human knowledge, healing, scientific irony, and perceptivity in a crisis.[42] He increased his teaching schedule and started playing golf again. A month after leaving the hospital, he discontinued all his medication and increased his physical activity until he was nearly back to his normal routine. Each subsequent medical test showed his heart getting stronger, until the previously recommended bypass operation was no longer necessary.

Cousins had a life-long healthy distrust in what the medical "experts" told him stemming from the misdiagnosis of tuberculosis that had put him in a sanatorium as a child. In 1954, at age thirty-nine, he was diagnosed (or perhaps misdiagnosed) with a "silent" coronary—a heart in very poor condition. Doctors then gave him eighteen months to live, but only if he gave up everything and lived a sedentary life. As he later wrote, "I looked down two roads. One road . . . I would give up everything important to me and try to squeeze out 18 vegetative and melancholy months." The other road, he explained, was that he might live eighteen minutes or eighteen months, but he was going to enjoy every moment of it by continuing to do the things he loved.[43]

Ultimately Cousins stayed on the UCLA faculty, working right up until his death in 1990. During his twelve years at UCLA he published an astonishing seven more books, most related to the medical field.[44] Cousins's own impact on the study of the brain-body connection is clear. The Brain Research Institute he was hired to help found at UCLA in 1978 is today called the Cousins Center for Psychoneuroimmunology.

While Cousins may have healed his heart physically, emotionally he was strained by the déjà vu that he must have felt. The *Saturday Review* was in crisis yet again. Shortly after Cousins retired, the magazine started to falter, with Tucker racking up a debt of nearly $1 million by 1980. Cousins's associates were furious. His friend Mary Swift scrambled to retrieve important files from the office before, as she wrote to Cousins's archivist, "those (*bleep*) new owners of SR do something irresponsible." She lamented that Tucker and his management team were "all arrogance and not a smidgen of humility. Even when they fail, it never occurs to them that the fault might be in part attributable to their own inadequacies."[45] They *did* do something irresponsible in the eyes of the former *Saturday Review* staffers: Tucker sold the magazine to the publisher of *Financial World.*

To save money, the new publisher cut weekly publication down to monthly. Even two years after his retirement, Norman Cousins was so strongly identified with the *Saturday Review* that reporters reached out to him for comment on this development. Cousins's concern was that the magazine had sealed its fate when it gave up weekly publication, so that it no longer had the ability to respond quickly to topical issues. Ultimately he was right. On August 16, 1982, the *Saturday Review* would close its doors forever. Reflecting on the news, Cousins told the *New York Times* that "something of value will go out of our life." He lamented the fact that such magazines were no longer a unifying national force and a forum for identifying and clarifying issues.[46]

Although he no longer had the *Saturday Review,* Cousins couldn't help but continue contributing to the intellectual churn of American society. He started writing a regular column for the *Christian Science Monitor* in which he engaged with whatever issue happened to catch his attention. As busy as he was in the medical field, he still found time to indulge his previous passion of advocating for peace. What inflamed his anger the most was the reporting in the mid-1980s about enormously wasteful military spending. At a time when the Reagan administration had increased the Pentagon's budget to the highest ever in peacetime, the Project on Military Procurement, a nonprofit organization that exposed defense industry fraud and waste, discovered some explosive news.

Front-page articles in national newspapers reported that the Pentagon was grossly overpaying for mundane everyday items. It spent $640 on a toilet seat, $7,600 on a coffee pot, and $659 on a single ashtray, to name only a few.[47] Cousins, naturally, was enraged. So enraged that he did more than just write a few articles on the subject; he published an entire book attacking the defense industry. *The Pathology of*

Power (1987) focused on the widely reported fraud and waste and argued that excessive and careless military spending allowed private contractors to earn huge profits in weapons making. He worried that the US economy was dangerously dependent on military spending. Cousins, beating his well-worn drum, argued that the solution to this problem was to strengthen world institutions like the United Nations. The foreign policy luminary George F. Kennan noted in a blurb on the book's jacket that it "reflects the wisdom of an honest and courageous spirit, accumulated over many years of involvement with public affairs as editor, educator, and commentator."[48]

But at the same time that Cousins continued to rail on the US national security stance and to advocate for global institutions, the world seemed to be moving in the opposite direction. The *Christian Science Monitor* noted in 1980 that "it can also be pointed out that almost every cause Mr. Cousins had championed has lately fallen on hard times." The author described how the Strategic Arms Limitation Treaty (SALT) seemed to have been permanently shelved; the death penalty had been reinstated; and environmental concerns were being trumped by the demand for energy.[49]

Perhaps by the mid-1980s Cousins was losing touch with the direction of events. He was seventy-two when *The Pathology of Power* came out, and while many of the columns he continued to write engaged with contemporary news, he also was increasingly coming across as an old man regaling the grandchildren with tales from his glory days. In an August 1989 article he reminisced about his relationship with Khrushchev, reminding readers that he had played badminton with the leader of the Soviet Union. He called for more "moral imagination" in the formulation of foreign policy. Again he made the case for optimism. He wanted to see more funding for education, more authority given to the United Nations, and he stressed the value and importance of individual actions in confronting politicians to enact changes. His time at the *Monitor* reads like a "Greatest Hits of Norman Cousins" column.

The world was passing Cousins by, and soon it would lose him forever. Ultimately, not even Cousins's eternal optimism and positive thinking could overcome the simple and relentless march of time and age. On November 30, 1990, Cousins collapsed at a hotel in Los Angeles. Paramedics rushed him to the nearby UCLA hospital, where he died of full cardiac arrest about twenty minutes later. He was seventy-five. He had outlived his doctor's initial prognosis by thirty-six years.

CONCLUSION

Cousins maintained his optimism even in his last will, where he told his mourners, "I would hope that any memorial service held for me will be liberated from the solemnity that has never sat well for me. I am suggesting an ambience that is compatible with my belief that no tragedy or sadness is to be attached to a life fully and joyously lived."[1] The joyousness and accomplishments of his life would reverberate well beyond his family circle.

News of Cousins's death sparked a round of newspaper obituaries from coast to coast that required multiple pages to describe his lifetime of wide-reaching achievements. The *Los Angeles Times* described Cousins as "a Renaissance Man in an era of specialists."[2] Even President George H. W. Bush penned a letter to Ellen Cousins in which he wrote, "Norman Cousins . . . [earned great] acclaim for the hope and inspiration he brought to millions of readers through his writings on the healing power of the human spirit. I'm sure that the people whose lives he touched will always cherish his memory."[3]

Throughout his public career, Cousins espoused his belief that a country as wealthy and powerful as the United States—a country with an abiding faith in liberal democracy and free market enterprise, morality and decency—should promote those philosophies and spread them to other nations. Not, however, at gunpoint, as many advocated (and, sadly, many presidents acquiesced to), but through a concern for the welfare and well-being of the world's people. Only if the world's peoples and governments worked together for international law and justice, he believed, could a more peaceful world truly be achieved. The prospect was imperative after 1945, with nuclear weapons having obliterated the notion of sovereign national borders.

The story of how one man was able to take often small and little-known humanitarian issues, bring them to public attention, and ultimately pressure governments around the world to do the "right" thing is one we should not forget. It is more important than ever to examine the success of the long-standing international agreements that citizen diplomats and individual peacemakers like Norman Cousins were able to achieve. They certainly were not easy or even successful (as Cousins's long fight against nuclear weapons shows), but they *did* make the world a far safer place. President Kennedy, in 1961, feared that by the end of the decade up to twenty countries might possess nuclear weapons. The fact that there are only nine today is a testament to the forward thinking of leaders like Kennedy and Khrushchev but especially to the tenacity of activists like Cousins, who worked for decades behind the scenes to make a safer world for all of us.

Norman Cousins relentlessly advocated for positivity and optimism. He fought hard to improve relations between the United States and its adversaries. He sought to introduce Americans to foreign cultures, and foreigners to Americans, in the hope that if people just knew one another a little better, they would see that they shared the same goals. Cousins pierced through the fear-mongering and anxiety and us-versus-them mentality that often prevailed during the Cold War with an example of hope, peace, and progress built on sustained dialogue. Those conversations Cousins had ultimately made the entire world a safer place. His lines of communication helped in some small part to defuse the Cuban Missile Crisis. While many criticized Cousins as being a Communist dupe, his communications with the so-called enemy proved to be extremely fruitful in furthering the Limited Nuclear Test Ban Treaty.

On balance, Cousins's entire life philosophy is perfectly reflected in the ideas he penned for the first draft of President John F. Kennedy's

American University Commencement Address. Sorensen took Cousins's ideals and polished them into the final draft to read that the challenge for politicians and civilians alike was "not to see only a distorted and desperate view of the other side, not to see conflict as inevitable, accommodation as impossible, and communication as nothing more than the exchange of threats. No government or social system is so evil that its people must be considered as lacking in virtue." Cousins, through his deep understanding of the fragility of human life, recognized that "in the final analysis, our most basic common link is that we all inhabit this small planet. We all breathe the same air. We all cherish our children's future. And we are all mortal."[4]

ACKNOWLEDGMENTS

Spending nearly a decade immersed in the life of someone I never met forced me to reflect deeply on my own life and the interactions and impressions I leave behind. In writing this book I have had many such interactions with countless people along the way who have helped me immensely. Their input improved this work greatly, and they warrant my thanks.

This book traces its origins to my dissertation at American University. From the very first days of my PhD program, my colleagues Amy Langford, Thomas Kenning, Lizzy Morse, Kelsey Fritz, Susan Perlman, Alison Jobe, Andrew Cox, Eddy Lucas, Nguyet Nguyen, and Andrew Chatfield served as my academic sounding board and personal support network. I want to say a special thanks to them for listening and providing sage advice while I tried to unravel the many stories of Norman Cousins.

As I embarked on my research, much financial support was provided by the American University College of Arts and Sciences as well as the History Department. Their well-timed and generous funding allowed me to go further in my research than I otherwise would have been able to do. I also want to thank my current institution, Trinity Washington University, for providing research funding and for fostering a congenial atmosphere in which to pursue my academic career. The Woodrow Wilson Center's Nuclear History Boot Camp, in which I was privileged to participate in 2018, was a formative experience and an inspiration to my research.

Thanks go especially to my academic mentors. They influenced this work in many ways. Dr. Peter Kuznick provided personal support and editing advice, suggested research paths to follow, and helped me to ply his vast network of contacts. It was on a 2011 trip to Hiroshima with Kuznick's Nuclear Studies Institute that I first met Koko Kondo, daughter of Kiyoshi Tanimoto and survivor of the atomic bombing, and, if I recall correctly, I first learned about the work of Norman Cousins. It was a life-changing trip in more ways than one.

I am indebted to Dr. Max Paul Friedman, who always returned early drafts with probing questions, the answers to which seemed so right that I was embarrassed not to have thought of them myself. Dr. Marty Sherwin's biography of J. Robert Oppenheimer, *American Prometheus*, was partly what sparked my interest in nuclear weapons and anti-nuclear activism and served as a model for my own work. I am especially grateful that I later came to know Marty personally and he became a cherished mentor and champion. Dr. Andrew Hunt deserves special mention for serving as an outside reader who provided thoughtful edits and encouragement. Dr. Eric Lohr's ongoing support and encouragement helped to open new opportunities for me, and alongside Dr. Anton Fedyashin, he helped to broaden my understanding of Russian and Soviet history. Dr. Tim Naftali first pointed me in the direction of the "secret" Tape 82 at the Kennedy Library, and Dr. James Hershberg helped me better understand Cousins's role in the Vietnam War.

I conducted the majority of my research in the UCLA Department of Special Collections, housed in the Charles E. Young Research Library, where the always cheery, knowledgeable, and helpful archivists and staff made my years of working in their windowless basement reading room much less dreadful. I thank them for their dedicated work. Thanks also to the archivists and staff at the Eisenhower and Kennedy Presidential Libraries and at the Peace Collection at Swarthmore College, where I also spent a good deal of time.

I would like to recognize and thank Norman Cousins's daughters Andrea, Candis, and Sarah for spending many hours with me talking about their father. They shared thoughtful insights and provided rich details about the more personal side of their father, who despite leading a very public life was a very private person. Candis also shared some photographs with me, some of which appear in this book.

The person who deserves perhaps the most thanks is my friend and colleague Dr. Lindsay MacNeill. This book would not have been possible without Lindsay, who, as the first editor of all my drafts, always provided constructive support while never hesitating to point out when my ideas, arguments, or writing left something to be desired. Thanks to Lindsay's thoughtfully unique perspective and deep knowledge, this book is far superior to what I could have managed on my own.

Of course, the unquestioning support and encouragement of my parents, Alex and Barb, and my sister, Heather, was the critical fuel for this whole endeavor. My continuing thanks go to my wife, Amelia. We had not met when I first embarked on writing this biography. We got married when I was halfway through the project, and throughout it all Amelia remained a calming influence, a patient listener, and a sharp editor. Our daughter, Esther, who arrived in this world in the project's final stages, is a constant reminder of the poignant need for that better, more peaceful world Norman Cousins dedicated his life to fostering. I am grateful for Cousins's work to make my world a better place, and I am indebted to all those who continue to advocate for peace, justice, a healthier planet, and the power of reasoned dialogue over violence and force.

NOTES

Abbreviations

ASP Adlai E. Stevenson Papers, Princeton University, Princeton, New Jersey

BArch Bundesarchiv (German Federal Archives), Berlin

BFC Benjamin B. Ferencz Collection (RG12.000), United States Holocaust Memorial Museum, Washington, DC

DDEL Dwight D. Eisenhower Presidential Library, Abilene, Kansas

JFKL John F. Kennedy Presidential Library, Boston

NACP National Archives, College Park, Maryland

NC Norman Cousins

NCP Norman Cousins Papers, Library Special Collections, Charles E. Young Research Library, UCLA

SCPC Swarthmore College Peace Collection, McCabe Library, Swarthmore, Pennsylvania

Prologue

1. "B29 Gunnery Brain Aims Six Guns at Once," *Popular Mechanics*, February 1945, 26.
2. This anecdote about Bob Caron is adapted from George R. Caron and Charlotte Meares, *Fire of a Thousand Suns: The George R. "Bob" Caron Story; Tail Gunner of the Enola Gay* (Westminster, CO: Web Publishing, 1995).

3. Norman Cousins Oral History, NCP, 119. There are two versions of this oral history. The original, typewritten version is paged differently than the digital PDF, which I cite here. See http://digital2.library.ucla.edu/dlcontent/oralhistory/pdf/masters/21198zz0008zkgn5master.pdf.
4. *New York Times*, August 7, 1945, 1.
5. Sarah Shapiro, "My Hiroshima," *San Francisco Chronicle*, September 4, 1994, 13.

Introduction

1. From 1924 until 1952 the magazine was called the *Saturday Review of Literature*. In 1952 the name was shortened to *Saturday Review*. Regardless of the year, in this book the magazine will be referred to as the *Saturday Review*.
2. "Norman Cousins: One of America's Great Editors," 92nd Cong., 1st sess., *Congressional Record* 117, pt. 33 (November 22, 1971), 42751. See also NCP, Box 1292, Folder: Treasure Letters—World.
3. Carter Wilkie to the president, August 17, 1993, Records of the Office of Communications (Clinton Administration), Series: Mark Gearan's Files, 19931995, https://catalo.archives.gov/id/55030702.
4. NC, speech at the Ochsner Distinguished Lectureship, September 29, 1987, NCP, Box 1328, transcript of VHS: Ochsner Distinguished Lectureship: "An Editor's Diary."
5. Fran Thompson to NC, September 1, 1968, NCP, Box 1194, Folder: Fran Thompson 1/4.
6. Adam Clymer and Don Van Natta Jr., "Family of Robert F. Kennedy Rethinks His Place at Library," *New York Times*, June 11, 2011, A1.
7. Mary Swift to Thompson, April 1981, NCP, Box 1194, Folder: Fran Thompson 1/4.
8. McGeorge Bundy, "For Norman Cousins," n.d., JFKL, McGeorge Bundy Personal Papers, Box 229, Folder: Speeches and Lectures [for Norman Cousins].
9. Arthur Herzog, *The War-Peace Establishment* (New York: Harper & Row, 1965), 206.
10. Andrea Cousins, interview by author, October 17, 2020.
11. Jeff Kingston, quoted in "Hiroshima Atomic Bombing Did Not Lead to Japanese Surrender, Historians Argue nearing 70th Anniversary," *ABC News*, August 4, 2015, https://www.abc.net.au/news/20150805/hiroshimabombing didnot-lead-japanese-surrender-anniversary/6672616.

Chapter 1. Educator for an Atomic Age

1. "Statement by the President Announcing the Use of the A-Bomb at Hiroshima," August 6, 1945, *Public Papers of the Presidents of the United States, Harry S. Truman, 1945–1953* (Washington, DC: GPO, 1966), doc. 93.
2. Norman Cousins Oral History, NCP, 119.
3. NC, *Modern Man Is Obsolete* (New York: Viking, 1945), 8.
4. NC, "Modern Man Is Obsolete," *Saturday Review of Literature*, August 18, 1945, 5.
5. NC, "Modern Man Is Obsolete," 5.
6. NC, editor's note, *Saturday Review of Literature*, September 1, 1945, 19.
7. Nat Schmulowitz, letter to the editor, *Saturday Review of Literature*, September 8, 1945, 20.
8. Carlos Romulo to NC, November 14, 1945, NCP, Box 1212, Folder: Romulo, Carlos, 1940s.
9. NC, editor's note, *Saturday Review of Literature*, September 22, 1945, 20.
10. Harold Ickes to NC, December 10, 1945, NCP, Box 1204, Folder: Executive Departments.
11. Sanford Gottlieb, conversation with author, May 16, 2013.
12. Joseph Bagnall, "Norman Cousins: The Man for the Nobel Peace Prize," January 1985, NCP, Box 1144, Folder: Nobel Nomination Materials, Jan 85.
13. Lawrence Wittner, *One World or None: A History of the World Nuclear Disarmament Movement through 1953* (Stanford, CA: Stanford University Press, 1993), 67.
14. Felix A. Morlion, "Freedom's Challenge and Pope John," unpublished manuscript, NCP, Box 968, Folder: f. 2 Morlion—[photocopy of manuscript, printed material, curriculum vitae], 66.
15. Norman Cousins Oral History, NCP, 128.

Chapter 2. The Formation of a Vision

1. NC to Teruaki Shimaguchi, October 9, 1953, NCP, Box 156, Folder: Teruaki #1.
2. Andrea Cousins, interview by author, October 17, 2020.
3. Candis Cousins Kerns, interview by author, October 25, 2020.
4. Norman Cousins Oral History, NCP, 50.
5. Kerns, interview.
6. Paul Edward Nelson, "Norman Cousins: Persuasion and the Moral Imagination" (PhD diss., University of Minnesota, 1968), 5.

7. Norman Cousins background data, September 28, 1966, Records of the Federal Bureau of Investigation, https://vault.fbi.gov/. Obtained through FOIA request by author.
8. Kerns, interview.
9. NC, interview by James Day, March 12, 1974, *Day at Night*, CUNY.
10. See "Only A Teacher: Schoolhouse Pioneers," PBS Online, pbs.org /onlyateacher/pioneers.html.
11. NC, interview by James Day.
12. Craig Kridel, "Toward a Theoretical Base for General Education Curricular Design" (PhD diss., Ohio State University, 1980), NCP, Box 1149, Folder: Craig Kridel Dissertation (3), 184, 186.
13. Kridel, "Toward a Theoretical Base," 186.
14. Kridel, "Toward a Theoretical Base," 186.
15. See Dolan Cummings, ed., *The Changing Role of the Public Intellectual* (New York: Routledge, 2005).
16. NC, "Confessions of A Universalist: One Man's Re-education," *Saturday Review of Literature*, August 6, 1949, 74.
17. Michael Kimmage, *The Conservative Turn: Lionel Trilling, Whittaker Chambers, and the Lessons of Anti-Communism* (Cambridge, MA: Harvard University Press, 2009).
18. Kerns, interview.
19. NC to Roland, n.d., NCP, Box 1150, Folder: Letters Biography Material.
20. NC to Barbara Smith, September 28, 1954, NCP, Box 142, Folder: Miscellaneous—1954—I–Z.
21. Andrea Cousins, interview.
22. Memo, Mr. Jones to Mr. Nichols, July 15, 1949, Records of the Federal Bureau of Investigation.
23. NC to Eugene Feingold, June 2, 1960, NCP, Box 218, Folder: FE–FH 1960.
24. NC, undated interview, NCP, Box 1150, Folder: Letters Biography Material.
25. NC, "Confessions of A Universalist," 75.
26. NC, "Antidotes to 'Mein Kampf,'" *Saturday Review of Literature*, March 4, 1944, 14.
27. NC, "Confessions of A Universalist," 75.
28. Kridel, "Toward a Theoretical Base," 211.
29. NC to F. Lyman Windolph, May 14, 1948, NCP, Box 1150, Folder: N.C. on Personal Philosophy.

30. Kerns, interview.
31. Kerns, interview.
32. Andrea Cousins, interview.
33. Kerns, interview.
34. Another founder of the *Saturday Review* was Henry Seidel Canby, considered to be a leading literary critic by many at the time.
35. Kerns, interview.
36. Kridel, "Toward a Theoretical Base," 192.

Chapter 3. World War II

1. Speech by NC at the Ochsher Distinguished Lectureship, September 29, 1987, NCP, Box 1328, transcript of VHS: Ochsher Distinguished Lectureship: "An Editor's Diary."
2. NC, "Not Recrimination But Resolve," *Saturday Review of Literature*, June 29, 1940, 8.
3. NC, "The One Indispensable," *Saturday Review of Literature*, October 12, 1940, 12.
4. NC, "Letter to a Novelist, 1960," *Saturday Review of Literature*, January 17, 1942, 3.
5. NC, *Who Speaks for Man?* (New York: Macmillan, 1953), 63.
6. Norman Cousins Oral History, NCP, 50.
7. NC to Selective Service Board 26B, May 29, 1944, NCP, Box 71, Folder: Cousins, Norman—Personal.
8. "Introduction of Norman Cousins by Allen Green," November 20, 1946, NCP, Box 1730, Folder: Lecture—Atomic Bomb vs. Human Intelligence Norwalk Town Hall—11/20/46.
9. NC to Selective Service Board 26B.
10. Michael Bess, *Choices under Fire: Moral Dimensions of World War II* (New York: Knopf, 2006), 93.
11. Bess, *Choices under Fire*, 95.
12. NC, "The Non-Obliterators," *Saturday Review of Literature*, April 8, 1944, 14.
13. NC, "Non-Obliterators," 14.
14. Norman Cousins Oral History, NCP, 116.
15. NC, "Waiting—For What?," *Saturday Review of Literature*, March 3, 1945, 20.
16. NC to Selective Service Board 26B.
17. Candis Cousins Kerns, interview by author, October 25, 2020.

18. Norman Cousins Oral History, NCP, 121.
19. Norman Cousins Oral History, NCP, 142.
20. NC, "Modern Man Is Obsolete," *Saturday Review of Literature*, August 18, 1945, 5.
21. Norman Cousins Oral History, NCP, 29.
22. NC, "Confessions of A Universalist: One Man's Re-education," *Saturday Review of Literature*, August 6, 1949, 80.
23. NC, "Confessions of A Universalist," 80.
24. Paul Boyer, *By the Bomb's Early Light: American Thought and Culture at the Dawn of the Atomic Age* (New York: Pantheon, 1985), 35.

Chapter 4. An Anti-Nuclear Crusade

1. NC to Andrew Hegre, August 12, 1952, NCP, Box 141, Folder: Miscellaneous—1952.
2. NC to Mrs. Kelley, December 5, 1949, NCP, Box 81, Folder: K.
3. NC to Elizabeth Schenk, November 22, 1948, NCP, Box 1150, Folder: N.C. on Personal Philosophy.
4. Candis Cousins Kerns, interview by author, October 25, 2020.
5. Harrison Smith to NC, July 3, 1946, NCP, Box 91, Folder: Memos, Misc. Etc. 1946–1949.
6. NC, "Where Do We Go From Here?," *Saturday Review of Literature*, May 5, 1945, 14.
7. NC, "The Paralysis of Conscience," *Saturday Review of Literature*, October 6, 1945, 14.
8. NC to Cecil W. Brown, April 24, 1950, NCP, Box 93, Folder: B—1950.
9. "Norman Cousins on Atomic Energy" (speech), November 20, 1946, NCP, Box 1730, Folder: Lecture—Atomic Bomb vs. Human Intelligence Norwalk Town Hall—11/20/46.
10. Geir Lundestad, "Empire By Invitation? The United States and Western Europe, 1945–1952," *Journal of Peace Research* 23, no. 3 (1986): 1.
11. NC, "For Murderers Only," *Saturday Review of Literature*, May 18, 1946, 18.
12. Stephen Wertheim, *Tomorrow, the World: The Birth of U.S. Global Supremacy* (Cambridge, MA: Belknap Press of Harvard University Press, 2020).
13. Wertheim, *Tomorrow, the World*, 17. This sentiment is also expressed in Paul Kennedy's review of this book, "'Tomorrow, the World' Review: From Isolation to American Empire," *Wall Street Journal*, January 8, 2021.

14. Unfortunately, Einstein's initial letter seems to be missing from Cousins's files. Their subsequent correspondence, however, exists. See NCP, Box 66, Folder: E—General—1946; and transcript of TV interview with NC, NCP, Box 1718, Folder: Potentials TV Interview 9/12/82 Barbara Hubbard.
15. Norman Cousins Oral History, NCP, 138.
16. The content of the Cousins-Einstein meeting is extrapolated here from point-form notes taken by Cousins during the meeting. See "Einstein," NCP, Box 1145, Folder: Einstein—Notes on NC's Visit in 1945.
17. A.L.A.S. to NC, October 29, 1945,NCP, Box 70, Folder: Cousins, Norman—Personal.
18. Norman Cousins Oral History, NCP, 137, first set of brackets in the original.
19. Federation of Atomic Scientists to NC, November 5, 1945, NCP, Box 70, Folder: Cousins, Norman—Personal.
20. See https://fas.org/about-fas/.
21. Memo, Mr. Jones to Mr. Nichols, July 15, 1949, Records of the Federal Bureau of Investigation.
22. Norman Cousins tax return, 1943, NCP, Box 71, Folder: Norman Cousins Personal.
23. "Income of Nonfarm Families and Individuals: 1946," January 28, 1948, Department of Commerce, Series P-60, No. 1. Available from www.census.gov.
24. Ulric Bell to Paul Tibbetts, November 19, 1945, NCP, Box 70, Folder: Cousins, Norman—Personal.
25. "Americans United and the Atomic Age Dinner—A Report for you," n.d., NCP, Box 70, Folder: Cousins, Norman—Personal.
26. "Address delivered by Paul Tibbets to the Atomic Age Dinner," November 28, 1945, NCP, Box 70, Folder: Atomic Age Dinner.
27. NC to Cord, December 13, 1945, NCP, Box 71, Folder: Cousins, Norman—Personal.
28. Lincoln Schuster to Sam Marx, December 11, 1945, NCP, Box 71, Folder: Atomic Age Misc.
29. Eugene Wigner, "Are We Making the Transition Wisely?," The Atomic Age, *Saturday Review of Literature*, November 17, 1945, 28–29.
30. J. Robert Oppenheimer, "Atomic Weapons and the Crisis in Science," The Atomic Age, *Saturday Review of Literature*, November 24, 1945, 9–12.

31. William M. Blair, "World Government Is Urged to Bar Ruin in Atomic War," *New York Times*, October 17, 1945, 1.
32. NC, "Selling Out Control," *Saturday Review of Literature*, October 20, 1945, 15.
33. Blair, "World Government Is Urged to Bar Ruin."
34. The most notable of the signers included Robert Bass (governor of New Hampshire,) Grenville Clark, Thomas Finletter, Edgar Ansel Mowrer, Foster Sterns (former member of Congress), and Alan Cranston.
35. "Declaration of the Dublin, N.H., Conference," *New York Times*, October 17, 1945, 4.
36. NC, "Notes on Visit to the President," December 21, 1945, NCP, Box 1145, Folder: Truman, Harry S.—Report of NC's Visit, Dec. 1945.
37. NC, "Notes on Visit to the President."
38. Norman Cousins Oral History, NCP, 143.
39. See "Daily Schedule of President Truman," January 20, 1948, http://www.trumanlibrary.org/calendar/main.php?currYear=1948&currMonth=1&currDay=20.
40. Robert Dallek, *The Lost Peace: Leadership in a Time of Horror and Hope, 1945–1953* (New York: Harper, 2011), 12.
41. NC, "A Memorandum to President Truman," *Saturday Review of Literature*, March 27, 1948, 20, 37.
42. NC to Howard Jones, February 3, 1948, NCP, Box 76, Folder: J General Correspondence 1948.

Chapter 5. 1946: A New Year in the Atomic Age

1. NC, "Reading Between the Lines," *Saturday Review of Literature*, January 12, 1946, 18.
2. NC, "For Murderers Only," *Saturday Review of Literature*, May 18, 1946.
3. George C. Marshall, "The Marshall Plan Speech," The George C. Marshall Foundation, accessed March 31, 2021, https://www.marshallfoundation.org/marshall/the-marshall-plan/marshall-plan-speech/.
4. NC, "The Paralysis of Conscience," *Saturday Review of Literature*, October 6, 1945, 18.
5. Andrea Cousins, interview by author, October 17, 2020.
6. Philip Bump, "In 1945, Americans Were Thrilled With Nuclear Weapons. That's No Longer True," *Washington Post*, May 27, 2016.

7. Samuel Harrell to NC, November 22, 1940, NCP, Box 952, Folder: Lectures 1939–1949.
8. Sarah Shapiro, email to author, January 5, 2021.
9. Shapiro, interview by author, September 22, 2020.
10. Candis Cousins Kerns, interview by author, October 25, 2020.
11. Sarah Shapiro, interview by author, October 19, 2020.
12. Shapiro, interview, September 22, 2020.
13. NC to Saul Cohn, November 1, 1946, NCP, Box 69, Folder: C—1946—1.
14. Norman Cousins Oral History, NCP, 139.
15. Shapiro, interview, September 22, 2020.
16. Shapiro, interview, October 25, 2020.
17. NC, "Blood, Sweat, Tears, and Iron Curtains," *Saturday Review of Literature*, March 30, 1946, 26.
18. NC, "Blood, Sweat, Tears, and Iron Curtains," 28.
19. "The Acheson-Lilienthal & Baruch Plans, 1946," US Department of State, Office of the Historian, accessed September 9, 2014, https://history.state.gov/milestones/1945-1952/baruch-plans.
20. NC and Thomas K. Finletter, "A Beginning for Sanity," *Saturday Review of Literature*, June 15, 1946, 5.
21. NC and Finletter, "Beginning for Sanity," 6.
22. Albert Speer, *Inside the Third Reich* (London: Weidenfeld & Nicolson, 1995), 314–20.
23. Norman Cousins Oral History, NCP, 139.
24. The Franck Report was a document prepared by James Franck and signed by a number of prominent nuclear physicists working on the Manhattan Project urging the United States not to use the atomic bomb in a military capacity.
25. NC and Finletter, "Beginning for Sanity," 7.
26. NC and Finletter, "Beginning for Sanity," 8.
27. Barton J. Bernstein, "Seizing the Contested Terrain of Early Nuclear History: Stimson, Conant, and Their Allies Explain the Decision to Use the Atomic Bomb," *Diplomatic History* 17, no. 1 (1993): 64. For Cousins's atomic diplomacy claim, see NC and Finletter, "Beginning for Sanity," 7. For the first scholarly argument for "atomic diplomacy," see Gar Alperovitz, *Atomic Diplomacy: Hiroshima and Potsdam; The Use of the Atomic Bomb and the American Confrontation with Soviet Power* (New York: Simon & Schuster, 1965).

28. Richard B. Frank, *Downfall: The End of the Japanese Imperial Empire* (New York: Random House, 1999), 133.
29. Michael Bess, *Choices under Fire: Moral Dimensions of World War II* (New York: Knopf, 2006), 212.
30. Frank, *Downfall*, 133.
31. Samuel Walker, *Prompt and Utter Destruction* (Chapel Hill: University of North Carolina Press, 1997).
32. Norman Cousins Oral History, NCP, 120.
33. Bess, *Choices under Fire*, 233.
34. P. M. S. Blackett, Lewis Mumford, and A. J. Muste quoted in Susan M. Lindee, *Suffering Made Real: American Science and the Survivors at Hiroshima* (Chicago: University of Chicago Press, 1994), 137.
35. John Hersey, "Hiroshima," *New Yorker*, August 31, 1946. It was later published as a book.
36. Lesley M. M. Blume, *Fallout* (New York: Simon & Schuster, 2020), 4.
37. Jon Michaud, "Eighty-five from the Archive: John Hersey," *New Yorker*, June 8, 2010.
38. Blume, *Fallout*, 146.
39. NC, "The Literacy of Survival," *Saturday Review of Literature*, September 14, 1946, 14.
40. Conant was the president of Harvard University and a wartime atomic policymaker. See Bernstein, "Seizing the Contested Terrain of Early Nuclear History," 37.
41. Blume, *Fallout*, 149.
42. See "The Atomic Bomb and the End of World War II," August 5, 2005, National Security Archive, http://www2.gwu.edu/~nsarchiv/NSAEBB/NSAEBB162/#_edn2.
43. Bernstein, "Seizing the Contested Terrain of Early Nuclear History," 37.
44. See John Mason Brown to NC, 1946, NCP, Box 65, Folder: B—General—1946.
45. See Henry L. Stimson, "The Decision to Use the Atomic Bomb," *Harper's Magazine* 194, no. 1161 (February 1947): 97–107.

Chapter 6. Witness to a Catastrophe

1. NC, "The $250,000,000 Reminder," n.d., NCP, Box 1702, Folder: MSS—Bikini Broadcasts.

2. Oliver Stone and Peter Kuznick, *The Untold History of the United States* (New York: Gallery Books, 2012), 198.
3. NC to David Lilienthal, June 11, 1946, NCP, Box 68, Folder: Lilienthal Report.
4. NC, "$250,000,000 Reminder."
5. Lesley M. M. Blume, *Fallout* (New York: Simon & Schuster, 2020), 56.
6. See *New York Times*, July 1, 1946, 1.
7. NC, "Atomic Bomb vs. Human Intelligence" (lecture),November 20, 1946, Box 1730, Folder: Lecture, Atomic Bomb vs. Human Intelligence Norwalk Town Hall—11/20/46.
8. NC, "The Standardization of Catastrophe," *Saturday Review of Literature*, August 10, 1946, 16.
9. NC, "Standardization of Catastrophe," 18.
10. See NC, editor's note, in Leo Szilard, "The Physicist Invades Politics," *Saturday Review of Literature*, May 3, 1947, 7.
11. NC, "I Dreamt I was Mr. Rockefeller," *Saturday Review of Literature*, April 12, 1947, 32.
12. NC, "I Dreamt I was Mr. Rockefeller," 32.
13. George Kennan ["X," pseud.], "The Sources of Soviet Conduct," *Foreign Affairs*, July 1947.
14. NC to Everette DeGoyler, March 14, 1951, NCP, Box 1198, Folder: DeGoyler, Everette.
15. Marc Selverstone, *Constructing the Monolith: The United States, Great Britain, and International Communism, 1945–1950* (Cambridge, MA: Harvard University Press, 2009).
16. NC to DeGoyler.
17. Stone and Kuznick, *Untold History of the United States*, 206.
18. NC, "I Dreamt I was Mr. Rockefeller," 33.
19. NC, "The Retreat from Washington," *Saturday Review of Literature*, December 6, 1947, 28.
20. NC, "Speaking of Tests," *Saturday Review of Literature*, July 9, 1949, 22.
21. NC, "Bystanders Are Not Innocent," *Saturday Review of Literature*, August 2, 1947, 7.
22. NC, "Now What We Need Is Education," *Saturday Review of Literature*, September 13, 1947, 20.
23. Paul Edward Nelson, "Norman Cousins: Persuasion and the Moral Imagination" (PhD diss., University of Minnesota, 1968), 20.

24. Memo, Mr. Jones to Mr. Nichols, July 15, 1949, Records of the Federal Bureau of Investigation.
25. NC, "Education and the Next War" (speech), [ca. 1944], NCP, Box 71, Folder: Cousins, Norman—Personal.

Chapter 7. An Educational Field Trip to Germany

1. Norman Cousins Oral History, NCP, 151.
2. Norman Cousins Oral History, NCP, 157.
3. NC, "An Apology for Living," *Saturday Review of Literature*, October 9, 1948, 9.
4. Norman Cousins Oral History, NCP, 154.
5. See "Berlin Broadcast—Town Hall," [1948], ABC Radio, NCP, Box 1702, Folder: Broadcast WJZ–Berlin.
6. NC, "Apology for Living."
7. NC, "The Case of Fritz Thyssen," *Saturday Review of Literature*, October 16, 1948, 21.
8. NC, ". . . But He's an American," *Saturday Review of Literature*, November 20, 1948, 22.
9. NC, "Dinner for 26 in Berlin," *Saturday Review of Literature*, December 18, 1948, 6–7.
10. NC, "Apology for Living," 58.
11. For the report, see "Memorandum to the State and Army Departments on Occupation Policies in Germany," [1948], NCP, Box 93, Folder: American Civil Liberties Union Correspondence.
12. Norman Cousins Oral History, NCP, 150.
13. "Peace: Everybody Wars over It," *Newsweek*, April 4, 1949, 19–22.
14. "Red Visitors Cause Rumpus," *Life*, April 4, 1949, 43.
15. NC, "Tell the Folks Back Home," *Saturday Review of Literature*, April 9, 1949, 20.
16. NC, "Tell the Folks Back Home," 20.
17. Eugene Rabinowitch, "The Three Points of Professor Joliot-Curie," *Bulletin of the Atomic Scientists*, June 6, 1950, 163.
18. Telegram, George V. Allen to NC, March 1949, NCP, Box 69, Folder: UWF—Unsorted.
19. NC to Allen, 28 March 1949, NCP, Box 69, Folder: UWF—Unsorted.
20. Memo, Mr. Jones to Mr. Nichols, July 15, 1949, Records of the Federal Bureau of Investigation.
21. NC, "Tell the Folks Back Home," 20.

22. Memo, Mr. Jones to Mr. Nichols.
23. NC to W. E. Mullins, June 24, 1954, NCP, Box 1192, Folder: Cousins—Marshall Fund.
24. "Red Visitors Cause Rumpus," 40.
25. Carter Clarke to NC, June 1, 1946, NCP, Box 91, Folder: Memos, Misc. Etc. 1946–1949.
26. Memo to Mr. Brown, "Norman Cousins." January 31, 1961, Records of the Federal Bureau of Investigation.

Chapter 8. From Editor's Desk to World Stage

1. Naoko Shibusawa, *America's Geisha Ally: Reimagining the Japanese Enemy* (Cambridge, MA: Harvard University Press, 2006), 214.
2. Kiyoshi Tanimoto, "Hiroshima's Idea," *Saturday Review of Literature*, March 12, 1949, 20.
3. Koko Kondo (daughter of Kyoshi Tanimoto), telephone conversation with author, November 11, 2014.
4. Tanimoto, "Hiroshima's Idea," 20.
5. Hiroshima Peace Center Associates was the entity that oversaw the Peace Center's US efforts.
6. Shibusawa, *America's Geisha Ally*, 214.
7. Craig Kridel, "Toward a Theoretical Base for General Education Curricular Design" (PhD diss., Ohio State University, 1980), NCP, Box 1149, Folder: Craig Kridel Dissertation (3), 201.
8. Alden Whitman, "Harrison Smith of the *Saturday Review* is Dead," *New York Times*, January 9, 1971, 30.
9. Nassrine Azimi, "Dare to Dream," *New York Times*, June 4, 2011.
10. NC, "Regeneration for What?," *Saturday Review of Literature*, September 3, 1949, 22.
11. NC, "Hiroshima—Four Years Later," *Saturday Review of Literature*, September 17, 1949, 10.
12. Kyoshi Tanimoto to NC, August 1, 1950, NCP, Box 96, Folder: Japanese Matters—1950.
13. NC, "Hiroshima—Four Years Later," 30.
14. Andrea Cousins, interview by author, October 17, 2020.
15. NC, "Notes from the Air," *Saturday Review of Literature*, August 20, 1949, 20.
16. Candis Cousins Kerns, interview by author, October 25, 2020.
17. NC to Mayor Shinzo Hamai, October 11, 1949, NCP, Box 96, Folder: Japanese Matters—1950.

18. Christina Klein, *Cold War Orientalism: Asia in the Middlebrow Imagination, 1945–1961* (Berkeley: University of California Press, 2003), 152.
19. NC, "Hiroshima—Four Years Later," 30.
20. Belinda Jelliffe, letter to the editor, *Saturday Review of Literature*, November 19, 1949, 28.
21. Alvin Frankenberg, letter to the editor, *Saturday Review of Literature*, November 19, 1949, 28.
22. NC, "On Being a 'Softie,'" *Saturday Review of Literature*, October 1, 1949, 20.
23. Stephen R. Best, letter to the editor, *Saturday Review of Literature*, October 29, 1949, 24.
24. Etta Delson, letter to the editor, *Saturday Review of Literature*, October 8, 1949, 22.
25. Genevieve Tiller Garland, letter to the editor, *Saturday Review of Literature*, November 5, 1949, 26.
26. Lawrence Malis, letter to the editor, *Saturday Review of Literature*, October 22, 1949, 20.
27. NC to Hamai.
28. Ninoshima Gakuen Island Orphanage to NC, July 15, 1950, NCP, Box 96, Folder: Japanese Matters—1950; NC, editor's note, *Saturday Review of Literature*, November 19, 1950, 24.
29. Helen Keller, letter to the editor, *Saturday Review of Literature*, June 3, 1950, 24.
30. Kathleen Sproul, "Genus: Parent—Species: Moral," *Saturday Review of Literature*, December 23, 1950, 26.
31. NC to Shimaguchi, October 9, 1953, NCP, Box 156, Folder: Teruaki #1.
32. Raymond Ciacio to NC, January 18, 1950, NCP, Box 79, Folder: C-1-1949.
33. Shibusawa, *America's Geisha Ally*, 216.
34. "Financial Report, Hiroshima Peace Center Associates," 1951, NCP, Box 96, Folder: Japanese Matters—1950.
35. *A Power Stronger than the Atom Bomb*, undated pamphlet, NCP, Box 407, Folder: HPCA 1963.
36. "Financial Report, Hiroshima Peace Center Associates," 1951, NCP, Box 96, Folder: Japanese Matters—1950.
37. NC to Shimaguchi, October 9, 1953.
38. Shimaguchi to NC, [likely 1956], NCP, Box 156, Folder: Teruaki #2.
39. NC to William Maloney, October 19, 1953, NCP, Box 156, Folder: Teruaki #1.

40. Sarah Shapiro, "How Hiroshima Came to a Daughter in Connecticut," *International Herald Tribune*, September 2, 1994.
41. Shapiro, "How Hiroshima Came to a Daughter in Connecticut."
42. Kerns, interview.
43. Sarah Shapiro, interview by author, September 22, 2020.
44. Shapiro, interview.
45. Kerns, interview.
46. Untitled notes by Fran Thompson, 1981, NCP, Box 1194, Folder: Francis Thompson 2.

Chapter 9. In Search of Peace, Cousins Rallies for War

1. NC to Lewis Mumford, August 27, 1947, NCP, Box 1208, Folder: Mumford, Lewis.
2. Mumford to NC, August 29, 1947, NCP, Box 1208, Folder: Mumford, Lewis.
3. NC to James Curtis, July 16, 1964, NCP, Box 1150, Folder: N.C. on Personal Philosophy.
4. NC to Curtis.
5. Memo, Jack Cominsky to NC, 1948, NCP, Box 91, Folder: Memos, Misc. Etc. 1946–1949.
6. David Halberstam, *The Coldest Winter: America and the Korean War* (New York: Hyperion, 2007), 89.
7. Jay Walz, "Truman Hurries to Capital; Meets Top Aids on Korea," *New York Times*, June 26, 1950, 1.
8. Halberstam, *Coldest Winter*, 93.
9. Halberstam, *Coldest Winter*, 1, 89.
10. Bruce Cummings. *The Korean War: A History* (New York: Modern Library, 2010), 6.
11. Halberstam, *Coldest Winter*, 94.
12. NC, "The 'Strange Banner,'" *Saturday Review of Literature*, July 22, 1950, 22.
13. NC, "Gettysburg and Korea," *Saturday Review of Literature*, December 2, 1950, 28.
14. A. J. Muste to NC, April 13, 1948, NCP, Box 75, Folder: F General Correspondence 1948.
15. NC to Muste, April 23, 1948, NCP, Box 75, Folder: F General Correspondence 1948.
16. "What Is Sovereignty?," transcript from undated, unidentified radio broadcast, NCP, Box 1703, Folder: UWF Broadcasts.

17. "What Is Sovereignty?"
18. NC to Everette DeGoyler, March 14, 1951, NCP, Box 1198, Folder: DeGoyler, Everette.
19. Cummings, *Korean War*, 13.
20. Cummings, *Korean War*, 12.
21. NC to DeGoyler.
22. "President Eisenhower's Remarks on the Importance of Indochina at the Governors' Conference, August 4, 1953," *Public Papers of the President, 1952–53* (Washington, DC: GPO, 1966), 540.
23. NC to DeGoyler.
24. NC to Albert Schaaf, October 7, 1954, NCP, Box 142, Folder: Miscellaneous—1954—I–Z.
25. NC, untitled speech, [likely 1964], NCP, Box 1733, Folder: LBJ Draft July '64.
26. NC to Elizabeth Schenk, November 22, 1948, NCP, Box 1150, Folder: N.C. on Personal Philosophy.
27. Lawrence Wittner, *One World or None: A History of the World Nuclear Disarmament Movement through 1953* (Stanford, CA: Stanford University Press, 1993), 66.
28. Wittner, *One World or None*, 70.
29. Wittner, *One World or None*, 70.
30. Wittner, *One World or None*, 321.
31. Wittner, *One World or None*, 314.
32. Untitled notes by Fran Thompson, 1970, NCP, Box: 1194, Folder: Francis Thompson 2.
33. Alan Cranston to NC, October 20, 1950, NCP, Box 51, Folder: UWF Correspondence 1950.
34. Quoted in Paul Edward Nelson, "Norman Cousins: Persuasion and the Moral Imagination" (PhD diss., University of Minnesota, 1968), 205.
35. Candis Cousins Kerns, interview by author, October 25, 2020; Sarah Shapiro, interview by author, September 22, 2020.
36. Mary Swift to Fran Thompson, mid-February 1981, NCP, Box 1194, Folder: Fran Thompson 1/4.
37. Candis Cousins Kerns, correspondence with author, October–December 2020.
38. NC employment agreement, February 1, 1961, NCP, Box 413, Folder: NC + SR Agreement.
39. Untitled notes by Fran Thompson, 1970.

40. Paul Boyer, *By the Bomb's Early Light: American Thought and Culture at the Dawn of the Atomic Age* (New York: Pantheon, 1985), 43.
41. NC, "Gettysburg and Korea," 28.
42. Gallup Poll #460, August 18, 1950, www.gallup.com.
43. Gallup Poll #481, October 12, 1951, www.gallup.com.
44. NC, "The Age of the Big Trap," *Saturday Review of Literature*, February 10, 1951, 22.
45. NC, "Age of the Big Trap," 23.
46. NC to DeGoyler.
47. NC to DeGoyler.
48. NC to DeGoyler.
49. Kerns, interview.
50. Oliver Stone and Peter Kuznick, *The Untold History of the United States* (New York: Gallery Books, 2012), 242.
51. Halberstam, *Coldest Winter*, 599.
52. NC, "What Goes On in America?," *Saturday Review of Literature*, May 5, 1951, 20.
53. "The Little Man Who Dared," *Time*, April 23, 1951.
54. "Nation Held in Great Danger," *Chicago Tribune*, April 11, 1951, 1.
55. "Forced Own Removal," *New York Herald-Tribune*, April 11, 1951, 1.
56. NC, "What Goes On in America?," 21.
57. "Transcript of General Douglas MacArthur's Address to Congress, April 19, 1951," President's Secretary's Files, Truman Papers, https://www.trumanlibrary.gov/library/research-files/transcript-general-douglas-macarthurs-address-congress.
58. NC, "What Goes On in America?," 21.

Chapter 10. Candidate of the Intellectuals

1. Jeff Broadwater, *Adlai Stevenson and American Politics: The Odyssey of a Cold War Liberal* (New York: Maxwell Macmillan International, 1994), 105.
2. Broadwater, *Adlai Stevenson and American Politics*, 111.
3. Broadwater, *Adlai Stevenson and American Politics*, 119.
4. Porter McKeever, *Adlai Stevenson: His Life and Legacy* (New York: William Morrow, 1989), 210.
5. McKeever, *Adlai Stevenson*, 210.
6. NC to Adlai Stevenson, September 22, 1952, ASP, Box 20, Folder: 10.
7. NC, "Speech for a Presidential Candidate," *Saturday Review*, August 2, 1952, 22. The magazine shortened its title in 1952.

8. Broadwater, *Adlai Stevenson and American Politics*, 128.
9. NC to Chester Bowles, October 9, 1952, NCP, Box 1196, Folder: Bowles, Chester, 1/6.
10. NC, "The Six Senses: Master Check-List Stevenson," undated memo to Stevenson, NCP, Box 1214, Folder: Stevenson, Adlai, E.
11. NC, "Six Senses."
12. NC, "Six Senses."
13. Stevenson to NC, September 17, 1952, ASP, Box 20, Folder: 10.
14. NC, "Six Senses."
15. Broadwater, *Adlai Stevenson and American Politics*, 125.
16. For the speeches that Cousins contributed to the Stevenson campaign, see NCP, Box 1214, Folder: Stevenson, Adlai, E. See also ASP, Box 20, Folder: 10.
17. NC to Stevenson, October 5, 1952, ASP, Box 20, Folder: 10.
18. NC to Bowles, October 9, 1952.
19. See NC to William Thompson, May 12, 1965, NCP, Box 1194, Folder: Fran Thompson Correspondence 3/4. See also NC to Richard Friedman, April 15, 1957, NCP, Box 158, Folder: Africa (Miscellaneous Correspondence) 1957.
20. Jean Edward Smith, *Eisenhower in War and Peace* (New York: Random House, 2012), 548.
21. William M. Blair, "Illinois G.O.P's Return to Power Held a Major Blow," *New York Times*, November 6, 1952, 17.
22. Broadwater, *Adlai Stevenson and American Politics*, 133, 137.
23. Broadwater, *Adlai Stevenson and American Politics*, 133–34.

Chapter 11. From Advocate to Diplomat

1. Benjamin P. Greene, *Eisenhower, Science Advice, and the Nuclear Test-Ban Debate, 1945–1963* (Stanford, CA: Stanford University Press, 2007), 25. I thank Benjamin Greene for sharing his research.
2. Greene, *Eisenhower, Science Advice*, 25.
3. For the "troublemaker" remark, see David Harley Serlin, "Built for Living: Imagining the American Body through Medical Science, 1945–1965" (PhD diss., New York University, 1999), 133.
4. J. D. Gregory, *On the Edge of Diplomacy: Rambles and Reflections, 1902–1928* (London: Hutchinson, 1931).
5. Giles Scott-Smith, "Private Diplomacy, Making the Citizen Visible," *New Diplomatic Studies* 8, no. 1 (2014): 5.

6. M. J. Zuckerman and Joseph Montville, “Can ‘Unofficial’ Talks Avert Disaster?,” *Carnegie Reporter* 3, no. 3 (Fall 1995).
7. Lawrence H. Chamberlain, “Who Speaks for Man?,” *Political Science Quarterly* 68 (December 1953): 627.
8. “The Critics Separate Wheat from Chaff,” *Saturday Review*, April 11, 1953, 24.
9. Maria Popova, “Carl Sagan’s Reading List,” *Atlantic*, July 11, 2012.
10. V. M. Zubok and Konstantin Pleshakov, *Inside the Kremlin’s Cold War: From Stalin to Khrushchev* (Cambridge, MA: Harvard University Press, 1996), 139.
11. Jean Edward Smith, *Eisenhower in War and Peace* (New York: Random House, 2012), 571.
12. Zubok and Pleshakov, *Inside the Kremlin’s Cold War*, 155.
13. Smith, *Eisenhower in War and Peace*, 572.
14. Quoted in Smith, *Eisenhower in War and Peace*, 572–73.
15. “Text of Speech by Eisenhower Outlining Proposals for Peace in World,” *New York Times*, April 17, 1953, 4.
16. Quoted in Smith, *Eisenhower in War and Peace*, 576.
17. NC, “Peace on a Silver Platter,” *Saturday Review*, May 9, 1953, 24.
18. Oliver Stone and Peter Kuznick, *The Untold History of the United States* (New York: Gallery Books, 2012), 253.
19. Dwight Eisenhower to NC, August 6, 1956, DDEL, Eisenhower Papers as President of the United States, 1953–1961, Ann Whitman File, Name Series, Box 7, Folder: Cousins, Norman (2).

Chapter 12. Eisenhower’s New Look

1. Martin J. Sherwin and Kai Bird, *American Prometheus: The Triumph and Tragedy of J. Robert Oppenheimer* (New York: Vintage Books, 2006), 470.
2. Steven E. Ambrose, *Eisenhower: The President* (New York: Simon & Schuster, 1984), 348.
3. Quoted in Oliver Stone and Peter Kuznick, *The Untold History of the United States* (New York: Gallery Books, 2012), 254.
4. Stone and Kuznick, *Untold History of the United States*, 254–55.
5. Benjamin P. Greene, *Eisenhower, Science Advice, and the Nuclear Test-Ban Debate, 1945–1963* (Stanford, CA: Stanford University Press, 2006), 24.
6. Stone and Kuznick, *Untold History of the United States*, 256.
7. Richard G. Hewlett and Jack M. Holl, *Atoms for Peace and War, 1953–1961: Eisenhower and the Atomic Energy Commission* (Berkeley: University of California Press, 1989), 209–10.

8. NC, "The Period of Total Danger," *Saturday Review*, March 17, 1954, 20.
9. Robert Divine, *Blowing on the Wind: The Nuclear Test Ban Debate, 1954–1960* (New York: Oxford University Press, 1978), 31.
10. NC, "Out of the Cave," *Saturday Review*, 27 November 1954, 24.
11. NC, "Out of the Cave."
12. William Benton to Robert Conger, September 18, 1956, NCP, Box 262, Folder: 1956, confidential, Benton, William.
13. Candis Cousins Kerns, interview by author, October 25, 2020.
14. Sarah Shapiro, interview by author, September 22, 2020.
15. Sarah Shapiro, interview.
16. Andrea Cousins, interview by author, October 22, 2020.
17. Laura McEnaney, *Civil Defense Begins at Home: Militarization Meets Everyday Life in the Fifties* (Princeton, NJ: Princeton University Press, 2000), 23.
18. Howard Ball, "Downwind from the Bomb," *New York Times*, February 9, 1986.
19. McEnaney, *Civil Defense Begins at Home*, 35–36.
20. "Their Sheltered Honeymoon," *Life*, August 10, 1959, 51.
21. Stone and Kuznick, *Untold History of the United States*, 255.
22. NC, "The Devil's Bargain Basement," *Saturday Review*, February 5, 1955, 22.
23. NC, "Devil's Bargain Basement," 22.
24. NC, "Letter to Administrator Peterson," *Saturday Review*, October 22, 1955, 24.
25. Andrea Cousins, interview.
26. NC to Everette DeGoyler, August 15, 1954, NCP, Box 1198, Folder: DeGoyler, Everette.
27. NC to DeGoyler, August 15, 1954.
28. Sarah Shapiro, "All The Way Home," *Aish*, August 30, 2008.
29. Untitled, undated notes by Fran Thompson, NCP, Box 1194, Folder: Francis Thompson 2.
30. Kerns, interview.

Chapter 13. A New Project

1. Koko Kondo (daughter of Kyoshi Tanimoto), telephone conversation with author, November 11, 2014.
2. NC, *Present Tense: An American Editor's Odyssey* (New York: McGraw-Hill, 1967), 325.

3. Shigeko Sasamori, telephone conversation with author, November 21, 2013.
4. "Medical Treatment for A-Bomb Victims 1953," undated memo, NCP, Box 330, Folder: Japan—1953.
5. Mrs. Richard Walsh (Pearl Buck) to NC, July 29, 1952, NCP, Box 1386, untitled folder.
6. Norman Cousins Oral History, NCP, 151.
7. Naoko Shibusawa, *America's Geisha Ally: Reimagining the Japanese Enemy* (Cambridge, MA: Harvard University Press, 2006), 228.
8. Shigeko Sasamori, telephone conversation.
9. NC, *Present Tense*, 325.
10. Kazuo Chujo, *Hiroshima Maidens: The Nuclear Holocaust Retold* (Tokyo: Asahi Shimbun, 1984), 57.
11. Notes from author's visit to and discussions with personnel at the Radiation Effects Research Foundation (formerly ABCC), August 8, 2009, Hiroshima, Japan. The ABCC's nontreatment policy is also discussed in many State Department documents. See, e.g., US Embassy, Tokyo (hereafter Tokyo) to State Department, May 1, 1956, RG 59, Department of State Records, 1955–59 Central Decimal File, Box 2876, NACP, 711.5611/5-156.
12. Telegram, Tokyo to Secretary of State, April 9, 1954, RG 59, Department of State Records, 1955–59 Central Decimal File, Box 2876, NACP, 711.5611/4-954. See also telegram, Tokyo to Secretary of State, April 21, 1954, RG 59, Department of State Records, 1955–59 Central Decimal File, Box 2876, NACP, 711.5611/4-2154.
13. Telegram, Tokyo to Secretary of State, April 9, 1954. See also telegram, Tokyo to Secretary of State, April 21, 1954.
14. Susan M. Lindee, *Suffering Made Real: American Science and the Survivors at Hiroshima* (Chicago: University of Chicago Press, 1994), 129.
15. Lindee, *Suffering Made Real*, 149.
16. NC, "Hiroshima—Four Years Later," *Saturday Review of Literature*, September 17, 1949, 30.
17. John Beatty, "Scientific Collaboration, Internationalism, and Diplomacy: The Case of the Atomic Bomb Casualty Commission," *Journal of the History of Biology* 26, no. 2 (Summer 1993): 217.
18. Beatty, "Scientific Collaboration, Internationalism, and Diplomacy," 217.
19. Rodney Barker, *The Hiroshima Maidens* (New York: Viking, 1985), 68.

20. Glenn D. Hook, "Evolution of the Anti-Nuclear Discourse in Japan," *Current Research on Peace and Violence* 10, no. 1 (1987): 35.
21. Lindee, *Suffering Made Real*, 132.
22. Robert Homes to Frank Waring, April 24, 1956, RG 59, State Department Records, 1955–59 Central Decimal File, Box 2876, NACP, 711.5611/10-655.
23. Barker, *Hiroshima Maidens*, 68.
24. NC, "The Maidens Are Coming," *Saturday Review*, April 9, 1955, 24–25.

Chapter 14. The Hiroshima Maidens

1. NC, "The Maidens Are Coming," *Saturday Review*, April 9, 1955, 24.
2. Civil Aeronautics Board to NC April 8, 1954, RG 59, Department of State Records, 1955–59 Central Decimal File, Box 2876, NACP, 711.5611/4-1154.
3. Max Bishop, memo, August 4, 1955, RG 59, Department of State Records, 1955–59 Central Decimal File, Box 2876, NACP, 711.5611/8-455. See also NC, "Maidens Are Coming."
4. See John E. Hull, *The Autobiography of General John Edwin Hull, 1895–1975* (n.p.: M. Anderson, 1978).
5. "Contract from Pan American Airlines to Norman Cousins," March 24, 1955, NCP, Box 330, Folder: Japan—1953.
6. Memo, Ambassador John Allison, Tokyo, to Secretary of State, May 1, 1956, RG 59, Department of State Records, 1955–59 Central Decimal File, Box 2876, NACP, 711.5611/5.156.
7. Max Bishop, memo, August 9, 1955, RG 59, Department of State Records, NACP, 711.5611/8-455.
8. Memo, Trent to Mosman, February 12, 1954, RG 59, Department of State Records, 1955–59 Central Decimal File, Box 2876, NACP, 711.5611/2.1254.
9. Friends Committee to NC, April 5, 1955, NCP, Box 330, Folder: Japan—1953.
10. Susan M. Lindee, *Suffering Made Real: American Science and the Survivors at Hiroshima* (Chicago: University of Chicago Press, 1994), 156.
11. Lawrence Wittner, *Resisting the Bomb: A History of the World Nuclear Disarmament Movement, 1954–1970* (Stanford, CA: Stanford University Press, 1997), 147.
12. Telegram, Tokyo to Secretary of State, April 21, 1954, RG 59, Department of State Records, 1955–59 Central Decimal File, Box 2876, NACP, 711.5611/4-2154.

13. Telegram, Tokyo to Secretary of State, April 23, 1954, RG 59, Department of State Records, 1955–59 Central Decimal File, Box 2876, NACP, 711.5611/4-2354.
14. NC, *Present Tense: An American Editor's Odyssey* (New York: McGraw-Hill, 1967), 327.
15. NC, *Present Tense*, 328.
16. NC, "Maidens Are Coming."
17. "Meeting Minutes," May 7, 1955, Department of Energy Records, Record Group 326, NACP, Box 3218, reprinted in Lindee, *Suffering Made Real*, 145n10.
18. Rodney Barker, *The Hiroshima Maidens* (New York: Viking, 1985), 80.
19. This account is paraphrased from Barker, *Hiroshima Maidens*, 82.
20. John E. Hull to NC, June 3, 1955, NCP, Box 1204, Folder: Executive Depts. Agencies, Armed Services.
21. Kazuo Chujo, *Hiroshima Maidens: The Nuclear Holocaust Retold* (Tokyo: Asahi Shimbun, 1984), 65.
22. Wittner, *Resisting the Bomb*, 157.
23. Memo, State Department to Tokyo, May 6, 1955, RG 59, State Department Records, NACP, 811.558/1-755.
24. Kiyoaki Maruta, "Operation Facelift," *Japan Times*, May 5, 1955, 1.
25. NC, "The Voyage of the Maidens," *Saturday Review*, May 14, 1955, 22–23.
26. *This Is Your Life*, episode 141, aired May 11, 1955, NBC.
27. Robert Jacobs, "Reconstructing the Perpetrator's Soul by Reconstructing the Victim's Body: The Portrayal of the 'Hiroshima Maidens' by the Mainstream Media in the United States," *Intersections: Gender and Sexuality in the Pacific* 24 (June 2010): 110.
28. Letter to NC, May 11, 1955, NCP, Box 82, Folder: T.
29. Memorandum of conversation between Walter Robertson and NC, June 2, 1955, RG 59, State Department Records, NACP, 811.588/1-755.
30. "Norman Cousins speech to the Jewish Welfare Board," April 19, 1958, NCP, Box 1725, Folder: Speech to the Jewish Welfare Board, April 19, 1958.
31. Memorandum of conversation between Robertson and NC.
32. David Harley Serlin, "Built for Living: Imagining the American Body through Medical Science, 1945–1965" (PhD diss., New York University, 1999), 139.
33. "Atomic Bomb Victims to Get More Care," *New York Times*, November 13, 1956, 10.

34. "10 of 24 Bomb Victims Start Back to Japan," *Chicago Tribune*, June 13, 1956, B9.
35. "13 Hiroshima Victims Guests of Friends Here," *Los Angeles Times*, October 27, 1956, 10.
36. Unidentified newspaper clipping from scrapbook, NCP, Box 1301.
37. Foster Hailey, "Hiroshima Victim Was Won by U.S.," *New York Times*, November 7, 1956, 47.
38. Letter to the editor, *New York Times*, September 18, 1955, E10.
39. Masunori Hiratsuka to NC, June 23, 1955, NCP, Box 146, Folder: Japan, Misc. Correspondence.
40. Toshikazu Kase to NC, October 20, 1955, NCP, Box 146, Folder: Japan, Misc. Correspondence.
41. Memo to Board of Trustees of Mt. Saini Hospital, May 27, 1955, NCP, Box 1386, untitled folder.
42. Memo, Ambassador John Allison, Tokyo, to Secretary of State, May 1, 1956.
43. Robert Homes to Frank Waring, April 24, 1956, RG 59, State Department Records, NACP, 711.5611/10-655.
44. Memo, Waring to Noel Hemmendinger, June 27, 1956, RG 59, State Department Records, 1955–59 Central Decimal File, Box 2876, NACP, 711.5611/6-2756.
45. "Meeting of Committee on Hiroshima Maidens," October 12, 1955, RG 59, State Department Records, 1955–59 Central Decimal File, Box 2876, NACP, 711.5611/9-2155.
46. "Treatment in United States of Japanese Atomic Bomb Victims," October 6, 1955, RG 59, State Department Records, 1955–59 Central Decimal File, Box 2876, NACP, 711.5611/10-655.
47. Sherman Adams to NC, November 15, 1956, DDEL, White House Central Files, Box 726, Folder: 195 Japan, Government and Embassy of.
48. NC to Dwight Eisenhower, November 19, 1956, NCP, Box 269, Folder: Confidential: Eisenhower, DD.
49. NC to Eisenhower, November 26, 1956, NCP, Box 269, Folder: Confidential: Eisenhower, DD.
50. Memo, Burke Wilkinson to Robinson McIlvaine, April 2, 1956, DDEL, White House Social Office Records, Box 54, Folder: Hiroshima Maidens Tour.
51. "Plan Welcomed in Hiroshima," *Japan Times*, June 17, 1956.

52. Gene Kramer, "Main Problem in Treating A-Victims Said Financial," *Japan Times*, June 22, 1956, 3.
53. "Surgery on 25 Is Only the Beginning: Cousins," *Japan Times*, November 15, 1956.
54. NC, "Report on a Homecoming," *Saturday Review*, December 15, 1956.
55. NC, *Present Tense*, 347–48.
56. Sarah Shapiro, "My Hiroshima," *San Francisco Chronicle*, September 4, 1994, 13.
57. Transcript of NC interview by Kono Hito, 1987, VHS, NCP, Box 1329.

Chapter 15. The Anti-Nuclear Agenda

1. Paul Boyer, *By the Bomb's Early Light: American Thought and Culture at the Dawn of the Atomic Age* (New York: Pantheon, 1985), 349.
2. Milton Katz, *Ban the Bomb: A History of SANE, the Committee for a Sane Nuclear Policy, 1957–1985* (New York: Praeger, 1987), 14.
3. Katz, *Ban the Bomb*, 15.
4. NC to Andrew Hegre, August 12, 1952, NCP, Box 141, Folder: Miscellaneous—1952.
5. NC, "Think of a Man," *Saturday Review*, August 4, 1956, 11.
6. NC, "Think of a Man," 9–14.
7. Dwight Eisenhower to NC, August 6, 1956, DDEL, Eisenhower Papers as President of the United States, 1953–1961, Ann Whitman File, Name Series, Box 7, Folder: Cousins, Norman (2).
8. Arthur Larson, *Eisenhower: The President Nobody Knew* (New York: Scribner, 1968), 172–73.
9. NC to Edison Dick, October 12, 1956, NCP, Box 156, Folder: Think of a Man, Letters in re: A–L, 1956.
10. NC to Lewis Mumford, November 18, 1957, SCPC, SANE Records, Series B, Box 4, Folder: Correspondence of Norman Cousins (1957–1958).
11. James Ledbetter, *Unwarranted Influence: Dwight D. Eisenhower and the Military Industrial Complex* (New Haven, CT: Yale University Press, 2011), 78.
12. Sarah Shapiro, interview by author, September 22, 2020.
13. Hubert Humphrey to NC, August 21, 1956, NCP, Box 156, Folder: Think of a Man, Letters in re: A–L, 1956.
14. Alfred Gray Reid to NC, August 26, 1956, NCP, Box 156, Folder: Think of a Man, Letters in re: M–Z, 1956.

15. NC to Reid, October 1, 1956, NCP, Box 156, Folder: Think of a Man, Letters in re: M–Z, 1956.
16. David Tal, *The American Nuclear Disarmament Dilemma, 1945–1963* (Syracuse, NY: Syracuse University Press, 2008), 70.
17. Katz, *Ban the Bomb*, 16.
18. "Remarks by Norman Cousins," May 1966, NCP, Box 1721, Folder: NC on Schweitzer, Schweitzer Convocation, Aspen, Colorado, June, 1966.
19. NC, *Present Tense: An American Editor's Odyssey* (New York: McGraw-Hill, 1967), 266.

Chapter 16. 1956: The Anti-Nuclear Election Campaign

1. Adlai Stevenson to NC, June 25, 1956, ASP, Box 20, Folder: 10.
2. McGeorge Bundy, *Danger and Survival: Choices about the Bomb in the First Fifty Years* (New York: Random House, 1988), 329.
3. Lawrence Wittner, *Resisting the Bomb: A History of the World Nuclear Disarmament Movement, 1954–1970* (Stanford, CA: Stanford University Press, 1997), 13.
4. Richard G. Hewlett and Jack M. Holl, *Atoms for Peace and War, 1953–1961: Eisenhower and the Atomic Energy Commission* (Berkeley: University of California Press, 1989), 364.
5. "Draft & H.Bomb Speech," September 25, 1956, NCP, Box 263, Folder: 1956—Confidential—A.E.S.
6. Stevenson to NC, December 15, 1956, ASP, Box 20, Folder: 10.
7. Wittner, *Resisting the Bomb*, 14.
8. Barry Steiner, "The Test Ban and the 1956 Election," *Arms Control Today*, December 2011, https://www.armscontrol.org/act/2011-12/test-ban-1956-election.
9. Stephen E. Ambrose, *Eisenhower: The President* (New York: Simon & Schuster, 1984), 348.
10. Robert Divine, *Blowing on the Wind: The Nuclear Test Ban Debate, 1954–1960* (New York: Oxford University Press, 1978), 208.
11. NC, *Talks with Nehru: India's Prime Minister Speaks Out on the Crisis of Our Time* (New York: J. Day, 1951).
12. NC to Jawaharlal Nehru, March 4, 1957, NCP, Box 1218, Folder: Test Ban Treaty Correspondence Nehru, Khrushchev 1/2.
13. Milton Katz, *Ban the Bomb: A History of SANE, the Committee for a Sane Nuclear Policy, 1957–1985* (New York: Praeger, 1987), 19.
14. NC, "It's Only Moral," *Saturday Review*, November 10, 1956, 22.

15. NC, *Dr. Schweitzer of Lambaréné* (New York: Harper Bros., 1960), 170.
16. Divine, *Blowing on the Wind*, 208.
17. David Tal, *The American Nuclear Disarmament Dilemma, 1945–1963* (Syracuse, NY: Syracuse University Press, 2008), 66.
18. Oliver Stone and Peter Kuznick, *The Untold History of the United States* (New York: Gallery Books, 2012), 282.
19. "Remarks by Norman Cousins," May 1966, NCP, Box: 1721, Folder: NC on Schweitzer, Schweitzer Convocation, Aspen, Colorado, June, 1966.
20. NC, *Dr. Schweitzer of Lambaréné*, 130.
21. "Remarks by Norman Cousins," May 1966.
22. NC, *Dr. Schweitzer of Lambaréné*, 165.
23. "Remarks by Norman Cousins," May 1966.
24. Bernard Shenley to NC, January 29, 1957, NCP, Box 1199, Folder: Eisenhower, Dwight, 1 of 2.
25. NC to Nehru, February 13, 1957, NCP, Box 1218, Folder: Test Ban Treaty Correspondence Nehru, Khrushchev 1/2.
26. Nehru to NC, February 19, 1957, NCP, Box 1218, Folder: Test Ban Treaty Correspondence Nehru, Khrushchev 1/2.
27. Wittner, *Resisting the Bomb*, 30–31.
28. NC to Nehru, May 29 1957, NCP, Box 1218, Folder: Test Ban Treaty Correspondence Nehru, Khrushchev 1/2.
29. "Schweitzer Urges World Opinion to Demand End of Nuclear Tests," *New York Times*, April 24, 1957, 1.
30. NC, "The Schweitzer Declaration," *Saturday Review*, May 18, 1957, 13–20.
31. NC, editor's note, *Saturday Review*, June 8, 1957, 23.
32. "What's Back of the Fallout Scare?," *U.S. News & World Report* 42, no. 23 (June 1957): 25. Cousins published a two-page rebuke of the article in NC, "An Open Letter to David Lawrence," *Saturday Review*, July 6, 1957, 20–21.
33. Katz, *Ban the Bomb*, 20.
34. Dr. Willard Libby, "An Open Letter to Dr. Schweitzer," *Saturday Review*, May 25, 1957, 8.
35. Dr. Harrison Brown, "What Is a 'Small' Risk?," *Saturday Review*, May 25, 1957, 9.
36. NC, "The Great Debate Opens," *Saturday Review*, June 15, 1957, 24.
37. Divine, *Blowing on the Wind*, 122.
38. Percy Ludlow to NC, July 22, 1957, SCPC, SANE Records, Series B, Box 6, Folder: Pre-SANE/Early Correspondence.

39. Vincent Glason to NC, June 9 1957, SCPC, SANE Records, Series B, Box 6, Folder: Pre-SANE/Early Correspondence.
40. Letter to NC, July 26, 1957, SCPC, SANE Records, Series B, Box 6, Folder: Pre-SANE/Early Correspondence.
41. NC to G. J. Watumull, September 10, 1957, SCPC, SANE Records, Series B, Box 6, Folder: Pre-SANE/Early Correspondence.
42. Benjamin P. Greene, *Eisenhower, Science Advice, and the Nuclear Test-Ban Debate, 1945–1963* (Stanford, CA: Stanford University Press, 2006), 125.
43. NC to Dwight Eisenhower, June 7, 1957, NCP, Box 269, Folder: Confidential: Eisenhower, DD.
44. Lewis Strauss to Eisenhower, June 18, 1956, DDEL, Eisenhower Papers as President of the United States, 1953–1961, Ann Whitman File, Name Series, Box 7, Folder: Cousins, Norman (2).
45. Eisenhower to NC, June 21, 1957, NCP, Box 1199, Folder: Eisenhower, Dwight, 1 of 2.
46. Greene, *Eisenhower, Science Advice*, 126.
47. NC to Eisenhower, June 27 1957, NCP, Box 1199, Folder: Eisenhower, Dwight, 1 of 2.
48. Untitled, undated note, DDEL, Eisenhower Papers as President of the United States, 1953–1961, Ann Whitman File, Name Series, Box 7, Folder: Cousins, Norman (2).
49. Dwight D. Eisenhower, *The Papers of Dwight D. Eisenhower*, vol. 19, *The Presidency: Keeping the Peace*, ed. Louis Galambos and Daun Van Ee (Baltimore: Johns Hopkins University Press, 2001), 287.
50. Strauss to Eisenhower, July 2, 1957, NCP, Box 1150, Folder: Oral History, 1989.
51. Eisenhower to NC, July 9, 1957, NCP, Box 1199, Folder: Eisenhower, Dwight, 1 of 2.
52. NC, "Dr. Teller and the Spirit of Adventure," *Saturday Review*, March 15, 1958, 26.
53. Eisenhower to NC, July 9, 1957, NCP, Box 1199, Folder: Eisenhower, Dwight, 1 of 2.
54. NC to Eisenhower, July 15, 1957, NCP, Box 1199, Folder: Eisenhower, Dwight, 1 of 2.
55. Ann Whitman to Strauss, July 20, 1957, NCP, Box 1150, Folder: Oral History, 1989.
56. Strauss to Whitman, July 23, 1957, NCP, Box 1150, Folder: Oral History, 1989.

57. *The Nature of Radioactive Fallout and its Effects on Man: Records of the Hearings of the Special Subcommittee on Radiation*, 85th Cong. (1957).
58. Chet Holifield to NC, June 3, 1957, NCP, Box 267, Folder: Holifield Hearings, 1957.
59. For a full written statement, see NC, "Reply to a Russian Invitation," *Saturday Review*, June 22, 1957, 20. For the Soviet broadcast version, see "Statement by Norman Cousins Editor of the Saturday Review in Reply to Radio Moscow Invitation to Comment on Nuclear Testing; as Edited by Radio Moscow," n.d., NCP, Box 267, Folder: Radio Moscow.
60. NC, "Double Disaster," *Saturday Review*, April 19, 1958, 26.
61. NC, "Neither Suicide Nor Surrender," *Saturday Review*, April 12, 1958, 26.
62. Divine, *Blowing on the Wind*, 212.

Chapter 17. SANE and the Anti-Testing Campaign

1. Herbert E. Moulton, "Prayer to God," *Saturday Review*, June 8, 1957, 23.
2. Lynn Brooks to NC, August 12, 1958, NCP, Box 1296, Folder: Letters from Fans and Readers 1941–1965.
3. Margaret S. Richardson, "Postcards to Washington," *Saturday Review*, June 8, 1957, 23.
4. Ettilie Wallace to NC, June 2, 1957, SCPC, SANE Records, Series B, Box 1, Folder: Correspondence of Norman Cousins, "W" 1957.
5. Milton Katz, *Ban the Bomb: A History of SANE, the Committee for a Sane Nuclear Policy, 1957–1985* (New York: Praeger, 1987), 23.
6. Sanford Gottlieb, conversation with author, May 16, 2013.
7. Katz, *Ban the Bomb*, xii–xiii.
8. NC to Dwight Eisenhower, November 13, 1957, NCP, Box 1199, Folder: Eisenhower, Dwight, 1 of 2.
9. Dwight D. Eisenhower, *The Papers of Dwight D. Eisenhower*, vol. 19, *The Presidency: Keeping the Peace*, ed. Louis Galambos and Daun Van Ee (Baltimore: Johns Hopkins University Press, 2001), 584.
10. Milton Katz, "Norman Cousins, Peace Activist and World Citizen," unpublished paper, n.d., NCP, Box 1149, Folder: 9, Katz.
11. NC to Homer Jack, March 7, 1962, NCP, Box 306, Folder: SANE, Confidential.
12. David Tal, *The American Nuclear Disarmament Dilemma, 1945–1963* (Syracuse, NY: Syracuse University Press, 2008), 138.
13. William Hitchcock, *The Age of Eisenhower: America and the World in the 1950s* (New York: Simon & Schuster, 2018), 376.

14. Steven E. Ambrose, *Eisenhower: The President* (New York: Simon & Schuster, 1984), 429–30.
15. NC, "Sense and Satellites," *Saturday Review*, October 19, 1957, 26.
16. NC, "Sense and Satellites," 26.
17. NC, "Sense and Satellites," 27.
18. Dwight Eisenhower, telephone call to John Foster Dulles, November 18, 1957, DDEL, Box 29, Folder: DDE Diary Series.

Chapter 18. The Ravensbrück Lapins and the Communist Connection

1. NC, *Present Tense: An American Editor's Odyssey* (New York: McGraw-Hill, 1967), 352.
2. Jesse Leavenworth, "Caroline and the Lapins," *Hartford Courant*, October 20, 2002.
3. Benjamin Ferencz, telephone conversation with author, September 2015.
4. Ferencz to Wilson E. Kaiser, June 5, 1957, BFC, RG-12.012.02.01.
5. Ferencz, conversation.
6. Ferencz to David Apter, April 15, 1957, BFC, RG-12.012.02.01.
7. Untitled, undated memo, BFC, RG-12.012.02.01.
8. Ferencz, conversation.
9. NC, "Dialogue in Warsaw: Report on the Ravensbrueck Lapins," *Saturday Review*, June 18, 1958, 11.
10. NC, "The Lapins Are Coming," *Saturday Review*, October 25, 1958, 22. They were referred to as the "lapins," which is the French word for rabbits, which, in turn, was translated from the German term "experimentation bunnies." In English it is the equivalent to calling them "human guinea pigs."
11. NC, unpublished manuscript, n.d., NCP, Box 1711, Folder: Scaffolding for Adventures Among the Humans, 44–45.
12. "Oral History of Benjamin B. Ferencz," BFC, RG-50.03*0259, 119.
13. "Memo: Compensation for Victims of Nazi Medical Experiments," April 7, 1959, BFC, RG-12.012.02.01.
14. German Embassy, Washington, to Bonn, December 19, 1958, BArch, B81/149.
15. German Embassy, Washington, to Bonn, December 19, 1958, BArch, B81/149.

16. Telegram, German Embassy, Washington, to German Ministry of Finance, December 20, 1958, BArch, B81/149.
17. Julius Klein to Dr. Knappstein, May 23, 1959, BArch, B81/149.
18. Jonathan S. Wiesen, "Germany's PR Man: Julius Klein and the Making of Transatlantic Memory," in *Coping with the Nazi Past: West German Debates on Nazism and Generational Conflict*, ed. Philipp Gassert and Alan E. Steinweis (New York: Berghahn Books, 2007), 294–308.
19. Cable, German Embassy, Washington, to German Press and Information Office, February 14, 1959, BArch, B81/149.
20. "Memo: Chronological Outline," March 1960, BFC, RG-12.012.02.01.
21. Ferencz to NC, April 24, 1959, BFC, RG-12.012.02.03.
22. German Embassy, Washington, to Rechtsabteilung, May 5, 1959, BArch, B81/149.
23. Memo, German Embassy, Washington, to Auswartiges Amt Ministerburo, April 24, 1959, BArch, B81/149.
24. Memo, German Press and Information Office, addressee unknown, April 17, 1959, BArch, B81/149.
25. Jarek Gajewski, "Regained Faith in People," unpublished paper, University of Toronto, http://individual.utoronto.ca/jarekg/Ravensbrück/Regainedfaith.pdf.
26. *Congressional Record* (Washington, DC: GPO, 1959), 8459.
27. Samuel A. Weiss, "Aid for Lapins Urged," letter to the editor, *New York Times*, June 12, 1959, 26.
28. "An End to Mass Guilt," *Washington Post*, May 31, 1959, E4.
29. Albert Shaft to German Embassy, Washington, March 22, 1960, BArch, B81/149.
30. "Bonn Wishes to Indemnify Polish Women. The Government is Still Examining International Legal and Political Questions," translated article from *Frankfurter Allgemeine*, May 28, 1960, BFC, RG-12.012.02.04.
31. Ferencz, conversation.
32. Telegram, NC to Konrad Adenauer, February 19, 1960, BArch, B81/149.
33. "Oral History of Benjamin B. Ferencz," BFC, RG-50.03*0259, 119.
34. NC, "The Ladies Depart," *Saturday Review*, June 13, 1959, 24.
35. Caroline Ferriday to Joachim Lipschitz, January 12, 1960, BFC, RG-12.012.02.04.
36. Ferencz to NC, April 24, 1959, BFC, RG-12.012.02.01.
37. Ferencz, conversation.

38. Telegram, NC to German Embassy, Washington, n.d., BFC, RG-12.012.02.04.
39. "Translation of: Minutes of the 112th Meeting of the German Parliament," May 5, 1960, BFC, RG-12.012.02.04.
40. "Tortured Women Win Late Justice," *News Chronicle*, August 10, 1960, BFC, RG-12.012.02.04.
41. Arthur J. Olsen, "73 Polish Women, Nazi Victims, to Get Indemnities from Bonn," *New York Times*, November 13, 1961, 1.
42. Bernard Ziffer, "Poland in 1961: Chronicle of Events January 1, 1961–December 31, 1961," *Polish Review* 7, no. 1 (Winter 1962): 107.
43. Ferriday to the National Archives and Records Administration, n.d., BFC, RG-12.012.02.01.
44. Mariah Dogroses to Ferencz, May 12, 1961, BFC, RG-12.012.02.01.
45. NC to L. D. Kislova, November 24, 1958, NCP, Box 208, Folder: Moscow—June 16–July 6.
46. NC, "The Toast of Warsaw," *Saturday Review*, June 7, 1958, 22.
47. "Degree is Conferred on Marian Anderson," *New York Times*, June 2, 1958, 23.
48. NC, "Is America Living Half a Life?," *Saturday Review*, November 17, 1957, 26.

Chapter 19. A Cultural Exchange of His Own

1. William Benton to NC, May 13, 1946, NCP, Box 1296, Folder: Letters from Fans and Readers 1941–1965.
2. Yale Richmond, *Cultural Exchange and the Cold War: Raising the Iron Curtain* (University Park: Pennsylvania State University Press, 2003), 16.
3. Dwight D. Eisenhower, *Waging Peace, 1956–1961* (New York: Doubleday, 1965), 410.
4. Robert Donaldson and Joseph Nogee, *The Foreign Policy of Russia: Changing Systems, Enduring Interests* (Armonk, NY: M. E. Sharp, 1998), 75.
5. Richmond, *Cultural Exchange and the Cold War*, 14–15.
6. George V. Allen to NC, August 25, 1958, NCP, Box 208, Folder: Moscow—June 16–July 6.
7. Alice Bobrysheva, *Thanks for the Memories: My Years with the Dartmouth Conference* (Dayton, OH: Kettering Foundation Press, 2003), 28, 5.
8. Bobrysheva, *Thanks for the Memories*, 5.
9. L. D. Kislova to NC, October 21, 1958, NCP, Box 208, Folder: Moscow—June 16–July 6.

10. James Voorhees, *Dialogue Sustained: The Multilevel Peace Process and the Dartmouth Conference* (Washington, DC: United States Institute of Peace Press, 2002), 24.
11. NC to Nina Popova, June 5, 1959, NCP, Box 208, Folder: Moscow—June 16–July 6.
12. NC to Dwight Eisenhower, May 22, 1959, NCP, Box 1199, Folder: Eisenhower, Dwight 1 of 2.
13. Eisenhower to NC, May 30, 1959, NCP, Box 1199, Folder: Eisenhower, Dwight 1 of 2.
14. Eisenhower to NC, June 10, 1959, NCP, Box 1199, Folder: Eisenhower, Dwight 1 of 2.
15. Lawrence Wittner, *A History of the World Nuclear Disarmament Movement through 1953* (Stanford, CA: Stanford University Press, 1993), 232.
16. NC, "An Address in Moscow," *Saturday Review*, July 25, 1959, 10, 27.
17. Bobrysheva, *Thanks for the Memories*, 7.
18. NC, "Some Marginal Notes on the Talk," *Saturday Review*, July 25, 1959, 28.
19. NC to Walter Lippmann, July 15, 1959, NCP, Box 208, Folder: Russia: After Effects.
20. NC, "Address in Moscow," 29.
21. NC, "Interview with a Soviet Official." *Saturday Review*, August 1, 1959, 33.
22. NC, "Address in Moscow," 27.
23. NC, untitled, undated report, NCP, Box 1354, Folder: NC Summary Report of Conferences I–III Prepared for Johnson Foundation.
24. Philip Stewart, conversation with author, September 28, 2015.
25. NC, "What Kind of Competition with the USSR?," *Saturday Review*, November 7, 1959, 26.
26. NC, "Tale of Two Exhibitions," *Saturday Review*, August 1, 1959, 24.
27. NC, "What Kind of Competition with the USSR?"; NC, "Tale of Two Exhibitions."
28. NC to Richard L. Neuberger, July 29, 1959, NCP, Box 208, Folder: Russia: After Effects.
29. NC to Allen Dulles, September 23 1959, General CIA Records. Available from: https://www.cia.gov/readingroom/document/cia-rdp80r01731r000200070028-7.
30. "Memorandum of Conference With the President," August 6, 1959, DDEL, Box 43, Folder: Staff Notes—Aug. 59 (1).
31. NC, "Report to the President: Observations About Trends in U.S.S.R.," August 6, 1959, DDEL, Box 43, Folder: Staff Notes—Aug. 59 (1).

32. NC, "Norman Cousins Speech: World Report," October 21, 1959, NCP, Box 1724, Folder: NC Speech World Report, 1959 Mills College.
33. NC to Kislova, July 23, 1959, NCP, Box 208, Folder: Russia: After Effects.
34. NC, "Norman Cousins Speech: World Report."
35. NC to Igor Bestushev, October 9, 1958, NCP, Box 208, Folder: Moscow, June 16.
36. NC, untitled, undated report.
37. Dr. Harold Saunders, conversation with author, September 21, 2015.
38. Nikolai Tikhonov and Mikhail Kotov to NC, November 10, 1959, NCP, Box 1348, Folder: 1960 Dartmouth Conf.
39. Bobrysheva, *Thanks for the Memories*, 15.
40. NC to William Hitzig, October 20, 1960, NCP, Box 1191, Folder: Hitzig, William—Conf. 1960.
41. "Soviet-U.S. Talks Held by Citizens," *New York Times*, November 5, 1960, 8.
42. NC to Eisenhower, July 1, 1960, NCP, Box 1199, Folder: Eisenhower, Dwight, 2 of 2.
43. Saunders, conversation.
44. "Draft for Joint Statement," n.d., NCP, Box 1348, Folder: Draft for Joint Statement.
45. NC, untitled, undated report.
46. Bobrysheva, *Thanks for the Memories*, 23.
47. Ralph A. Jones to NC, November 21, 1960, NCP, Box 1349, Folder: Soviet Peace Committee—Conf. 1960.
48. Stewart, conversation.
49. "The Search for Peace," *New York Times*, November 14, 1960, 30.
50. Oleg Bykov to NC, December 6, 1960, NCP, Box 1348, Folder: 1960 Dartmouth Conf.
51. "Russians Hail U.S. for Warm Welcome," *New York Times*, December 15, 1960, 49.
52. Leslie S. Brady to NC, December 15, 1960, NCP, Box 1351, Folder: Correspondence with State.
53. Jones to NC, February 13, 1960, NCP, Box 1351, Folder: Correspondence with State.
54. Stephen E. Ambrose, *Eisenhower: The President* (New York: Simon & Schuster, 1984), 564.
55. Robert Divine, *Blowing on the Wind: The Nuclear Test Ban Debate, 1954–1960* (New York: Oxford University Press, 1978), 300.

56. Ambrose, *Eisenhower*, 565.
57. Telegram, NC to Eisenhower, March 18, 1960, NCP, Box 1199, Folder: Eisenhower, Dwight, 1 of 2.
58. Bruce Geelhoed and Anthony Edmonds, *Eisenhower, Macmillan and Allied Unity, 1957–1961* (New York: Palgrave Macmillan, 2003), 98.
59. NC, "The Long Road Back," *Saturday Review*, June 18, 1960, 24.
60. NC, "Should the President Travel?," *Saturday Review*, July 9, 1960, 22.
61. NC, "What Do We Do When We Are Wrong?," *Saturday Review*, May 21, 1960, 30.
62. NC, *The Pathology of Power* (New York: Norton, 1987), 75–77.
63. Ambrose, *Eisenhower*, 611.
64. NC, *Pathology of Power*, 81.
65. "Draft of Ike's Farewell Speech," n.d., NCP, Box 1731, Folder: Eisenhower Speeches.
66. Eisenhower (via Ann Whitman) to NC, January 16, 1961, NCP, Box 1199, Folder: Eisenhower, Dwight, 2 of 2.
67. Arthur Larson, *Eisenhower: The President Nobody Knew* (New York: Scribner, 1968), 172–73.
68. James Ledbetter, *Unwarranted Influence: Dwight D. Eisenhower and the Military Industrial Complex* (New Haven, CT: Yale University Press, 2011), 80.

Chapter 20. The Dawn of the Kennedy Administration

1. NC to Adlai Stevenson, August 17, 1960, NCP, Box 1214, Folder: Stevenson, Adlai—conf. 1960.
2. Candis Cousins Kerns, interview by author, October 25, 2020.
3. Sarah Shapiro, interview by author, September 22, 2020.
4. Richard Nixon to NC, January 11, 1961, NCP, Box 1296, Folder: Letters from Fans and Readers 1941–1965.
5. NC, "Diary of a Change," *Saturday Review*, February 18, 1961, 28.
6. NC, *Present Tense: An American Editor's Odyssey* (New York: McGraw-Hill, 1967), 68.
7. NC to Dwight Eisenhower, March 30, 1961, NCP, Box 1199, Folder: Eisenhower, Dwight, 1 of 2.
8. Eisenhower (via Ann Whitman) to NC, May 20, 1961, NCP, Box 1199, Folder: Eisenhower, Dwight, 1 of 2.
9. NC to Lenore Marshall, May 4, 1960, NCP, Box 1192, Folder: Marshall-Cousins, Misc. papers, letters.

10. NC to Marshall, May 1, 1961, NCP, Box 1192, Folder: Cousins-Marshall Fund. RAND was a policy think tank founded by the Douglass Aircraft Company primarily to offer research and analysis to the US military.
11. NC to Marshall, May 1, 1961.
12. NC to Marshall, May 1, 1961.
13. NC to Marshall, May 1, 1961.
14. Homer Jack to Frank Elliot (Harper Publishers), November 14, 1960, SCPC, SANE Records, Series B, Box 36, Folder: Cousins, Norman (re: In Place of Folly).
15. Ernest Hacly to Richard Baltzell, January 8, 1961, SCPC, SANE Records, Series B, Box 36, Folder: Cousins, Norman (re: In Place of Folly).
16. Edward Meyerding to NC, n.d., SCPC, SANE Records, Series B, Box 36, Folder: Cousins, Norman (re: In Place of Folly).
17. Transcript of "The Nation's Future," May 17, 1961, NCP, Box 1702, Folder: Nation's Future, NBC, 4/15/61.
18. Jack M. Straus to NC, June 30, 1959, NCP, Box 231, Folder: SR–ST 1960.
19. Memo, Hal Bowser to NC, n.d., NCP, Box 231, Folder: SR–ST 1960.
20. Memo, Mary Harvey to NC, January 2, 1960, NCP, Box 231, Folder: SR–ST 1960.
21. "Norman Cousins Script #5: Russia & Revisionism," broadcast week of May 8, 1961, NCP, Box 1702, Folder: Syndicated Broadcast, May 1961.
22. Arthur Larson, "The Cuba Incident and the Rule of Law," *Saturday Review*, May 13, 1961, 28.
23. "Norman Cousins Script #4: Cuba," broadcast week of May 8, 1961, NCP, Box 1702, Folder: Syndicated Broadcast, May 1961.
24. "Curtains for Now in Cuba," *Chicago Tribune*, April 22, 1961, 10.
25. "The Collapse in Cuba," *Wall Street Journal*, April 21, 1961, 12.

Chapter 21. Flashpoints: Berlin and the Congo

1. Oliver Stone and Peter Kuznick, *The Untold History of the United States* (New York: Gallery Books, 2012), 295–96.
2. William Taubman, *Khrushchev: The Man and His Era* (New York: Norton, 2003), 499.
3. Ted Sorensen, *Kennedy: The Classic Biography* (1965; reprint, New York: Harper Perennial, 2013), 586.
4. Stone and Kuznick, *Untold History of the United States*, 296.
5. Taubman, *Khrushchev*, 495.

6. Kenneth D. Rose, *One Nation Underground: The Fallout Shelter in American Culture* (New York: New York University Press, 2001), 4.
7. Rose, *One Nation Underground*, 3.
8. Taubman, *Khrushchev*, 502.
9. NC, "Berlin: No Extermination Without Representation," *Saturday Review*, August 5, 1961, 20.
10. Rose, *One Nation Underground*, 1–4.
11. "A Message to You from the President," *Life*, September 15, 1961, 95.
12. NC, "Nuclear War: The Life and Death Questions," *Saturday Review*, September 30, 1961, 24.
13. "Shelters in Big Cities Sought by Kennedy," *New York Times*, July 27, 1961, 1.
14. Walter H. Waggoner, "Thousands Seek Aid on Shelters," *New York Times*, September 5, 1961, 5.
15. NC, "Shelters, Survival, and Common Sense," *Saturday Review*, October 21, 1961, 66.
16. "Religion: Gun Thy Neighbor?," *Time*, August 18, 1961.
17. NC, "Shelters, Survival, and Common Sense, Part II," *Saturday Review*, October 28, 1961, 26.
18. NC, "Shelters, Survival, and Common Sense, Part III," *Saturday Review*, November 4, 1961, 28.
19. NC, "Shelters, Survival, and Common Sense, Part IV," *Saturday Review*, November 25, 1961, 31.
20. Quoted in Aleksandr Fursenko and Timothy Naftali, *Khrushchev's Cold War: The Inside Story of an American Adversary* (New York: Norton, 2006), 384.
21. NC, "One Year Later," *Saturday Review*, March 3, 1962, 20.
22. Memo, Secretary of State Rusk to President Kennedy, January 18, 1962, in *Foreign Relations of the United States, 1961–1963*, Vol. XXV, *Organization of Foreign Policy; Information Policy; United Nations; Scientific Matters*, ed. David Patterson, Paul Claussen, Evan Duncan, and Jeffery Soukup (Washington, DC: GPO, 2001), 415.
23. Laurence Burd, "Kennedy Flies Home to Push U.N. Bond Deal," *Chicago Daily Tribune*, January 30, 1962, 10.
24. Kennedy to NC, February 1, 1962, NCP, Box 1206, Folder: Kennedy, John, 1962.
25. NC, untitled meeting notes, March 13, 1962, NCP, Box 1206, Folder: Kennedy, John, NC Visit 3/13/62.

26. NC, "The Vital Services," *Saturday Review*, July 21, 1962, 18.
27. NC to Kennedy, March 20, 1962, NCP, Box 1206, Folder: Kennedy, John, 1962.
28. McGeorge Bundy, "For Norman Cousins," n.d., JFKL, McGeorge Bundy Personal Papers, Box 229, Folder: Speeches and Lectures [for Norman Cousins].
29. Bundy, "For Norman Cousins."
30. NC, "Force as a Language," *Saturday Review*, May 19, 1962, 24.
31. NC, "To Lead or to Follow?," *Saturday Review*, June 9, 1962, 18.
32. Philip Stewart, conversation with author, September 28, 2015.

Chapter 22. Cousins, the Vatican, and the Cuban Missile Crisis

1. NC, "Modern Man Is Obsolete," *Saturday Review of Literature*, August 18, 1945.
2. NC to E. Christinson, November 9, 1960, NCP, Box 227, Folder: OI–ON 1960.
3. Khrushchev's thinking is from Sergei Khrushchev, conversation with author, 2013.
4. Vatican memo, "Conclusions," December 10, 1962, NCP, Box 911, Folder: Morlion, 1962–1964.
5. Karim Schelkens, "Vatican Diplomacy After the Cuban Missile Crisis: New Light on the Release of Josyf Slipyj," *Catholic Historical Review* 97, no. 4 (October 2011): 680.
6. Felix Morlion to NC, December 10, 1962, NCP, Box 912, Folder: f. 9 Morlion 1962, Father Morlion—pre-trip plus reports—1962.
7. Giancarlo Zizola, *The Utopia of Pope John XXIII* (Maryknoll, NY: Orbis Books, 1979), 238.
8. "Occasion of the Contacts of F.M. with N.C.," n.d., NCP, Box 912, Folder: f. 9 Morlion 1962, Father Morlion—pre-trip plus reports—1962, 5.
9. Felix A. Morlion, "Freedom's Challenge and Pope John," unpublished manuscript, [1964?], NCP, Box 968, Folder: f. 2 Morlion—[photocopy of manuscript, printed material, curriculum vitae], 64–66.
10. "Occasion of the Contacts of F.M. with N.C."
11. Morlion, "Freedom's Challenge and Pope John," 68.
12. NC, *The Improbable Triumvirate: John F. Kennedy, Pope John, Nikita Khrushchev* (New York: Norton, 1972), 11. Although this particular quote is sourced from Cousins, the sequence of events and discussions of this

first meeting are confirmed and elaborated upon in Morlion's independent report back to the Vatican. See "Occasion of the Contacts of F.M. with N.C."

13. NC, address, "The New Realities," Emory and Henry College: November 19, 1963, NCP, Box 1722, Folder: NC Speech "The New Realities" Nov. 19, 1963 Emory & Henry College Emory, Virginia.
14. Pope John XXIII, *Ad Petri Cathedram,* https://www.vatican.va/content/john-xxiii/en/encyclicals/documents/hf_j-xxiii_enc_29061959_ad-petri.html.
15. Pope John XXIII, *Princeps Pastorum,* https://www.vatican.va/content/john-xxiii/en/encyclicals/documents/hf_j-xxiii_enc_28111959_princeps.html.
16. NC, *Improbable Triumvirate,* 11.
17. Morlion, "Freedom's Challenge and Pope John," 70.
18. Aleksandr Fursenko and Timothy Naftali, *One Hell of a Gamble: Khrushchev, Castro, and Kennedy, 1958–1964; The Secret History of the Cuban Missile Crisis* (New York: Norton, 1998), 198–99.
19. Graham Allison and Philip Zelikow, *Essence of Decision* (Boston: Little, Brown, 1971), 60.
20. Zizola, *Utopia of Pope John,* 4.
21. NC, *Improbable Triumvirate,* 13.
22. "Why an Urgent First Step Was Made with our Headquarters," undated restricted memo, NCP, Box 912, Folder: f. 9 Morlion 1962, Father Morlion—pre-trip plus reports—1962.
23. "Why an Urgent First Step Was Made with our Headquarters."
24. The full text of the pope's message reads: "I beg heads of state not to remain insensitive to the cry of humanity, peace, peace. Let them do all that is in their power to save peace; in this way they will avoid the horrors of a war, the appalling consequences of which no one could predict. Let them continue to negotiate. History will see this loyal and open attitude as a witness to conscience. To promote, encourage, and accept negotiations, always and on every level, is a rule of wisdom that draws down both heavenly and earthly blessings." Peter Hebblethwaite and Margaret Hebblethwaite, *Pope John XXIII: Pope of the Century* (London: Continuum, 2000), 231.
25. "Why an Urgent First Step Was Made with our Headquarters."
26. Morlion, "Freedom's Challenge and Pope John," 75–80.
27. "Why an Urgent First Step Was Made with our Headquarters."

28. "Address of Senator John F. Kennedy to the Greater Houston Ministerial Association," September 12, 1960, JFKL, https://www.jfklibrary.org/archives/other-resources/john-f-kennedy-speeches/houston-tx-19600912-houston-ministerial-association.
29. "Why an Urgent First Step Was Made with our Headquarters."
30. Memo, Salinger to the president, October 30, 1962, JFKL, Digital Collection, Series: Staff Memoranda, Collection: President's Office Files.
31. Si Frumkin, "Getting a Telephone Call Through to the Soviet Union," *Los Angeles Times*, January 18, 1986.
32. NC, *Improbable Triumvirate*, 18.
33. NC, *Improbable Triumvirate*, 25.
34. Memo, Salinger to the president, November 16, 1962, JFKL, Digital Collection, Series: Staff Memoranda, Collection: President's Office Files.
35. "Why an Urgent First Step Was Made with our Headquarters."
36. Hebblethwaite and Hebblethwaite, *Pope John XXIII*, 446–47.
37. Giuseppe Alberigo and Joseph Komonchak, *History of Vatican II* (Maryknoll, NY: Orbis Books, 2006), 99.
38. Although the pope's statement appeared on page 5 of *Pravda*, the White House may have given it even more weight because Pierre Salinger mistakenly wrote in a memo to Kennedy that it appeared on the front page. See memo, Salinger to the president, November 16, 1962.
39. Untitled notes by NC, [ca. September 1966], NCP, Box 1721, Folder: The Critic—on Pope John.
40. Memo, "Visit of Mr. Norman Cousins to the Soviet Union," April 2, 1963, JFKL, National Security Files, Box 188, Folder: USSR Subjects Khrushchev Talks—Norman Cousins, Gardner Cowles, 4/20/62–4/22/63. Obtained through FOIA request by author.
41. Untitled report, February 12, 1963, NCP, Box 912, Folder: f. 3 Father Morlion post trip.
42. Memo, Salinger to the president, November 16, 1962.
43. Memo, Salinger to the president, October 30, 1962. See also "M.C. February 12, 1963," NCP, Box 912, Folder: f. 3 Father Morlion—post trip.
44. Sergei Khrushchev (discussant), "The Strength of Dialogue in Russian-American Relations," Symposium, Initiative for Russian Culture, American University, Washington, DC, April 13, 2013.

45. "War and Peace in the Nuclear Age; At the Brink; Interview with Norman Cousins, 1986," March 3, 1986, pt. 1 of 3, WGBH Media Library and Archives, https://openvault.wgbh.org/catalog/V_329C06A5E8FA47C5AAE40EF0BD66C4BD.
46. Fursenko and Naftali, *One Hell of a Gamble*, 283.
47. Oliver Stone and Peter Kuznick, *The Untold History of the United States* (New York: Gallery Books, 2012), 310.
48. Fursenko and Naftali, *One Hell of a Gamble*, 284.
49. Stone and Kuznick, *Untold History of the United States*, 311.
50. Much more than the basic story outlined here happened in the intervening period, including some exchange of letters before the agreement. See Fursenko and Naftali, *One Hell of a Gamble*, for the pertinent details.
51. "Letter from Chairman Khrushchev to President Kennedy," in *Foreign Relations of the United States, 1961–1963*, Vol. VI, *Kennedy-Khrushchev Exchanges*, ed. Charles S. Sampson and Glenn W. LaFantsie (Washington, DC: GPO, 1996), Doc. 68, p. 183, https://history.state.gov/historicaldocuments/frus1961-63v06/d68, emphasis added.
52. Memo, Salinger to the president, October 30, 1962. See also "M.C. February 12, 1963."
53. "Second Private Conversation with E.F. and G.S.," undated memo, NCP, Box 912, Folder: f. 9 Morlion 1962, Father Morlion—pre-trip plus reports—1962, 9.

Chapter 23. The Crisis Abates but Contacts Continue

1. "Second Private Conversation with E.F. and G.S.," undated memo, NCP, Box 912, Folder: f. 9 Morlion 1962, Father Morlion—pre-trip plus reports—1962, 9.
2. "The Line of Further Possibilities," November 1962, NCP, Box 912, Folder: f. 9 Morlion 1962, Father Morlion—pre-trip plus reports—1962, 9.
3. Felix Morlion to NC, December 10, 1962, NCP, Box 912, Folder: f. 9 Morlion 1962, Father Morlion—pre-trip plus reports—1962.
4. NC, *The Improbable Triumvirate: John F. Kennedy, Pope John, Nikita Khrushchev* (New York: Norton, 1972), 20.
5. Memorandum II, [ca. February 1963], NCP, Box 909, Folder: Morlion—1963.
6. Memo, Pierre Salinger to the president, October 30, 1962, JFKL, Digital Collection, Series: Staff Memoranda, Collection: President's Office

Files. See also "M.C. February 12, 1963," NCP, Box 912, Folder: f. 3 Father Morlion—post trip.

7. "Line of Further Possibilities."
8. Aleksandr Fursenko and Timothy Naftali, *One Hell of a Gamble: Khrushchev, Castro, and Kennedy, 1958–1964; The Secret History of the Cuban Missile Crisis* (New York: Norton, 1998), 126–27.
9. Nikita Khrushchev to SANE, February 25, 1961, SCPC, SANE Records, Series B, Box 36, Folder: National Committee for a SANE Nuclear Policy, Correspondence and Related Papers, 1961–1962.
10. Matthew Evangelista, *Unarmed Forces: The Transnational Movement to End the Cold War* (Ithaca, NY: Cornell University Press, 1999), 47.
11. Morlion to NC, 10 December 1962.
12. Memo, Salinger to the president, October 30, 1962. See also "M.C. February 12, 1963," NCP, Box 912, Folder: f. 3 Father Morlion—post trip.
13. NC, *Improbable Triumvirate*, 24–25.
14. "Robert Kennedy Article on Cuban Missile Crisis Brings $1 Million," September 20, 1968, *Washington Evening Star*.
15. Robert F. Kennedy, "Lessons of the Cuban Missile Crisis," *Saturday Review*, October 26, 1986, 22–25; Robert F. Kennedy, *Thirteen Days: A Memoir of the Cuban Missile Crisis* (New York: McCall, 1968).
16. NC, "Memo: Budget Request for first Dartmouth," n.d., NCP, Box 1348, Folder: NC Speech Soviet Peace Committee 1959.
17. Memo, "Concrete Signs of Peaceful Coexistence," December 10, 1962, NCP, Box 912, Folder: f. 9 Morlion 1962, Father Morlion—pre-trip plus reports—1962.
18. NC, *Improbable Triumvirate*, 30.
19. NC, untitled memo, December 14, 1962, NCP, Box 909, Folder: Morlion—1963.
20. Cousins did not speak Russian and was accompanied by his translator Oleg Bykov.
21. "Interview with Norman Cousins," WBBM Radio, Chicago, October 21, 1968, NCP, Box 1702, Folder: WBBM NC Interview.
22. Fursenko and Naftali, *Khrushchev's Cold War*, 508.
23. "Interview with Norman Cousins," WBBM Radio, Chicago, October 21, 1968.
24. NC to Khrushchev, July 17, 1963, NCP, Box 1219, Folder: NC/Khrushchev Corresp.

25. NC, untitled memo, December 14, 1962.
26. NC, Memorandum II, n.d., NCP, Box 909, Folder: Morlion—1963, 6.
27. NC, Memorandum II, 9–10.
28. Cousins's account of his meeting with the pope is detailed in NC, *Improbable Triumvirate*, 62–66.
29. NC, *Improbable Triumvirate*, 66.
30. NC to Khrushchev, December 21, 1962, NCP, Box 1219, Folder: NC/Khrushchev Corresp.
31. NC to Angelo Dell'Acqua, January 24, 1963, NCP, Box 911, Folder: f. 2 Morlion 1962–1964.
32. NC to Angelo Dell'Acqua, January 24, 1963.

Chapter 24. The Breakthrough to the Limited Nuclear Test Ban Treaty

1. Matthew Evangelista, *Unarmed Forces: The Transnational Movement to End the Cold War* (Ithaca, NY: Cornell University Press, 1999), 46.
2. NC, *The Improbable Triumvirate: John F. Kennedy, Pope John, Nikita Khrushchev* (New York: Norton, 1972).
3. NC, *Improbable Triumvirate*, 10.
4. David Tal, *The American Nuclear Disarmament Dilemma, 1945–1963* (Syracuse, NY: Syracuse University Press, 2008), 165.
5. Tal, *American Nuclear Disarmament Dilemma*, 166–70.
6. Robert Dallek, *An Unfinished Life: John F. Kennedy, 1917–1963* (Boston: Little, Brown, 2003), 343.
7. Tal, *American Nuclear Disarmament Dilemma*, 181.
8. NC, "Soviet Scientists and Soviet Tests," *Saturday Review*, November 18, 1961, 31.
9. Tal, *American Nuclear Disarmament Dilemma*, 182.
10. NC, "One Year Later," *Saturday Review*, March 3, 1962, 20.
11. Candis Cousins Kerns, interview by author, October 25, 2020.
12. NC to Homer Jack, March 7, 1962, NCP, Box 306, Folder: SANE Confidential.
13. NC to Jack.
14. Lawrence Wittner, *Resisting the Bomb: A History of the World Nuclear Disarmament Movement, 1954–1970* (Stanford, CA: Stanford University Press, 1997), 427.
15. Memo, "Geneva Nuclear Test Detection Negotiations," June 17, 1959, RG 59, Department of State Records, NACP, 711.5611/5-156.

16. Aleksandr Fursenko and Timothy Naftali, *Khrushchev's Cold War: The Inside Story of an American Adversary* (New York: Norton 2006), 508.
17. Vojtech Mastny, "The 1963 Nuclear Test Ban Treaty: A Missed Opportunity for Détente?," *Journal of Cold War Studies* 10, no. 1 (Winter 2010): 8.
18. Nikita Khrushchev, *Khrushchev Remembers* (Boston: Little, Brown, 1970), 410–12.
19. Tal, *American Nuclear Disarmament Dilemma*, 215.
20. Mastny, "1963 Nuclear Test Ban Treaty," 9.
21. Ronald Terchek, *The Making of the Test Ban Treaty* (The Hague: M. Nijhoff, 1970), 16.
22. NC, *Improbable Triumvirate*, 54–55.
23. Wittner, *Resisting the Bomb*, 417.
24. Khrushchev to Kennedy, December 19, 1962, JFKL, National Security Files, Box 183, Folder: Union of Soviet Socialist Republics: Subjects, Khrushchev Correspondence, 11/25/62–12/30/62.
25. NC to Ralph Dungan, [early January 1963?], JFKL, National Security Files, Box 191A, Folder: Vatican General, From Dungan's Files: 7/2/62-9/21/64.
26. Dungan to John F. Kennedy, January 19, 1963, JFKL, National Security Files, Box 191A, Folder: Vatican General, From Dungan's Files: 7/2/62-9/21/64.
27. NC to Dungan, January 28, 1963, JFKL, National Security Files, Box 191A, Folder: Vatican General, From Dungan's Files: 7/2/62–9/21/64.
28. *Foreign Relations of the United States, 1961–1963*, Vol. VI, *Kennedy-Khrushchev Exchanges*, ed. Charles S. Sampson and Glenn W. LaFantasie (Washington, DC: GPO, 1996), 238–40.
29. Tape 82 (2 of 3), JFKL, President's Office Files, Presidential Recordings.
30. Anatoly Dobrynin, *In Confidence: Moscow's Ambassador to America's Six Cold War Presidents (1962–1986)* (New York: Random House, 1995), 102.
31. Ambassador James Goodby (discussant), "The Test Ban Treaty 50 Years On: New Perspectives on Nuclear Arms Control and the Cold War," Society for Historians of American Foreign Relations, Arlington, VA, 20 June 2013.
32. NC, *Improbable Triumvirate*, 78.
33. Memorandum of conversation between Dean Rusk and NC, February 19, 1963, JFKL, National Security Files, Box 188, Folder: USSR Subjects, Khrushchev talks—Norman Cousins, Item 1A, 4.

34. Kendrick Oliver, *Kennedy, Macmillan and the Nuclear Test-Ban Debate, 1961–63* (London: Macmillan, 1998), 153–63.
35. "Private Discussion with the President," March 12, 1963, NCP, Box 1206, Folder: Kennedy, John F. & Staff.
36. NC to Kennedy, March 13, 1963, NCP, Box 1206, Folder: Kennedy, John F. & Staff.
37. "Memorandum from Attorney General Robert Kennedy to John F. Kennedy," April 3, 1963, in *Foreign Relations of the United States, 1961–1963*, Vol. VI, *Kennedy-Khrushchev Exchanges*, ed. Charles S. Sampson and Glenn W. LaFantasie (Washington, DC: GPO, 1996), 262.
38. William Taubman, *Khrushchev: The Man and His Era* (New York: Norton, 2003), 584.
39. Harold Macmillan, *At the End of the Day, 1961–1963* (New York: Harper & Row, 1973), 463.
40. Fursenko and Naftali, *Khrushchev's Cold War*, 517.
41. Mastny, "1963 Nuclear Test Ban Treaty," 15.
42. NC, *Improbable Triumvirate*, 80.

Chapter 25. A Sojourn with Khrushchev

1. Candis Cousins Kerns, email to author, January 14, 2021.
2. Kerns, interview by author, October 25, 2020.
3. Kerns, email to author.
4. This account of the meeting with Khrushchev is drawn from the author's personal interviews with Andrea and Candis as well as from notes by Norman and Andrea Cousins found in NCP, Box 1220.
5. See NC, *Improbable Triumvirate*, 82–97. See also Lawrence Wittner, *Resisting the Bomb: A History of the World Nuclear Disarmament Movement, 1954–1970* (Stanford, CA: Stanford University Press, 1997), 49.
6. Memo, "Visit of Mr. Norman Cousins to the Soviet Union," April 22, 1963, JFKL, National Security Files, Box 188, Folder: USSR Subjects Khrushchev Talks—Norman Cousins, Gardner Cowles, 4/20/62–4/22/63.
7. Franklyn Griffiths, "The Soviet Experience of Arms Control," *International Journal* 44, no. 2 (Spring 1989): 319.
8. Tape 82 (3 of 3), JFKL, President's Office Files, Presidential Recordings.
9. "War and Peace in the Nuclear Age; At the Brink; Interview with Norman Cousins, 1986," March 3, 1986, pt. 1 of 3, WGBH Media Library

and Archives, https://openvault.wgbh.org/catalog/V_329C06A5E8FA47C5AAE40EF0BD66C4BD.

10. Tape 82 (3 of 3), JFKL.
11. NC, *Improbable Triumvirate,* 110.
12. Tape 82 (3 of 3), JFKL.
13. Tape 82 (3 of 3), JFKL.
14. David Tal, *The American Nuclear Disarmament Dilemma, 1945–1963* (Syracuse, NY: Syracuse University Press, 2008), 225.
15. "Private Discussion with the President," March 12, 1963, NCP, Box 1206, Folder: Kennedy, John F. & Staff.
16. Vojtech Mastny, "The 1963 Nuclear Test Ban Treaty: A Missed Opportunity for Détente?," *Journal of Cold War Studies* 10, no. 1 (Winter 2010): 15.
17. Memorandum on meeting with Anatoly Dobrynin, April 26, 1963, NCP, Box 1206, Folder: Kennedy, John F. & Staff.
18. Ted Sorensen, *Counselor: A Life at the Edge of History* (New York: Harper, 2008), 326.
19. NC to John F. Kennedy, April 30, 1963, JFKL, Theodore Sorensen Papers, Subject Files 1961–64, Box 36.
20. Norman Cousins Oral History, NCP, 276.
21. Ted Sorensen, *Kennedy: The Classic Biography* (1965; reprint, New York: Harper Perennial, 2013), 730.
22. NC to Kennedy, April 30, 1963, NCP, Box 1206, Folder: Kennedy, John F. (13).
23. "An Evening with Ted Sorensen," May 28, 2008, JFKL, Library Forums, Transcripts, https://www.jfklibrary.org/events-and-awards/forums/past-forums/transcripts/an-evening-with-ted-sorensen.
24. "Theodore Sorensen Oral History Interview," April 15, 1964, JFKL, John F. Kennedy Oral History Collection.
25. A copy of NC's draft can be found in NCP, Box 1149, Folder 15: Kennedy Staff.
26. Sorensen, *Kennedy,* 729–30.
27. "Theodore Sorensen Oral History Interview," April 15, 1964.
28. Letter from Carl Kaysen, addressee unknown, June 7, 1963, JFKL, National Security Files, Box: 305A, Folder: President's Speeches, American University Speech 6/10/63; 6/7/63–6/11/63.
29. Andreas Wagner and Marcel Gerber, "John F. Kennedy and the Limited Test Ban Treaty: A Case Study of Presidential Leadership," *Presidential Studies Quarterly* 29, no. 2 (June 1999): 472.

30. NC, untitled, undated draft of Kennedy's American University speech, NCP, Box 1149, Folder 15: Kennedy Staff.
31. John F. Kennedy, "Commencement Address at American University," June 10, 1963, JFKL, https://www.jfklibrary.org/archives/other-resources/john-f-kennedy-speeches/american-university-19630610.
32. NC, untitled, undated draft of Kennedy's American University speech.
33. Kennedy, "Commencement Address at American University."
34. NC, untitled, undated draft of Kennedy's American University speech.
35. Kennedy, "Commencement Address at American University."
36. Norman Cousins Oral History, NCP, 276.
37. Sorensen, *Counselor*, 326.
38. Wittner, *Resisting the Bomb*, 421.
39. Edward R Murrow to Kennedy, June 13, 1963, JFKL, National Security Files, Box 305A, Folder: President's Speeches, American University Speech 6/10/63–6/13/63.
40. Special memo, "Foreign Radio and Press Reaction," June 12, 1963, JFKL. National Security Files, Box 305A, Folder: President's Speeches, American University Speech 6/10/63–6/12/63.
41. Telegram, US Embassy, Belgrade, to Secretary of State, June 12, 1963, JFKL, National Security Files, Box 305A, Folder: President's Speeches, American University Speech 6/7/63–6/11/63.
42. William Taubman, *Khrushchev: The Man and His Era* (New York: Norton, 2003), 602.
43. "CIA Information Report," June 11, 1963, JFKL, National Security Files, Box 305A, Folder: President's Speeches, American University Speech 6/10/63–6/13/63.
44. Telegram, US Embassy, Moscow, to Secretary of State, June 11, 1963, JFKL, National Security Files, Box 305A, Folder: President's Speeches, American University Speech 6/7/63–6/11/63.
45. NC to Khrushchev, June 17, 1963, NCP, Box 1219, Folder: NC/Khrushchev Correspondence.
46. "CIA Information Report."
47. US Embassy, Moscow, to Kennedy, July 26, 1963, JFKL, National Security Files, Box 305A, Folder: President's Speeches, American University Speech 6/16/63–6/26/63.
48. Tape 82 (2 of 3), JFKL, President's Office Files, Presidential Recordings.
49. Roderick MacFarquhar, *Origins of the Cultural Revolution, Volume 3* (New York: Columbia University Press, 1999), 357.

50. Griffiths, "Soviet Experience of Arms Control," 320.
51. Tal, *American Nuclear Disarmament Dilemma*, 194.

Chapter 26. The Fight to Ratify

1. NC to Nikita Khrushchev, June 24, 1963, NCP, Box 1218, Folder: Test Ban Treaty Correspondence Nehru, Khrushchev 2/2.
2. William Burr and Hector Montford, eds., "The Making of the Limited Test Ban Treaty, 1958–1963," National Security Archive, www.nsarchive2.gwu.edu/NSAEBB/NSAEBB94/.
3. "Confidential Report by FM," July 24, 1963, NCP, Box 912, Folder: 1963. Confidential report from FM.
4. Norman Cousins Oral History, NCP, 280.
5. Norman Cousins Oral History, NCP, 285.
6. NC to Khrushchev, August 12, 1963, NCP, Box 1218, Folder: Test Ban Treaty Correspondence Nehru, Khrushchev 2/2.
7. Thurston Clarke, *JFK's Last Hundred Days: The Transformation of a Man and the Emergence of a Great President* (New York: Penguin, 2013), 13.
8. Ronald Terchek, *The Making of the Test Ban Treaty* (The Hague: M. Nijhoff, 1970).
9. NC, untitled meeting notes, August 2, 1963, NCP, Box 1355, Folder: Ad hoc meeting, Washington, D.C. August 2, 1963.
10. "Theodore Sorensen Oral History Interview," April 15, 1964, JFKL, John F. Kennedy Oral History Collection.
11. Charles E. Johnson, notes on meeting with Ambassador Wadsworth, August 6, 1963, JFKL, National Security Files, Box 264A, Folder: ACDA [Arms Control and Disarmament Agency] Disarmament Subjects Nuclear Test Ban Treaty Citizens Committee, 8/63.
12. Clarke, *JFK's Last Hundred Days*, 22–30.
13. Frederick G. Dutton to McGeorge Bundy, August 12, 1963, JFKL, National Security Files, Box 264A, Folder: ACDA Disarmament Subjects Nuclear Test Ban Treaty Citizens Committee, 8/63.
14. Norman Cousins Oral History, NCP, 285.
15. NC, untitled speech, September 1963, NCP, Box 1722, Folder: NC Speech (draft) Congressman—Test Ban Treaty.
16. Norman Cousins Oral History, NCP, 286.
17. Clarke, *JFK's Last Hundred Days*, 19.
18. Terchek, *Making of the Test Ban Treaty*, 198.
19. Norman Cousins Oral History, NCP, 289.

20. "War and Peace in the Nuclear Age; At the Brink; Interview with Norman Cousins, 1986," March 3, 1986, pt. 1 of 3, WGBH Media Library and Archives, https://openvault.wgbh.org/catalog/V_329C06A5E8FA47C5AAE40EF0BD66C4BD.
21. Norman Cousins Oral History, NCP, 289.
22. Glenn Seaborg, *Kennedy, Khrushchev, and the Test Ban* (Berkeley: University of California Press, 1981), 207.
23. Clarke, *JFK's Last Hundred Days*, 4.
24. NC, *The Improbable Triumvirate: John F. Kennedy, Pope John, Nikita Khrushchev* (New York: Norton, 1972), 24.
25. NC, "The Box Score Is the Thing," *Saturday Review*, January 30, 1960, 24.
26. Norman Cousins Oral History, NCP, 294.
27. "Confidential Report by FM," July 24, 1963.
28. Telegram from NC, addressee unknown, November 22, 1963, NCP, Box 330, Folder: Far East Itinerary 1963–64.
29. NC to Carlos P. Romulo, November 26, 1963, NCP, Box 1212, Folder: Romulo, Carlos, 1960s.
30. Sarah Shapiro, interview by author, September 22, 2020.
31. Norman Cousins Oral History, NCP, 294–95.
32. NC, "The Legacy of John F. Kennedy," *Saturday Review*, December 7, 1963, 27.
33. J. Wayne Fredericks to NC, December 12, 1963, NCP, Box 1203, Folder: Pres & VP.
34. Ted Sorensen to NC, December 18, 1963, NCP, Box 1213, Folder: Sorensen, Theodore.
35. NC, "Can Civilization be Assassinated?," *Saturday Review*, December 21, 1963, 14.

Chapter 27. 1964: Near Death and Rebirth

1. Senator Joseph Clark to NC, December 17, 1963, NCP, Box 376, Folder: CI–CN 1964.
2. NC, "The White House Revisited," *Saturday Review*, February 8, 1964, 20.
3. James Voorhees, *Dialogue Sustained: The Multilevel Peace Process and the Dartmouth Conference* (Washington, DC: United States Institute of Peace Press, 2002), 53.
4. Voorhees, *Dialogue Sustained*, 54.
5. NC, "By Way of General Background," n.d., NCP, Box 1222, Folder: Bundy—Peace Mission.

6. Norman Cousins Oral History, NCP, 295.
7. Voorhees, *Dialogue Sustained*, 53–55.
8. "Rapporteur's Notes Fourth Dartmouth Conference, July 25–31, 1964," NCP, Box 1354, Folder: Rapporteur's Notes: Fourth Dartmouth Conf: Leningrad, July 25–31, 1964.
9. Norman Cousins Oral History, NCP, 295.
10. David Rockefeller, *Memoirs* (New York: Random House, 2002), 223–24.
11. Rockefeller, *Memoirs*, 231.
12. Lyndon B. Johnson, "By Lyndon B. Johnson: Bombing North after Tonkin Attack," *New York Times*, October 20, 1971, 40.
13. Norman Cousins Oral History, NCP, 295.
14. Norman Cousins Oral History, NCP, 296.
15. NC, *Anatomy of an Illness: As Perceived by the Patient* (New York: Norton, 1979), 36.
16. NC, *Anatomy of an Illness*, 36.
17. Norman Cousins Oral History, NCP, 298.
18. Norman Cousins Oral History, NCP, 298.
19. William Hitzig, "TO WHOM IT MAY CONCERN," August 29, 1974, NCP, Box1191, Folder: Friends, Hitzig.
20. William Hitzig, untitled, undated medical notes, NCP, Box 1191, Folder: Friends, Hitzig.
21. Norman Cousins Oral History, NCP, 298.
22. NC to Ralph Dungan, October 7, 1964, NCP, Box 377, Folder: DU–DZ 1964.
23. Untitled, undated notes by Fran Thompson, NCP, Box 1194, Folder: Fran Thompson 1/4.
24. Candis Cousins Kerns, interview by author, October 25, 2020; Sarah Shapiro interview by author, September 22, 2020.
25. Edward Lowman to Hitzig, October 5, 1964, NCP, Box 902, Folder: Correspondence 1964–1971, NC—Personal.
26. "Cousins Medical Record compiled by Dr. David Globus," October 10, 1964, NCP, Box 1192, Folder: Hitzig, Dr. William, Health.
27. NC to Agnes McManus, October 27, 1964, NCP, Box 385, Folder: MC. Today Butazolidin is recognized as toxic and no longer approved for human use.
28. NC, *Anatomy of an Illness*, 32–33.
29. Untitled, undated notes by Fran Thompson.
30. Untitled, undated notes by Fran Thompson.

31. Shapiro, interview.
32. Untitled notes by Dr. William Hitzig, January 20, 1983, NCP, Box 1191, Folder: Friends: Hitzig.
33. Untitled notes by Dr. William Hitzig.
34. Untitled, undated notes by Fran Thompson.
35. Pauling later published two books on the topic, *Vitamin C and the Common Cold* (1970) and *Cancer and Vitamin C* (1979).
36. NC, *Anatomy of an Illness*, 43.
37. Untitled notes by Dr. William Hitzig.
38. NC, *Anatomy of an Illness*, 96.
39. Bill Hitzig to Alan Funt, September 11, 1964, NCP, Box 902, Folder: Correspondence 1964–1971, NC—personal.
40. NC, *Anatomy of an Illness*, 44.
41. Untitled notes by Dr. William Hitzig.
42. NC, "Life Begins at Twenty-Five," *Saturday Review*, April 24, 1965, 26.
43. NC to Gaea McCormick, October 1, 1964, NCP, Box 385, Folder: MC.
44. Untitled, undated notes by Fran Thompson.
45. NC to Fran Thompson, October 15, 1964, NCP, Box 1191, Folder: Fran Thompson Correspondence.
46. NC to Thompson, May 12, 1965, NCP, Box 1191, Folder: Fran Thompson Correspondence.
47. NC to Thompson, October 15, 1964.
48. Transcript of "Adlai E. Stevenson United World Federalists Dinner Publius Award to Norman Cousins," November 18, 1964, NCP, Box 1299, Folder: Publius Award Dinner.
49. "Six Hundred Acclaim Norman Cousins," *New York Federalist*, January 1965, NCP, Box 1299, Folder: Publius Award Dinner.
50. Transcript of "Adlai E. Stevenson United World Federalists Dinner."
51. Beverly Beyette, "L.A. Renaissance of Norman Cousins," *Los Angeles Times*, January 28, 1979, G1.

Chapter 28. Crusade against Dirty Air

1. Untitled notes by Fran Thompson, 1970, NCP, Box 1194, Folder: Fran Thompson 1/4.
2. NC to C. E. Eble, April 12, 1965, NCP, Box 356, Folder: EA–ED, 1965.
3. Fred J. Cook, "Murk, Smog, Smoke—Needed: Fresh Air," *New York Times*, December 29, 1963, 126.
4. NC to C. E. Eble.

5. NC, "The Fouling of the American Environment," *Saturday Review*, May 22, 1965, 31.
6. Bernard Stengren, "It Was a Clear and Windy Day for a Look at the Smoke Problem Here," *New York Times*, September 14, 1963, 27.
7. Cook, "Murk, Smog, Smoke."
8. Jim Dwyer, "Remembering a City Where Smog Could Kill," *New York Times*, February 28, 2017.
9. Stengren, "It Was a Clear and Windy Day."
10. "A Drive on Air Pollution," *New York Times*, September 24, 1963, 38.
11. Eliza Griswold, "How 'Silent Spring' Ignited the Environmental Movement," *New York Times Magazine*, September 21, 2012.
12. "The Story of Silent Spring," August 13, 2015, Natural Resources Defense Council, www.nrdc.org/stories/story-silent-spring.
13. Griswold, "How 'Silent Spring' Ignited the Environmental Movement."
14. Arthur Weinberg and Lila Weinberg, "Where Are Today's Muckrakers?," *Saturday Review*, July 9, 1966, 55.
15. "Rachel Carson and Nuclear War," Rachel Carson Council, https://rachelcarsoncouncil.org/rachel-carson-nuclear-war/.
16. C. W. Griffin, "America's Airborne Garbage," *Saturday Review*, May 22, 1965, 32.
17. Robert Rienow and Leona Train Rienow, "Last Chance for the Nation's Waterways," *Saturday Review*, May 22, 1965, 35.
18. Charles G. Bennett, "New York: Too Little, Too Late?," *Saturday Review*, May 22, 1965, 45.
19. Nelson Rockefeller, letter to the editor, *Saturday Review*, June 26, 1965, 21.
20. Joseph Clark and Richard McCarthy, letters to the editor, *Saturday Review*, June 26, 1965, 21.
21. *Firing Line*, January 22, 1990, PBS.
22. Charles Grutzner, "Lindsay Blames City for Dirty Air," *New York Times*, June 24, 1965, 22.
23. "Cousins Will Head New Panel to Study City's Air Pollution," *New York Times*, January 13, 1966, 41.
24. NC, notes on Air Pollution Task Force meeting, February 25, 1966, NCP, Box 334, Folder: Task Force Misc. NC Notes.
25. NC, notes on Air Pollution Task Force meeting.
26. NC, "The Mayor's Task Force on Air Pollution," May 9, 1966, NCP, Box 334, Folder: N.C.

27. Peter Kihss, "Air Study Finds Pollution Here Worst in Nation," *New York Times*, May 10, 1966, 1.
28. NC, "Mayor's Task Force on Air Pollution."
29. NC, "Mayor's Task Force on Air Pollution."
30. "Smog Here Nears the Danger Point; Patients Warned," *New York Times*, November 25, 1966, 1.
31. Peter Kihss, "City and Con Edison Agree on Air Pollution Plan," *New York Times*, May 18, 1966, 48.
32. Carolyn Konheim, "Performance on Clean Air," *New York Times*, June 3, 1966, 37.
33. John Kifner, "Mayor Announces 5-Year Plan to End Air Pollution Here," *New York Times*, October 12, 1966, 1.
34. Untitled notes by Fran Thompson, 1970.

Chapter 29. Days of Apprehension and Confusion

1. Sarah Shapiro, interview by author, September 22, 2020.
2. Shapiro, interview; Andrea Cousins, interview by author, October 17, 2020; Candis Kerns Cousins, interview by author, October 25, 2020.
3. Memo on May 7 editorial committee luncheon with John Steinbeck, May 11, 1964, NCP, Box 414, Folder: McCalls—1964.
4. NC, "Black Wind Rising," *Saturday Review*, May 30, 1964, 22.
5. Andrea Cousins, interview.
6. Robert Buzzanco, *Masters of War: Military Dissent and Politics in the Vietnam Era* (Cambridge: Cambridge University Press, 1996), 169.
7. Buzzanco, *Masters of War*, 153–55.
8. Fredrik Logevall, *Choosing War: The Lost Chance for Peace and the Escalation of War in Vietnam* (Berkeley: University of California Press, 2001), 196–97.
9. Logevall, *Choosing War*, 198.
10. *The Fog of War: Eleven Lessons from the Life of Robert S. McNamara*, dir. Errol Morris (2003; Culver City, CA: Sony Pictures Classics, 2015), DVD.
11. NC, "Vietnam: Miscalculations and Alternatives," *Saturday Review*, December 12, 1964, 32.
12. David Halberstam, "Taylor Expected to Ask Expansion of Vietnam War," *New York Times*, November 32, 1964, 1.
13. Memo, NC to Bill Moyers, November 29, 1964, NCP, Box 1221, Folder: Vietnam Memo 11/29/64 White House.

14. NC to Lyndon Johnson, November 29, 1964, NCP, Box 1221, Folder: Vietnam Memo 11/29/64 White House.
15. NC, "Vietnam and the American Conscience," *Saturday Review*, February 27, 1965, 23.
16. Buzzanco, *Masters of War*, 192–93.
17. NC, "How America Can Help Vietnam," *Saturday Review*, March 20, 1965, 20.
18. Gabriel Kolko, *Vietnam: Anatomy of a War, 1940–1975* (New York: HarperCollins, 1986), 89.
19. NC, "How America Can Help Vietnam," 20.
20. NC, "How America Can Help Vietnam," 20.
21. Max Frankel, "U.S. Reveals Use of Nonlethal Gas against Vietcong," *New York Times*, March 23, 1965, 1.
22. NC, "How to Lose the World," *Saturday Review*, April 10, 1965, 28.
23. "The President's Address at Johns Hopkins University: Peace Without Conquest." *Public Papers of the Presidents of the United States: Lyndon B. Johnson, 1965*, 2 vols. (Washington, DC: GPO, 1966), 1:394–99.
24. Memorandum of conversation with Ambassador Anatoly Dobrynin, April 8, 1965, NCP, Box 1222, Folder: Dobrynin—4/8/65.
25. NC, "How America Can Help Vietnam," 20.
26. NC, "The President and Vietnam," *Saturday Review*, May 15, 1965, 22.
27. Memorandum of conversation with Ambassador Anatoly Dobrynin.
28. James Voorhees, *Dialogue Sustained: The Multilevel Peace Process and the Dartmouth Conference* (Washington, DC: United States Institute of Peace Press, 2002), 69.
29. Memorandum of conversation with Ambassador Anatoly Dobrynin.
30. Memorandum of conversation with Ambassador Anatoly Dobrynin.
31. NC to Hubert Humphrey, April 12, 1965, NCP, Box 1732, Folder: Letters to Humphrey.
32. NC, untitled, undated notes, NCP, Box 1221, Folder: NC Meetings with Valenti, Lewandowski, Trip to the Philippines, LBJ, Mac Bundy, Goldberg, Wyzner.
33. Untitled notes by Fran Thompson, 1970, NCP, Box 1194, Folder: Francis Thompson 2.
34. NC, dictated notes, January 30, 1966, NCP, Box 1221, Folder: Negotiations—N.C. Meeting with Lewandowski, 10 Park Ave 12/13/65.
35. NC, untitled, undated notes.

36. Notes from NC meeting with Ambassador Janusz Lewandowsi at United Nations, January 30, 1966, NCP, Box 1221, Folder: NC Negotiations Re Vietnam Research & Xeroxes.
37. NC, "Some on-the-spot impressions," January 3, 1966, NCP, Box 1322, Folder: NC's written account of trip with HHH to Philippines for Inauguration of President Marcos
38. Norman Cousins Oral History, NCP, 132.
39. Lien-Hang T. Nguyen, *Hanoi's War: An International History of the War for Peace in Vietnam* (Chapel Hill: University of North Carolina Press, 2012), 78.

Chapter 30. "The Humphrey Mission"

1. NC, notes on briefing with the president, January 3, 1966, NCP, Box 1322, Folder: NC's written account of trip with HHH to Philippines for Inauguration of President Marcos.
2. Memo, NC to Lyndon Johnson, January 6, 1966, NCP, Box 1322, Folder: NC's written account of trip with HHH to Philippines for Inauguration of President Marcos.
3. NC, untitled, undated notes, NCP, Box 1221, Folder: NC Meetings with Valenti, Lewandowski, Trip to the Philippines, LBJ, Mac Bundy, Goldberg, Wyzner.
4. Norman Cousins Oral History, NCP, 132.
5. NC, untitled notes from January 3, 1966,, NCP, Box 1322, Folder: NC's written account of trip with HHH to Philippines for Inauguration of President Marcos
6. NC, untitled notes from January 3, 1966.
7. "Speech by Norman Cousins," May 9, 1967, NCP, Box 1720, Folder: NC Speech, UWF Congressional Breakfast, Washington D.C.
8. Memo, NC to Johnson, January 6, 1966.
9. NC, untitled, undated notes.
10. "Speech by Norman Cousins," May 9, 1967.
11. Norman Cousins background data, September 28, 1966, Records of the Federal Bureau of Investigation, https://vault.fbi.gov/. Obtained through FOIA request by author.
12. "Speech by Norman Cousins," May 9, 1967.
13. Lien-Hang T. Nguyen, *Hanoi's War: An International History of the War for Peace in Vietnam* (Chapel Hill: University of North Carolina Press, 2012), 80.

14. NC, dictated notes, n.d., NCP, Box 1222, Folder: Negotiations—NC meetings with Bundy, Valenti. . . .
15. NC, dictated notes.
16. NC, untitled, undated notes.
17. NC, dictated notes.
18. NC, dictated notes.
19. NC, dictated notes.
20. NC, dictated notes.
21. The above exchange can be found in NC, dictated notes.
22. NC, untitled, undated notes.
23. Fredrik Logevall, *Choosing War: The Lost Chance for Peace and the Escalation of War in Vietnam* (Berkeley: University of California Press, 2001).
24. NC, dictated notes.
25. James Hershberg, conversation with author, 2012.
26. NC, dictated notes.
27. NC, dictated notes.
28. NC, dictated notes.
29. NC, dictated notes.
30. NC, dictated notes.
31. NC, dictated notes.
32. NC, untitled, undated notes.
33. NC, dictated notes.

Chapter 31. The Scramble to Prevent a Bombing

1. NC, dictated notes, n.d., NCP, Box 1222, Folder: Negotiations—NC meetings with Bundy, Valenti. . . .
2. NC, untitled, undated notes, NCP, Box 1221, Folder: Negotiations: NC Meetings with Valenti, Lewandowski, Trip to the Philippines, LBJ, Mac Bundy, Goldberg, Wyzner. . . .
3. NC, untitled, undated notes.
4. NC, untitled, undated notes.
5. Seymour Topping, "Ho Chi Minh Calls Peace Bids by U.S. 'Impudent Threat,'" *New York Times*, January 29, 1966, 1.
6. NC, untitled, undated notes.
7. The above exchange with Thant can be found in NC notes, "Insert A," n.d., NCP, Box 1221, Folder: Negotiations—N.C. Meeting with U Thant at his home, Riverdale, NY, 1/30/66—Telephone calls to Lewandowski, Mac Bundy. etc.

8. NC notes, "Insert A."
9. NC, untitled, undated notes.
10. NC notes, "Insert A."
11. NC notes, "Insert A."
12. NC notes, "Insert A."

Chapter 32. Campaigning against (and during) a War

1. NC to Hubert Humphrey, November 10, 1966, NCP, Box 1206, Folder: Hubert Humphrey Correspondence.
2. NC, "Vietnam and the Fourth Group," *Saturday Review*, April 1, 1967, 22.
3. Eric Goldman to NC, April 13, 1965, NCP, Box 1206, Folder: LBJ Staff.
4. Goldman to NC.
5. NC to Jack Valenti, December 14, 1965, NCP, Box 1206, Folder: LBJ Staff.
6. Untitled, undated memo, NCP, Box 416, Folder: Editorial Committee.
7. NC, untitled notes, April 6, 1967, NCP, Box 1222, Folder: NC Conf.
8. NC, untitled notes.
9. NC, untitled notes.
10. NC, "The Pentagon Papers," *Saturday Review*, July 3, 1971, 16.
11. See, e.g., NC to William Wheeler (Pitney-Bowes chairman), April 13, 1967, NCP, Box 419, Folder: SANE Correspondence.
12. Stuart Loory, "Interview with Norman Cousins," September 27, 1967, Stuart Loory Collection, Box 15, American Heritage Center, University of Wyoming, Laramie.
13. Loory, "Interview with Norman Cousins."
14. NC, "Visit to the White House March 15, 1968," n.d., NCP, Box 1145, Folder: NC Visit to White House (LBJ).
15. NC, "Visit to the White House March 15, 1968."
16. "Cousins Hits Grades as Factor in Draft," *New York Times*, April 18, 1966, 23.
17. Howard Hays to Donald Keys, August 22, 1976, NCP, Box 1146, Folder: Cousins for President.
18. Richard Travis to Hays, September 21, 1967, NCP, Box 1146, Folder: Cousins for President.
19. NC to Hays, November 21, 1967, NCP, Box 1146, Folder: Cousins for President.
20. Norman Cousins Oral History, NCP, 240.
21. "Final Words: Cronkite's Vietnam Commentary," *All Things Considered*, July 18, 2009, NPR.

22. Robert Buzzanco, *Masters of War: Military Dissent and Politics in the Vietnam Era* (Cambridge: Cambridge University Press, 1996), 311.
23. "Speech by Norman Cousins," undated draft, NCP, Box 1731, Folder: NC Draft Speech HHH Entry race Democratic Nomination 1968.
24. NC to Humphrey, [date illegible], NCP, Box 1206, Folder: Humphrey, Hubert H. 1968 Campaign.
25. William Benton to Douglass Carter, October 7, 1968, NCP, Box 1206, Folder: Humphrey, Hubert H. 1968 Campaign.
26. NC to Fran Thompson, May 12, 1965, NCP, Box 1191, Folder: Fran Thompson Correspondence.
27. NC, "The Arms Race and the Candidates," *Saturday Review*, October 26, 1968, 30.
28. Summary of dinner with former vice president Nixon, February 14, 1964, NCP, Box 414, Folder: McCalls—1964.
29. Telegram, NC to Humphrey, November 6, 1968, NCP, Box 1206, Folder: Humphrey, Hubert H. Correspondence.

Chapter 33. The Biafran War

1. Barnaby Philips, "Biafra: Thirty Years On," *BBC News*, January 13, 2000, http://news.bbc.co.uk/2/hi/africa/596712.stm.
2. *Foreign Relations of the United States, 1964–1968*, Vol. XXIV, *Africa*, ed. Nina Davis Howland and David S. Patterson (Washington, DC: GPO, 1999), Doc. 387.
3. *Foreign Relations of the United States, 1964–1968*, Vol. XXIV, Doc. 385.
4. *Foreign Relations of the United States, 1964–1968*, Vol. XXIV, Doc. 390.
5. *Foreign Relations of the United States, 1964–1968*, Vol. XXIV, Doc.t 395.
6. NC, "ABC," *Saturday Review*, February 1, 1969, 21.
7. NC, "ABC," 21.
8. *Foreign Relations of the United States, 1969–1976*, Vol. E-5, Pt. 1, *Sub-Saharan Africa*, ed. Joseph Hilts, David C. Humphrey, and Edward C. Keefer (Washington, DC: GPO, 2005), Doc. 25.
9. *Foreign Relations of the United States, 1969–1976*, Vol. E-5, Pt. 1, Doc. 38.
10. *Foreign Relations of the United States, 1969–1976*, Vol. E-5, Pt. 1, Doc. 44.
11. *Foreign Relations of the United States, 1969–1976*, Vol. E-5, Pt. 1, Doc. 65.
12. *Foreign Relations of the United States, 1969–1976*, Vol. E-5, Pt. 1, Doc. 90.
13. *Foreign Relations of the United States, 1969–1976*, Vol. E-5, Pt. 1, Doc. 92.
14. *Foreign Relations of the United States, 1969–1976*, Vol. E-5, Pt. 1, Doc. 118.

15. NC to Henry Kissinger, August 25, 1969, NCP, Box 1295, Folder: Biafra 1969.
16. *Foreign Relations of the United States, 1969–1976*, Vol. E-5, Pt. 1, Doc. 112.
17. *Foreign Relations of the United States, 1969–1976*, Vol. E-5, Pt. 1, Doc. 113.
18. "Press Statement by Dr. Ifegwu Eke, Commissioner of Information, Republic of Biafra," September 17, 1969, NCP, Box 1295, Folder: Biafra 1969.
19. G. A. Onyegbula to NC, September 8, 1969, NCP, Box 1295, Folder: Biafra 1969.
20. *Foreign Relations of the United States, 1969–1976*, Vol. E-5, Pt. 1, Doc. 118.
21. *Foreign Relations of the United States, 1969–1976*, Vol. E-5, Pt. 1, Doc. 118.
22. Onyegbula to Kissinger, September 24, 1969, NCP, Box 1295, Folder: Biafra 1969.
23. *Foreign Relations of the United States, 1969–1976*, Vol. E-5, Pt. 1, Doc. 112.
24. NC to Yakubu Gowon, October 7, 1969, NCP, Box 1295, Folder: Biafra 1969.
25. Michael Gould, *The Struggle for Modern Nigeria: The Biafran War, 1967–1970* (London: I. B. Tauris, 2012), 106.
26. Gould, *Struggle for Modern Nigeria*, 107.
27. Lasse Heerten, *The Biafran War and Postcolonial Humanitarianism* (Cambridge: Cambridge University Press, 2017), 293.
28. *Foreign Relations of the United States, 1969–1976*, Vol. E-5, Pt. 1, Doc. 165.
29. *Foreign Relations of the United States, 1969–1976*, Vol. E-5, Pt. 1, Doc. 166.
30. Timothy Naftali, "Ronald Reagan's Long-Hidden Racist Conversation with Richard Nixon," *Atlantic*, July 30, 2019.
31. *Foreign Relations of the United States, 1969–1976*, Vol. E-5, Pt. 1, Doc. 172.
32. *Foreign Relations of the United States, 1969–1976*, Vol. E-5, Pt. 1, Doc. 178.
33. Sarah Shapiro, email to author, December 17, 2020.
34. NC, "Cambodia," *Saturday Review*, May 16, 1970, 24.
35. NC, "The Weekend Everyone Went to School," *Saturday Review*, May 23, 1970, 33.
36. NC, "The Taming of Individuals and the State," *Saturday Review*, January 17, 1970, 26.
37. Andrea Cousins, interview by author, October 17, 2020.
38. NC to Lenore Marshall, May 4, 1960, NCP, Box 1192, Folder: Marshall-Cousins, Misc. papers, letters.
39. Candis Cousins Kerns, interview by author, October 25, 2020.

40. NC to Ralph Silberman, October 11, 1972, NCP, Box 1292, Folder: Treasure Letters—World.

Chapter 34. The Saturday Review*'s Final Crisis*

1. NC to Mrs. John Lindley, September 19, 1975, NCP, Box 1292, Folder: Letters from Readers re: Resignation.
2. Sarah Shapiro, interview by author, September 22, 2020.
3. NC to Rita Libin, October 15, 1975, NCP, Box 1297, Folder: Letters from Readers.
4. Miscellaneous notes by Fran Thompson, n.d., NCP, Box 1194, Folder: Francis Thompson 2.
5. NC, "Report to the Readers," *Saturday Review*, July 31, 1971, 16.
6. NC, "Report to the Readers," 17.
7. "Saturday Review Talks Confirmed by Cascade," *New York Times*, July 1, 1971, 79.
8. NC to Hubert Humphrey, December 15, 1971, NCP, Box 1292, Folder: Treasure Letters—World.
9. Stanley Brock to Nicholas Charney, November 23, 1971, NCP, Box 1295, Folder: Saturday Review/World Merger Congratulatory Letters to NC
10. NC, "Final Report to the Readers," *Saturday Review*, November 27, 1971, 32.
11. NC, "Final Report to the Readers," 32.
12. Henry Raymont, "Saturday Review Will Expand by Starting Four Monthlies," *New York Times*, November 15, 1971, 37.
13. NC to James Kilpatrick, December 14, 1971, NCP, Box 1292, Folder: Treasure Letters—World.
14. NC, "Final Report to the Readers," 32.
15. NC, "Final Report to the Readers," 32.
16. John Corry, "It's a New World for Norman Cousins," *New York Times*, June 22, 1972, 48.
17. Lawrence Van Gelder, "Unyielding Editor," *New York Times*, November 17, 1971, 53.
18. "Editor Cousins Leaves Saturday Review Post," *Los Angeles Times*, November 17, 1971, A4.
19. "Saturday Review Gets a New Editor," *New York Times*, November 19, 1971, 41.
20. Susan Aitel to NC, November 22, 1971, NCP, Box 1297, Folder: Letters from Readers.

21. Virginia Avery to NC, January 7, 1972, NCP, Box 1297, Folder: Letters from Readers.
22. Ellen Asher to NC, November 24, 1971, NCP, Box 1297, Folder: Letters from Readers.
23. "Norman Cousins: One of America's Great Editors," 92nd Cong., 1st sess., *Congressional Record* 117, pt. 33 (November 22, 1971), 42751. See also NCP, Box 1292, Folder: Treasure Letters—World.
24. NC to Humphrey, December 15, 1971, NCP, Box 1292, Folder: Treasure Letters re: Resignation.
25. NC to Kilpatrick, December 14, 1971.
26. Van Gelder, "Unyielding Editor," 53.
27. NC to Kilpatrick, December 14, 1971.
28. Van Gelder, "Unyielding Editor," 53.
29. NC to Humphrey, December 15, 1971.
30. Miscellaneous notes by Fran Thompson.
31. Martin Bernheimer, "Can't Beat Critics, So Craft Joins 'Em." *Los Angeles Times*, June 30, 1972, G8.
32. NC, "Birth of SR/W," *World*, July 31, 1973, 14.
33. Bernheimer, "Can't Beat Critics, So Craft Joins 'Em."
34. Corry, "New World for Norman Cousins."
35. Miscellaneous notes by Fran Thompson.
36. Philip Dougherty, "Advertising: Unsuccess Story," *New York Times*, April 26, 1973, 72.
37. Eric Pace, "Saturday Review Seeks Funds as Reports of 'Crisis' Circulate," *New York Times*, March 23, 1973, 28.
38. Eric Pace, "Saturday Review in Bankruptcy; Norman Cousins to Run It Again," *New York Times*, April 25, 1973, 89.
39. NC, "Birth of SR/W," 14.
40. Miscellaneous notes by Fran Thompson.
41. NC, "Birth of SR/W," 14.
42. Eric Pace, "Cousins's World Will Be Expanded," *New York Times*, July 6, 1973, 9.
43. NC, "Report to the Readers," *Saturday Review*, April 16, 1977, 4.
44. Pace, "Cousins's World Will Be Expanded."

Chapter 35. The Third Act

1. Lawrence K. Altman, "Behind the Bestsellers," *New York Times*, December 16, 1979, BR8.

2. Don Colburn, "Norman Cousins, Still Laughing," *Washington Post*, October 21, 1986.
3. Robert D. McFadden, "R. Peter Straus, Radio Pioneer, Dies at 89," *New York Times*, August 8, 2012, B23.
4. NC, "An Open Letter to Carll Tucker," *Saturday Review*, April 15, 1978, 5.
5. Sarah Shapiro, "All the Way Home," *Aish*, August 30, 2008.
6. Untitled, undated notes by Fran Thompson, NCP, Box 1194, Folder: Fran Thompson 1/4.
7. NC, "Open Letter to Carll Tucker," 5.
8. NC, "Report to the Readers." *Saturday Review*, April 16, 1977, 5.
9. NC, "How the Patients Appraise Physicians," *New England Journal of Medicine* 314, n. 20 (November 28, 1985): 1422.
10. "Norman Cousins Will Conduct UCLA Seminars," *Los Angeles Times*, April 4, 1978, A29.
11. NC, *Head First: The Biology of Hope and the Healing Power of the Human Spirit* (New York: Penguin, 1990), 6. See also Beverly Beyette, "L.A. Renaissance of Norman Cousins," *Los Angeles Times*, January 28, 1979, G1.
12. NC, *Head First*, 11.
13. NC to Dr. Gordon Hunter Grant, September 7, 1978, NCP, Box 1584, Folder: Letters Re: Anatomy.
14. Untitled, undated notes by Fran Thompson.
15. Candis Cousins Kerns, interview by author, October 25, 2020.
16. NC to William Hitzig, December 14, 1983, NCP, Box 1191, Folder: Friends, Hitzig.
17. "Dr. Richard Selzer Letter to the Editor," *Commentary*, August 1980, 12.
18. NC, "Norman Cousins Talks on Positive Emotions and Health," KCRW-FM Los Angeles, August 1983. Transcript provided by Bob Rosenbaum.
19. NC, *The Healing Heart: Antidotes to Panic and Helplessness* (New York: Norton, 1983), 128.
20. NC, *Head First*, 2.
21. Raffi Khatchadourian, "The Laughing Guru," *New Yorker*, August 30, 2010.
22. Francisco Tausk Ilia Elenkov, and Jan Moynihan, "Psychoneuroimmunology," *Dermatologic Therapy* 21 (2008): 21.
23. Harold Benjamin, "Norman Cousins and the Wellness Community," *Los Angeles Times*, December 16, 1990.
24. Shari Roan, "The Positive Influence of Norman Cousins," *Los Angeles Times*, December 6, 1990.

25. Untitled notes by Fran Thompson, November 21, 1981, NCP, Box 1194, Folder: Fran Thompson 1/4.
26. Constance Holden, "Cousins's Account of Self-Cure Rapped," *Science*, November 20, 1981, 892.
27. Florence Ruderman, "Medical World News Rounds," *Medical World News*, August 18, 1980.
28. "Dr. Richard Selzer Letter to the Editor."
29. "Dr. Martin Goldner Letter to the Editor," *Commentary*, August 1980, 14.
30. Holden, "Cousins's Account of Self-Cure Rapped."
31. NC to Florence Ruderman, July 8, 1981, NCP, Box 1584, Folder: Anatomy—Critics.
32. Khatchadourian, "Laughing Guru."
33. Roan, "Positive Influence of Norman Cousins."
34. NC, "Norman Cousins Talks on Positive Emotions and Health."
35. Bob Rosenbaum, email to author, August 4, 2017.
36. NC, "Norman Cousins Talks on Positive Emotions and Health."
37. NC, *Healing Heart*, 36.
38. NC, *Healing Heart*, 35.
39. NC, *Healing Heart*, 37.
40. NC, *Healing Heart*, 44.
41. NC, *Healing Heart*, 75.
42. NC, *The Physician in Literature* (New York: W. B. Saunders, 1982).
43. NC, *Healing Heart*, 41.
44. Roan, "Positive Influence of Norman Cousins."
45. Mary Swift to Thompson, May 4, 1982, NCP, Box 1194, Folder: Fran Thompson 1/4.
46. Jonathan Friendly, "Saturday Review Shuts Down," *New York Times*, August 17, 1982, D1.
47. Fred Hiatt, "Now, the $600 Toilet Seat," *Washington Post*, February 5, 1985, A5.
48. NC, *The Pathology of Power* (New York: Norton, 1987).
49. Christopher Swan, "Norman Cousins in Search of Statesmen," *Christian Science Monitor*, September 4, 1980.

Conclusion

1. NC, "1988 Letter of Request," NCP, Box 1153, Folder: D.C. Memorial Service, April 26, 1991.

2. Burt Folkart, "Norman Cousins, 75; Editor, Author, Philosopher," *Los Angeles Times,* December 1, 1990, A36.
3. George H. W. Bush to Ellen Cousins, December 10, 1990, NCP, Box 1153, Folder: D.C. Memorial Service, April 26, 1991.
4. John F. Kennedy, "American University Commencement Address," June 10, 1963, https://www.jfklibrary.org/archives/other-resources/john-f-kennedy-speeches/american-university-19630610.

INDEX

Page numbers in *italics* refer to illustrations.